Acknowledgments

To my readers—The IT Pro Solutions series is a new adventure. Thank you for being there with me through many books and many years.

To my wife—for many years, through many books, many millions of words, and many thousands of pages she's been there, providing support and encouragement and making every place we've lived a home.

To my kids—for helping me see the world in new ways, for having exceptional patience and boundless love, and for making every day an adventure.

To everyone I've worked with at Microsoft—thanks for the many years of support and for helping out in ways both large and small.

Special thanks to my son Will for his extensive contributions to this book. You've made many contributions previously, but now I can finally give you the cover credit you've earned and deserved for so long.

—William R. Stanek

Windows Server 2016:

Server Infrastructure

IT Pro Solutions

William R. Stanek

Author & Series Editor

William R. Stanek, Jr.

Contributor

Windows Server 2016:
Server Infrastructure

IT Pro Solutions

Published by Stanek & Associates
PO Box 362, East Olympia, WA, 98540-0362
www.williamrstanek.com.

Stanek & Associates publishes in a variety of formats, including print, electronic and by print-on-demand. Some materials included with standard print editions may not be included in electronic or print-on-demand editions or vice versa.

Country of First Publication: United States of America.

Cover Design: Creative Designs Ltd.
Editorial Development: Andover Publishing Solutions
Technical Review: L & L Technical Content Services

You can provide feedback related to this book by emailing the author at williamstanek @ aol.com. Please use the name of the book as the subject line.

Version: 1.0.1.2b

> **Note**   I may periodically update this text and the version number shown above will let you know which version you are working with. If there's a specific feature you'd like me to write about in an update, message me on Facebook (http://facebook.com/williamstanekauthor). Please keep in mind readership of this book determines how much time I can dedicate to it.

Table of Contents

How to Use This Guide

This book was designed to provide the tools and guidance you need to get the most out of your Windows Server 2016 experience. The first chapter, *Deploying Windows Server 2016,* takes you through the essentials for working with the product. Following this are chapters that will take an in-depth look at specific tasks and aspects of Windows Server 2016.

William Stanek has been developing expert solutions and writing professionally for Microsoft Windows Server since 1995. In this book, William shares his extensive knowledge of the product, delivering ready answers for day-to-day management and zeroing in on core commands and techniques.

As with all books in the IT Pro Solutions series, this book is written especially for IT professionals working with, supporting, and managing a specific version of a product or products. Here, the product written about is Windows Server 2016, including nano server, core, and full GUI deployments.

Print Readers

Print editions of this book include an index and some other elements not available in the digital edition. Updates to this book are available online. Visit http://www.williamrstanek.com/server2016admin/ to get any updates. This content is available to all readers.

Digital Book Readers

Digital editions of this book are available at all major retailers, at libraries upon request and with many subscription services. If you have a digital edition of this book that you downloaded elsewhere, such as a file sharing site, you should know that the author doesn't receive any royalties or income from such downloads. Already downloaded this book or others? Donate here to ensure William can keep writing the books you need:

https://www.paypal.com/cgi-bin/webscr?cmd=_s-xclick&hosted_button_id=CPSBGLZ35AB26

Support Information

Every effort has been made to ensure the accuracy of the contents of this book. As corrections are received or changes are made, they will be added to the online page for the book available at:

http://www.williamrstanek.com/server2016admin/

If you have comments, questions, or ideas regarding the book, or questions that are not answered by visiting the site above, send them via e-mail to:

williamstanek@aol.com

Other ways to reach the author:

Facebook: http://www.facebook.com/William.Stanek.Author

Twitter: http://twitter.com/williamstanek

It's important to keep in mind that Microsoft software product support is not offered. If you have questions about Microsoft software or need product support, please contact Microsoft.

Microsoft also offers software product support through the Microsoft Knowledge Base at:

http://support.microsoft.com/

Conventions & Features

This book uses a variety of elements to help keep the text clear and easy to follow. You'll find code terms and listings in `monospace`, except when I tell you to actually enter or type a command. In that case, the command appears in **bold**. When I introduce and define a new term, I put it in *italics*.

The first letters of the names of menus, dialog boxes, user interface elements, and commands are capitalized. Example: the Add Roles And Features Wizard. This book also has notes, tips and other sidebar elements that provide additional details on points that need emphasis.

Keep in mind that throughout this book, where William has used click, right-click and double-click, you also can use touch equivalents: tap, press and hold, and double tap. Also, when using a device without a physical keyboard, you are able to enter text by using the onscreen keyboard. If a device has no physical keyboard, simply touch an input area on the screen to display the onscreen keyboard.

Share & Stay in Touch

The marketplace for technology books has changed substantially over the past few years. In addition to becoming increasingly specialized and segmented, the market has been shrinking rapidly, making it extremely difficult for books to find success. If you want William to be able to continue writing and write the books you need for your career, raise your voice and support his work.

Without support from you, the reader, future books by William will not be possible. Your voice matters. If you found the book to be useful, informative or otherwise helpful, please take the time to let others know by sharing about the book online.

To stay in touch with William, visit him on Facebook or follow him on Twitter. William welcomes messages and comments about the book, especially suggestions for improvements and additions. If there is a topic you think should be covered in the book, let William know.

Chapter 1. Deploying Windows Server 2016

Welcome to *Windows Server 2016: Server Infrastructure*, your guide to managing Microsoft's newest server operating system. Before getting into the specifics of deploying and managing Windows servers, take a few seconds to familiarize yourself with the deployment options available, including

- **Physical server**   A server deployment on a physical machine. You use a physical machine when you need a standalone installation of the operating system.
- **Virtual server**   A server deployment to a virtual machine. You use a virtual server when you have an existing host server and want to install the operating system as a guest operating system.
- **Containerized server**   A server deployment that uses containers. You use a container when you have an existing host server and want to establish the base image for a container stack as part of an application or service.

Physical servers are a standard deployment approach; virtual servers are the traditional type of virtualization. Virtual servers create virtual environments that run their own operating systems and manage their own memory, processors and resources. Containers, on the other hand, virtualize the operating system layer rather than simulate the underlying physical machine.

Regardless of which deployment approach you use, you have three options for setting up the operating system:

- **Full-Server installation**   This approach, referred to in the GUI as Server With Desktop Experience, configures a server with all user interfaces and management tools. You'll most often use a full-server installation with a physical server deployment and then primarily when you need to use roles or features not supported by the other installation options.
- **Server Core installation**   This approach configures a server with a limited user interface that is designed to be managed locally using a command line and remotely using either graphical or command-line tools. Server Core supports a limited set of roles and features, primarily those for Active Directory, DHCP, DNS, and Hyper-V as well as file, print and media services. You use Server Core when you need a reduced-footprint installation.
- **Nano Server installation**   This approach configures a server with a minimal footprint that is designed to be managed remotely. For local management, there is only the Recovery Console. Nano Server supports a very limited set of roles and

features, primarily those for file servers, DNS servers and web servers. You use Nano Server when you need a minimal-footprint installation.

> **NOTE** This book is designed to be used with *Windows Server 2016: Administration Essentials*. While this book focuses on infrastructure services, including those for file services, print services, DHCP and DNS, the latter book focuses on management and configuration of servers, setting up Active Directory and Group Policy and more. Chapter 1 of that book is where you'll find a complete discussion of configuration options, Nano Server and containers.

Together, the deployment and setup options give you many possibilities. Full Server is optimized for manageability; Server Core and Nano Server are optimized for performance. However, only a Full Server deployment provides the full graphical shell and the full desktop experience. As part of the graphical shell, user interfaces, graphical management tools, ink and handwriting services, and the server media foundation are installed. As part of the desktop experience, desktop themes, media player, Disk Cleanup and other Windows desktop tools are installed.

Preparing for Windows Server 2016

You can install Windows Server 2016 by performing a clean installation or an upgrade. With a clean installation, Setup replaces any existing operating system on the computer, and all user or application settings are lost. With an upgrade, Setup performs a clean installation of the operating system and then migrates user settings, documents, and applications from the earlier version of Windows.

Working with Windows Server 2016

Windows Server 2016 is available in two primary editions: Standard and Datacenter. While both editions provide the same core functionality, support for containers and nano servers, only Datacenter Edition supports storage replicas, shielded virtual machines and the extended networking stack. Further, with Standard Edition, servers are limited to two virtualized, Hyper-V environments and you must re-license the server for every two additional environments. In contrast, the license for Datacenter Edition allows an unlimited number of virtualized environments.

Before you install Windows Server 2016, you should be sure that your server meets the minimum requirements of the edition you plan to use. Windows Server 2016 requires a 64-bit processor that supports NX and DEP, which all current processors do. For core and nano server deployments, servers should have at least 512 MB of RAM and at least 32 GB of disk space for installation of the base operating system. For full-server deployments, servers should have at least 2 GB of RAM and at least 32 GB of disk space for the operating system.

> **NOTE** For optimal performance, you should have at least 10 percent of free space on a server's disks at all times. Additional disk space is required for paging and dump files and also for the features, roles, and role services you install as well.

When you install Windows Server 2016, Setup automatically makes recovery options available on your server as an advanced boot option. In addition to a command line for troubleshooting and options for changing the startup behavior, you can use System Image Recovery to perform a full recovery of the computer by using a system image created previously. If other troubleshooting techniques fail to restore the computer and you have a system image for recovery, you can use this feature to restore the computer from the backup image.

After you install a server, you can configure it using the integrated management tools. The one you'll use the most for handling core configuration tasks is Server Manager. Server Manager provides setup and configuration options for the local server in addition to options for managing roles, features, and related settings on any remotely manageable server in the enterprise.

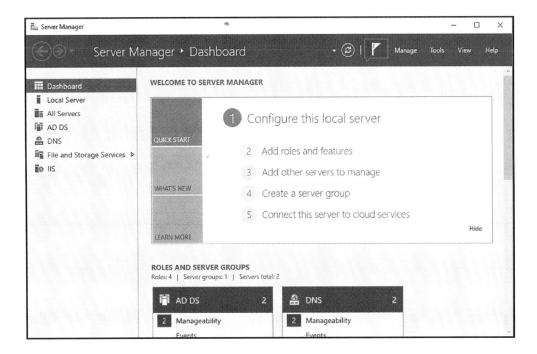

Tasks you can use Server Manager to perform include the following:

- Adding servers for remote management
- Initiating remote connections to servers
- Configuring the local server
- Managing installed roles and features
- Managing volumes and shares on file servers
- Configuring Network Interface Card (NIC) Teaming
- Viewing events and alerts
- Restarting servers

Server Manager is great for general system administration, but you also need a tool that gives you granular control over system environment settings and properties. This is where the Settings app comes into the picture. The Settings app is replacing the System utility as the preferred tool for managing a computer's basic configuration.

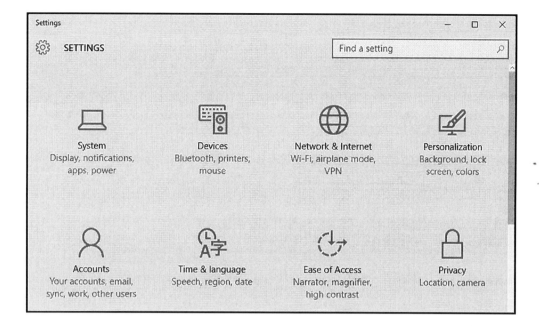

When you are working remotely, you'll need to use command-line tools for these tasks instead. Windows Server 2016 supports two command-line environments, regardless of whether you are working with a Server Core, nano server or full-server deployment:

- Windows Command Processor (cmd.exe)
- Windows PowerShell (powershell.exe)

Windows Server 2016 uses the same configuration architecture as Windows Server 2012 and Windows Server 2012 R2. You prepare servers for deployment by installing and configuring the following components:

- **Server roles**   A *server role* is a related set of software components that allows a server to perform a specific function for users and other computers on a network. A computer can be dedicated to a single role, such as Active Directory Domain Services (AD DS), or provide multiple roles.
- **Role services**   A *role service* is a software component that provides the functionality for a server role. Each role can have one or more related role services. Some server roles, such as Domain Name System (DNS) and Dynamic Host Configuration Protocol (DHCP), have a single function, and installing the role installs this function. Other roles, such as Network Policy and Access Services, and Active Directory Certificate Services (AD CS), have multiple role services that you can install. With these server roles, you can choose which role services to install.

- **Features** A *feature* is a software component that provides additional functionality. Features, such as BitLocker Drive Encryption and Windows Server Backup, are installed and removed separately from roles and role services. A computer can have zero or more features installed, depending on its configuration.

You configure roles, role services, and features by using Server Manager. Some roles, role services, and features are dependent on other roles, role services, and features. As you install roles, role services, and features, Server Manager prompts you to install other roles, role services, or features that are required. Similarly, if you try to remove a required component of an installed role, role service, or feature, Server Manager warns that you cannot remove the component unless you also remove dependent roles, role services, or features.

Because adding or removing roles, role services, and features can change hardware requirements, you should carefully plan any configuration changes and determine how they affect a server's overall performance. Although you typically want to combine complementary roles, doing so increases the workload on the server, so you need to optimize the server hardware accordingly. Unlike early releases of Windows, Windows Server 2016 does not install some important server features automatically. For example, you must add Windows Server Backup to use the built-in backup and restore features of the operating system.

Managing Server Core

Server Core is designed to be managed locally using the command line or remotely using either command-line or graphical tools. You use Server Core when you don't need a desktop and want to reduce the overall footprint of the server. A server running in a core configuration doesn't have the Windows shell, Internet Explorer or local GUI management.

With a Server Core installation, you get a user interface that includes a limited desktop environment for local console management of the server. This minimal interface includes the following:

- Windows Logon screen for logging on and logging off
- Notepad (Notepad.exe) for editing files
- Registry Editor (Regedit.exe) for managing the registry
- Task Manager (Taskmgr.exe) for managing tasks and starting new tasks
- Command prompt (Cmd.exe) for administration using the command line

- Windows PowerShell prompt for administration using Windows PowerShell
- File Signature Verification tool (Sigverif.exe) for verifying digital signatures of system files
- System Information (Msinfo32.exe) for getting system information
- Windows Installer (Msiexec.exe) for managing Windows Installer
- Date And Time control panel applet (Timedate.cpl) for viewing or setting the date, time, and time zone
- Region And Language control panel applet (Intl.cpl) for viewing or setting regional and language options, including formats and the keyboard layout
- Server Configuration utility (Sconfig.cmd), which provides a text-based menu system for managing a server's configuration

When you start a server with a Server Core installation, you can use the Windows Logon screen to unlock the server and log on. The first time you press Ctrl+Alt+Delete you are prompted to enter and confirm a password for the Administrator account. Afterward, when you press Ctrl+Alt+Delete to unlock the server, you are prompted to enter the password for the Administrator account or press Esc to switch users or log-in methods.

In a domain, the standard restrictions apply for logging on to servers, and anyone with appropriate user rights and logon permissions can log on to the server. On servers that are not acting as domain controllers and for servers in workgroup environments, you can use the NET USER command to add users, and the NET LOCALGROUP command to add users to local groups for the purposes of logging on locally.

After you log on to a Server Core installation, you have a limited desktop environment with an administrator command prompt. You can use the command prompt for administration of the server and to run PowerShell. One way to open a PowerShell prompt is to enter powershell in the command prompt window.

While you are logged in, you can press Ctrl+Alt+Delete to display the Logon UI. You navigate this text-based menu using the Up/Down arrow keys or Tab to move between options and Enter to select an option. The menu has the following options:

- Change a password
- Lock
- Sign out
- Task Manager
- Cancel

> **NOTE** When you are logged on locally, you'll also have the option to switch users. If you are working remotely using Remote Desktop, you can't send the Ctrl+Alt+Delete keystroke combination to the remote computer. Here, use Ctrl+Alt+End instead.

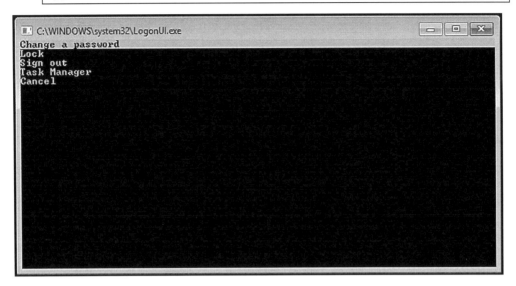

At the command prompt, you have all the standard commands and command-line utilities available for managing the server. However, commands, utilities, and programs run only when all of their dependencies are available in the Server Core installation. If you accidentally close the default command prompt, you can open a new command prompt by following these steps:

1. Press Ctrl+Alt+Delete (or Ctrl+Alt+End when working remotely) and then select Task Manager.

2. In Task Manager, click More Details.

3. On the File menu, click Run New Task.

4. In the Create New Task dialog box, enter **cmd.exe** in the Open box, and then click OK.

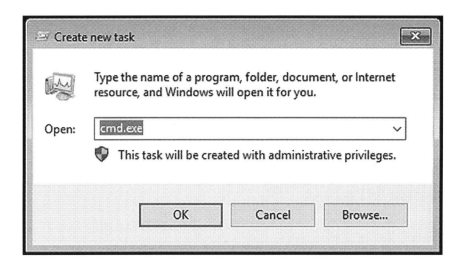

You can use this technique to open additional Command Prompt windows, too. Although you can work with Notepad and Regedit by entering **notepad.exe** or **regedit.exe** instead of **cmd.exe**, you can also start Notepad and Regedit directly from a command prompt by entering **notepad.exe** or **regedit.exe** as appropriate.

The Server Configuration utility (Sconfig.cmd) provides a text-based menu system that makes it easy to do the following:

- Configure domain or workgroup membership
- Change a server's name
- Add a local Administrator account
- Configure remote management features
- Configure Windows Update settings
- Download and install Windows updates
- Enable or disable Remote Desktop
- Configure network settings for TCP/IP
- Configure the date and time
- Activate Windows Server
- Change CEIP participation options
- Log off, restart, or shut down

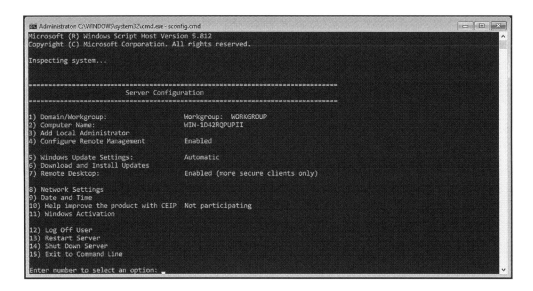

Although a Server Core installation supports a limited set of roles and role services, you can install most features. Server Core also supports the .NET Framework and Windows Remote Management (WinRM). This support allows you to perform local and remote administration by using PowerShell. Some of the common tasks you might want to perform when you are logged on include the following:

Cscript Scregedit.wsf   Configure the operating system. Use the *cli* parameter to list available configuration areas.

ipconfig /all   List information about the computer's IP address configuration.

Netdom RenameComputer   Set the server's name.

Netdom Join   Join the server to a domain.

Netsh   Provide multiple contexts for managing the configuration of networking components. Enter **netsh interface ipv4** to configure IPv4 settings. Enter **netsh interface ipv6** to configure IPv6 settings.

Pnputil.exe   Install or update hardware device drivers.

Sc query type=driver   List installed device drivers.

Serverweroptin.exe   Configure Windows Error Reporting.

Slmgr /ato   Windows Software Licensing Management tool used to activate the operating system. Runs `Cscript slmgr.vbs –ato`.

Slmgr /ipk   Install or replace the product key. Runs `Cscript slmgr.vbs –ipk`.

SystemInfo   List the system configuration details.

Wecutil.exe   Create and manage subscriptions to forwarded events.

Wevtutil.exe   View and search event logs.

Winrm quickconfig   Configure the server to accept -WS-Management requests from other computers. Runs `Cscript winrm.vbs quickconfig`. Enter without the *quickconfig* parameter to see other options.

Wmic datafile where name="FullFilePath" get version   List a file's version.

Wmic nicconfig index=9 call enabledhcp   Set the computer to use dynamic IP addressing rather than static IP addressing.

Wmic nicconfig index=9 call enablestatic("IPAddress"), ("SubnetMask")   Set a computer's static IP address and network mask.

Wmic nicconfig index=9 call setgateways("GatewayIPAddress")   Set or change the default gateway.

Wmic product get name /value   List installed Windows Installer (MSI) applications by name.

Wmic product where name="Name" call uninstall   Uninstall an MSI application.

Wmic qfe list   List installed updates and hotfixes.

Wusa.exe PatchName.msu /quiet   Apply an update or hotfix to the operating system.

Managing Nano Server

Nano Server provides a fully custom environment with just the components your server needs to support the applications and services you want to deploy. You use Nano Server when you don't need 32-bit support, the graphical desktop interface or other graphical components.

Nano Server is designed to be managed remotely using either command-line or graphical tools. As Nano Server doesn't have the Windows logon interface, this means you can't log in to servers using this configuration as you do other servers. With a Nano Server installation, the only interface available when you log on locally is the Recovery Console.

Recovery Console provides features similar to the Logon UI for Server Core with options similar to Sconfig.cmd. With a keyboard and monitor connected to a nano server, you can log in to the recovery console using an administrator account. The console runs automatically and has a basic text-based menu that is navigated using the keyboard. You use the arrow keys or Tab to navigate between options and Enter to select an option. To go back a screen or a page, you press Esc.

Although the console is meant to help you diagnose and resolve networking issues that prevent you from connecting to a server, you can use the recovery features at any time to work with basic settings of the server, including

- Network adapters
- TCP/IP settings
- Server naming

You also can use the console to restart or shutdown the server.

As Nano Server doesn't have the remote desktop, you can't remotely manage a server using this configuration in the same way as you can a full-server or server core installation. Not supporting remote desktop, however, isn't the same as not being able to use remote management tools or other options.

Although you can't remote in to a nano server and nano server doesn't have the graphical interfaces, you can use the graphical administration tools to remotely manage a server using this configuration. Thus, the easiest way to manage a nano server remotely is to install the Remote Server Administration Tools (RSAT) on your management computer and then use the tools to manage the server.

You also can manage a nano server using Windows PowerShell Remoting. Start by opening an administrator command prompt. If you haven't added the server as a trusted host on your computer, do so by entering the following command:

```
Set-Item WSMan:\localhost\Client\TrustedHosts NanoServerIPAddress
```

Where NanoServerIPAddress is the IP address of the nano server. You can then establish a remote session with the server. The basic syntax is:

```
$Cred = Get-Credential
$Session = New-PSSession -ComputerName IPAddress -Credential $Cred
```

To establish a connection to the nano server, you must pass in your user name and password. This example stores credentials in a Credential object and then uses Get-Credential to prompt for the required credentials. You also could specify the credentials explicitly, as shown here:

```
$Session = New-PSSession -ComputerName IPAddress
```

After you establish a session with the nano server, you must import the server-side PowerShell session into your client-side session by running the following command:

```
Import-PSSession $Session
```

You can then work with the nano server remotely. When you are finished, you should disconnect the remote shell from the nano server.

> **NOTE** Beginning with Windows PowerShell 3.0, sessions are persistent by default. When you disconnect from a session, any command or scripts that are running in the session continue running, and you can later reconnect to the session to pick up where you left off. You also can reconnect to a session if you were disconnected unintentionally, such as by a temporary network outage.

To disconnect a session without stopping commands or releasing resources, run the following command:

```
Disconnect-PSSession $Session
```

The $Session object was instantiated when you created the session. As long as you don't exit the PowerShell window in which this object was created, you can use this object to reconnect to the session by entering:

```
Connect-PSSession $Session
```

When you are completely finished with the session, you should remove it. Removing a session stops any commands or scripts that are running, ends the session, and releases the resources the session was using. Remove a session by running the following command:

```
Remove-PSSession $Session
```

Performing a Clean Installation

Before you start an installation, you need to consider whether you want to manage the computer's drives and partitions during the setup process. If you want to use the advanced drive setup options that Setup provides for creating and formatting partitions, you need to start the computer by using the distribution media. If you don't start by using the distribution media, these options won't be available, and you'll be able to manage disk partitions at a command prompt only by using the DiskPart utility.

You can perform a clean installation of Windows Server 2016 by following these steps:

1. Use one of the following techniques to start the Setup program:

- To perform a new installation, start the computer with the Windows Server 2016 distribution media in the computer's disc drive, and then press any key when prompted to start Setup from your media. If you are not prompted to boot from the disc drive, you might need to access the boot manager or select advanced boot options and then boot from the media rather than from the hard disk, or you might need to change the computer's firmware settings to allow starting and loading the operating system from media.
- To perform a clean installation over an existing installation, you can boot from the distribution media, or you can start the computer and log on by using an account with administrator privileges. When you insert the Windows Server 2016 distribution media into the computer's disc drive, Setup should start automatically. If Setup doesn't start automatically and you are trying to boot from media, you might need to select advanced boot options or change firmware settings to allow booting from media. If you are logged in to an existing installation, you can start use File Explorer to access the distribution media, and then double-click Setup.exe.

```
F2  = System Setup
F10 = Lifecycle Controller (Config iDRAC, Update FW, Install OS
F11 = Boot Manager
F12 = PXE Boot


Initializing Serial ATA devices...
  Port A: TOSHIBA DT01ACA050
  Port B: ST31000340AS
  Port C: ST3500630AS
  Port E: HL-DT-ST DVD-ROM DU90N
```

> **NOTE** If you are installing Windows Server 2016 as a guest operating system on a host server, you'll need to allocate resources beforehand, including those for memory, processors and disks. Although the operating system can operate in a minimal installation with only 512 MB RAM, you may need to allocate more RAM than this initially to complete the setup process.

2. If you started the computer by using the distribution media, you'll next need to choose your language, time and currency formats, and keyboard layout when prompted. Only one keyboard layout is available during installation. If your keyboard language and the language edition of Windows Server 2016 you are installing are different, you might see unexpected characters as you type. To avoid this, be sure that you select the correct keyboard language. When you are ready to continue with the installation, click Next.

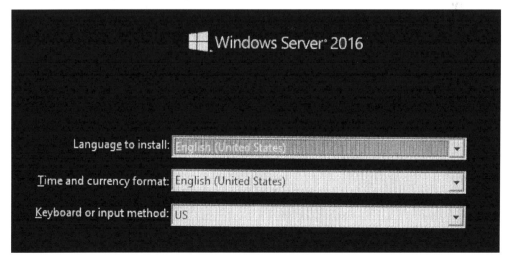

3. If you are starting the installation from an existing operating system and are connected to a network or the Internet, choose whether to get updates during the installation. Click either Download And Install Updates or Not Right Now.

Get important updates

These updates will help the installation go smoothly, and can include important fixes and updated device drivers. If you don't install these updates now, you will get them later from Windows Update.

○ Download and install updates (recommended)

● Not right now

4. With volume and enterprise licensed editions of Windows Server 2016, you might not need to provide a product key during installation. With retail editions, however, you need to enter a product key when prompted. Click Next to continue.

Product key

The product key should be with the box the DVD came in or on your email receipt. When you connect to the Internet, we'll activate Windows for you.

It looks similar to this: XXXXX-XXXXX-XXXXX-XXXXX-XXXXX

Enter Product key

Dashes will be added automatically

> **NOTE** Don't worry about using the correct letter case or entering dashes. Setup enters all letters you type in uppercase. When a dash is needed, Setup enters the dash automatically. If you started Setup from an existing installation, you can copy the key from a document and then paste it into the Product key text box. If you enter an invalid product key, Setup will continue to display a warning and you'll need to correct the issue. Sometimes it's easier to re-enter the product key than try to identify a mistyped value.

5. Choose whether to perform a standard (Server Core) installation or a full-server (with Desktop Experience) installation. Keep in mind the edition of the operating system listed is based on the product key you entered previously. If you entered a product key for the wrong edition, you can go back and enter a product key for the edition you want to use. Click Next.

Select Image

Please select the image you want to install.

Operating System:	Language:
Windows Server 2016 Datacenter	en-US
Windows Server 2016 Datacenter (Desktop Experience)	en-US

6. The license terms for Windows Server 2016 have changed from previous releases of Windows. After you review the license terms, click Accept to continue.

7. If you started the installation while logged on to an existing installation, you'll next see the Choose What To Keep page. Generally, you won't be able to keep any existing files, apps or settings and the Nothing selection will be your only option. Before continuing make sure you really don't need any files or other data on the system drive. If necessary, you can cancel the installation and restart Setup once you've backed up important files and data. Click Next and then click Install to begin the installation process. Skip the remaining steps.

Choose what to keep

● Keep personal files and apps
   You will be able to manage your Windows settings.

○ Nothing
   Everything will be deleted, including files, apps, and settings.

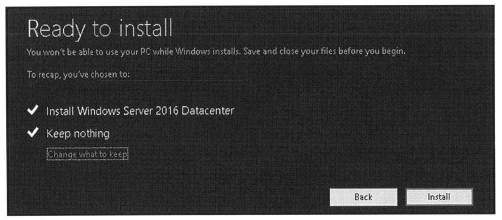

Ready to install

You won't be able to use your PC while Windows installs. Save and close your files before you begin.

To recap, you've chosen to:

✔ Install Windows Server 2016 Datacenter

✔ Keep nothing

  Change what to keep

[Back] [Install]

8. If you booted from distribution media, you'll need to continue through the remaining steps of this procedure to complete the installation. When prompted, select the type of installation you want Setup to perform. Because you are performing a clean installation to replace an existing installation completely or configure a new computer, select Custom: Install Windows Only (Advanced) as the installation type.

9. You'll next be able to select the disk or disk and partition on which you want to install the operating system. There are two versions of the related page, so you need to keep the following in mind:

* When a computer has a single hard disk with a single partition encompassing the whole disk or a single area of unallocated space, the whole disk partition is selected by default, and you can click Next to choose this as the install location and continue. With a disk that is completely unallocated, you might want to create the necessary partition before installing the operating system, as discussed in the "Managing Disk Partitions During Installation" section later in this chapter.

* When a computer has multiple disks or a single disk with multiple partitions, you need to select an existing partition to use for installing the operating system or create a partition. You can create and manage partitions, as discussed in the "Managing Disk Partitions During Installation" section later in this chapter.

* If a disk has not been initialized for use or if the firmware of the computer does not support starting the operating system from the selected disk, you need to initialize it by creating one or more partitions on the disk. You cannot select or format a hard disk partition that uses FAT or FAT32 or has other incompatible settings. To work around this issue, you might want to convert the partition to NTFS.

* When working with this page, you can access a command prompt to perform any necessary preinstallation tasks. See the "Using the Command Line During Installation" section later in this chapter.

10. If the partition you select contains a previous Windows installation, Setup provides a prompt stating that existing user and application settings will be moved to a folder named Windows.old and that you must copy these settings to the new installation to use them. Click OK.

11. Click Next. Setup starts the installation of the operating system. During this procedure, Setup copies the full disk image of Windows Server 2016 to the location you selected and then expands it. Afterward, Setup installs features based on the computer's configuration and the hardware it detects. This process requires several automatic restarts.

When Setup finishes the installation, the operating system will be loaded, and you can perform initial configuration tasks such as setting the administrator password and server name. If you encounter any issues during the installation, you may need to go through the Setup process again. See "Performing Additional Tasks During Installation" for tips and guidance.

REAL WORLD Servers running core installations of Windows Server are configured to use DHCP by default. As long as the server has a network card and a connected network cable, a Server Core installation should be able to connect to your organization's DHCP servers and obtain the correct network settings. You can configure the server by using Sconfig, which provides menu options for configuring domain/workgroup membership, the computer name, remote management, Windows Update, Remote Desktop, network settings, date and time, logoff, restart, and shutdown.

Alternatively, you can configure the server by using individual commands. If you want to use a static IP address, use Netsh to apply the settings you want. After networking is configured correctly, enter **Slmgr –ipk** to set the product key and **Slmgr –ato** to activate Windows. Enter **timedate.cpl** to set the server's date and time. If you want to enable remote management by using the WS-Management protocol, enter **winrm quickconfig**.

Next, you'll probably want to set the name of the computer. To view the default computer name, enter **echo %computername%**. To rename the computer, use Netdom RenameComputer with the following syntax: **netdom renamecomputer** *currentname* **/newname:***newname*, where *currentname* is the current name of the computer and *newname* is the name you want to assign. An example is **netdom renamecomputer win-k4m6bnovlhe /newname:server18**. You'll need to restart the computer, and you can do this by entering **shutdown /r**.

When the computer restarts, you can join it to a domain by using Netdom Join. For the syntax, enter **netdom join /?**.

As part of a server's post-installation configuration, you'll also want to configure networking settings. Chapter 2 provides a detailed discussion of the related options, including details on how to team adapters for load balancing. Once you've finalized the TCP/IP configuration, you may need to join the server to a domain and Windows Server 2016 provides several ways to do this.

In PowerShell, you can add a server to a domain using Add-Computer. The basic syntax is:

```
$Cred = Get-Credential
Add-Computer –Domain DomainName -Credential $Cred
```

where DomainName is the name of the domain to which the local computer should be added. When you are joining a computer to a domain, you must provide the credentials of a user account that has permission to join computers to the specified domain.

> **TIP** You don't have to be logged on to the server to add it to the domain using PowerShell. When working remotely, use the –ComputerName parameter to specify the name or IP address of the server to join to the domain.

If you have any problem adding the server to a domain, you may want to:

* Check the TCP/IP settings and ensure the IP address, subnet mask, gateway and DNS server addresses are correct.
* Check the date and time of the server to ensure these settings are correct and as close to world time as possible.

Sometimes, it may seem like you are doing everything right and you still not be able to join a server to a domain. In this case, you can perform an offline domain join that doesn't require the server to communicate directly with a domain controller. Here, you:

1. Run the following command on a computer that is a member of the domain to create a provisioning file:

```
djoin /provision /domain DomainName /machine TargetName /savefile FileName
```

where DomainName is the name of the domain to which the server should be added, TargetName is the name of the server, and FileName is the name for the provisioning file. The following example creates a provisioning file called fs97-join.txt to allow FileServer97 to join the ImaginedLands.local domain:

```
djoin /provision /domain imaginedlands.local /machine fileserver97
/savefile fs97-join.txt
```

2. When you run the /provision command, a computer account is created in the domain for the server and then a provisioning file is generated. Copy the provisioning file to the target server. This text-based file contains encrypted strings that allow the server to join the domain without using TCP/IP networking for authentication.

3. Run the following command to provision the target server:

```
djoin /requestodj /localos /loadfile FilePath /windowspath WinPath
```

Here, you perform an offline domain request of the local operating system by loading a provisioning file. FileName specifies the path and name of the provisioning file and WinPath specifies the location of the Windows directory on the server. The following example loads the provisioning file created previously and use the %SystemRoot% environment variable to specify the location of the Windows directory:

```
djoin /requestodj /localos /loadfile f:\fs97-join.txt /windowspath
%systemroot%
```

4. After you restart the target server, the server will be a joined to the previously specified domain and you'll be able to logon to the server using a domain account. As no domain user credentials are cached initially, the server will need an active network connection for logon to occur.

Provisioning can fail for a variety of reasons. If a server with the same name as the one you want to join to the domain was previously provisioned or added to the domain, provisioning will fail and you'll need to confirm whether the name is actually available for use. If no other domain joined computer is actually using the name, you can force DJoin to re-provision the name and create a provisioning file by adding the /Reuse parameter, as shown in the following example:

```
djoin /provision /domain tvpress.local /machine webserver23
/savefile ws23-join.txt /reuse
```

> **TIP** Copying the provisioning file to a core server using a USB drive? Use DiskPart to determine the drive letter. Enter **diskpart** to start the utility and then enter **list volume** to list all available volumes.

Performing an Upgrade Installation

You can upgrade servers running Windows Server 2012 R2 to Windows Server 2016. During an upgrade, Setup attempts to keep Windows settings, user files and apps. If the server has apps installed that don't support Windows Server 2016, you should uninstall the apps before continuing. Because of the challenges presented with upgrading a server hosting services and application software, it often is more efficient to migrate services and applications a server is hosting to other servers and then perform a clean installation.

You can perform an upgrade installation of Windows Server 2016 by following these steps:

1. Start the computer, and log on by using an account with administrator privileges. When you insert the Windows Server 2016 distribution media into the computer's DVD-ROM drive, Setup should start automatically. If Setup doesn't start automatically, use File Explorer to access the distribution media and then double-click Setup.exe.

2. Because you are starting Setup from the current operating system, you are not prompted to choose your language, time and currency formats, or keyboard layout, and only the current operating system's keyboard layout is available during installation. If your keyboard language and the language of the edition of Windows Server 2016 you are installing are different, unexpected characters might be displayed as you type.

3. If the computer is connected to a network or the Internet, choose whether to get updates during the installation. Click either Download And Install Updates or Not Right Now.

Get important updates

These updates will help the installation go smoothly, and can include important fixes and updated device drivers. If you don't install these updates now, you will get them later from Windows Update.

○ Download and install updates (recommended)

● Not right now

4. With volume-licensed and enterprise-licensed editions of Windows Server 2016, you might not need to provide a product key during installation of the operating system. With retail editions, however, you are prompted to enter a

product key. If you enter an invalid product key, Setup will display a warning and you'll need to correct the issue before you can continue.

5. Choose whether to perform a standard (Server Core) installation or a full-server (with Desktop Experience) installation. Keep in mind the edition of the operating system listed is based on the product key you entered previously. If you entered a product key for the wrong edition, you can go back and enter a product key for the edition you want to use. Click Next.

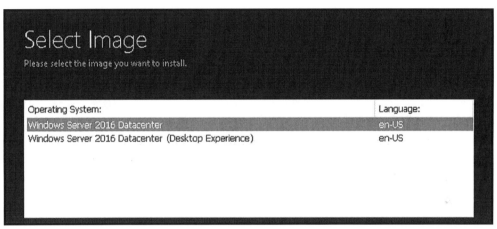

6. The license terms for Windows Server 2016 have changed from previous releases of Windows. After you review the license terms, click Accept to continue.

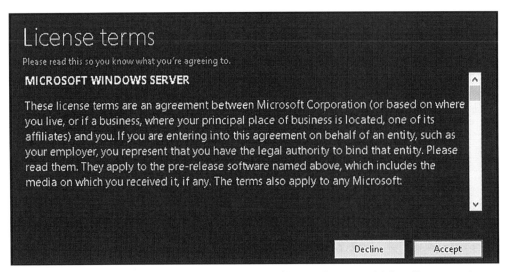

7. Next, specify that you want to keep files and apps, which tells Setup that you want to perform an upgrade. This ensures that Setup will try to keep Windows settings, user files and apps.

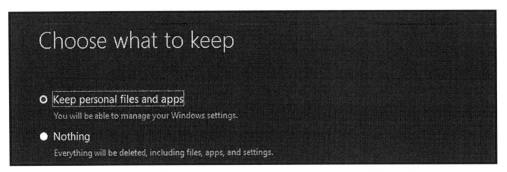

8. If there are any issues that need your attention, you'll be asked to take corrective action, confirm that you understand the issues or both before you can continue. After taking a corrective action, click Refresh to have Setup perform the preinstallation checks again. If there are no other issues, Setup will continue. If you are asked for confirmation, clicking Confirm will also continue the Setup process, provided there are no other issues that need your attention.

9. Click Install. Setup will then start the installation. Because you are upgrading the operating system, you do not need to choose an installation location. During this process, Setup copies the full disk image of Windows Server 2016 to the system disk. Afterward, Setup installs features based on the computer's configuration and the hardware it detects.

Ready to install

You won't be able to use your PC while Windows installs. Save and close your files before you begin.

To recap, you've chosen to:

✔ Install Windows Server 2016 Datacenter
✔ Keep personal files and apps

Change what to keep

[Back] [Install]

When Setup finishes the installation, the operating system will be loaded, and you can perform initial configuration tasks such as setting the administrator password and server name. If you encounter any issues during the installation, you may need to go through the Setup process again. See "Performing Additional Tasks During Installation" for tips and guidance.

Performing Additional Tasks During Installation

Sometimes you might forget to perform a preinstallation task prior to starting the installation. Rather than restarting the computer, you can access a command prompt from Setup or use advanced drive options to perform the necessary tasks.

Using the Command Line During Installation

When you access a command prompt from Setup, you access the Windows Preinstallation Environment (Windows PE) used by Setup to install the operating system. During installation, on the Where Do You Want To Install Windows page, you can access a command prompt by pressing Shift+F10. The Windows PE gives you access to many of the same command-line tools that are available in a standard installation of Windows Server 2016. These tools include:

- **ARP** Displays and modifies the IP-to-physical address translation tables used by the Address Resolution Protocol (ARP).
- **ASSOC** Displays and modifies file extension associations.
- **ATTRIB** Displays and changes file attributes.
- **CALL** Calls a script or script label as a procedure.
- **CD/CHDIR** Displays the name of or changes the current directory.

- **CHKDSK**   Checks a disk for errors and displays a report.
- **CHKNTFS**   Displays the status of volumes. Sets or excludes volumes from automatic system checking when the computer is started.
- **CHOICE**   Creates a list from which users can select one of several choices in a batch script.
- **CLS**   Clears the console window.
- **CMD**   Starts a new instance of the Windows command shell.
- **COLOR**   Sets the colors of the command-shell window.
- **CONVERT**   Converts FAT volumes to NTFS.
- **COPY**   Copies or combines files.
- **DATE**   Displays or sets the system date.
- **DEL**   Deletes one or more files.
- **DIR**   Displays a list of files and subdirectories within a directory.
- **DISKPART**   Invokes a text-mode command interpreter so that you can manage disks, partitions, and volumes by using a separate command prompt and commands that are internal to DISKPART.
- **DISM**   Services and manages Windows images.
- **DOSKEY**   Edits command lines, recalls Windows commands, and creates macros.
- **ECHO**   Displays messages or turns command echoing on or off.
- **ENDLOCAL**   Ends localization of environment changes in a batch file.
- **ERASE**   Deletes one or more files.
- **EXIT**   Exits the command interpreter.
- **EXPAND**   Uncompresses files.
- **FIND**   Searches for a text string in files.
- **FOR**   Runs a specified command for each file in a set of files.
- **FORMAT**   Formats a drive or USB flash device.
- **FTP**   Transfers files.
- **FTYPE**   Displays or modifies file types used in file- name extension associations.
- **GOTO**   Directs the Windows command interpreter to a labeled line in a script.
- **HOSTNAME**   Prints the computer's name.
- **IF**   Performs conditional processing in batch programs.
- **IPCONFIG**   Displays TCP/IP configuration.
- **LABEL**   Creates, changes, or deletes the volume label of a disk.
- **MD/MKDIR**   Creates a directory or subdirectory.
- **MORE**   Displays output one screen at a time.
- **MOUNTVOL**   Manages a volume mount point.
- **MOVE**   Moves files from one directory to another directory on the same drive.
- **NBTSTAT**   Displays the status of NetBIOS.
- **NET ACCOUNTS**   Manages user account and password policies.
- **NET COMPUTER**   Adds or removes computers from a domain.
- **NET CONFIG SERVER**   Displays or modifies the configuration of a server service.
- **NET CONFIG WORKSTATION**   Displays or modifies the configuration of a workstation service.

- **NET CONTINUE**   Resumes a paused service.
- **NET FILE**   Displays or manages open files on a server.
- **NET GROUP**   Displays or manages global groups.
- **NET LOCALGROUP**   Displays or manages local group accounts.
- **NET NAME**   Displays or modifies recipients for messenger service messages.
- **NET PAUSE**   Suspends a service.
- **NET PRINT**   Displays or manages print jobs and shared queues.
- **NET SEND**   Sends a messenger service message.
- **NET SESSION**   Lists or disconnects sessions.
- **NET SHARE**   Displays or manages shared printers and directories.
- **NET START**   Lists or starts network services.
- **NET STATISTICS**   Displays workstation and server statistics.
- **NET STOP**   Stops services.
- **NET TIME**   Displays or synchronizes network time.
- **NET USE**   Displays or manages remote connections.
- **NET USER**   Displays or manages local user accounts.
- **NET VIEW**   Displays network resources or computers.
- **NETSH**   Invokes a separate command prompt that allows you to manage the configuration of various network services on local and remote computers.
- **NETSTAT**   Displays the status of network connections.
- **PATH**   Displays or sets a search path for executable files in the current command window.
- **PATHPING**   Traces routes, and provides packet-loss information.
- **PAUSE**   Suspends the processing of a script, and waits for keyboard input.
- **PING**   Determines whether a network connection can be established.
- **POPD**   Changes to the directory stored by PUSHD.
- **PRINT**   Prints a text file.
- **PROMPT**   Modifies the command prompt.
- **PUSHD**   Saves the current directory and then changes to a new directory.
- **RD/RMDIR**   Removes a directory.
- **RECOVER**   Recovers readable information from a bad or defective disk.
- **REG ADD**   Adds a new subkey or entry to the registry.
- **REG COMPARE**   Compares registry subkeys or entries.
- **REG COPY**   Copies a registry entry to a specified key path on a local or remote system.
- **REG DELETE**   Deletes a subkey or entries from the registry.
- **REG QUERY**   Lists the entries under a key and the names of subkeys (if any).
- **REG RESTORE**   Writes saved subkeys and entries back to the registry.
- **REG SAVE**   Saves a copy of specified subkeys, entries, and values to a file.
- **REGSVR32**   Registers and unregisters DLLs.
- **REM**   Adds comments to scripts.
- **REN**   Renames a file.
- **ROUTE**   Manages network routing tables.

- **SET**   Displays or modifies Windows environment variables. Also used to evaluate numeric expressions at the command line.
- **SETLOCAL**   Begins the localization of environment changes in a batch file.
- **SFC**   Scans and verifies protected system files.
- **SHIFT**   Shifts the position of replaceable parameters in scripts.
- **START**   Starts a new command-shell window to run a specified program or command.
- **SUBST**   Maps a path to a drive letter.
- **TIME**   Displays or sets the system time.
- **TITLE**   Sets the title for the command-shell window.
- **TRACERT**   Displays the path between computers.
- **TYPE**   Displays the contents of a text file.
- **VER**   Displays the Windows version.
- **VERIFY**   Tells Windows whether to verify that your files are written correctly to a disk.
- **VOL**   Displays a disk volume label and serial number.

Forcing Disk Partition Removal During Installation

During installation, you might be unable to select the hard disk you want to use. This issue can arise if the hard-disk partition contains an invalid byte offset value. To resolve this issue, you need to remove the partitions on the hard disk (which destroys all associated data) and then create the necessary partition by using the advanced options in the Setup program. During installation, on the Where Do You Want To Install Windows page, you can remove unrecognized hard-disk partitions by following these steps:

1. Press Shift+F10 to open a command prompt.
2. At the command prompt, enter **diskpart**. This starts the DiskPart utility.
3. To view a list of disks on the computer, enter **list disk**.
4. Select a disk by entering **select disk *DiskNumber***, where *DiskNumber* is the number of the disk you want to work with.
5. To permanently remove the partitions on the selected disk, enter **clean**.
6. When the cleaning process is finished, enter **exit** to exit the DiskPart utility.
7. Enter **exit** to exit the command prompt.

> ***CAUTION***   Do not clean a disk if there are any files or other data on the disk that may be needed. Cleaning a disk removes all partitions on the selected disk, which in turn causes all data on the disk to be lost.

To get Setup to recognize the changes you've made, you'll need to go back to the previous window and then continue with the installation process. You'll then be able to select the disk you previously cleaned and use it for installation. With the disk selected, click the Disk Options link to display the partition configuration options and then click New. In the Size box, set the size of the partition in megabytes, and then click Apply. This creates a partition on the disk you cleaned. Make sure the partition is at least 32 GB (32768 MB).

Loading Device Drivers During Installation

During installation, on the Where Do You Want To Install Windows page, you can use the Load Driver option to load the device drivers for disks and disk controllers. Typically, you use this option when a storage subsystem or disk drive you want to use for installing the operating system isn't available for selection.

To load the device drivers and make the disk available, follow these steps:

1. During installation, on the Where Do You Want To Install Windows page, click Load Driver.

2. When prompted, insert the installation media into a DVD drive or USB flash drive, and then click OK. Setup then searches the computer's removable media drives for the device drivers.

- If Setup finds multiple device drivers, select the driver to install, and then click Next.
- If Setup doesn't find the device driver, click Browse to use the Browse For Folder dialog box to select the device driver to load, click OK, and then click Next.

You can click the Rescan button to have Setup rescan the computer's removable media drives for the device drivers. If the driver is found, you'll be able to select and install it. If you are unable to install a device driver successfully, click the back arrow button in the upper-left corner of the Install Windows dialog box to go back to the previous page and then try to continue the installation. If this doesn't work, you'll need to determine which disk or storage subsystem drivers are needed and obtain them before you can continue.

Managing Disk Partitions During Installation

When you are performing a clean installation and have started the computer from the distribution media, the Where Do You Want To Install Windows page is displayed during setup. This page has options for working with drives and partitions, including:

- **New**   Creates a partition. You must then format the partition.
- **Format**   Formats a new partition so that you can use it for installing the operating system.
- **Delete**   Deletes a partition that is no longer wanted.
- **Extend**   Extends a partition to increase its size.

The sections that follow discuss how to use each of these options. If these options aren't available, you can still work with the computer's disks. On the Where Do You Want To Install Windows page, press Shift+F10 to open a command prompt. At the command prompt, enter **diskpart** to start the DiskPart utility.

Creating Disk Partitions During Installation

Creating a partition allows you to set the partition's size. Because you can create new partitions only in areas of unallocated space on a disk, you might need to delete existing partitions to be able to create a partition of the size you want. After you create a partition, you can format the partition so that you can use it to install a file system. If you don't format a partition, you can still use it for installing the operating system. In this case, Setup formats the partition when you continue installing the operating system.

You can create a new partition by following these steps:

1. During installation, on the Where Do You Want To Install Windows page, click the disk on which you want to create the partition, and then click New.

2. In the Size box, set the size of the partition in megabytes, and then click Apply to have Setup create a partition on the selected disk.

After you create a partition, you need to format the partition to continue with the installation.

Formatting Disk Partitions During Installation

Formatting a partition creates a file system on the partition. When formatting is complete, you have a formatted partition on which you can install the operating system. Keep in mind that formatting a partition destroys all data on the partition. You should format existing partitions (rather than ones you just created) only when you want to remove an existing partition and all its contents so that you can start the installation from a freshly formatted partition.

You can format a partition by following these steps:

1. During installation, on the Where Do You Want To Install Windows page, click the partition that you want to format.
2. Click Format. When prompted to confirm that you want to format the partition, click OK. Setup then formats the partition.

Deleting Disk Partitions During Installation

Deleting a partition removes a partition you no longer want or need. When Setup finishes deleting the partition, the disk space previously allocated to the partition becomes unallocated space on the disk. Deleting the partition destroys all data on the partition. Typically, you need to delete a partition only when it is in the wrong format or when you want to combine areas of free space on a disk.

You can delete a partition by following these steps:

1. During installation, on the Where Do You Want To Install Windows page, click the partition you want to delete.
2. Click Delete. When prompted to confirm that you want to delete the partition, click OK. Setup then deletes the partition.

Extending Disk Partitions During Installation

Windows Server 2016 requires at least 10 GB of disk space for installation, and at least 32 GB of available disk space is recommended. If an existing partition is too small, you won't be able to use it to install the operating system. To resolve this, you can extend a partition to increase its size by using areas of contiguous, unallocated space on the current disk. You can extend a partition with an existing file system only if it is formatted with NTFS 5.2 or later. New partitions created in Setup can be extended also, provided that the disk on which you create the partition has unallocated space.

You can extend a partition by following these steps:

1. During installation, on the Where Do You Want To Install Windows page, click the partition you want to extend.

2. Click Extend. In the Size box, set the size of the partition in megabytes, and then click Apply to extend the selected partition.

3. When prompted to confirm that you want to extend the partition, click OK. Setup then extends the partition.

Chapter 2. Implementing TCP/IP Networking

You enable networked computers to communicate by using the basic networking protocols built into Windows Server 2016. The key protocol you use is TCP/IP, which is a suite of protocols and services used for communicating over a network and is the primary protocol used for internetwork communications. Compared to configuring other networking protocols, configuring TCP/IP communications is fairly complicated, but TCP/IP is the most versatile protocol available.

> **NOTE** Group Policy settings can affect your ability to install and manage TCP/IP networking. The key policies you should examine are in User Configuration\Administrative Templates\Network\Network Connections and Computer Configuration\Administrative Templates\System\Group Policy. Group Policy is discussed in Chapter 13, "Using Group Policy for Administration."

Navigating Networking Options

TCP/IP is the primary networking protocol used by Windows computers. Modern computers use IP version 4 (IPv4) and IP version 6 (IPv6) addressing.

Networking Tools & Essentials

Windows Server 2016 has an extensive set of tools for managing networking, including:

- **Network Connections**   Lists the available network adapters and their status.
- **Network And Sharing Center**   Provides a central console for viewing and managing a computer's networking and sharing configuration.
- **Network Diagnostics**   Provides automated diagnostics to help diagnose and resolve networking problems.

You use Network Connections to view and manage a server's network adapters. To access Network Connections, follow these steps:

1. Open Settings by clicking Start and then selecting Settings.
2. On the Settings home page, click Network & Internet and then click Ethernet.
3. On the Ethernet page, click Change Adapter Options.

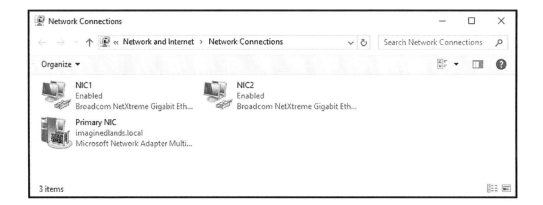

While you are working with Network Connections, you can:

- Double-click a network adapter to display its status.
- Right-click a network adapter and then select Properties to view the related Properties dialog box.
- Right-click a network adapter and then select Diagnose to begin troubleshooting networking problems.

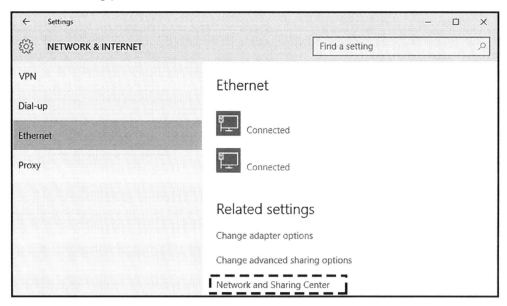

Network And Sharing Center provides an overview of the network. The value below the network name shows the category of the current network. The three categories of networks are defined as follows:

- **Domain network** Designates a network in which computers are connected to the corporate domain to which they are joined

- **Private network** Designates a network in which computers are configured as members of a homegroup or workgroup and are not connected directly to the public Internet
- **Public network** Designates a network in a public place, such as a coffee shop or an airport, rather than an internal network

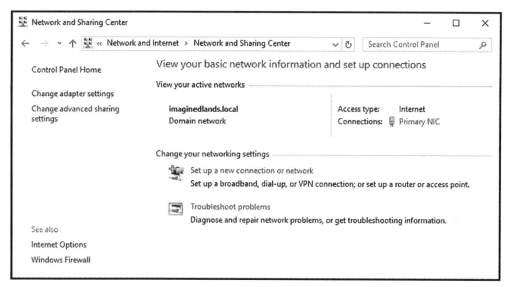

The Access Type box specifies whether and how the computer is connected to its current network. Values for this option are No Network Access, No Internet Access, or Internet. If you click the name of a network connection, you can display the related status dialog box.

You can access Network And Sharing Center by following these steps:

1. Open Settings by clicking Start and then selecting Settings.
2. On the Settings home page, click Network & Internet and then click Ethernet.
3. On the Ethernet page, click Network And Sharing Center.

Clicking Change Adapter Settings displays Network Connections, which you can use to manage network connections. Clicking Change Advanced Sharing Settings provides options for configuring the computer's sharing and discovery settings for each network profile.

However, with Windows Server 2016, network discovery generally is turned off for all network categories by default, while file and print sharing are turned on for all network categories by default. Thus, the category is mostly applicable to firewall settings, which are used to block or allow applications according to the network category.

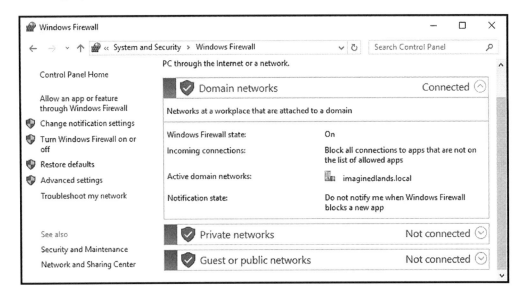

You can use Windows Firewall to manage which apps are blocked or allowed by following these steps:

1. Open Settings by clicking Start and then selecting Settings.
2. On the Settings home page, click Network & Internet and then click Ethernet.
3. On the Ethernet page, click Windows Firewall. In the Windows Firewall app, the active network is listed as Connected.
4. Click Allow An App Or Feature Through Windows Firewall. Then on the Allowed Apps page, click Change Settings.
5. Use the options provided to specify which apps and features are allowed. If an app or feature is allowed for a particular network category, select the related checkbox. Otherwise, clear the related checkbox.

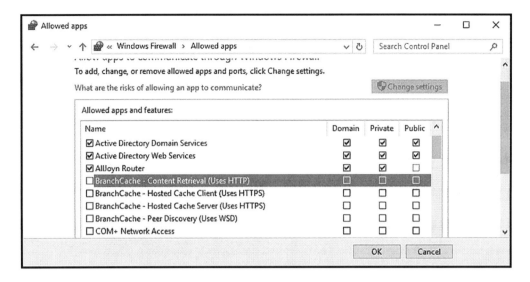

When you connect a computer's network adapter to a network for the first time, Windows sets the network category based on the configuration of the computer. Typically, you will find that a network adapter is set as public before you join a computer to a domain.

If the category is set incorrectly, one way to fix the problem is to click Troubleshoot Problems while working with Network And Sharing Center and then follow the prompts to allow the network troubleshooter to detect the problem and help you resolve it. Another way to resolve the problem is to use Windows PowerShell to make the change. For example, the default alias for the first network connection on a device typically is "Ethernet". If so, you can use the following command to change the network category of this connection to private:

```
Get-NetConnectionProfile -InterfaceAlias "Ethernet" |
Set-NetConnectionProfile -NetworkCategory Private
```

From Network And Sharing Center, you can attempt to diagnose a networking problem. To do this, click Troubleshoot Problems, and then click a troubleshooter to run, such as Incoming Connections or Network Adapter, and then follow the prompts. Windows Network Diagnostics then attempts to identify the network problem and provide a possible solution.

Network Interfaces & Teaming

A network connection is created automatically if a computer has a network adapter and is connected to a network. If a computer has multiple network adapters, one network connection is created for each adapter that is connected to a network. Each network connection can be configured in the following ways:

- **Manually** IP addresses that are assigned manually are called *static IP addresses*. Static IP addresses are fixed and don't change unless you change them. You usually assign static IP addresses to Windows servers, and when you do this, you need to configure additional information to help the server navigate the network.
- **Dynamically** A DHCP server (if one is installed on the network) assigns dynamic IP addresses at startup, and the addresses might change over time. Dynamic IP addressing is the default configuration.
- **Alternate addresses (IPv4 only)** When a computer is configured to use DHCP and no DHCP server is available, Windows Server 2016 assigns an alternate private IP address automatically. The alternate address is in the range 169.254.0.1 to 169.254.255.254 with a subnet mask of 255.255.0.0. You can also specify a user-configured alternate address.

By default, servers use dynamic IPv4 addressing, if a DHCPv4 server is available, or autoconfiguration using alternate addressing otherwise. The alternate address is in the range 169.254.0.1 to 169.254.255.254 with a subnet mask of 255.255.0.0. You can also specify a user-configured alternate address.

Unlike IPv4, a DHCPv6 server is not required to dynamically configured IPv6. IPv6 can autoconfigure itself without DHCP or any other stateful configuration protocol. Computers autoconfigure link-local addresses for each network adapter configured to use IPv6 through router discovery, which also sets the addresses of routers and other essential configuration parameters automatically.

> **TIP** The default link-local address is based on the FE80::/64 prefix and the 64-bit identifier of the network adapter itself. This default address is used as long as it is unique and valid for the network. However, if for some reason the default address is not unique, you will need to manually specify another IPv6 address.

You can configure the TCP/IP settings for each individual network adapter available on a sever by following these steps:

1. Open Settings. On the Settings home page, click Network & Internet and then click Ethernet.

2. On the Ethernet page, click Change Adapter Options. In Network Connections, right-click the connection with which you want to work, and then click Properties. This displays a Properties dialog box for the connection.

3. In the Properties dialog box for the network connection, be sure that Internet Protocol Version 6 (TCP/IPv6), Internet Protocol Version 4 (TCP/IPv4), or both are selected.

4. As appropriate, follow the instructions in the next section for configuring static or dynamic IP addressing.

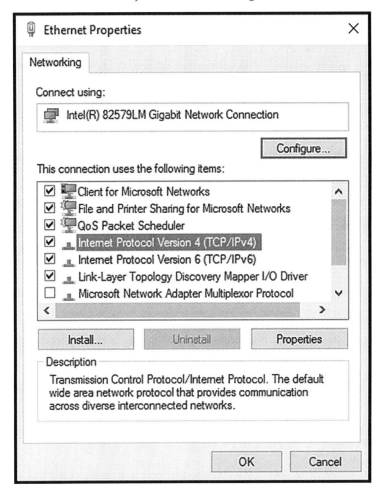

Although you generally must configure each network adapter available on a server separately, network interface teaming (NIC teaming) allows you to group adapters together for the purposes of load balancing. If a server has teamed adapters, you'll find that IPv4 and IPv6 are disabled on individual adapters and that the Microsoft Network Adapter Multiplexor Protocol is enabled instead.

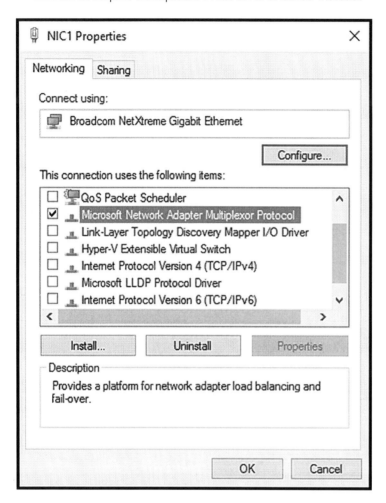

The reason for this is that you configure TCP/IP addressing for teamed adapters by using the multiplexed interface rather than individual adapters. The IP addressing options available are the same as those for standard adapters. This means you use the IPv4 options in the adapter's properties dialog box to configure IPv4 and the related IPv6 options to configure IPv6.

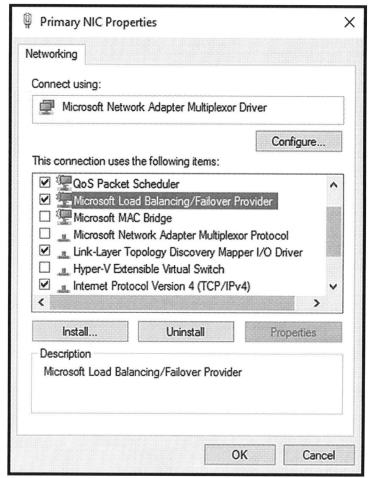

Other options of the multiplexed adapter, however, such as whether load balancing is enabled, should be configured by using the NIC Teaming interface. In Server Manager, you can access the NIC Teaming interface by clicking the related Enabled or Disabled link on the Local Server page.

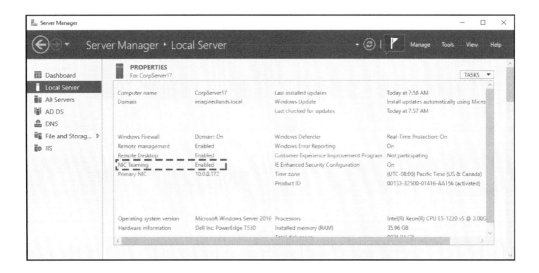

You also can access the NIC Teaming interface by entering the following in the Search box or at a prompt:

```
Lbfoadmin.exe /servers .
```

The /servers command passed to Lbfoadmin specifies the server or servers you want to work with. In the example, you use a period (.) to specify that you want to work with the local server. You also could pass in a comma-separated list of servers to work with, such as:

```
Lbfoadmin.exe /servers corpserver28, corpserver31
```

Configuring TCP/IP Networking

As discussed previously, you configure TCP/IP settings using the Properties dialog box for the network adapter. If a server has multiple adapters and those adapters are teamed, you configure network teaming settings using the NIC Teaming app.

Configuring Static IP Addresses

When you assign a static IP address, you need to tell the computer the IP address you want to use, the subnet mask for this IP address, and, if necessary, the default gateway to use for internetwork communications. An IP address is a numeric identifier for a computer. IP addressing schemes vary according to how your network is configured, but they're typically assigned based on a particular network segment.

IPv6 addresses and IPv4 addresses are very different. With IPv6, the first 64 bits represent the network ID and the remaining 64 bits represent the network interface. With IPv4, a variable number of the initial bits represent the network ID and the rest of the bits represent the host ID. For example, if you're working with IPv4 and a computer on the network segment 10.0.10.0 with a subnet mask of 255.255.255.0, the first three octets (8-bit groups) represent the network ID, and the address range you have available for computer hosts is 10.0.10.1 to 10.0.10.254. In this range, the address 10.0.10.255 is reserved for network broadcasts.

If you're on a private network that is indirectly connected to the Internet, you should use private IPv4 addresses. Table 2-1 summarizes private network IPv4 addresses.

TABLE 2-1 Private IPv4 network addressing

PRIVATE NETWORK ID	SUBNET MASK	NETWORK ADDRESS RANGE
10.0.0.0	255.0.0.0	10.0.0.0–10.255.255.255
172.16.0.0	255.240.0.0	172.16.0.0–172.31.255.255
192.168.0.0	255.255.0.0	192.168.0.0–192.168.255.255

All other IPv4 network addresses are public and must be leased or purchased. If the network is connected directly to the Internet and you've obtained a range of IPv4 addresses from your Internet service provider, you can use the IPv4 addresses you've been assigned.

Using the *Ping* Command to Check an Address

Before you assign a static IP address, you should make sure that the address isn't already in use or reserved for use with DHCP. With the *ping* command, you can check whether an address is in use. Open a command prompt and enter **ping**, followed by the IP address you want to check.

To test the IPv4 address 10.0.10.12, you would use the following command:

```
ping 10.0.10.12
```

To test the IPv6 address FEC0::02BC:FF:BECB:FE4F:961D, you would use the following command:

```
ping FEC0::02BC:FF:BECB:FE4F:961D
```

If you receive a successful reply from the ping test, the IP address is in use and you should try another one. If the request times out for all four ping attempts, the IP address isn't active on the network at this time and probably isn't in use; however, a firewall could be blocking your ping request. Your company's network administrator would also be able to confirm whether an IP address is in use.

Configuring a Static IPv4 or IPv6 Address

One network connection is available for each network adapter installed. These connections are created automatically. To configure static IP addresses for a particular connection, follow these steps:

1. In Network And Sharing Center, click Change Adapter Settings. In Network Connections, right-click the connection with which you want to work, and then click Properties.
2. Double-click Internet Protocol Version 6 (TCP/IPv6) or Internet Protocol Version 4 (TCP/IPv4) as appropriate for the type of IP address you are configuring.
3. For an IPv6 address, do the following:

- Click Use The Following IPv6 Address, and then enter the IPv6 address in the IPv6 Address text box. The IPv6 address you assign to the computer must not be in use anywhere else on the network.
- The Subnet Prefix Length option ensures that the computer communicates over the network properly. Windows Server 2016 should insert a default value for the subnet prefix into the Subnet Prefix Length text box. If the network doesn't use variable-length subnetting, the default value should suffice, but if it does use variable-length subnets, you need to change this value as appropriate for your network.

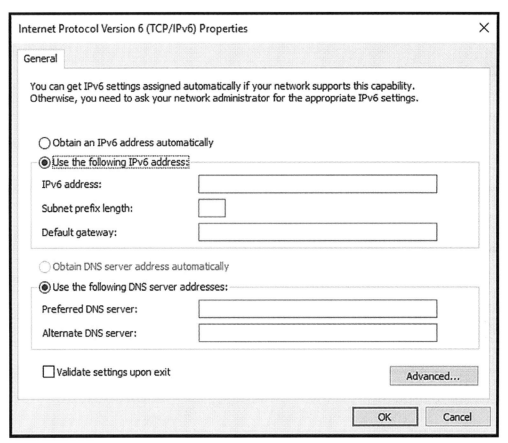

4. For an IPv4 address, do the following:

- Click Use The Following IP Address, and then enter the IPv4 address in the IP Address text box. The IPv4 address you assign to the computer must not be in use anywhere else on the network.
- The Subnet Mask option ensures that the computer communicates over the network properly. Windows Server 2016 should insert a default value for the subnet mask into the Subnet Mask text box. If the network doesn't use variable-length subnetting, the default value should suffice, but if it does use variable-length subnets, you need to change this value as appropriate for your network.

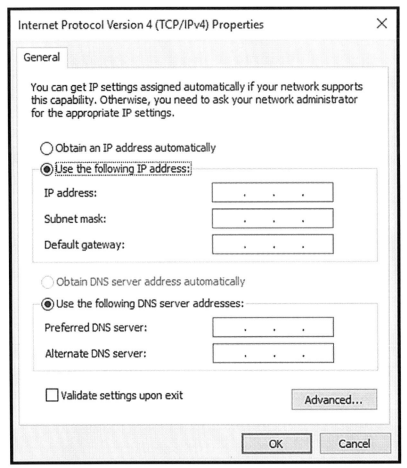

5. If the computer needs to access other TCP/IP networks, the Internet, or other subnets, you must specify a default gateway. Enter the IP address of the network's default router in the Default Gateway text box.

6. Domain Name System (DNS) is needed for domain name resolution. Enter a preferred address and an alternate DNS server address in the text boxes provided.

7. When you have finished, click OK twice. Repeat this process for other network adapters and IP protocols you want to configure.

8. With IPv4 addressing, configure WINS as necessary.

Configuring Dynamic IP Addresses and Alternate IP Addressing

Although most servers have static IP addresses, you can configure servers to use dynamic addressing, alternate IP addressing, or both. You configure dynamic and alternate addressing by following these steps:

1. In Network And Sharing Center, click Change Adapter Settings. In Network Connections, one LAN connection is shown for each network adapter installed. These connections are created automatically. If you don't find a LAN connection for an installed adapter, check the driver for the adapter. It might be installed incorrectly. Right-click the connection with which you want to work, and then click Properties.

2. Double-click Internet Protocol Version 6 (TCP/IPv6) or Internet Protocol Version 4 (TCP/IPv4) as appropriate for the type of IP address you are configuring.

3. Select Obtain An IPv6 Address Automatically or Obtain An IP Address Automatically as appropriate for the type of IP address you are configuring. You can select Obtain DNS Server Address Automatically, or you can select Use The Following DNS Server Addresses, and then enter a preferred and alternate DNS server address in the text boxes provided.

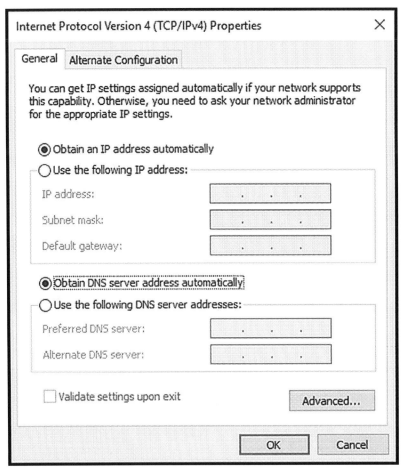

4. When you use dynamic IPv4 addressing, you can configure an automatic alternate address or manually configure the alternate address. To use an automatic configuration, on the Alternate Configuration tab, select Automatic Private IP Address. Click OK, click Close, and then skip the remaining step.

5. To use a manual configuration, on the Alternate Configuration tab, select User Configured, and then enter the IP address you want to use in the IP Address text box. The IP address you assign to the computer should be a private IP address, and it must not be in use anywhere else when the settings are applied. Complete the alternate configuration by entering a subnet mask, default gateway, DNS server, and Windows Internet Name Service (WINS) settings. When you have finished, click OK, and then click Close.

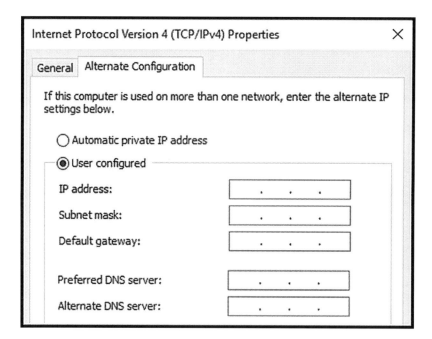

Configuring Multiple Gateways

To provide fault tolerance in case of a router outage, you can choose to configure Windows Server 2016 computers so that they use multiple default gateways. When you assign multiple gateways, Windows Server 2016 uses the gateway metric to determine which gateway is used and at what time. The gateway metric indicates the routing cost of using a gateway. The gateway with the lowest routing cost, or metric, is used first. If the computer can't communicate with this gateway, Windows Server 2016 tries to use the gateway with the next lowest metric.

The best way to configure multiple gateways depends on the configuration of your network. If your organization's computers use DHCP, you probably want to configure the additional gateways through settings on the DHCP server. If computers use static IP addresses or you want to set gateways specifically, assign them by following these steps:

1. In Network And Sharing Center, click Change Adapter Settings. In Network Connections, right-click the connection with which you want to work, and then click Properties.

2. Double-click Internet Protocol Version 6 (TCP/IPv6) or Internet Protocol Version 4 (TCP/IPv4) as appropriate for the type of IP address you are configuring.

3. Click Advanced to open the Advanced TCP/IP Settings dialog box.

4. The Default Gateways panel shows the current gateways that have been manually configured (if any). You can enter additional default gateways as necessary. Click Add, and then enter the gateway address in the Gateway text box. By default, Windows Server 2016 automatically assigns a metric to the gateway. You can also assign the metric yourself. To do this, clear the Automatic Metric check box, enter a metric in the text box provided, and then click Add. Repeat this process for each gateway you want to add.

5. Click OK, and then click Close.

Configuring Networking for Hyper-V

After you install Hyper-V and create an external virtual network, your server uses a virtual network adapter to connect to the physical network. When you work with the

Network Connections page, you will find the original network adapter and a new virtual network adapter. The original network adapter will have nothing bound to it except the Microsoft Virtual Network Switch Protocol, and the virtual network adapter will have all the standard protocols and services bound to it. The virtual network adapter that appears under Network Connections will have the same name as the virtual network switch with which it is associated.

> **NOTE** As part of the Hyper-V configuration, you can create an internal virtual network, which enables communications only between the server and hosted virtual machines. This configuration exposes a virtual network adapter to the parent server without the need to have a physical network adapter associated with it and isolates the virtual machine from the Internet and the rest of the LAN. Hyper-V binds the virtual network service to a physical network adapter only when an external virtual network is created. An external virtual network is required for communications on the LAN and the Internet.

Following this, when you install Hyper-V on a server and enable external virtual networking, you'll find that virtual network switching is being used. The server will have a network connection with the Hyper-V Extensible Virtual Switch Protocol enabled and all other networking components not enabled and an entry for a virtual connection with the key networking components enabled and the Hyper-V Extensible Virtual Switch Protocol disabled. This is the configuration you want to use to ensure proper communications for the server and any hosted virtual machines that use networking. If this configuration is changed, virtual machines won't be able to connect to the external network.

Using NIC Teaming

NIC teaming allows you to optimize the way a server uses multiple network interfaces. When you add interfaces to a team, you group them together for load balancing, designating a standby interface or both. By load balancing interfaces, you can increase the available bandwidth for networking and reduce the likelihood that the capacity of a server's network card is a limiting factor with respect to overall performance. By designating a standby interface, you can ensure user can connect to a server in the event an adapter fails.

Understanding NIC Teaming

By default, NIC teaming is disabled on Windows servers. A NIC team can be configured in a switch dependent or independent mode. A switch dependent mode requires configuration of a switch and the server to identify which links are part of the team. A switch independent mode only requires configuration of a server to identify the interfaces associated with the team.

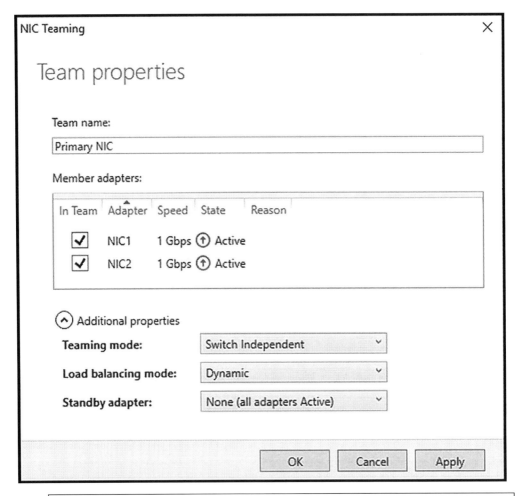

REAL WORLD   The benefit of using switch dependent teaming is that the overhead associated with load balancing is shifted to the switch, rather than requiring the server to manage the load balancing. The drawback is that you typically need enterprise-class switches and must either enable teaming on the switches or specifically configure the switches for teaming.

Up to 32 interfaces can be added to a team. Windows Server 2016 supports two switch dependent teaming modes:

- LACP, also referred to as dynamic teaming
- Static teaming, also referred to as generic teaming

Dynamic teaming, which is supported by most enterprise-class switches and based on IEEE 802.1ax, allows for the automatic creation of a team. Here, Windows Server dynamically identifies links between a server and a particular switch using the Link Aggregation Control Protocol (LACP) and adds them to the team automatically. Generally, enabling LACP on the switch and then creating a team that uses dynamic teaming is all you need to do to configure this mode.

Static teaming, which is also supported by most enterprise-class switches and based on IEEE 802.3ad, requires manual configuration of the server and switch to identify the links that are part of the team. Here, you configure the switch to use static teaming and then creating a team that uses static teaming for specific interfaces on the server.

Windows Server 2016 also supports a switch independent mode, which requires only that you creating a team on the server for specific interfaces. As switches don't participate in the team when using this mode, links connected to multiple switches can be used if necessary.

Regardless of which teaming mode a server uses, you have three choices for load balancing across the participating interfaces:

- Dynamic
- Hyper-V port
- Address hash

Each traffic distribution algorithm has its pros and cons. Dynamic load balancing is the default mode and it is arguably the most efficient when you want to try to distribute the load evenly across all available interfaces. With dynamic load balancing, traffic distribution also is similar regardless of whether you use a switch dependent or switch independent mode as well.

Hyper-V port traffic distribution is based on the MAC address of a particular virtual machine hosted on a server or the port to which the virtual machine is connected. If a server has many virtual machines, this approach can be useful to achieve balanced distribution over the interfaces used in the team. However, if a server has few virtual machines or several high bandwidth using virtual machines, traffic distribution may favor a select few interfaces rather than all interfaces and thus may not be balanced appropriately.

With Hyper-V port distribution, the available bandwidth of any particular MAC address or Hyper-V port is always limited to the bandwidth available on a single interface. Additionally, it's important to note that inbound and outbound traffic for the virtual machine occur over the same interface. Thus, you should use this distribution mode when the number of virtual machines on the server is a multiple to the number of available interfaces and the sharing of inbound and outbound traffic for a particular virtual machine won't be a limiting factor.

Address hash distribution is based on a hash from the address components of a TCP or UDP packet stream, including the source and destination MAC addresses, the source and destination IP addresses, and the source and destination TCP or UDP ports. If a server has a heavy outbound workload, this approach can achieve good load balancing across all interfaces in a team. However, as an IP address can only be associated with a specific, designated MAC address for routing, all inbound traffic is received only on the primary interface of the team. Thus, inbound traffic is limited in terms of total available bandwidth and cannot exceed the bandwidth of the primary interface. With these limitations, you'll find that address hash distribution is best used when you have heavy outbound traffic and light inbound traffic.

Configuring NIC Teaming

You enable teaming by creating a new team using either the NIC Teaming app or the cmdlets associated with the Netlbfo module in Windows Powershell. To list all of the cmdlets for the Netlbfo module, enter **Get-Command –Module Netlbfo** at a PowerShell prompt.

In Server Manager, access the NIC Teaming app by clicking the related Enabled or Disabled link on the Local Server page. Alternatively, while working with Windows Server 2016, enter **Lbfoadmin.exe /servers .** in the Search box or at a command prompt.

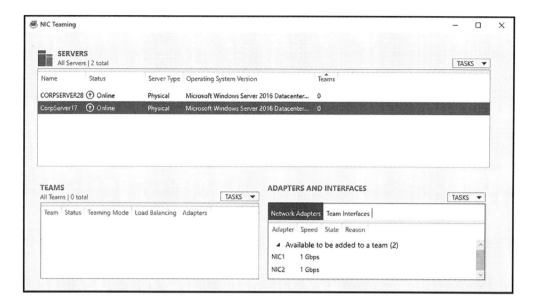

In most cases, you'll find it's easier to work directly with the server you want to configure for NIC teaming by logging on locally or accessing the server using Remote Desktop. That said, the NIC Teaming interface does support configuration of remote servers and virtual machines running on a host server. If the server or virtual machine you want to work with is listed on the Servers panel, click on it to select it. Otherwise, add the server by selecting the related Tasks option, clicking Add Servers and then using the dialog box provided to specify the name or IP address of the server or servers you want to work with. You can add a server by name on the Active Directory panel or by name or IP address on the DNS panel. For example, on the Active Directory panel, type the computer name or fully qualified domain name of a remote Windows server that is in a trusted domain and then click Find Now. In the Name list, double-click a server to add it to the Selected list.

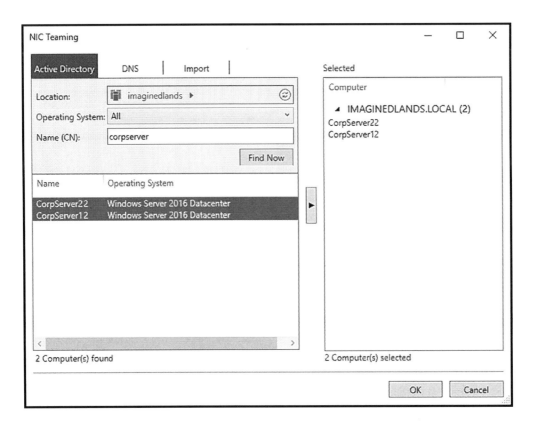

Once you've selected the server you want to work with on the Servers panel, you can use the option on the Teams panel to create the NIC team. Select the related Tasks button and then select New Team. In the New Team dialog box, type a name of the team, such as Primary NIC or Primary NIC Team and select the interfaces that should be part of the team.

Next, expand the Additional Properties panel by clicking on the panel heading. You'll then be able to specify the teaming and load balancing modes. By default, all network interfaces are active. If the team should have a standby adapter for failover purposes, click the Standby Adapter option and then select the standby adapter. Only one interface can be designated as the standby.

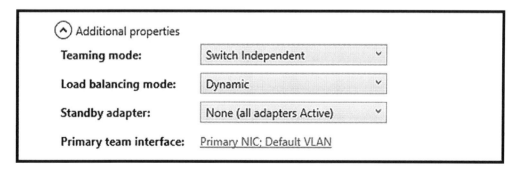

Close the New Team dialog box and create the team by clicking OK. If you are remotely accessing the server that you are configuring, your connection with the server will be lost and you will need to reestablish your connection.

When you create the team, the interfaces that are part of the team will be configured as discussed previously. This means the Microsoft Network Adapter Multiplexor Protocol will be enabled on the interfaces while all other protocols are disabled. A multiplexed interface will also be added and configured for the server. Generally, this interface will have the same TCP/IP settings as the server's primary adapter had previously. Open the Properties dialog box for the multiplexed adapter to view or change the TCP/IP settings.

Chapter 3. Data Storage: The Essentials

A hard drive is the most common storage device used on network workstations and servers. Users depend on hard drives to store their documents, spreadsheets, and other types of data. Drives are organized into file systems that users can access either locally or remotely.

Local file systems are installed on a user's computer and can be accessed without remote network connections. The C drive, which is available on most workstations and servers, is an example of a local file system. You access the C drive by using the file path C:\.

On the other hand, you access remote file systems through a network connection to a remote resource. You can connect to a remote file system by using the Map Network Drive feature of File Explorer.

Wherever disk resources are located, your job as an IT professional is to manage them. The tools and techniques you use to add, prepare and work with drives are discussed in this chapter. Later chapters discuss techniques for partitioning drives, implementing storage management and more.

Deploying File Services

A file server provides a central location for storing and sharing files across the network. When many users require access to the same files and application data, you should configure file servers in the domain. Although all servers are configured with basic file and storage services, you must still configure any additional services and features that may be needed using the File And Storage Services role.

The role services associated with the File And Storage Services include:

- **BranchCache For Network Files** Enables computers in a branch office to cache commonly used files from shared folders. It takes advantage of data deduplication techniques to optimize data transfers over the wide area networks (WAN) to branch offices.
- **Data Deduplication** Uses subfile variable-size chunking and compression to achieve greater storage efficiency. This works by segmenting files into 32-KB to 128-KB chunks, identifying duplicate chunks, and replacing the duplicates with

references to a single copy. Optimized files are stored as reparse points. After deduplication, files on the volume are no longer stored as data streams and instead are replaced with stubs that point to data blocks within a common chunk store.

- **DFS Namespaces**   Enables you to group shared folders located on different servers into one or more logically structured namespaces. Each namespace appears as a single shared folder with a series of subfolders; however, the underlying structure of a namespace can come from shared folders on multiple servers in different sites.
- **DFS Replication**   Enables you to synchronize folders on multiple servers across local or WAN connections by using a multimaster replication engine. The replication engine uses the Remote Differential Compression (RDC) protocol to synchronize only the portions of files that have changed since the last replication. You can use DFS Replication with DFS Namespaces or by itself. When a domain is running in a Windows 2008 domain functional level or higher, domain controllers use DFS Replication to provide more robust and granular replication of the SYSVOL directory.
- **File Server**   Enables you to manage file shares that users can access over the network.
- **File Server Resource Manager (FSRM)**   Installs a suite of tools that administrators can use to better manage data stored on servers. By using FSRM, administrators can generate storage reports, configure quotas, and define file-screening policies.
- **File Server VSS Agent Service**   Enables VSS-aware backup utilities to create consistent shadow copies (snapshots) of applications that store data files on the file server.
- **iSCSI Target Server**   Turns any Windows Server into a network-accessible block storage device, which can be used for testing of applications prior to deploying storage area network (SAN) storage. It supports shared storage on both Windows iSCSI initiators and those iSCSI initiators that are not based on Windows as well as network/diskless boot for diskless servers.
- **iSCSI Target Storage Provider**   Supports managing iSCSI virtual disks and shadow copies (snapshots) from an iSCSI initiator.
- **Server for NFS**   Provides a file-sharing solution for enterprises with a mixed Windows and UNIX environment. When you install Server for Network File System (NFS), users can transfer files between Windows Server and UNIX operating systems by using the NFS protocol.
- **Storage Services**   Enables you to manage storage, including storage pools and storage spaces. Storage pools group disks so that you can create virtual disks from the available capacity. Each virtual disk you create is a storage space.
- **Work Folders**   Enables users to synchronize their corporate data to their devices and vice versa. Those devices can be joined to the corporate domain or a workplace.

When you add any needed role services to a file server, you might also want to install the following optional features, available through the Add Roles And Features Wizard:

- **BitLocker Drive Encryption**   Prevents unauthorized access to data by wrapping entire drives or only the used portion of volumes in tamper-proof encryption. Used with Trust Platform Module (TPM), BitLocker can validate the integrity of a server's boot manager and boot files at startup to guarantee that a hard disk has not been tampered with while the operating system was offline.
- **BitLocker Network Unlock**   Enables a protected system volume to be automatically unlocked on startup when a computer is joined to a domain and using TPM.
- **Enhanced Storage**   Supports additional functions made available by devices that support hardware encryption and enhanced storage. Enhanced storage devices support Institute of Electrical and Electronics Engineers (IEEE) standard 1667 to provide enhanced security, which can include authentication at the hardware level of the storage device.
- **Multipath I/O**   Provides support for using multiple data paths between a file server and a storage device. Servers use multiple I/O paths for redundancy in case of the failure of a path and to improve transfer performance.
- **SMB Bandwidth Limit**   Tracks SMB traffic by source category, either default, virtual machine or Live Migration, and allows you to limit the amount of traffic for each category by setting a bytes per second limitation.
- **Storage Replica**   Enables block-level replication between servers, with or without clustering. When you install and configure storage replica, you can mirror the data in physical sites to safeguard data at the filesystem level using a synchronous or asynchronous technique.
- **Windows Server Backup**   The standard backup utility included with Windows Server 2016.

Binaries needed to install roles and features are referred to as *payloads*. With Windows Server 2016, payloads are stored in subfolders of the %SystemDrive%\Windows\WinSXS folder. If the binaries for the tools have been removed, you might need to install the tools by specifying a source.

> **IMPORTANT**   If payloads have been removed and you don't specify a source, payloads are restored via Windows Update by default. However, Group Policy can be used to control whether Windows Update is used to restore payloads and to provide alternate source paths for restoring payloads. The policy with which you want to work is Specify Settings For Optional Component Installation And Component Repair, which is under Computer Configuration\Administrative Templates\System. This policy also is used for obtaining payloads needed to repair components.

You can configure the File And Storage Services role on a server by following these steps:

1. In Server Manager, click Manage, and then click Add Roles And Features, or select Add Roles And Features in the Quick Start pane. This starts the Add Roles And Features Wizard. If the wizard displays the Before You Begin page, read the Welcome text, and then click Next.

2. On the Installation Type page, Role-Based Or Feature-Based Installation is selected by default. Click Next.

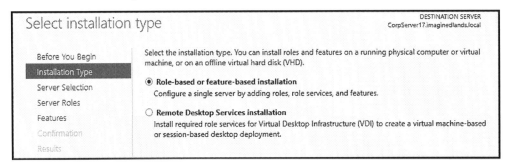

3. On the Server Selection page, you can choose to install roles and features on running servers or virtual hard disks. Either select a server from the server pool or select a server from the server pool on which to mount a virtual hard disk (VHD). If you are adding roles and features to a VHD, click Browse and then use the Browse For Virtual Hard Disks dialog box to locate the VHD. When you are ready to continue, click Next.

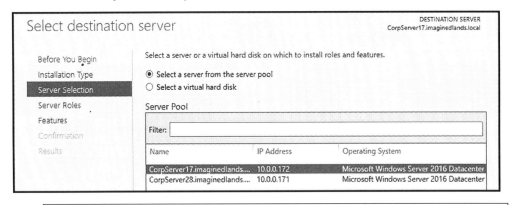

NOTE Only servers that are running Windows Server 2012 or later and that have been added for management in Server Manager are listed.

4. On the Server Roles page, select File And Storage Services. Expand the related node, and select the additional file services to install. If additional features are required to install a role, you'll see an additional dialog box. Click

Add Features to close the dialog box and add the required features to the server installation. When you are ready to continue, click Next.

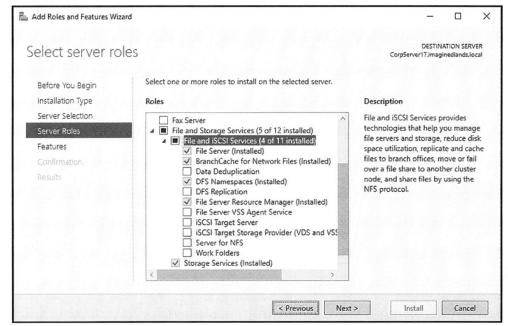

5. On the Features page, select the features you want to install. If additional functionality are required to install a feature you selected, you'll see an additional dialog box. Click Add Features to close the dialog box and add the required features to the server installation. When you are ready to continue, click Next. Depending on the added feature, there may be additional steps before you get to the Confirm page.

6. Optionally, on the Confirm page, click the Export Configuration Settings link to generate an installation report that can be displayed in Internet Explorer.

> **REAL WORLD** If the server on which you want to install roles or features doesn't have all the required binary source files, the server gets the files via Windows Update by default or from a location specified in Group Policy.
>
> You can also specify an alternate path for the required source files. To do this, click the Specify An Alternate Source Path link, enter that alternate path in the box provided, and then click OK. For network shares, enter the UNC path to the share, such as \\CorpServer25\WinServer2016\. For mounted Windows images, enter the WIM path prefixed with WIM: and including the index of the image to use, such as WIM:\\CorpServer25\WinServer2016\install.wim:4.

7. After you review the installation options and save them as necessary, click Install to begin the installation process. The Installation Progress page tracks the progress of the installation. If you close the wizard, click the Notifications icon in Server Manager, and then click the link provided to reopen the wizard.

8. When Setup finishes installing the server with the roles and features you selected, the Installation Progress page will be updated to reflect this. Review the installation details to ensure that all phases of the installation were completed successfully.

   Note any additional actions that might be required to complete the installation, such as restarting the server or performing additional installation tasks.

   If any portion of the installation failed, note the reason for the failure. Review the Server Manager entries for installation problems, and take corrective actions as appropriate.

Adding Drives

Windows Server 2016 supports both hard disk drives and solid state drives. Before you make a drive available to users, you need to configure it and consider how it will be used. With Windows Server 2016, you can configure drives in a variety of ways. The technique you choose depends primarily on the type of data with which you're working and the needs of your network environment. For general user data stored on workstations, you might want to configure individual drives as standalone storage devices. In that case, user data is stored on a workstation's drive, where it can be accessed and stored locally.

Although storing data on a single drive is convenient, it isn't the most reliable way to store data. To improve reliability and performance, you might want a set of drives to work together. Windows Server 2016 supports drive sets and arrays by using various storage technologies, including Storage Spaces.

Physical Drives

Whether you use individual drives or drive sets, you need physical drives. Physical drives are the actual hardware devices that are used to store data. The amount of data a drive can store depends on its size and whether it uses compression. Windows Server 2016 supports both Standard Format and Advanced Format drives. Standard Format drives have 512 bytes per physical sector and are also referred to as 512 native sector or *512b drives*. Advanced Format drives have 4096 bytes per physical sector and are available in both 4K native and *512* emulation versions. 4K native and 512e drives represent a significant shift for the drive industry, and it allows for large, multiterabyte drives.

Disks perform physical media updates in the granularity of their physical sector size. 512b disks work with data 512 bytes at a time; native 4K and 512e disks work with data 4096 bytes at a time. At an administrator prompt, you can use the command-line utility Fsutil to determine bytes per physical sector by entering the following:

Fsutil fsinfo ntfsinfo *DriveDesignator*

where DriveDesignator is the designator of the drive to check, such as:

Fsutil fsinfo sectorinfo c:

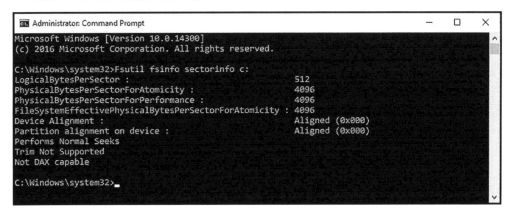

Having a larger physical sector size is what allows drive capacities to jump well beyond previous physical capacity limits. When there is only a 512-byte write, drives must perform additional work to complete the sector write. For best performance, applications must be updated to read and write data properly in this new level of granularity (4096 bytes).

Windows Server 2016 supports many drive interface architectures, including

- Small Computer System Interface (SCSI)
- Parallel ATA (PATA), also known as IDE
- Serial ATA (SATA)

The terms SCSI, IDE, and SATA designate the interface type used by the drives. The interface is used to communicate with a drive controller. SCSI drives use SCSI controllers, IDE drives use IDE controllers, and so on.

SCSI is one of the most commonly used interfaces, and there are multiple bus designs for SCSI and multiple interface types. Parallel SCSI (also called SPI) has largely been replaced by Serial Attached SCSI (SAS). Internet SCSI (iSCSI) uses the SCSI architectural model, but it uses TCP/IP as the transport rather than the traditional physical implementation.

SATA was designed to replace IDE. SATA drives are increasingly popular as a low-cost alternative to SCSI. SATA II and SATA III, the most common SATA interfaces, are designed to operate at 3 gigabits per second and 6 gigabits per second, respectively. In addition, eSATA (also known as external SATA) is meant for externally connected drives.

Various improvements to SATA are available, including revision 3.3, which includes support for SATA Express. SATA Express combines two PCI Express 3.0 ports to achieve speeds of up to 12 gigabits per second and is designed to be used with high performance solid state drives. With Serial Attached Storage (SAS), which leverages SCSI commands, enterprise hard disk drives are also achieving speeds of up to 12 gigabits per second.

When setting up a new server, you should give considerable thought to the drive configuration. Start by choosing drives or storage systems that provide the appropriate level of performance. There really is a substantial difference in speed and performance among various drive specifications.

You should consider not only the capacity of the drive but also the following:

- **Rotational speed**   A measurement of how fast the disk spins
- **Average seek time**   A measurement of how long it takes to seek between disk tracks during sequential I/O operations

Generally speaking, when comparing drives that conform to the same specification, such as Ultra640 SCSI or SATA III, the higher the rotational speed (measured in thousands of rotations per minute) and the lower the average seek time (measured in milliseconds, or msecs), the better. As an example, a drive with a rotational speed of 15,000 RPM gives you 45–50 percent more I/O per second than the average 10,000 RPM drive, all other things being equal. A drive with a seek time of 3.5 msecs gives you a 25–30 percent response time improvement over a drive with a seek time of 4.7 msecs.

Other factors to consider include the following:

- **Maximum sustained data transfer rate**   A measurement of how much data the drive can continuously transfer
- **Mean time to failure (MTTF)**   A measurement of how many hours of operation you can expect to get from the drive before it fails
- **Nonoperational temperatures**   Measurements of the temperatures at which the drive fails

Most drives of comparable quality have similar transfer rates and MTTF. For example, if you compare enterprise SAS drives with 15,000 RPM rotational speed from different vendors, you will probably find similar transfer rates and MTTF. Transfer rates can be expressed in megabytes per second (MBps) or gigabits per second (Gbps). A rate of 1.5 Gbps is equivalent to a data rate of 187.5 MBps, and 3.0 Gbps is equivalent to 375 MBps. Sometimes you'll get a maximum external transfer rate (per the specification to which the drive complies) and an average sustained transfer rate. The average sustained transfer rate is the most important factor.

> **NOTE**   Don't confuse MBps and Mbps. MBps is megabytes per second. Mbps is megabits per second. Because there are 8 bits in a byte, a 100 MBps transfer rate is equivalent to an 800 Mbps transfer rate.

Power requirements and temperature are other important factors to consider when you're selecting a drive, but they're factors few administrators take into account. Typically, the faster a drive rotates, the more power it uses and the hotter it runs. This is not always the case, but it is certainly something you should consider when making your choice. For example, 15K drives tend to use more power and run hot, and you must be sure sufficient power is available while also carefully regulating temperature. Be sure to compare average operating power and temperature specifications. While a typical 10K drive may use 7.87 watts of power, a typical 15K drive may use 8.68 watts of power. Typical 15K drives can become nonoperational at temperatures of 70 degrees Centigrade or higher (as would most other drives).

Windows Server 2016 adds support for disk drives with hardware encryption (referred to as encrypted drives). Encrypted drives have built-in processors that shift the encryption-decryption activities from the operating system to hardware, freeing up operating system resources. Windows Server 2016 will use hardware encryption with BitLocker when available. Other security features available in Windows Server 2016 include Secure Boot and Network Unlock. Secure Boot provides boot integrity by validating Boot Configuration Data (BCD) settings according to the Trusted Platform Module (TPM) validation profile settings. Network Unlock can be used to automatically unlock the operating system drive on domain-joined computers.

Preparing a Physical Drive for Use

After you install a drive, you need to configure it for use. You configure the drive by partitioning it and creating file systems in the partitions as needed. A *partition* is a section of a physical drive that functions as if it were a separate unit. After you create a partition, you can create a file system in the partition.

The MBR and GPT Partition Styles

Two partition styles are used for disks: master boot record (MBR) and GUID partition table (GPT). The MBR contains a partition table that describes where the partitions are located on the disk. With this partition style, the first sector on a drive contains the master boot record and a binary code file called the *master boot code* that's used to boot the system. This sector is unpartitioned and hidden from view to protect the system.

With the MBR partitioning style, disks traditionally support volumes of up to 4 terabytes (TB) and use one of two types of partitions: primary or extended. Each MBR drive can have up to four primary partitions or three primary partitions and one extended partition. Primary partitions are drive sections you can access directly for file storage. You make a primary partition accessible to users by creating a file system on it. Although you can access primary partitions directly, you can't access extended partitions directly. Instead, you can configure extended partitions with one or more logical drives that are used to store files. Being able to divide extended partitions into logical drives allows you to divide a physical drive into more than four sections.

GPT was originally developed for high-performance computers using Intel's Itanium processors. The key difference between the GPT partition style and the MBR partition style has to do with how partition data is stored. With GPT, critical partition data is stored in the individual partitions, and redundant primary and backup partition tables are used for improved structural integrity. Additionally, GPT disks support volumes of up to 18 exabytes (1 exabyte equals 1024x1024 terabytes) and as many as 128 partitions. Although the GPT and MBR partitioning styles have underlying differences, most disk-related tasks are performed in the same way.

Legacy and Protective Mbrs

Most computers ship with Unified Extensible Firmware Interface (UEFI). Although UEFI is replacing BIOS and EFI as the top-level firmware interface, UEFI doesn't replace all the functionality in either BIOS or EFI and typically is wrapped around BIOS or EFI. With respect to UEFI, GPT is the preferred partitioning scheme and a protective MBR may be located on any disk that uses the GPT disk layout. A legacy MBR and a protective MBR differ in many important ways.

A legacy MBR is located at the first logical block on a disk that is not using the GPT disk layout. The first 512 bytes on an MBR disk have the following layout:

- The MBR begins with a 424-byte boot code, which is used to select an MBR partition record and load the first logical block of that partition. The boot code on the MBR is not executed by UEFI.
- The boot code is followed by a 4-byte unique MBR disk signature, which can be used by the operating system to identify the disk and distinguish the disk from other disks on the system. The unique signature is written by the operating system and not used by UEFI.
- A 2-byte separator follows the disk signature. At byte offset 446, there is an array of four MBR partition records, with each record being 16 bytes in length. Block 510 contains 0x55 and block 511 contains 0xAA. Block 512 is reserved.

The four partition records each define the first and last logical blocks that a particular partition uses on a disk:

- Each 16-byte MBR partition record begins with a 1-byte boot indicator. For example, a value of 0x80 identifies a bootable legacy partition. Any other value indicates that this is not a bootable legacy partition. This value is not used by UEFI.
- The boot indicator is followed by a 3-byte address identifying the start of the partition. At byte offset 4, there's a 1-byte value that indicates the operating system type, which is followed by a 3-byte value that identifies the end of the partition. These values are not used by UEFI.
- At byte offset 8, there is a 4-byte value indicating the first logical block of the partition, and this is followed by a 4-byte value indicating size of the partition in units of logical blocks. Both of these values are used by UEFI.

> **NOTE**   If an MBR partition has an operating system type value of 0xEF, firmware must add the UEFI system partition GUID to the handle for the MBR partition. This allows boot applications, operating system loaders, drivers, and other lower-level tools to locate the UEFI system partition, which must physically reside on the disk.

A protective MBR may be located at the first logical block on a disk that is using the GPT disk layout. The protective MBR precedes the GUID Partition Table Header and is used to maintain compatibility with tools that do not understand GPT partition structures. The purpose of the protective MBR is to protect the GPT partitions from boot applications, operating system loaders, drivers, and other lower-level tools that don't understand the GPT partitioning scheme. The protective MBR does this by defining a fake partition covering the entire disk. When a disk has a protective MBR, the first 512 bytes on the disk have the following layout:

- The protective MBR begins with a 424-byte boot code, which is not executed by UEFI.
- The boot code is followed by a 4-byte disk signature, which is set to zero and not used by UEFI.
- A 2-byte separator follows the disk signature. This separator is set to zero and not used by UEFI.
- At byte offset 446, there is an array of four MBR partition records, with each record being 16-bytes in length. Only the first partition record—the protective partition record—is used. The other partition records are set to zero.
- Block 510 contains 0x55 and block 511 contains 0xAA. Block 512 is reserved.

The protective partition record reserves the entire space on the disk after the first 512 bytes for the GPT disk layout. The protective partition record begins with a 1-byte boot indicator that is set to 0x00, which indicates a non-bootable partition. The boot indicator is followed by a 3-byte address identifying the start of the partition at 0x000200, which is the first usable block on the disk.

At byte offset 4, there's a 1-byte value set to 0xEE to indicate the operating system type as GPT Protective. This is followed by a 3-byte value that identifies the last usable block on the disk, which is the end of the partition (or 0xFFFFFF if it is not possible to represent this value).

At byte offset 8, there is a 4-byte value set to 0x00000001, which identifies the logical block address of the GPT partition header. This is followed by a 4-byte value indicating size of the disk minus one block (or 0xFFFFFFFF if the size of the disk is too large to be represented).

Disk Types and File Systems

In addition to a partition style, physical drives have a disk type, which is either basic or dynamic, as discussed later in the chapter under "Working with Disks." After you set the partition style and disk type for a physical drive, you can format free areas of the drive to establish logical partitions. Formatting creates a file system on a partition. Windows Server 2016 supports the following file systems:

* FAT
* FAT32
* exFAT
* NTFS
* ReFS

With FAT, the number of bits used with the file allocation table determines the variant with which you are working and the maximum volume size. FAT16, also known simply as FAT, defines its file allocation tables using 16 bits. Volumes that are 4 gigabytes (GB) or less in size are formatted with FAT16.

FAT32 defines its file allocation tables using 32 bits, and you can create FAT32 volumes that are 32 GB or less by using the Windows format tools. Although Windows can mount larger FAT32 volumes created with third-party tools, you should use NTFS for volumes larger than 32 GB.

Extended FAT is an enhanced version of FAT. Technically, exFAT could have been called FAT64 (and is called that by some). Because exFAT defines its file allocation tables by using 64 bits, it can overcome the 4-GB file-size limit and the 32-GB volume-size limit of FAT32 file systems. The exFAT format supports allocation unit sizes of up to 128 KB for volumes up to 256 TB.

NTFS volumes have a very different structure and feature set than FAT volumes. The first area of the volume is the boot sector, which stores information about the disk layout, and a bootstrap program executes at startup and boots the operating system. Instead of a file allocation table, NTFS uses a relational database called the master file table (MFT) to store information about files.

The MFT stores a file record of each file and folder on the volume, pertinent volume information, and details about the MFT itself. NTFS gives you many advanced options, including support for the Encrypting File System, compression, and the option to configure file screening and storage reporting. File screening and storage reporting are available when you add the File Server Resource Manager role service to a server as part of the File Services role.

At an administrator prompt, you can use Fsutil to get information about an NTFS volume by entering the following:

`Fsutil fsinfo ntfsinfo` *DriveDesignator*

where DriveDesignator is the designator of the drive to check, such as:

`Fsutil fsinfo ntfsinfo c:`

```
Administrator: Command Prompt                                            —  □  ×

C:\Windows\system32>Fsutil fsinfo ntfsinfo c:
NTFS Volume Serial Number :        0x9a4ab50e4ab4e7e1
NTFS Version    :                  3.1
LFS Version     :                  2.0
Number Sectors :                   0x00000000218d17ff
Total Clusters :                   0x000000000431a2ff
Free Clusters  :                   0x0000000003e70120
Total Reserved :                   0x0000000000027b95
Bytes Per Sector   :               512
Bytes Per Physical Sector :        4096
Bytes Per Cluster :                4096
Bytes Per FileRecord Segment    :  1024
Clusters Per FileRecord Segment :  0
Mft Valid Data Length :            0x00000000070c0000
Mft Start Lcn  :                   0x00000000000c0000
Mft2 Start Lcn :                   0x0000000000000002
Mft Zone Start :                   0x00000000000c70c0
Mft Zone End   :                   0x00000000000cc820
Max Device Trim Extent Count :     0
Max Device Trim Byte Count :       0x0
Max Volume Trim Extent Count :     62
Max Volume Trim Byte Count :       0x40000000
Resource Manager Identifier :      8BB7E6FA-1161-11E6-9B2D-FE362480C635

C:\Windows\system32>_
```

Resilient File System (ReFS) can be thought of as the next generation of NTFS. As such, ReFS remains compatible with core NTFS features while cutting noncore features to focus relentlessly on reliability. This means disk quotas, Encrypting File System (EFS), compression, file screening, and storage reporting are not available but built-in reliability features have been added.

One of the biggest reliability features in ReFS is a data integrity scanner, also called a *data scrubber*. The scrubber provides proactive error identification, isolation, and correction. If the scrubber detects data corruption, a repair process is used to localize the area of corruption and perform automatic online correction. Through an automatic online salvage process, corrupted areas that cannot be repaired, such as those caused by bad blocks on the physical disk, are removed from the live volume so that they cannot adversely affect good data. Because of the automated scrubber and salvage processes, a Check Disk feature is not needed when you use ReFS (and there's no Check Disk utility for ReFS).

> **NOTE** When you are working with File And Storage Services, you can group available physical disks into storage pools so that you can create virtual disks from available capacity. Each virtual disk you create is a storage space. Because only NTFS and ReFS support storage spaces, you'll want to keep that in mind when you are formatting volumes on file servers. For more information about storage spaces, see Chapter 6 "Using Storage Spaces".

Like NTFS, ReFS has been revised several times since it was introduced. Windows Server 2016 RTM supports ReFS 3.0, which has different features and enhancements than earlier releases of the file system.

> **TIP**   Although you can use the Convert utility to convert a FAT volume to NTFS, there currently is no utility available to convert NTFS volumes to ReFS or vice versa. If you upgrade from an earlier release of Windows Server or move drives to a server running Windows Server 2016, you may find that volumes that use older versions of ReFS are unavailable. This is because the different versions of ReFS are incompatible with each other. To recover the data, you'll need to move the drive to a computer running a version of Windows Server that supports the file system.

At an administrator prompt, you can use the command-line utility Fsutil to get information about an ReFS volume by entering the following:

```
Fsutil fsinfo refsinfo DriveDesignator
```

where DriveDesignator is the designator of the drive to check, such as:

```
Fsutil fsinfo refsinfo d:
```

```
Administrator: Command Prompt                                    —    □    ×

C:\Windows\system32>Fsutil fsinfo refsinfo g:
REFS Volume Serial Number :     0xa0162ca3162c7d02
REFS Version    :               3.0
Number Sectors :                0x0000000018680000
Total Clusters :                0x00000000030d0000
Free Clusters  :                0x0000000002fc67d1
Total Reserved :                0x000000000004a50c
Bytes Per Sector  :             512
Bytes Per Physical Sector :     4096
Bytes Per Cluster :             4096
Checksum Type:                  CHECKSUM_TYPE_NONE


C:\Windows\system32>_
```

Using Disk Management

You use Disk Management to configure drives. Disk Management is included as part of the Computer Management console. You can also add it to custom MMCs.

In Computer Management, you can access Disk Management by expanding the Storage node, and then selecting Disk Management. Alternatively, you can type **diskmgmt.msc** in the Search box and then press Enter.

Disk Management has three views: Disk List, Graphical View, and Volume List. With remote systems, you're limited in the tasks you can perform with Disk Management. Remote management tasks you can perform include viewing drive details, changing drive letters and paths, and converting disk types. With removable media drives, you can also eject media remotely. To perform more advanced manipulation of remote drives, you can use the DiskPart command-line utility.

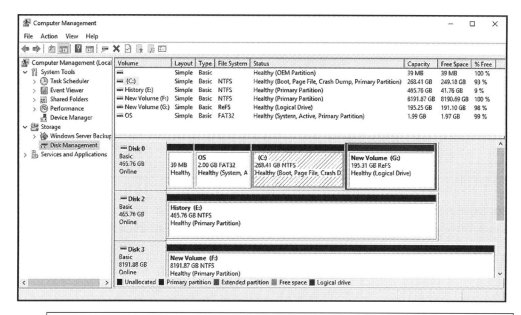

> **NOTE** You should be aware that if you create a partition but don't format it, the partition is labeled as Free Space. In addition, if you haven't assigned a portion of the disk to a partition, this section of the disk is labeled Unallocated.

In the default configuration, the Volume List view is in the upper-right corner, and the Graphical View is in the lower-right corner. This is the default configuration. You can change the view for the top or bottom pane as follows:

- To change the top view, select View, choose Top, and then select the view you want to use.
- To change the bottom view, select View, choose Bottom, and then select the view you want to use.
- To hide the bottom view, select View, choose Bottom, and then select Hidden.

Windows Server 2016 supports four types of disk configurations:

- **Basic** The standard fixed disk type. Basic disks are divided into partitions and are the original disk type for early Windows operating systems.

- **Dynamic**   An enhanced fixed disk type that you can update without having to restart the operating system (in most cases). Dynamic disks are divided into volumes.
- **Removable**   The standard disk type associated with removable storage devices.
- **Virtual**   The virtual hard disk (VHD) disk type associated with virtualization. Computers can use VHDs just like they use regular fixed disks and can even be configured to boot from a VHD.

These disk configurations can be used with legacy storage approaches as well as standards-based storage. From the Disk Management window, you can get more detailed information on a drive section by right-clicking it, and then selecting Properties. When you do this, you get a dialog box. The example that follows shows the dialog boxes for two fixed disks. The one on the left uses NTFS, and the one on the right uses ReFS. Both disks have additional tabs based on the server configuration.

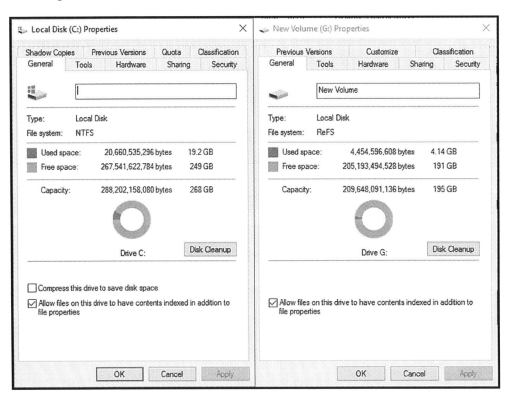

If you've configured remote management through Server Manager and MMCs, you can use Disk Management to configure and work with disks on remote computers. Keep in mind, however, that your options are slightly different from when you are working with the disks on a local computer. Tasks you can perform include the following:

- Viewing limited disk properties, but not volume properties. When you are viewing disk properties, you'll see only the General and Volumes tabs. You won't be able to see volume properties.
- Changing drive letters and mount paths.
- Formatting, shrinking, and extending volumes. With mirrored, spanned, and striped volumes, you are able to add and configure related options.
- Deleting volumes (except for system and boot volumes).
- Creating, attaching, and detaching VHDs. When you create and attach VHDs, you need to enter the full file path and won't be able to browse for the .vhd file.

Some tasks you perform with disks and volumes depend on the Plug and Play and Remote Registry services.

Using Removable Storage Devices

Removable storage devices can be formatted with ReFS, NTFS, FAT, FAT32, or exFAT. You connect external storage devices to a computer rather than installing them inside the computer. This makes external storage devices easier and faster to install than most fixed disk drives. Most external storage devices have either a USB, FireWire or eSATA interface.

Working with removable disks is similar to working with fixed disks. You can do the following:

- Right-click a removable disk, and then select Open or Explore to examine the disk's contents in File Explorer.
- Right-click a removable disk, and then select Format to format a removable disk as discussed in "Formatting partitions" later in this chapter. Removable disks generally are formatted with a single partition.
- Right-click a removable disk, and then select Properties to view or set properties. On the General tab of the Properties dialog box, you can set the volume label.

When you work with removable disks, you can customize disk and folder views. To do this, right-click the disk or folder, select Properties, and then click the Customize tab. You can then specify the default folder type to control the default details displayed. For example, you can set the default folder type as Documents or Pictures And Videos. You can also set folder pictures and folder icons.

With exFAT, FAT, or FAT32, folders and files stored on a removable disk do not have any security permissions or features other than the basic read-only or hidden attribute flags that you can set. With NTFS, removable disks support network file and folder sharing. You configure sharing on removable disks in the same way you configure standard file sharing. You can assign share permissions, configure caching options for offline file use, and limit the number of simultaneous users. You can share an entire removable disk as well as individual folders stored on the removable disk. You can also create multiple share instances.

Installing and Checking for a New Drive

Hot swapping is a feature that allows you to remove internal devices without shutting off the computer. Typically, hot-swappable internal drives are installed and removed from the front of the computer. If your computer supports hot swapping of internal drives, you can install drives without having to shut down. After you have installed a new drive, open Disk Management, and then choose Rescan Disks from the Action menu. New disks that are found are added with the appropriate disk type. If a disk that you've added isn't found, restart the computer.

If the computer doesn't support hot swapping of internal drives, you must turn the computer off and then install the new drives. Then you can scan for new disks as described previously. If you are working with new disks that have not been initialized—meaning they don't have disk signatures—Disk Management will start the Initialize Disk dialog box as soon it starts up and detects the new disks. You can then initialize the disks by following these steps:

1. Each disk you install needs to be initialized. In the Initialize Disk dialog box, select the disk or disks you installed.

2. Disks can use either the MBR or GPT partition style. Select the partition style you want to use for the disk or disks you are initializing.

3. Click OK. If you elected to initialize disks, Windows writes a disk signature to the disks and initializes the disks with the basic disk type.

If you don't want to use the Initialize Disk dialog box, you can close it and use Disk Management instead to view and work with the new disk. In the Disk List view, the new disk is marked with a red downward-pointing arrow icon, the disk's type is listed as Unknown, and the disk's status is listed as Not Initialized. Right-click the disk's icon and select Online. Right-click the disk's icon again, and select Initialize Disk. You can then initialize the disk as discussed previously.

> **NOTE** At an administrator PowerShell prompt, you can use Get-Disk to list available disks and Initialize-Disk to initialize new disks.

Understanding Drive Status

Knowing the status of a drive is useful when you install new drives or troubleshoot drive problems. Disk Management shows the drive status in Graphical View and Volume List view. Here are the most common status values and the techniques you can use to resolve error conditions:

- **Online** The normal disk status. It means the disk is accessible and doesn't have problems. Both dynamic disks and basic disks display this status. The drive doesn't have any known problems. You don't need to take any corrective action.
- **Online (Errors)** I/O errors have been detected on a dynamic disk. You can try to correct temporary errors by right-clicking the disk and selecting Reactivate Disk. If this doesn't work, the disk might have physical damage or you might need to run a thorough check of the disk.
- **Offline** The disk isn't accessible and might be corrupted or temporarily unavailable. If the disk name changes to Missing, the disk can no longer be located or identified on the system. Check for problems with the drive, its controller, and cables. Make sure that the drive has power and is connected properly. Use the Reactivate Disk command to bring the disk back online (if possible).
- **Foreign** The disk has been moved to your computer but hasn't been imported for use. A failed drive brought back online might sometimes be listed as Foreign. Right-click the disk, and then click Import Foreign Disks to add the disk to the system.
- **Unreadable** The disk isn't accessible currently, which can occur when disks are being rescanned. Both dynamic and basic disks display this status. With FireWire and USB card readers, you might get this status if the card is unformatted or improperly formatted. You might also get this status after the card is removed from the reader. Otherwise, if the drives aren't being scanned, the drive might be corrupted or have I/O errors. Right-click the disk, and then click Rescan Disk (on the Action menu) to try to correct the problem. You might also want to restart the system.
- **Unrecognized** The disk is of an unknown type and can't be used on the system. A drive from a system that is not based on Windows might display this status. If the disk is from another operating system, don't do anything. Normally, you can't use the drive on the computer without initializing and formatting it, so try a different drive.

- **Not Initialized**   The disk doesn't have a valid signature. A drive from a system not based on Windows might display this status. If the disk is from another operating system, don't do anything. You can't use the drive on the computer, so try a different drive. To prepare the disk for use on Windows Server 2016, right-click the disk, and then click Initialize Disk.
- **No Media**   No media has been inserted into the DVD or removable drive, or the media has been removed. Only DVD and removable disk types display this status. Insert a DVD or a removable disk to bring the disk online. With FireWire and USB card readers, this status is usually (but not always) displayed when the card is removed.

Working with Disks

Windows Server 2016 supports both legacy storage approaches and standards-based storage approaches. Legacy storage uses software-based RAID. Standards-based storage uses Storage Spaces.

Disk Management Essentials

Basic, dynamic, and virtual disk configurations can be used with both legacy storage approaches and standards-based storage. Normally, Windows Server 2016 disk partitions are initialized as basic disks. The exception is when you want to use software-based RAID instead of standards-based storage.

With software-based RAID, you can't create new fault-tolerant drive sets by using the basic disk type. You need to convert to dynamic disks and then create volumes that use striping, mirroring, or striping with parity (referred to as RAID 0, 1, and 5, respectively). The fault-tolerant features and the ability to modify disks without having to restart the computer are the key capabilities that distinguish dynamic disks from basic disks. Other features available on a disk depend on the disk formatting.

You can use both basic and dynamic disks on the same computer; however, volume sets must use the same disk type and partitioning style. For example, if you want to mirror drives C and D using software RAID, both drives must have the dynamic disk type and use the same partitioning style, which can be either MBR or GPT. Note that Disk Management allows you to start many disk configuration tasks regardless of whether the disks with which you are working use the dynamic disk type. The catch is that during the configuration process, Disk Management will convert the disks to the dynamic disk type. To learn how to convert a disk from basic to dynamic, see "Changing Drive Types" on the next page.

You can perform different disk configuration tasks with basic and dynamic disks. With basic disks, you can do the following:

- Format partitions, and mark them as active
- Create and delete primary and extended partitions
- Create and delete logical drives within extended partitions
- Convert from a basic disk to a dynamic disk

With dynamic disks, you can do the following:

- Create and delete simple, striped, spanned, mirrored, and RAID-5 volumes
- Remove a mirror from a mirrored volume
- Extend simple or spanned volumes
- Split a volume into two volumes
- Repair mirrored or RAID-5 volumes
- Reactivate a missing or offline disk
- Revert to a basic disk from a dynamic disk (requires deleting volumes and restoring from backup)

With either disk type, you can do the following:

- View properties of disks, partitions, and volumes
- Make drive-letter assignments
- Configure security and drive sharing
- Use Storage Spaces to implement standards-based storage

Special Considerations for Basic and Dynamic Disks

Whether you're working with basic or dynamic disks, you need to keep in mind five special types of drive sections:

- **Active**   The active partition or volume is the drive section for system caching and startup. Some devices with removable storage might be listed as having an active partition.
- **Boot**   The boot partition or volume contains the operating system and its support files. The system and boot partition or volume can be the same.
- **Crash dump**   The partition to which the computer attempts to write dump files in the event of a system crash. By default, dump files are written to the %SystemRoot% folder, but they can be located on any partition or volume.

- **Page file**   A partition containing a paging file used by the operating system. Because a computer can page memory to multiple disks, according to the way virtual memory is configured, a computer can have multiple page file partitions or volumes.
- **System**   The system partition or volume contains the hardware-specific files needed to load the operating system. The system partition or volume can't be part of a striped or spanned volume.

Volume	Layout	Type	File System	Status	Capacity	Free Space	% Free
	Simple	Basic		Healthy (Recovery Partition)	450 MB	450 MB	100 %
(C:)	Simple	Basic	NTFS	Healthy (System, Boot, Page File, Active, Crash Dump, Primary Partition)	160.22 GB	118.73 GB	74 %
New Volume (D:)	Simple	Basic	ReFS	Healthy (Primary Partition)	72.19 GB	71.77 GB	99 %

REAL WORLD   GPT is becoming more common. With Windows Server 2016, a disk with the GPT partition style will have a recovery partition and an EFI system partition. The only Disk Management view that shows the partition style is the Disk list view. While you are working with the Graphical view, you can determine the partition style by right-clicking a disk (not a volume on the disk), and selecting Properties. In the Properties dialog box, the partition style is listed on the Volumes tab.

NOTE   You can mark a partition as active by using Disk Management. In Disk Management, right-click the primary partition you want to mark as active, and then click Mark Partition As Active. You can't mark dynamic disk volumes as active. When you convert a basic disk containing the active partition to a dynamic disk, this partition becomes a simple volume that's active automatically.

Changing Drive Types

You can use dynamic disks with any current version of Windows and many other operating systems, including most UNIX variants. However, keep in mind that you need to create a separate volume for any operating system not based on Windows.

You can't use dynamic disks on portable computers. When you are working with non-portable computers and servers, you only can use dynamic disks with drives connected to internal controllers (as well as some eSATA controllers). Although you can't use dynamic disks with portable or removable drives on these computers, you can connect such a drive to an internal controller or a recognized eSATA controller, and then use Disk Management to import the drive.

Windows Server 2016 provides the tools you need to convert a basic disk to a dynamic disk and to change a dynamic disk back to a basic disk. When you convert to a dynamic disk, partitions are changed to volumes of the appropriate type automatically. You can't change these volumes back to partitions. Instead, you must delete the volumes on the dynamic disk, and then change the disk back to a basic disk. Deleting the volumes destroys all the information on the disk.

Converting a Basic Disk to a Dynamic Disk

Before you convert a basic disk to a dynamic disk, you should make sure that you don't need to boot the computer to an operating system that doesn't support dynamic disks. With MBR disks, you should also make sure that the disk has 1 MB of free space at the end of the disk. Although Disk Management reserves this free space when creating partitions and volumes, disk management tools on other operating systems might not. Without the free space at the end of the disk, the conversion will fail.

With GPT disks, you must have contiguous, recognized data partitions. If the GPT disk contains partitions that Windows doesn't recognize, such as those created by another operating system, you can't convert to a dynamic disk.

With either type of disk, the following holds true:

- There must be at least 1 MB of free space at the end of the disk. Disk Management reserves this free space automatically, but other disk management tools might not.
- You can't use dynamic disks on portable computers or with removable media. You can configure these drives only as basic drives with primary partitions.
- You shouldn't convert a disk if it contains multiple installations of the Windows operating system. If you do, you might be able to start the computer only by using the installation which did the conversion.

To convert a basic disk to a dynamic disk, follow these steps:

1. In Disk Management, right-click a basic disk that you want to convert, either in the Disk List view or in the left pane of the Graphical View. Then click Convert To Dynamic Disk.

NOTE Make sure you right-click a disk and not a volume on a disk. If you right-click a volume, you won't have the same options.

2. In the Convert To Dynamic Disk dialog box, select the check boxes for the disks you want to convert.

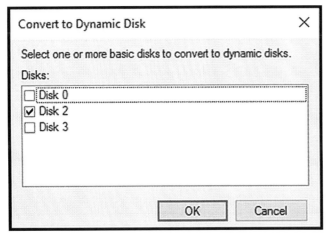

3. Click OK to continue. This displays the Disks To Convert dialog box, which shows the disks you're converting.

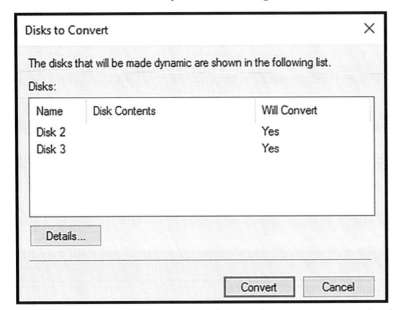

The buttons and columns in this dialog box contain the following information:

- **Name** Shows the disk number.
- **Disk Contents** Shows the type and status of partitions, such as boot, active, or in use.
- **Will Convert** Specifies whether the drive will be converted. If the drive doesn't meet the criteria, it won't be converted, and you might need to take corrective action, as described previously.
- **Details** Shows the volumes on the selected drive.
- **Convert** Starts the conversion.

4. To begin the conversion, click Convert. Disk Management warns you that after the conversion is complete, you won't be able to start previous versions of Windows from volumes on the selected disks. Click Yes to continue.

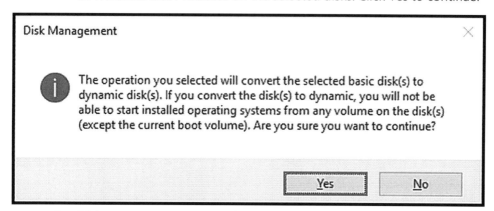

Disk Management ✕

The operation you selected will convert the selected basic disk(s) to dynamic disk(s). If you convert the disk(s) to dynamic, you will not be able to start installed operating systems from any volume on the disk(s) (except the current boot volume). Are you sure you want to continue?

Yes   No

5. Disk Management restarts the computer if a selected drive contains the boot partition, system partition, or a partition in use.

Changing a Dynamic Disk Back to a Basic Disk

Before you can change a dynamic disk back to a basic disk, you must delete all dynamic volumes on the disk. After you do this, right-click the disk and select Convert To Basic Disk to change the dynamic disk to a basic disk. You can then create new partitions and logical drives on the disk.

Reactivating Dynamic Disks

If the status of a dynamic disk is Online (Errors) or Offline, you can often reactivate the disk to correct the problem. You reactivate a disk by following these steps:

1. In Disk Management, right-click the dynamic disk you want to reactivate, and then click Reactivate Disk. Confirm the action when prompted.

2. If the drive status doesn't change, you might need to reboot the computer. If this still doesn't resolve the problem, check for problems with the drive, its controller, and the cables. Also make sure that the drive has power and is connected properly.

Rescanning Disks

Rescanning all drives on a system updates the drive configuration information on the computer. Rescanning can sometimes resolve a problem with drives that show a status of Unreadable. You rescan disks on a computer by choosing Rescan Disks from the Action menu in Disk Management.

Moving a Dynamic Disk to a New System

An important advantage of dynamic disks over basic disks is that you can easily move dynamic disks from one computer to another. For example, if after setting up a computer you decide that you don't really need an additional drive, you can move it to another computer where it can be better used.

Windows Server 2016 greatly simplifies the task of moving drives to a new system. Before moving disks, you should follow these steps:

1. Open Disk Management on the system where the dynamic disks are currently installed. Check the status of the disks, and ensure that they're marked as Healthy. If the status isn't Healthy, you should repair partitions and volumes before you move the disks.

> **NOTE** Drives with BitLocker Drive Encryption cannot be moved by using this technique. BitLocker Drive Encryption wraps drives in a protected seal so that any offline tampering is detected and results in the disk being unavailable until an administrator unlocks it.

2. Check the drive subsystems on the original computer and the computer to which you want to transfer the disk. Both computers should have identical drive subsystems. If they don't, the Plug and Play ID on the system drive from the original computer won't match what the destination computer is expecting. As a result, the destination computer won't be able to load the right drivers, and the boot attempt might fail.

3. Check whether any dynamic disks you want to move are part of a spanned, extended, or striped set. If they are, you should make a note of which disks are part of which set and plan on moving all disks in a set together. If you are moving only part of a disk set, you should be aware of the consequences. For spanned, extended, or striped volumes, moving only part of the set will make the related volumes unusable on the current computer and on the computer to which you are planning to move the disks.

When you are ready to move the disks, follow these steps:

1. On the original computer, start Computer Management. Then, in the left pane, select Device Manager. In the Device list, expand Disk Drives. This

shows a list of the physical disk drives on the computer. Right-click each disk you want to move, and then click Uninstall. If you are unsure which disks to uninstall, right-click each disk and click Properties. In the Properties dialog box, click the Volumes tab and then select Populate to show the volumes on the selected disk.

2. Next, on the original computer, select the Disk Management node in Computer Management. If the disk or disks you want to move are still listed, right-click each disk, and then click Remove Disk.

3. After you perform these procedures, you can move the dynamic disks. If the disks are hot-swappable disks and this feature is supported on both computers, remove the disks from the original computer, and then install them on the destination computer. Otherwise, turn off both computers, remove the drives from the original computer, and then install them on the destination computer. When you have finished, restart the computers.

4. On the destination computer, access Disk Management, and then choose Rescan Disks from the Action menu. When Disk Management finishes scanning the disks, right-click any disk marked Foreign, and then click Import. You should now be able to access the disks and their volumes on the destination computer.

NOTE   In most cases, the volumes on the dynamic disks should retain the drive letters they had on the original computer. However, if a drive letter is already used on the destination computer, a volume receives the next available drive letter. If a dynamic volume previously did not have a drive letter, it does not receive a drive letter when moved to the destination computer. Additionally, if automounting is disabled, the volumes aren't automatically mounted, and you must manually mount volumes and assign drive letters.

Managing Virtual Hard Disks

Virtual hard disks (VHDs) provide alternate storage locations that function similar to traditional disks while requiring some additional setup prior to use. Before you can use a VHD, you must create, attach and initialize it using Disk Management or another management tool. You must also partition the virtual disk and then format this partition.

Creating Virtual Hard Disks

In Disk Management, you can create a VHD by choosing Create VHD from the Action menu. In the Create And Attach Virtual Hard Disk dialog box, specify whether you want to use the standard VHD format or the newer VHDX format. As the VHDX format has many enhancements over the VHD format, including resiliency for power failure events and support for very large virtual disks, you'll typically want to use this format. The only time you wouldn't want to use this format is when you may move the virtual disk to an early Windows or Windows Server operating system.

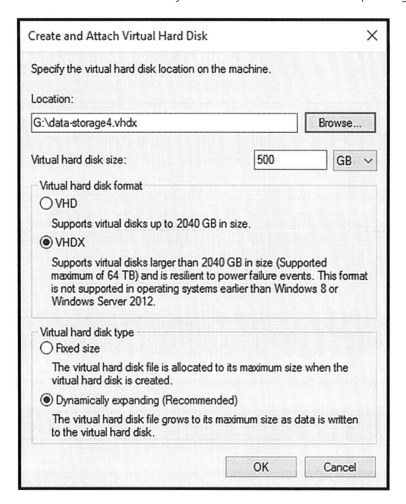

Next, click Browse. Use the Browse Virtual Disk Files dialog box to select the location where you want to create the .vhd or .vhdx file for the VHD. After you enter a file name for the virtual disk, such as data-storage, click in the Save As Type list and select Virtual Disk Files (*.vhd) or Virtual Disk Files (*.vhdx) as appropriate for the virtual disk format you are using. Click Save to close the Browse... dialog box.

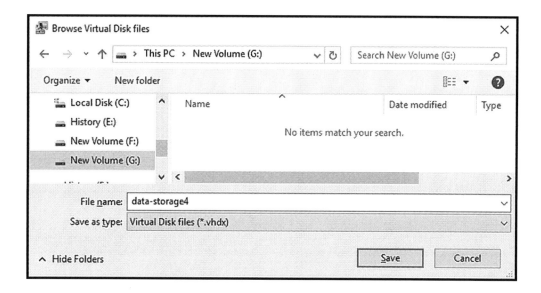

After you specify the storage location, size the virtual disk using the Virtual Hard Disk Size options. You can enter the size of the disk in megabytes, gigabytes, or terabytes. Complete the configuration by specifying whether the size of the VHD dynamically expands to its fixed maximum size as data is saved to it or instead uses a fixed amount of space regardless of the amount of data stored on it. When you click OK, Disk Management creates the VHD.

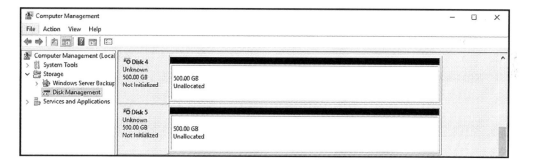

The VHD is attached automatically and added as a new disk. To initialize the disk for use, right-click the disk entry in Graphical View, and then click Initialize Disk. In the Initialize Disk dialog box, the disk is selected for initialization. Specify the disk type as MBR or GPT, and then click OK.

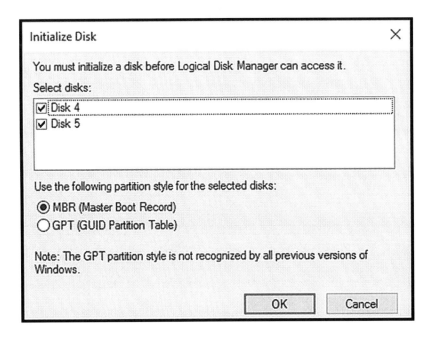

After initializing the disk, you can create a volume on the disk using the unpartitioned space. Right-click the unpartitioned space on the disk and select New Simple Volume. Use the New Simple Volume wizard to create the volume, as discussed in the section of this chapter entitled "Creating Volumes and Volume Sets." After you create the volume, the VHD is available for use.

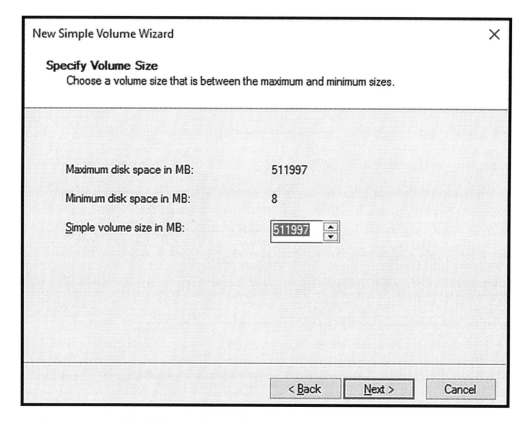

Working with Virtual Hard Disks

After you've created, attached, initialized, and formatted a VHD, you can work with a virtual disk in much the same way as you work with other disks. You can write data to and read data from a VHD. You can boot the computer from a VHD.

You are able to take a VHD offline or put a VHD online by right-clicking the disk entry in Graphical View and selecting Offline or Online, respectively. If you no longer want to use a VHD, you can detach it by right-clicking the disk entry in Graphical View, selecting Detach VHD, and then clicking OK in the Detach Virtual Hard Disk dialog box.

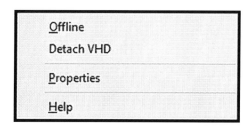

You can use VHDs created with other programs as well. If you created a VHD using another program or have a detached VHD you want to attach, you can work with the VHD by completing the following steps:

1. In Disk Management, click the Attach VHD option on the Action menu.

2. In the Attach Virtual Hard Disk dialog box, click Browse. Use the Browse Virtual Disk Files dialog box to select the .vhd or .vhdx file for the virtual disk, and then click Open.

3. If you want to attach the VHD in read-only mode, select Read-Only. Click OK to attach the VHD.

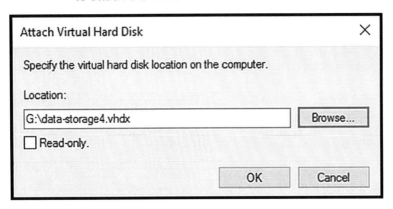

Chapter 4. Partitioning and Optimizing Drives

Whether you are working with hard disk drives (HDDs) or solid state drives (SSDs), you can use disks with either the basic or dynamic disk type. Basic disks use partitions, while dynamic disks use volumes, and both of which can be compressed or encrypted. Compression allows you to store more information on a drive, but shouldn't be used with some types of data, such as professionally-produced audio. Encryption protects sensitive data by making it unreadable if files are copied to another computer without first being decrypted. In addition to standard encryption, Windows Server 2016 also supports BitLocker Drive Encryption, a drive encryption technology discussed in Chapter 5.

Using Basic Disks and Partitions

When you install a new computer or update an existing computer, you often need to partition the drives on the computer. You partition drives by using Disk Management.

Partitioning Essentials

In Windows Server 2016, a physical drive using the MBR partition style can have up to four primary partitions and one extended partition. This allows you to configure MBR drives in one of two ways: by using one to four primary partitions, or by using one to three primary partitions and one extended partition. A primary partition can fill an entire disk, or you can size it as appropriate for the workstation or server you're configuring. Within an extended partition, you can create one or more logical drives. A logical drive is simply a section of a partition with its own file system. Generally, you use logical drives to divide a large drive into manageable sections. With this in mind, you might want to divide a 600-GB extended partition into three logical drives of 200 GB each. Physical disks with the GPT partition style can have up to 128 partitions.

After you partition a drive, you format the partitions. This is high-level formatting that creates the file system structure rather than low-level formatting that sets up the drive for initial use. You're probably very familiar with the C drive used by Windows Server 2016. Well, the C drive is simply the designator for a disk partition. If you partition a disk into multiple sections, each section can have its own drive letter. You use the drive letters to access file systems in various partitions on a physical drive.

Unlike MS-DOS, which assigns drive letters automatically starting with the letter C, Windows Server 2016 lets you specify drive letters. Generally, the drive letters C through Z are available for your use.

> **NOTE** The drive letter A used to be assigned to a system's floppy disk drive. If the system had a second floppy disk drive, the letter B was assigned to it, so you could use only the letters C through Z. Don't forget that DVD drives and other types of media drives need drive letters as well. The total number of drive letters you can use at one time is 24. If you need additional volumes, you can create them by using drive paths.

By using drive letters, you can have only 24 active volumes. To get around this limitation, you can mount disks to drive paths. A drive path is set as a folder location on another drive. For example, you might mount additional drives as E:\Data1, E:\Data2, and E:\Data3. You can use drive paths with basic and dynamic disks. The only restriction for drive paths is that you mount them on empty folders that are on NTFS drives.

To help you differentiate between primary partitions and extended partitions with logical drives, Disk Management color codes the partitions. For example, primary partitions might be color coded with a dark-blue band and logical drives in extended partitions might be color coded with a light-blue band. The key for the color scheme is shown at the bottom of the Disk Management window. You can change the colors in the Settings dialog box by choosing Settings from the View menu.

Creating Partitions and Simple Volumes

Windows Server 2016 simplifies the Disk Management user interface by using one set of dialog boxes and wizards for both partitions and volumes. The first three volumes on a basic drive are created automatically as primary partitions. If you try to create a fourth volume on a basic drive, the remaining free space on the drive is converted automatically to an extended partition with a logical drive of the size you designate by using the new volume feature in the extended partition. Any subsequent volumes are created in the extended partitions as logical drives automatically.

In Disk Management, you create partitions, logical drives, and simple volumes by following these steps:

1. In Disk Management's Graphical View, right-click an unallocated or free area, and then click New Simple Volume. This starts the New Simple Volume Wizard. Read the Welcome page, and then click Next.

2. The Specify Volume Size page in the New Simple Volume Wizard specifies the minimum and maximum size for the volume in megabytes and lets you size the volume within these limits. Size the partition in megabytes in the Simple Volume Size In MB box, and then click Next.

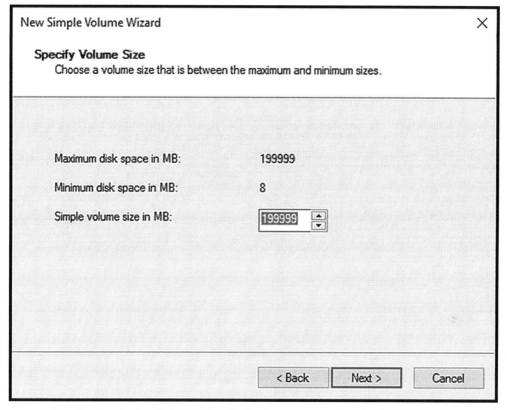

3. On the Assign Drive Letter Or Path page, specify whether you want to assign a drive letter or path, and then click Next. The following options are available:

- **Assign The Following Drive Letter** Choose this option to assign a drive letter. Then select an available drive letter in the list provided. By default, Windows Server 2016 selects the lowest available drive letter and excludes reserved drive letters as well as those assigned to local disks or network drives.
- **Mount In The Following Empty NTFS Folder** Choose this option to mount the partition in an empty NTFS folder. You must then type the path to an existing folder or click Browse to search for or create a folder to use.
- **Do Not Assign A Drive Letter Or Drive Path** Choose this option if you want to create the partition without assigning a drive letter or path. If you later want the

partition to be available for storage, you can assign a drive letter or path at that time.

> **NOTE** You don't have to assign volumes a drive letter or a path. A volume with no designators is considered to be unmounted and is for the most part unusable. An unmounted volume can be mounted by assigning a drive letter or a path at a later date. See "Assigning Drive Letters and Paths" in Chapter 8.

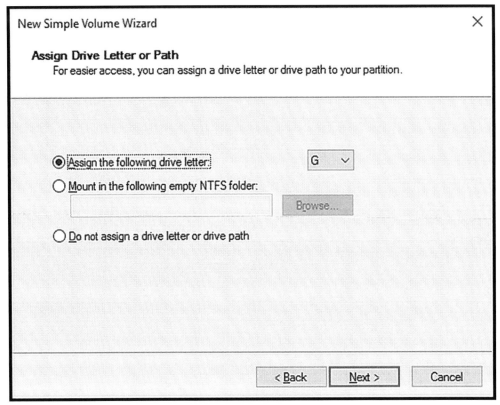

4. On the Format Partition page, determine whether and how the volume should be formatted. If you want to format the volume, select Format This Volume With The Following Settings, and then configure the following options:

- **File System**   Sets the file system type as FAT, FAT32, exFAT, NTFS, or ReFS. The file system types available depend on the size of the volume you are formatting. If you use FAT32, you can later convert to NTFS with the Convert utility. You can't, however, convert NTFS partitions to FAT32.
- **Allocation Unit Size**   Sets the cluster size for the file system. This is the basic unit in which disk space is allocated. The default allocation unit size is based on the size of the volume and is set dynamically prior to formatting by default. To override this feature, you can set the allocation unit size to a specific value. If you use many small files, you might want to use a smaller cluster size, such as 512 or

1024 bytes. With these settings, small files use less disk space. Note that ReFS volumes have a fixed allocation unit size.

- **Volume Label**   Sets a text label for the partition. This label is the partition's volume name and is set to New Volume by default. You can change the volume label at any time by right-clicking the volume in File Explorer, clicking Properties, and typing a new value in the Label box provided on the General tab.
- **Perform A Quick Format**   Tells Windows Server 2016 to format without checking the partition for errors. With large partitions, this option can save you a few minutes. However, it's usually better to check for errors, which enables Disk Management to mark bad sectors on the disk and lock them out.
- **Enable File And Folder Compression**   Turns on compression for the disk. Built-in compression is available only for NTFS (and is not supported for FAT, FAT32, exFAT, or ReFS). Under NTFS, compression is transparent to users and compressed files can be accessed just like regular files. If you select this option, files and directories on this drive are compressed automatically. For more information on compressing drives, files, and directories, see "Compressing Drives and Data" later in this chapter.

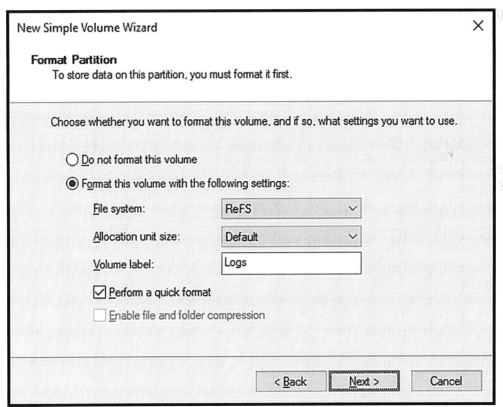

Formatting Partitions

Formatting creates a file system on a partition and permanently deletes any existing data. This is high-level formatting that creates the file system structure rather than low-level formatting that initializes a drive for use. To format a partition, right-click the partition, and then click Format. This opens the Format dialog box.

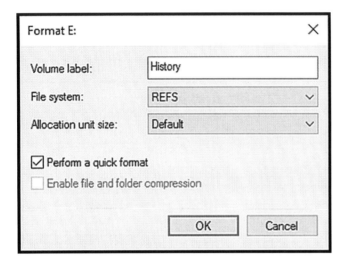

You use the formatting options as follows:

- **Volume Label**   Specifies a text label for the partition. This label is the partition's volume name.
- **File System**   Specifies the file system type as FAT, FAT32, exFAT, NTFS, or ReFS. The file system types available depend on the size of the volume you are formatting.
- **Allocation Unit Size**   Specifies the cluster size for the file system. This is the basic unit in which disk space is allocated. The default allocation unit size is based on the size of the volume and is set dynamically prior to formatting. To override this feature, you can set the allocation unit size to a specific value. If you use lots of small files, you might want to use a smaller cluster size, such as 512 or 1024 bytes. With these settings, small files use less disk space.
- **Perform A Quick Format**   Tells Windows Server 2016 to format without checking the partition for errors. With large partitions, this option can save you a few minutes. However, it's more prudent to check for errors, which allows Disk Management to mark bad sectors on the disk and lock them out.

When you're ready to proceed, click OK. Because formatting a partition destroys any existing data, Disk Management gives you one last chance to cancel the procedure.

Click OK to start formatting the partition. Disk Management changes the drive's status to reflect the formatting and the percentage of completion. When formatting is complete, the drive status changes to reflect this.

Using Volumes and Volume Sets

You create volume sets and RAID arrays on dynamic drives. With a volume set, you can create a single volume that spans multiple drives. Users can access this volume as if it were a single drive, regardless of how many drives the volume is spread over. A volume that's on a single drive is referred to as a *simple volume*. A volume that spans multiple drives is referred to as a *spanned volume*.

With a RAID array, you can protect important business data and sometimes improve the performance of drives. RAID can be implemented by using the built-in features of the operating system (a software approach) or by using hardware. Windows Server 2016 supports three levels of software RAID: 0, 1, and 5. RAID arrays are implemented as mirrored, striped, and striped with parity volumes.

You create and manage volumes in much the same way in which you create and manage partitions. A *volume* is a drive section you can use to store data directly.

> **NOTE** With spanned and striped volumes on basic disks, you can delete a volume but you can't create or extend volumes. With mirrored volumes on basic disks, you can delete, repair, and resync the mirror. You can also break the mirror. For striped with parity volumes (RAID-5) on basic disks, you can delete or repair the volume, but you can't create new volumes.

Understanding Volume Basics

Disk Management color codes volumes by type, much like it does partitions. Volumes also have the following properties:

- **Layout** Volume layouts include simple, spanned, mirrored, striped, and striped with parity.
- **Type** Volumes always have the type *dynamic*. Partitions always have the type *basic*.
- **File System** Like partitions, each volume can have a different file system type, such as FAT or NTFS file system. Note that FAT16 is available only when the partition or volume is 2 GB or less in size.

- **Status**   The state of the drive. In Graphical View, the state is shown as Healthy, Failed Redundancy, and so on. The next section, "Understanding volume sets," discusses volume sets and the various states you might see.
- **Capacity**   The total storage size of the drive.
- **Free Space**   The total amount of available space on the volume.
- **% Free**   The percentage of free space out of the total storage size of the volume.

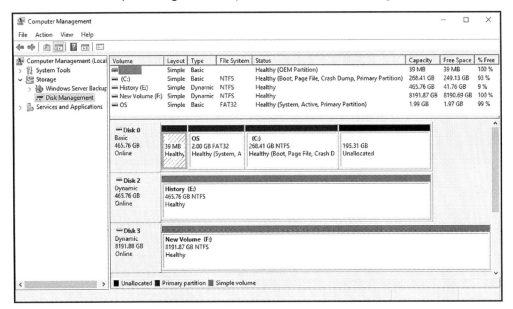

An important advantage of dynamic volumes over basic volumes is that dynamic volumes enable you to make changes to volumes and drives without having to restart the system (in most cases). Volumes also let you take advantage of the fault-tolerance enhancements of Windows Server 2016. You can install other operating systems and dual boot a Windows Server 2016 system by creating a separate volume for the other operating system. For example, you could install Windows Server 2016 on volume C and Windows 10 on volume D.

With volumes, you can do the following:

- Assign drive letters and drive paths as discussed in "Assigning Drive Letters and Paths" later in Chapter 8
- Create any number of volumes on a disk as long as you have free space
- Create volumes that span two or more disks and, if necessary, configure fault tolerance
- Extend volumes to increase the volumes' capacity
- Designate active, system, and boot volumes as described in "Special considerations for basic and dynamic disks" in Chapter 3, "Data Storage: The Essentials"

Understanding Volume Sets

With volume sets, you can create volumes that span several drives by using free space on different drives to create what users see as a single volume. Files are stored on the volume set segment by segment, with the first segment of free space being used to store files before other segments. When the first segment fills up, the second segment is used, and so on.

You can create a volume set using free space on up to 32 hard disk drives. The key advantage to volume sets is that they let you tap into unused free space and create a usable file system. The key disadvantage is that if any hard disk drive in the volume set fails, the volume set can no longer be used, which means that essentially all the data on the volume set is lost.

Understanding the volume status is useful when you install new volumes or are trying to troubleshoot problems. Disk Management shows the drive status in Graphical View and Volume List view. Status values for dynamic volumes and the resolution for error states follow:

- **Data Incomplete** Spanned volumes on a foreign disk are incomplete. You must have forgotten to add the other disks from the spanned volume set. Add the disks that contain the rest of the spanned volumes, and then import all the disks at one time.
- **Data Not Redundant** Fault-tolerant volumes on a foreign disk are incomplete. You must have forgotten to add the other disks from a mirror or RAID-5 set. Add the remaining disks, and then import all the disks at one time.
- **Failed** An error disk status. The disk is inaccessible or damaged. Ensure that the related dynamic disk is online. As necessary, right-click the volume, and then click Reactivate Volume. For a basic disk, you might need to check the disk for a faulty connection.
- **Failed Redundancy** An error disk status. One of the disks in a mirror or RAID-5 set is offline. Ensure that the related dynamic disk is online. If necessary, reactivate the volume. Next, you might need to replace a failed mirror or repair a failed RAID-5 volume.
- **Formatting** A temporary status that indicates the volume is being formatted. The progress of the formatting is indicated as the percent complete unless you choose the Perform A Quick Format option.
- **Healthy** The normal volume status. The volume doesn't have any known problems. You don't need to take any corrective action.

- **Healthy (At Risk)**   Windows had problems reading from or writing to the physical disk on which the dynamic volume is located. This status appears when Windows encounters errors.   Right-click the volume, and then click Reactivate Volume. If the disk continues to have this status or has this status periodically, the disk might be failing, and you should back up all data on the disk.
- **Healthy (Unknown Partition)**   Windows does not recognize the partition. This can occur because the partition is from a different operating system or is a manufacturer-created partition used to store system files.   No corrective action is necessary.
- **Initializing**   A temporary status that indicates the disk is being initialized.   The drive status should change after a few seconds.
- **Regenerating**   A temporary status that indicates that data and parity for a RAID-5 volume are being regenerated.   Progress is indicated as the percent complete. The volume should return to Healthy status.
- **Resynching**   A temporary status that indicates that a mirror set is being resynchronized.   Progress is indicated as the percent complete. The volume should return to Healthy status.
- **Stale Data**   Data on foreign disks that are fault tolerant are out of sync.   Rescan the disks or restart the computer, and then check the status. A new status should be displayed, such as Failed Redundancy.
- **Unknown**   The volume cannot be accessed. It might have a corrupted boot sector.   The volume might have a boot sector virus. Check it with an up-to-date antivirus program. Rescan the disks or restart the computer, and then check the status.

Creating Volumes and Volume Sets

You can format simple volumes as exFAT, FAT, FAT32, or NTFS. To make management easier, you should format volumes that span multiple disks as NTFS, which enables you to expand the volume set if necessary. If you find you need more space on a volume, you can extend simple and spanned volumes by selecting an area of free space and adding it to the volume. You can extend a simple volume within the same disk, and you can also extend a simple volume onto other disks. When you do this, you create a spanned volume, which you must format as NTFS.

You create volumes and volume sets by following these steps:

1. In Disk Management's Graphical View, right-click an unallocated area, and then click New Spanned Volume or New Striped Volume as appropriate. Read the Welcome page, and then click Next.

2. Select the disks that you want to be part of the volume, and then size the volume segments on those disks.

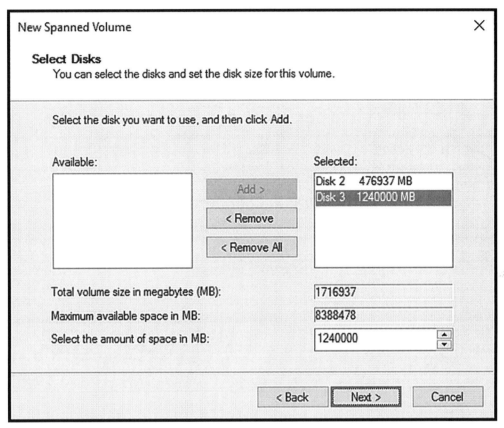

3. Available disks are shown in the Available list. If necessary, select a disk in this list, and then click Add to add the disk to the Selected list. If you make a mistake, you can remove disks from the Selected list by selecting the disk, and then clicking Remove.

> **CAUTION** The disk wizards in Windows Server 2016 show both basic and dynamic disks with available disk space. If you add space from a basic disk, the wizard converts the disk to a dynamic disk before creating the volume set. Before clicking Yes to continue, be sure you really want to do this because it can affect how the disk is used by the operating system.

4. Select a disk in the Selected list, and then specify the size of the volume on the disk in the Select The Amount Of Space In MB box. The Maximum Available Space In MB box shows you the largest area of free space available on the disk. The Total Volume Size In Megabytes box shows you the total disk space selected for use with the volume. Click Next.

> **TIP** Although you can size a volume set any way you want, consider how you'll use volume sets on the system. Simple and spanned volumes aren't fault tolerant; rather than creating one monstrous volume with all the available free space, you might want to create several smaller volumes to help ensure that losing one volume doesn't mean losing all your data.

5. Specify whether you want to assign a drive letter or path to the volume, and then click Next. You use the available options as follows:

- **Assign The Following Drive Letter** To assign a drive letter, choose this option, and then select an available drive letter in the list provided.
- **Mount In The Following Empty NTFS Folder** To assign a drive path, choose this option, and then type the path to an existing folder on an NTFS drive, or click Browse to search for or create a folder.
- **Do Not Assign A Drive Letter Or Drive Path** To create the volume without assigning a drive letter or path, choose this option. You can assign a drive letter or path later if necessary.

6. Specify whether the volume should be formatted. If you elect to format the volume, set the following formatting options:

- **File System** Specifies the file system type, such as NTFS or ReFS.
- **Allocation Unit Size** Specifies the cluster size for the file system. This is the basic unit in which disk space is allocated. The default allocation unit size is based on the volume's size and is set dynamically prior to formatting. Although you can't change the default size if you select ReFS, you can set the allocation unit size to a specific value with other formats. If you use a lot of small files, you might want to use a smaller cluster size, such as 512 or 1024 bytes. With these settings, small files use less disk space.
- **Volume Label** Specifies a text label for the partition. This label is the partition's volume name.
- **Perform A Quick Format** Tells Windows to format without checking the partition for errors. With large partitions, this option can save you a few minutes. However, it's more prudent to check for errors, which allows Disk Management to mark bad sectors on the disk and lock them out.
- **Enable File And Folder Compression** Turns on compression for the disk. Compression is transparent to users, and compressed files can be accessed just like regular files. If you select this option, files and directories on this drive are compressed automatically. For more information on compressing drives, files, and directories, see "Compressing Drives and Data" in Chapter 4. (NTFS only)

7. Click Next, and then click Finish.

Deleting Volumes and Volume Sets

You use the same technique to delete all volumes, whether they're simple, spanned, mirrored, striped, or RAID-5 (striped with parity). Deleting a volume set removes the associated file system, and all associated data is lost. Before you delete a volume set, you should back up any files and directories the volume set contains.

You can't delete a volume that contains the system, boot, or active paging files for Windows Server 2016.

To delete volumes, follow these steps:

1. In Disk Management, right-click any volume in the set, and then click Delete Volume. You can't delete a portion of a spanned volume without deleting the entire volume.
2. Click Yes to confirm that you want to delete the volume.

Managing Volumes

You manage volumes much like you manage partitions. Follow the techniques outlined in Chapter 8.

Compressing Drives and Data

When you format a drive for NTFS, Windows Server 2016 allows you to turn on the built-in compression feature. With compression, all files and directories stored on a drive are automatically compressed when they're created. Because this compression is transparent to users, compressed data can be accessed just like regular data. The difference is that you can store more information on a compressed drive than you can on an uncompressed drive.

> **IMPORTANT** File Explorer shows the names of compressed resources in blue. It's also important to point out that ReFS does not support NTFS compression.
>
> **REAL WORLD** Although compression is certainly a useful feature when you want to save disk space, you can't encrypt compressed data. Compression and encryption are mutually exclusive alternatives for NTFS volumes, which means you have the choice of using compression or using encryption. You can't use both techniques. For more information on encryption, see "Encrypting Drives and Data" later in this chapter. If you try to compress

encrypted data, Windows Server 2016 automatically decrypts the data and then compresses it. Likewise, if you try to encrypt compressed data, Windows Server 2016 uncompresses the data, and then encrypts it.

Compressing Drives

To compress a drive and all its contents, follow these steps:

1. In File Explorer or Disk Management, right-click the drive you want to compress, and then click Properties.

2. On the General tab, select Compress Drive To Save Disk Space, and then click OK.

3. In the Confirm Attribute Changes dialog box, select whether to apply the changes to subfolders and files, and then click OK.

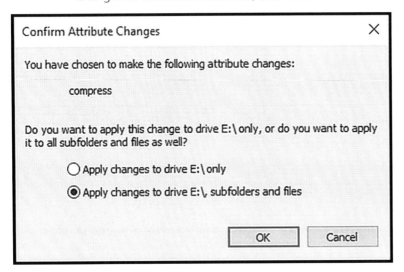

Compressing Directories and Files

If you decide not to compress a drive, Windows Server 2016 lets you selectively compress directories and files. To compress a file or directory, follow these steps:

1. In File Explorer, right-click the file or directory you want to compress, and then click Properties.

2. On the General tab of the Properties dialog box, click Advanced. In the Advanced Attributes dialog box, select the Compress Contents To Save Disk Space check box. Click OK twice.

For an individual file, Windows Server marks the file as compressed, and then compresses it. For a directory, Windows Server marks the directory as compressed and then compresses all the files in it. If the directory contains subfolders, Windows Server displays a dialog box that allows you to compress all the subfolders associated with the directory. Simply select Apply Changes To This Folder, Subfolders, And Files, and then click OK. After you compress a directory, any new files added or copied to the directory are compressed automatically.

> **NOTE** If you move an uncompressed file from a different drive, the file is compressed. However, if you move an uncompressed file to a compressed folder on the same NTFS drive, the file isn't compressed. Note also that you can't encrypt compressed files.

Expanding Compressed Drives

File Explorer shows the names of compressed files and folders in blue. You can remove compression from a drive by following these steps:

1. In File Explorer or Disk Management, right-click the drive that contains the data you want to expand, and then click Properties.
2. Clear the Compress Drive To Save Disk Space check box, and then click OK.

3. In the Confirm Attribute Changes dialog box, select whether to apply the change to subfolders and files, and then click OK.

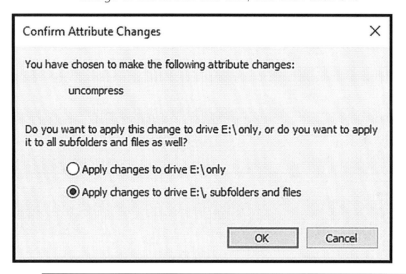

> **TIP** Windows always checks the available disk space before expanding compressed data. You should, too. If less free space is available than used space, you might not be able to complete the expansion. For example, if a compressed drive uses 150 GB of space and has 70 GB of free space available, you won't have enough free space to expand the data. Generally, you need about 1.5 to 2 times as much free space as you have compressed data.

Expanding Compressed Directories and Files

If you decide that you want to expand a compressed file or directory, follow these steps:

1. Right-click the file or directory in File Explorer, and then click Properties.
2. On the General tab of the Properties dialog box, click Advanced. Clear the Compress Contents To Save Disk Space check box. Click OK twice.

With files, Windows Server removes compression and expands the file. With directories, Windows Server expands all the files within the directory. If the directory contains subfolders, you also have the opportunity to remove compression from the subfolders. To do this, select Apply Changes To This Folder, Subfolders, And Files when prompted, and then click OK.

> **TIP**   Windows Server also provides command-line utilities for compressing and uncompressing data. The compression utility is called Compact (Compact.exe). The uncompression utility is called Expand (Expand.exe).

Encrypting Drives and Data

NTFS has many advantages over other file systems you can use with Windows Server. One advantage is the capability to automatically encrypt and decrypt data by using the Encrypting File System (EFS). When you encrypt data, you add an extra layer of protection to sensitive data, and this extra layer acts as a security blanket blocking all other users from reading the contents of the encrypted files. Indeed, one of the great benefits of encryption is that only the designated user can access the data. This benefit is also a disadvantage in that the user must remove encryption before authorized users can access the data.

> **NOTE**   As discussed previously, you can't compress encrypted files. The encryption and compression features of NTFS are mutually exclusive. You can use one feature or the other, but not both. Note also that ReFS doesn't support this type of encryption.

Understanding Encryption and the Encrypting File System

File encryption is supported on a per-folder or per-file basis. Any file placed in a folder marked for encryption is automatically encrypted. Files in encrypted format can be read only by the person who encrypted the file. Before other users can read an encrypted file, the user must decrypt the file or grant special access to the file by adding a user's encryption key to the file.

Every encrypted file has the unique encryption key of the user who created the file or currently has ownership of the file. An encrypted file can be copied, moved, backed up, restored, or renamed just like any other file, and in most cases these actions don't affect the encryption of the data. (For details, see "Working With Encrypted Files and Folders" later in this chapter.) The user who encrypts a file always has access to the file, provided that the user's public-key certificate is available on the computer that she is using. For this user, the encryption and decryption process is handled automatically and is transparent.

EFS is the process that handles encryption and decryption. The default setup for EFS allows users to encrypt files without needing special permission. Files are encrypted by using a public/private key that EFS automatically generates on a per-user basis.

Encryption certificates are stored as part of the data in user profiles. If a user works with multiple computers and wants to use encryption, an administrator needs to configure a roaming profile for that user. A roaming profile ensures that the user's profile data and public-key certificates are accessible from other computers. Without this, users won't be able to access their encrypted files on another computer.

> **SECURITY ALERT**   An alternative to a roaming profile is to copy the user's encryption certificate to the computers that the user uses. You can do this by using the certificate backup and restore process. Simply back up the certificate on the user's original computer, and then restore the certificate on each of the other computers the user logs on to.

EFS has a built-in data recovery system to guard against data loss. This recovery system ensures that encrypted data can be recovered if a user's public-key certificate is lost or deleted. The most common scenario for this is when a user leaves the company and the associated user account is deleted. A manager might have been able to log on to the user's account, check files, and save important files to other folders, but if the user account has been deleted, encrypted files will be accessible only if the encryption is removed or if the files are moved to an exFAT, FAT, or FAT32 volume (where encryption isn't supported).

To access encrypted files after the user account has been deleted, you need to use a recovery agent. Recovery agents have access to the file encryption key necessary to unlock data in encrypted files. To protect sensitive data, however, recovery agents don't have access to a user's private key or any private key information.

Windows Server won't encrypt files without designated EFS recovery agents. Therefore, recovery agents are designated automatically, and the necessary recovery certificates are generated automatically as well. This ensures that encrypted files can always be recovered.

EFS recovery agents are configured at two levels:

- **Domain**   The recovery agent for a domain is configured automatically when the first Windows Server domain controller is installed. By default, the recovery agent is the domain administrator. Through Group Policy, domain administrators can designate additional recovery agents. Domain administrators can also delegate recovery agent privileges to designated security administrators.

- **Local computer** When a computer is part of a workgroup or in a standalone configuration, the recovery agent is the administrator of the local computer by default. Additional recovery agents can be designated. Further, if you want local recovery agents in a domain environment rather than domain-level recovery agents, you must delete the recovery policy from Group Policy for the domain.

You can delete recovery agents if you don't want them to be used. However, if you delete all recovery agents, EFS will no longer encrypt files. One or more recovery agents must be configured for EFS to function.

Encrypting Directories and Files

With NTFS volumes, Windows Server lets you select files and folders for encryption. When a file is encrypted, the file data is converted to an encrypted format that can be read only by the person who encrypted the file. Users can encrypt files only if they have the proper access permissions. When you encrypt folders, the folder is marked as encrypted, but only the files within it are actually encrypted. All files that are created in or added to a folder marked as encrypted are encrypted automatically. Note that File Explorer shows names of encrypted resources in green.

To encrypt a file or directory, follow these steps:

1. In File Explorer, right-click the file or directory you want to encrypt, and then click Properties.

2. On the General tab of the Properties dialog box, click Advanced, and then select the Encrypt Contents To Secure Data check box. Click OK twice.

NOTE You can't encrypt compressed files, system files, or read-only files. If you try to encrypt compressed files, the files are automatically uncompressed and then encrypted. If you try to encrypt system files, you get an error.

For an individual file, Windows Server marks the file as encrypted, and then encrypts it. For a directory, Windows Server marks the directory as encrypted, and then encrypts all the files in it. If the directory contains subfolders, Windows Server displays a dialog box that allows you to encrypt all the subfolders associated with the directory. Simply select Apply Changes To This Folder, Subfolders, And Files, and then click OK.

NOTE On NTFS volumes, files remain encrypted even when they're moved, copied, or renamed. If you copy or move an encrypted file to an exFAT, FAT, or FAT32 volume, the file is automatically decrypted before being copied or moved. Thus, you must have proper permissions to copy or move the file.

You can grant special access to an encrypted file or folder by right-clicking the file or folder in File Explorer, and then selecting Properties. On the General tab of the Properties dialog box, click Advanced. In the Advanced Attributes dialog box, click Details. In the Encryption Details For dialog box, users who have access to the encrypted file are listed by name. To allow another user access to the file, click Add. If a user certificate is available for the user, select the user's name in the list provided, and then click OK. Otherwise, click Find User to locate the certificate for the user.

Working with Encrypted Files and Folders

Previously, I said you can copy, move, and rename encrypted files and folders just like any other files. This is true, but I qualified this by saying "in most cases." When you work with encrypted files, you'll have few problems as long as you work with NTFS volumes on the same computer. When you work with other file systems or other computers, you might run into problems. Two of the most common scenarios are the following:

- **Copying between volumes on the same computer**   When you copy or move an encrypted file or folder from one NTFS volume to another NTFS volume on the same computer, the files remain encrypted. However, if you copy or move encrypted files to a FAT volume, the files are decrypted before transfer and then transferred as standard files, and therefore end up in their destination as unencrypted files. FAT doesn't support encryption.
- **Copying between volumes on a different computer**   When you copy or move an encrypted file or folder from one NTFS volume to another NTFS volume on a different computer, the files remain encrypted as long as the destination computer allows you to encrypt files and the remote computer is trusted for delegation. Otherwise, the files are decrypted and then transferred as standard files. The same is true when you copy or move encrypted files to a FAT volume on another computer. FAT doesn't support encryption.

After you transfer a sensitive file that has been encrypted, you might want to confirm that the encryption is still applied. Right-click the file, and then select Properties. On the General tab of the Properties dialog box, click Advanced. The Encrypt Contents To Secure Data option should be selected.

Configuring Recovery Policies

Recovery policies are configured automatically for domain controllers and workstations. By default, domain administrators are the designated recovery agents for domains, and the local administrator is the designated recovery agent for a standalone workstation.

Group Policy Management Console (GPMC) is a feature you can add to any installation of Windows Server 2016 by using the Add Roles And Features Wizard. The

GPMC is also available on Windows desktops when you install the Remote Server Administration Tools (RSAT). After you add the GPMC to a computer, it is available on the Tools menu in Server Manager. Through the Group Policy console, you can view, assign, and delete recovery agents by following these steps:

1. With the GPMC, you can edit a Group Policy Object (GPO) by right-clicking the GPO, and then selecting Edit on the shortcut menu. The GPMC then opens the Group Policy Management Editor, which you use to manage policy settings.

2. Open the Encrypted Data Recovery Agents node in Group Policy. To do this, access the Administrative Templates policies for Computer Configuration under Windows Settings, Security Settings, Public Key Policies, and then select Encrypting File System.

3. The pane at the right lists the recovery certificates currently assigned. Recovery certificates are listed according to who issued them, who they are issued to, expiration date, purpose, and more.

4. To designate an additional recovery agent, right-click Encrypting File System, and then click Add Data Recovery Agent. This starts the Add Recovery Agent Wizard, which you can use to select a previously generated certificate that has been assigned to a user and mark it as a designated recovery certificate. Click Next.

5. On the Select Recovery Agents page, you can select certificates published in Active Directory or use certificate files. If you want to use a published certificate, click Browse Directory and then—in the Find Users, Contacts, And Groups dialog box—select the user with which you want to work. You'll then be able to use the published certificate of that user. If you want to use a certificate file, click Browse Folders. In the Open dialog box, use the options provided to select and open the certificate file you want to use.

> **SECURITY ALERT** Before you designate additional recovery agents, you should consider setting up a root certificate authority (CA) in the domain. Then you can use the Certificates snap-in to generate a personal certificate that uses the EFS Recovery Agent template. The root CA must then approve the certificate request so that the certificate can be used.

6. To delete a recovery agent, select the recovery agent's certificate in the right pane, and then press Delete. When prompted to confirm the action, click Yes to permanently and irrevocably delete the certificate. If the recovery policy is empty (meaning that it has no other designated recovery agents), EFS will be turned off so that files can no longer be encrypted; existing EFS-encrypted resources won't have a recovery agent.

Decrypting Files and Directories

File Explorer shows names of encrypted resources in green. If you want to decrypt a file or directory, follow these steps:

1. In File Explorer, right-click the file or directory, and then click Properties.
2. On the General tab of the Properties dialog box, click Advanced. Clear the Encrypt Contents To Secure Data check box. Click OK twice.

With files, Windows Server decrypts the file and restores it to its original format. With directories, Windows Server decrypts all the files within the directory. If the directory contains subfolders, you also have the option to remove encryption from the subfolders. To do this, select Apply Changes To This Folder, Subfolders, And Files when prompted, and then click OK.

> **TIP** Windows Server also provides a command-line utility called Cipher (Cipher.exe) for encrypting and decrypting your data. Entering **cipher** at a command prompt without additional parameters shows you the encryption status of all folders in the current directory.

Chapter 5. Using TPM and BitLocker Drive Encryption

Windows Server 2016 has many built-in features designed to protect servers from attacks by individuals accessing a server over a network or from the Internet. But what about when individuals have direct physical access to a server or your data? In these instances, Windows security safeguards don't apply. If someone can start a server—even if it's to another operating system he's installed—he could gain access to any data stored on the server, perhaps even your organization's most sensitive data. In addition, with the increased use of USB flash drives, users often take their data with them, and if they lose the USB flash drive, the data typically has no protection, meaning that anyone who finds the flash drive could read and access the data.

To protect servers and data in these instances, Windows Server 2016 includes Measured Boot, BitLocker Drive Encryption, BitLocker To Go, and the Trusted Platform Module (TPM) Services architecture. Together these features help protect servers and your data whether stored on fixed or removable drives. BitLocker Drive Encryption is a full-volume encryption technology. BitLocker To Go is a virtual-volume encryption technology for USB flash drives. TPM is a feature you can use with BitLocker Drive Encryption to enhance security.

Creating Trusted Platforms

A server running Windows Server 2016 must be equipped with a compatible TPM in addition to compatible firmware to take advantage of TPM Services. Windows Server 2016 supports TPM version 2.0 or later and requires Trusted Computing Group (TCG)–compliant firmware. Firmware that is TCG-compliant supports the Static Root of Trust Measurement as defined by the TCG. For some configurations of TPM and BitLocker Drive Encryption, you also need to be sure that the firmware supports reading USB flash drives at startup.

Navigating TPM Essentials

As discussed in the previous chapter, Windows Server 2016 includes the Encrypting File System (EFS) for encrypting files and folders. By using EFS, users can protect sensitive data so that it can be accessed only with their public key certificate.

Encryption certificates are stored as part of the data in a user's profile. So long as users have access to their profiles and the encryption keys they contain, they can access their encrypted files.

Although EFS offers excellent data protection, it doesn't safeguard a server from attack by someone who has direct physical access. In a situation in which a user loses a server, a server is stolen, or an attacker is logging on to a server, EFS might not protect the data because the attacker might be able to gain access to the server before it boots. He could then access the server from another operating system and change the server's configuration. He might then be able to hack into a logon account on the original operating system and log on as the user, or configure the server so that he can log on as a local administrator. Either way, the attacker could eventually gain full access to a server and its data.

To seal a server from physical attack and wrap it in an additional layer of protection, Windows Server 2016 includes the TPM Services architecture. TPM Services protect a server by using a dedicated hardware component called a TPM. A TPM is a microchip that is usually installed on the motherboard of a server, where it communicates with the rest of the system by using a hardware bus. Servers running Windows Server 2016 can use a TPM to provide enhanced protection for data, to ensure early validation of the boot file's integrity, and to guarantee that a disk has not been tampered with while the operating system was offline.

A TPM has the ability to create cryptographic keys and encrypt them so that they can be decrypted only by the TPM. This process, referred to as *wrapping* or *binding*, protects the key from disclosure. A TPM has a master "wrapping" key called the Storage Root Key (SRK). The SRK is stored within the TPM to ensure that the private portion of the key is secure.

Servers that have a TPM can create a key that has been not only wrapped but sealed. The process of sealing the key ensures that the key is tied to specific platform measurements and can be unwrapped only when those platform measurements have the same values they had when the key was created. This is what gives TPM-equipped servers increased resistance to attack.

Because TPM stores private portions of key pairs separately from memory controlled by the operating system, keys can be sealed to the TPM to provide absolute assurances about the state of a system and its trustworthiness. TPM keys are unsealed only when the integrity of the system is intact. Further, because the TPM uses its own internal firmware and logic circuits for processing instructions, it does not rely on the operating system and is not subject to external software vulnerabilities.

The TPM can also be used to seal and unseal data that is generated outside the TPM, and this is where the true power of the TPM lies. In Windows Server 2016, the feature that accesses the TPM and uses it to seal a server is called BitLocker Drive Encryption. Although BitLocker Drive Encryption can be used in both TPM and non-TPM configurations, the most secure method is to use TPM.

When you use BitLocker Drive Encryption and a TPM to seal the boot manager and boot files of a server, the boot manager and boot files can be unsealed only if they are unchanged since they were last sealed. This means that you can use the TPM to validate a server's boot files in the pre–operating system environment. When you seal a hard disk by using TPM, the hard disk can be unsealed only if the data on the disk is unchanged since it was last sealed. This guarantees that a disk has not been tampered with while the operating system was offline.

When you use BitLocker Drive Encryption but do not use a TPM to seal the boot manager and boot files of a server, TPM cannot be used to validate a server's boot files in the pre–operating system environment. This means that in this instance, there is no way to guarantee the integrity of the boot manager and boot files of a server.

TPM Management and Policies

Windows Server 2016 provides several tools for working with a TPM, including the following:

- **Trusted Platform Module Management**   A console for configuring and managing a TPM. You can access this tool by typing **tpm.msc** in the Apps Search box, and then pressing Enter.
- **Manage The TPM Security Hardware**   A wizard for creating the required TPM owner password. You can access this tool by typing **tpminit** in the Apps Search box, and then pressing Enter.

> **REAL WORLD**   Access to the Trusted Platform Module Management console can be restricted in Group Policy. If you are unable to open the console, check if a Group Policy Object (GPO) being processed includes Management Console restrictions under Windows Components\Microsoft Management Console.

To perform TPM management tasks on a local server, you must be a member of the local server's Administrators group or be logged on as the local server administrator. When you are working with Trusted Platform Module Management, you can determine the exact state of the TPM. If you try to start Trusted Platform Module Management without turning on TPM, you'll get an error stating this. You'll also get an error if you try to run the Initialize The TPM Security Hardware Wizard without turning on TPM.

You will be able to perform management tasks with the TPM tools only when you've turned on TPM in firmware. When you are working with the Trusted Platform Module Management console, you should note the TPM status and the TPM manufacturer information. The TPM manufacturer information shows the version supported. If you want to use TPM with BitLocker Drive Encryption, TPM version 2.0 or later is required.

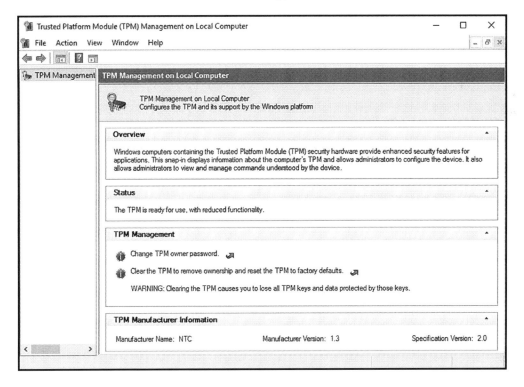

> **NOTE** Although earlier releases of Windows showed the exact TPM state, Windows Server 2016 typically shows either a status of "The TPM is ready for use" or "The TPM is not ready for use." If the TPM is ready for use, the TPM is on and ownership has been taken.

By default, Windows Server 2016 stores full TPM owner authorization information in the registry of the local server. This significant change enables administrators of the local server to perform TPM management tasks without having to provide the TPM owner password.

The Configure The Level Of TPM Owner Authorization Information Available To The Operating System policy controls the level of authorization information stored in the registry. This policy is found in the Administrative Templates policies for Computer Configuration under System\Trusted Platform Module Services. This policy has three enabled settings:

- **Full** The full TPM owner authorization, the TPM administrative delegation blob, and the TPM user delegation blob are stored in the registry. This setting enables a TPM to be used without requiring remote or external storage of the TPM owner authorization. Note that TPM-based applications designed for earlier versions of Windows or that rely on TPM anti-hammering logic might not support full TPM owner authorization in the registry.
- **Delegated** Only the TPM administrative delegation blob and the TPM user delegation blob are stored in the registry. This level is appropriate for TPM-based applications that rely on TPM anti-hammering logic. When you use this setting, Microsoft recommends that you remotely or externally store the TPM owner authorization.
- **None** No TPM owner authorization information is stored in the registry. Use this setting for compatibility with earlier releases of Windows and for applications that require external or remote storage of the TPM owner authorization. When using this setting, remote or external storage of the TPM owner authorization is required, just as it was in earlier releases of Windows.

> **CAUTION** If you change the policy setting from Full to Delegated or vice versa, the full TPM owner authorization value is regenerated and any copies of the original TPM value will be invalid.

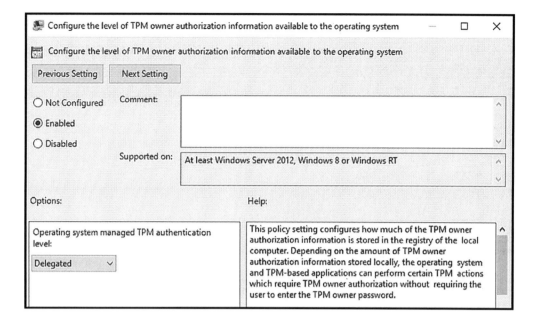

When this policy is set to Delegated or None, you'll be prompted for the TPM owner password before you are able to perform most TPM administration tasks.

With earlier releases of Windows, Microsoft recommended remotely storing the TPM owner authorization in Active Directory Domain Services (AD DS) for domain-joined servers, which could be accomplished by enabling the Turn On TPM Backup To Active Directory Domain Services policy, extending schema for the directory, and setting appropriate access controls.

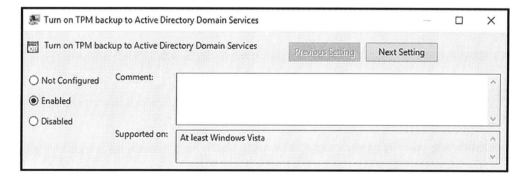

Enabling backup to Active Directory changes the default way TPM owner information is stored. Specifically, when Turn On TPM Backup To Active Directory Domain Services is enabled and Configure The Level Of TPM Owner Authorization Information Available To The Operating System is disabled or not configured, only the TPM administrative delegation blob and the TPM user delegation blob are stored in the registry. Here, to store the full TPM owner information, you must use the enabled setting of Full (or disable Active Directory backup of the TPM owner authorization).

Related policies under System\Trusted Platform Module Services include:

- Ignore The Default List Of Blocked TPM Commands
- Ignore The Local List Of Blocked TPM Commands
- Standard User Lockout Duration
- Standard User Individual Lockout Threshold
- Standard User Total Lockout Threshold

These policies control the way command block lists are used and when lockout is triggered after multiple failed authorization attempts. An administrator can fully reset all lockout-related parameters in the Trusted Platform Module Management console. On the Action menu, click Reset TPM Lockout. When the full TPM owner authorization is stored in the registry, you don't need to provide the TPM owner password. Otherwise, follow the prompts to provide the owner password or select the file containing the TPM owner password.

Enabling TPM in Firmware

The TPM Services architecture in Windows Server 2016 provides the basic features required to configure and deploy TPM-equipped servers. This architecture can be extended with a feature called BitLocker Drive Encryption, which is discussed in the section "BitLocker Drive Encryption: the Essentials" later in this chapter.

Before you can use TPM, you must enable TPM in firmware. In many cases, servers that have TPM ship with it already enabled. Sometimes, however, you'll find TPM is not enabled and you'll need to enable it in firmware. With one of my servers, I needed to do the following:

1. Start the server, and then press F2 startup to access the firmware. In the firmware, I accessed the System BIOS screen and then the System Security screen.
2. On the System Security screen, TPM Security was listed as an option and I set it to On using the mouse. When I enabled TPM, the storage of TPM hierarchies was also enabled, which typically is what you want.

```
System BIOS Settings • System Security

Intel(R) AES-NI ........................................................    Enabled
System Password ......................................................   [                    ]
Setup Password .......................................................   [                    ]
Password Status ......................................................   ◉ Unlocked      ○ Locked
TPM Security .........................................................   ○ Off      ◉ On
   TPM Information ...................................................    Type: 2.0  NTC
   TPM Firmware ......................................................    1.3.0.1
   TPM Hierarchy ....................................................    ◉ Enabled     ○ Disabled     ○ Clear
TPM Advanced
Intel(R) TXT ........................................................    ◉ Off      ○ On
Power Button .......................................................    ◉ Enabled      ○ Disabled
AC Power Recovery ................................................    ◉ Last     ○ On      ○ Off
```

3. To save the changes to the setting and exit the firmware, I clicked Exit. When prompted to confirm whether I wanted to save the changes, I clicked Yes, and the server then rebooted.

With a different server, I needed to do the following:

1. Start the server, and then press F2 during startup to access the firmware. In the firmware, I accessed the Security menu and then the TPM Security screen.

2. On the TPM Security screen, I needed to select the TPM Security check box, and click Apply.

3. A prompt reminded me that I needed to turn off and then restart the server for TPM security to be fully enabled.

4. When I exited firmware, the server rebooted.

Next, you need to initialize and prepare the TPM for first use in software. As part of this process, you take ownership of the TPM, which sets the owner password on the TPM. After TPM is enabled, you can manage the TPM configuration.

Initializing and Preparing a TPM for First Use

Initializing a TPM configures it for use on a server so that you can use the TPM to secure volumes on the server's hard drives. The initialization process involves turning on the TPM and then setting ownership of the TPM. By setting ownership of the TPM, you assign a password that helps ensure that only the authorized TPM owner can access and manage the TPM. The TPM password is required to turn off the TPM if you no longer want to use it, and to clear the TPM before the server is recycled. In an Active Directory domain, you can configure Group Policy to save TPM passwords.

By using an administrator account, you can initialize the TPM and create the owner password by completing the following steps:

1. Start the Trusted Platform Module Management console. On the Action menu, click Prepare The TPM to start the Manage The TPM Security Hardware Wizard (tpminit).

> **NOTE** If the Initialize The TPM Security Hardware Wizard detects firmware that does not meet Windows requirements for a TPM or a TPM is not found, you will not be able to continue and should check that the TPM has been turned on in firmware.

2. When the wizard finishes its initial tasks, the TPM owner password is set and you are notified that the TPM is ready for use.

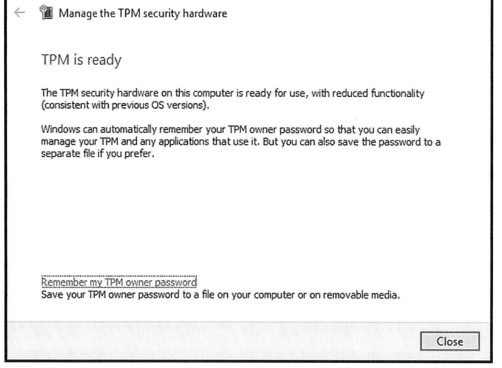

3. Before clicking Close, you should save the TPM owner password. Click Remember My TPM Owner Password. In the Save As dialog box, select a location to save the password backup file, and then click Save.

4. In the TPM Management console, the status should be listed as "The TPM is ready for use."

> **NOTE** By default, the password backup file is saved as *ServerName*.tpm. Ideally, you should save the TPM ownership password to removable media,

such as a USB flash drive, and store the media in a secure location. In a domain where the TPM Backup To Active Directory Domain Services policy is applied, you won't have the option to save the TPM password. Here, the password is saved to Active Directory automatically.

Clearing the TPM

Clearing the TPM erases information stored on the TPM and cancels the related ownership of the TPM. You should clear the TPM when a TPM-equipped server is to be recycled. Clearing the TPM invalidates any stored keys, and data encrypted by these keys can no longer be accessed.

After clearing the TPM, you should take ownership of the TPM. This will write new information to the TPM. You might then want to turn off the TPM so it isn't available for use.

By using an administrator account, you can clear the TPM, take ownership, and then turn off TPM by completing the following steps:

1. Start the Trusted Platform Module Management console. On the Action menu, click Clear TPM. This starts the Manage the TPM Security Hardware Wizard.

CAUTION   Clearing the TPM resets it to factory defaults. As a result, you lose all keys and data protected by those keys. You do not need the TPM owner password to clear the TPM.

2. Read the warning on the Clear The TPM Security Hardware page, and then click Restart. Click Cancel to exit without clearing the TPM.

Manage the TPM security hardware

Clear the TPM security hardware

You must restart your computer to configure your TPM security hardware settings so that your TPM can be cleared. To do so:

Click the Restart button below.

Be Physically present at the computer to follow the instructions that appear during the startup process.

Log on to Windows to continue the wizard automatically.

Restart   Cancel

3. Typically, hardware designed for Windows Server 2016 can automatically complete the re-initialization process. On other hardware, you'll need physical access to the server to respond to the manufacturer's firmware confirmation prompt. For example, you may need to press F12 during startup to clear, enable, and activate the TPM, or press ESC to reject the change request and continue loading the operating system.

Changing the TPM Owner Password

You can change the TPM password at any time. The key reason to do this is if you suspect that the TPM owner password has been compromised. Your company's security policy also might require TPM owner password changes in certain situations.

To change the TPM owner password, complete the following steps:

1. Start the Trusted Platform Module Management console. On the Action menu, click Change Owner Password. This starts the Manage The TPM Security Hardware Wizard.

2. When the full TPM owner authorization is stored in the registry, you don't need to provide the TPM owner password. Otherwise, follow the prompts to

provide the owner password or select the file containing the TPM owner password.

3. On the Create The TPM Owner Password page, you can elect to create the password automatically or manually.

4. If you want the wizard to create the password for you, select Automatically Create The Password (Recommended). The new TPM owner password is displayed. Click Change Password.

5. If you want to create the password, select Manually Create The Password. Enter and confirm a password of at least eight characters, and then click Change Password.

6. Before clicking Close, you might want to save the TPM owner password. Click Remember My TPM Owner Password. In the Save As dialog box, select a location to save the password backup file, and then click Save.

BitLocker Drive Encryption: the Essentials

BitLocker is built into all editions of Windows Server 2016 and added as a feature for all editions of Windows Server. Although BitLocker Drive Encryption and BitLocker To Go are often referred to simply as BitLocker, they are separate but similar features. BitLocker Drive Encryption is designed to protect the data on the internal hard drives of lost, stolen, or inappropriately decommissioned servers and is a volume-level encryption technology. BitLocker To Go is designed to protect the data on removable data drives, such as external hard drives and USB flash drives, and is a virtual-volume encryption technology. Standard BitLocker encrypts by wrapping the entire volume or only the used portion of the volume in protected encryption. BitLocker To Go, on the other hand, creates a virtual volume on a USB flash drive. This virtual volume is encrypted by using an encryption key stored on the USB flash drive.

Understanding BitLocker Drive Encryption

On a server without BitLocker Drive Encryption, a user with direct physical access to the server has a variety of ways he could gain full control and then access the server's data, whether that data is encrypted with EFS or not. For example, a user could use a boot disk to boot the server and reset the administrator password. A user could also install and then boot to a different operating system and then use this operating system to unlock the other installation.

BitLocker Drive Encryption prevents all access to a server's drives except by authorized personnel by wrapping entire drives or only the used portion of drives in tamper-proof encryption. If an unauthorized user tries to access a BitLocker-encrypted drive, the encryption prevents the user from viewing or manipulating the protected data in any way. This dramatically reduces the risk of an unauthorized person gaining access to confidential data through offline attacks.

IMPORTANT   BitLocker Drive Encryption is meant to be used when a server is not in a physically secure location and requires additional protection. However, the encryption processes can reduce disk throughput, which in turn can affect a server's overall performance.

BitLocker Drive Encryption can use a TPM to validate the integrity of a server's boot manager and boot files at startup and to guarantee that a server's hard disk has not been tampered with while the operating system was offline. BitLocker Drive Encryption also stores measurements of core operating system files in the TPM.

Every time the server is started, Windows validates the boot files, the operating system files, and any encrypted volumes to ensure that they have not been modified while the operating system was offline. If the files have been modified, Windows alerts the user and refuses to release the key required to access Windows. The server then goes into Recovery mode, prompting the user to provide a recovery key before it permits access to the boot volume. The Recovery mode is also used if a BitLocker-encrypted disk drive is transferred to another system.

BitLocker Drive Encryption can be used in both TPM and non-TPM servers. If a server has a TPM, BitLocker Drive Encryption uses the TPM to provide enhanced protection for your data and to ensure early boot file integrity. These features together help prevent unauthorized viewing and accessing of data by encrypting the entire Windows volume and by safeguarding the boot files from tampering. If a server doesn't have a TPM or its TPM isn't compatible with Windows, BitLocker Drive Encryption can be used to encrypt entire volumes, and in this way protect the volumes from tampering. This configuration, however, doesn't offer the added security of early boot file integrity validation.

On servers with a compatible TPM that is initialized, BitLocker Drive Encryption typically uses one of the following TPM modes:

* **TPM-Only**   In this mode, only TPM is used for validation. When the server boots, TPM is used to validate the boot files, the operating system files, and any encrypted volumes. Because the user doesn't need to provide an additional startup key, this mode is transparent to the user, and the user logon experience is unchanged. However, if the TPM is missing or the integrity of files or volumes has changed, BitLocker enters Recovery mode and requires a recovery key or password to regain access to the boot volume.
* **TPM and PIN**   In this mode, both TPM and a user-entered numeric key are used for validation. When the server boots, TPM is used to validate the boot files, the operating system files, and any encrypted volumes. The user must enter a PIN when prompted to continue startup. If the user doesn't have the PIN or is unable to provide the correct PIN, BitLocker enters Recovery mode instead of booting to the operating system. As before, BitLocker also enters Recovery mode if the TPM is missing or the integrity of boot files or encrypted volumes has changed.
* **TPM and Startup Key**   In this mode, both TPM and a startup key are used for validation. When the server boots, TPM is used to validate the boot files, the operating system files, and any encrypted volumes. The user must have a USB flash drive with a startup key to log on to the server. If the user doesn't have the startup key or is unable to provide the correct startup key, BitLocker enters Recovery mode. As before, BitLocker also enters Recovery mode if the TPM is missing or the integrity of boot files or encrypted volumes has changed.
* **TPM and Smart Card Certificate**   In this mode, both TPM and a smart card certificate are used for validation. When the server boots, TPM is used to validate the boot files, the operating system files, and any encrypted volumes. The user must have a smart card with a valid certificate to log on to the server. If the user doesn't have a smart card with a valid certificate and is unable to provide one, BitLocker enters Recovery mode. As before, BitLocker also enters Recovery mode if the TPM is missing or the integrity of boot files or encrypted volumes has changed.

Network unlock enables the system volume on a server with TPM to be automatically unlocked on startup, if the server is joined and connected to a domain. When not joined and connected to a domain, other means of validation can be used, such as a startup PIN.

On servers without a TPM or on servers that have incompatible TPMs, Windows Server 2016 can be configured to use an unlock password for the operating system drive. To configure this, you must enable the Configure Use Of Passwords For Operating System Drives policy in the Administrative Templates policies for Computer Configuration under Windows Components\BitLocker Drive Encryption\Operating System Drives. The unlock password can be configured with minimum length and complexity requirements. The default minimum password length is 8 characters, meaning the password must be at least 8 characters. Complexity requirements can be:

- Always validated using the Require Password Complexity setting.
- Validated if possible using the Allow Password Complexity setting.
- Not validated using the Do Now Allow Password Complexity setting.

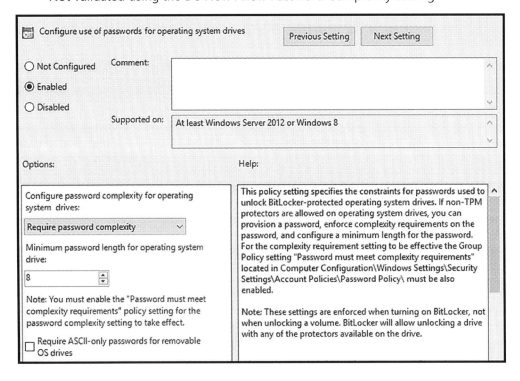

The unlock password is validated when you enable BitLocker Drive Encryption and set the password, and whenever the password is changed by a user. With required complexity, you can only set a password (and enable encryption) when the server can connect to a domain controller and validate the complexity of the password. With allowed complexity, the server will attempt to validate the complexity of the password when you set it but will allow you to continue and enable encryption if no domain controllers are available.

On servers without a TPM or on servers that have incompatible TPMs, BitLocker Drive Encryption also can use Startup Key Only or Smart Card Certificate Only mode. Startup Key Only mode requires a USB flash drive containing a startup key. The user inserts the USB flash drive in the server before turning it on. The key stored on the flash drive unlocks the server.

Smart Card Certificate Only mode requires a smart card with a valid certificate. The user validates the smart card certificate after turning on the server. The certificate unlocks the server.

It's also important to point out that standard users can reset the BitLocker PIN and password on operating system drives, fixed data drives, and removable data drives. If you don't want standard users to be able to perform these tasks, enable the Disallow Standard Users From Changing The PIN Or Password policy. This Computer Configuration policy is found under Windows Components\BitLocker Drive Encryption\Operating System Drives.

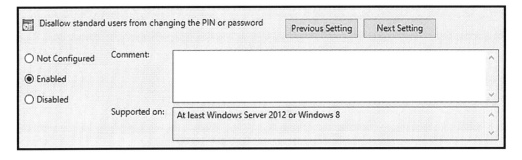

Several important changes have been made to BitLocker Drive Encryption since the technology was first implemented. Specifically, you can do the following:

- Encrypt FAT volumes and NTFS volumes. When you encrypt FAT volumes, you have the option of specifying whether encrypted volumes can be unlocked and viewed.

This option is configured through Group Policy and is enabled when you turn on BitLocker. In the Administrative Templates policies for Computer Configuration under Windows Components\BitLocker Drive Encryption, there are separate policies for earlier versions of Windows that allow FAT-formatted fixed drives and FAT-formatted removable drives to be unlocked and viewed.

* Allow a data-recovery agent to be used with BitLocker Drive Encryption. This option is configured through Group Policy. The data-recovery agent allows an encrypted volume to be unlocked and recovered by using a recovery agent's personal certificate or a 48-digit recovery password. You can optionally save the recovery information in Active Directory. In the Administrative Templates policies for Computer Configuration, there are separate policies for operating system volumes, other fixed drives, and removable drives.

* Deny write access to removable data drives not protected with BitLocker. This option is configured through Group Policy. If you enable this option, users have read-only access to unencrypted removable data drives and read/write access to encrypted removable data drives.

In a domain, domain administrators are the default data-recovery agents. A homegroup or workgroup has no default data-recovery agent, but you can designate one. Any user you want to designate as a data-recovery agent needs a personal encryption certificate. You can generate a certificate by using the Cipher utility and then use the certificate to assign the data-recovery agent in Local Security Policy under Public Key Policies\BitLocker Drive Encryption.

Earlier releases of Windows support AES encryption with a diffuser. Windows 8 and Windows Server 2016 move away from this to support standard AES with 128-bit encryption by default or 256-bit encryption (if you enable the Choose Drive Encryption Method And Cipher Strength policy to set the cipher strength to 256-bit encryption). The cipher strength must be set prior to turning on BitLocker. Changing the cipher strength has no effect if the drive is already encrypted or encryption is in progress.

Hardware Encryption, Secure Boot, and Network Unlock

Most BitLocker-related settings are controlled with the Administrative Templates policies for Computer Configuration under Windows Components\BitLocker Drive Encryption. Windows Server 2016 supports disk drives with hardware encryption (referred to as *encrypted hard drives*). Encryption in hardware is faster and moves the processing burden from the server's processor to the hardware processor on the hard disk. By default, if a server has hardware encryption, Windows Server 2016 will use it with BitLocker.

In Group Policy, you can precisely control whether to permit software-based encryption when hardware encryption is not available and whether to restrict encryption to those algorithms and cipher strengths supported by hardware. Do this by enabling the Configure Use Of Hardware-Based Encryption For Fixed Data Drives policy and configuring the related options. When the policy is enabled, you must specifically allow software-based encryption when hardware-based encryption isn't available.

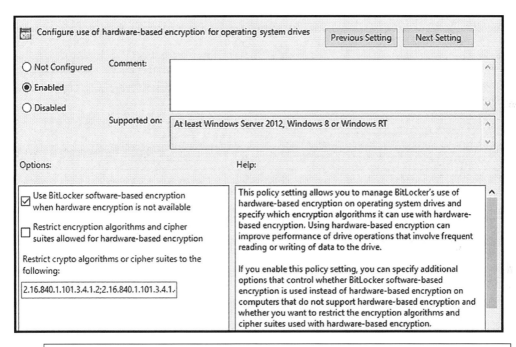

MORE INFO   The Choose Drive Encryption Method And Cipher Strength policy doesn't apply to hardware-based encryption. You can set the encryption methods you want for hardware-based policy under Fixed Data Drives, in the Configure Use Of Hardware-Based Encryption For Fixed Data Drives policy. With hardware-based encryption, the encryption algorithm is set when the drive is partitioned.

Next, you might want to configure policy to control the permitted encryption types. Windows Server 2016 allows users to encrypt full volumes or used space only. Encrypting full volumes takes longer, but it's more secure because the entire volume is protected. Encrypting used space protects only the portion of the drive used to store data. By default, either option can be used. If you want to allow only one type or the other, enable and configure related Enforce Drive Encryption Type policy for BitLocker. There are separate Enforce Drive Encryption Type policies for the operating system, fixed data, and removable data drives.

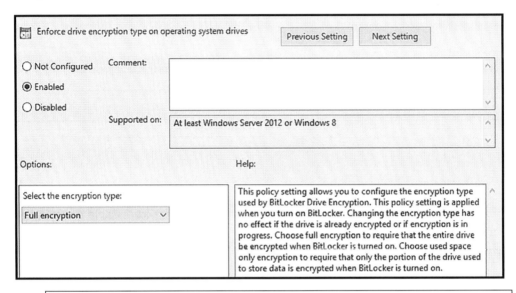

REAL WORLD In high-security environments, you will want to encrypt entire volumes. At the time of this writing, and unless fixed with a future update or service pack, deleted files appear as free space when you encrypt used space only. As a result, until the files are wiped or overwritten, information in the files could be recovered with certain tools.

Operating system drives are handled as special cases. Windows Server 2016 enables you to pre-provision BitLocker so that you can turn on encryption prior to installation. Windows Server 2016 also can be configured to do the following:

* Require additional authentication at startup. If you enable and configure the related policy, Require Additional Authentication At Startup, user input is required, even if the platform lacks a pre-boot input capability. To enable a USB keyboard to be used on such a platform in the pre-boot environment, you should set the Enable Use Of BitLocker Authentication Requiring Preboot Keyboard Input On Slates policy to Enabled.
* Allow secure boot for integrity validation. Secure boot is used by default to verify boot configuration data (BCD) settings according to the TPM validation profile settings (also referred to as Secure Boot policy). When you use secure boot, the settings of the Use Enhanced Boot Configuration Data Validation Profile policy are ignored (unless you specifically disable secure boot support by setting Allow Secure Boot For Integrity Validation to Disabled).

You set TPM validation profile settings by platform. For BIOS-based firmware, you use the Configure TPM Platform Validation Profile For BIOS-Based Firmware Configurations policy. For Unified Extensible Firmware Interface (UEFI)–based firmware, you use the Configure TPM Platform Validation Profile For Native UEFI Firmware Configurations policy. When you enable these policies, you specify exactly which platform configuration registers to validate during boot.

For BIOS-based firmware, Microsoft recommends validating Platform Configuration Registers (PCRs) 0, 2, 4, 8, 9, 10, and 11. For UEFI firmware, Microsoft recommends validating PCRs 0, 2, 4, 7, and 11. In both instances, PCR 11 validation is required for BitLocker protection to be enforced. PCR 7 validation is required to support secure boot with UEFI (and you'll need to enable this by selecting the related option).

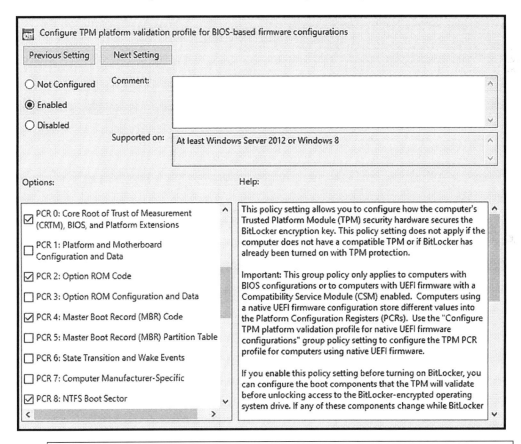

IMPORTANT Windows Server 2016 is designed to be run on servers with UEFI. UEFI doesn't replace all the functionality in either BIOS or EFI and can, in fact, be wrapped around BIOS or EFI. When a server has UEFI and is running Windows Server 2016, UEFI is the first link in the chain of trust for secure boot. UEFI 2.3.1 and later are able to run internal integrity checks that verify the firmware's digital signature before running it. If the firmware's digital signature has been modified or replaced (as an example, by a firmware rootkit), the firmware will not load.

With Secure Boot, firmware also verifies the digital signature on the Windows boot loader as part of initialization. If a rootkit is installed and the Windows boot loader has been modified, the server will be prevented from starting. After the Secure Boot, the boot loader verifies the digital signature of the operating system kernel as part of Trusted Boot. Also as part of Trusted Boot, the kernel in turn verifies all remaining boot components, including boot drivers and startup files. Finally, Measured Boot allows third-party software running on a remove server to verify the security of every startup component as well.

When you protect a server with BitLocker, you can require additional authentication at startup. Typically, this means a user is required to have a startup key on a USB flash drive, a startup PIN, or both. The Network Unlock feature provides this additional layer of protection without requiring the startup key, startup PIN, or both by automatically unlocking the operating system drive when a server is started, if the following conditions are met:

* The BitLocker-protected server has an enabled TPM.
* The server is on a trusted, wired network.
* The server is joined to and connected to a domain.
* A Network Unlock server with an appropriate Network Unlock certificate is available.

Because the server must be joined to and connected to the domain for network unlock to work, user authentication is still required when a server is not connected to the domain. When connected to the domain, the client server connects to a Network Unlock server to unlock the system drive. Typically, the Network Unlock server is a domain controller configured to use and distribute Network Unlock certificates to clients. The Network Unlock certificates in turn are used to create the network unlock keys.

You can configure a domain controller to distribute this certificate to clients. To do this, create an X.509 certificate for the server, for example by using Certmsg.mc, then use the BitLocker Driver Encryption Network Unlock Certificate setting to add this certificate to a GPO applied to the domain controller. You'll find this Computer Configuration setting under Windows Settings\Security Settings\Public Key Policies.

Finally, Windows Server 2016 also enables you to provision BitLocker during operating system deployment. You can do this from the Windows PreInstallation Environment (Windows PE). It's important to point out that Windows PowerShell includes a DISM module. As this module doesn't support wildcards when searching for feature names, you can use the Get-WindowsOptionalFeature cmdlet to list feature names, as shown in this example:

```
get-windowsoptionalfeature -online | ft
```

To completely install BitLocker and related management tools, use the following command:

```
enable-windowsoptionalfeature -online -featurename bitlocker,bitlocker-
utilities, bitlocker-networkunlock -all
```

Deploying BitLocker Drive Encryption

Deploying BitLocker Drive Encryption in an enterprise changes the way administrators and users work with servers. A server with BitLocker Drive Encryption usually requires user intervention to boot to the operating system—a user must enter a PIN, insert a USB flash drive containing a startup key, or use a smart card with a valid certificate. Because of this requirement, after you deploy BitLocker Drive Encryption, you can no longer be assured that you can perform remote administration that requires a server to be restarted without having physical access to the server—someone might need to be available to enter the required PIN, insert the USB flash drive with the startup key, or use a smart card with a valid certificate.

To work around this issue, you can configure network unlock on your trusted, wired networks. Before you use BitLocker Drive Encryption, you should perform a thorough evaluation of your organization's servers. You need to develop plans and procedures for the following:

- Evaluating the various BitLocker authentication methods and applying them as appropriate
- Determining whether servers support TPM, and thus whether you must use TPM or non-TPM BitLocker configurations
- Storing, using, and periodically changing encryption keys, recovery passwords, and other validation mechanisms used with BitLocker

You need to develop procedures for tasks such as these:

- Performing daily operations with BitLocker-encrypted drives
- Providing administrative support for BitLocker-encrypted drives
- Recovering servers with BitLocker-encrypted drives

These procedures need to take into account the way BitLocker encryption works and the requirements to have PINs, startup keys, smart cards, and recovery keys available whenever you work with BitLocker-encrypted servers. After you evaluate your organization's servers and develop basic plans and procedures, you need to develop a configuration plan for implementing BitLocker Drive Encryption.

Several implementations of BitLocker Drive Encryption are available. Although servers running Windows Server 2016 can work with any of the available versions, earlier versions of Windows can't necessarily work with the latest version of BitLocker. For example, you might need to configure Group Policy to allow access from earlier versions of Windows.

To turn on BitLocker Drive Encryption on the drive containing the Windows operating system, the drive must have at least two partitions:

- The first partition is for BitLocker Drive Encryption. This partition, designated as the active partition, holds the files required to start the operating system and is not encrypted.
- The second is the primary partition for the operating system and your data. This partition is encrypted when you turn on BitLocker.

When you install Windows Server 2016, an additional partition is created automatically during setup. By default, this additional partition is used by the Windows Recovery Environment (Windows RE). However, if you enable BitLocker on the system volume, BitLocker usually moves Windows RE to the system volume and then uses the additional partition for BitLocker. Because of this, during BitLocker setup, you'll typically see a notification that a new system drive will be created from free space on the original system drive and also be notified that the new drive will not have a drive letter.

> **← BitLocker Drive Encryption (C:)**
>
> Preparing your drive for BitLocker
>
> An existing drive or unallocated free space on the hard drive will be used to turn on BitLocker.
>
> ⌃ Details
>
> A new system drive will be created from free space on drive C:. The new drive will not have a drive letter.

Using BitLocker on a hard disk is easy. On a server with a compatible TPM, you must initialize the TPM as discussed in the "Initializing and Preparing a TPM for First Use" section earlier in this chapter, and then you need to enable BitLocker. On a server without a compatible TPM, you need to enable BitLocker only on your hard disk.

You can use local Group Policy and Active Directory–based Group Policy to help manage and maintain TPM and BitLocker configurations. Group Policy settings for TPM Services are found in Administrative Templates policies for Computer Configuration under System\Trusted Platform Module Services. Group Policy settings for BitLocker are found in Administrative Templates policies for Computer Configuration under Windows Components\BitLocker Drive Encryption. There are separate subfolders for fixed data drives, operating system drives, and removable data drives.

Policies you might want to configure include the following:

Trusted Platform Module Services policies

- Configure The Level of TPM Owner Authorization Information Available To The Operating System
- Configure The List Of Blocked TPM Commands
- Ignore The Default List Of Blocked TPM Commands
- Ignore The Local List Of Blocked TPM Commands
- Standard User Individual Lockout Threshold
- Standard User Lockout Duration
- Standard User Total Lockout Threshold
- Turn On TPM Backup To Active Directory Domain Services

BitLocker Drive Encryption policies

- Choose Default Folder For Recovery Password

- Choose Drive Encryption Method And Cipher Strength
- Prevent Memory Overwrite On Restart
- Provide The Unique Identifiers For Your Organization
- Validate Smart Card Certificate Usage Rule Compliance

Fixed Drive policies

- Allow Access To BitLocker-Protected Fixed Data Drives From Earlier Versions Of Windows
- Choose How BitLocker-Protected Fixed Drives Can Be Recovered
- Configure Use Of Hardware-Based Encryption For Fixed Data Drives
- Configure Use Of Passwords For Fixed Data Drives
- Configure Use Of Smart Cards On Fixed Data Drives
- Deny Write Access To Fixed Drives Not Protected By BitLocker
- Enforce Drive Encryption Type On Fixed Data Drives

Operating System Drive policies

- Allow Enhanced PINs For Startup
- Allow Network Unlock At Startup
- Allow Secure Boot For Integrity Validation
- Choose How BitLocker-Protected Operating System Drives Can Be Recovered
- Configure Minimum PIN Length For Startup
- Configure TPM Platform Validation Profile For BIOS-Based Firmware Configurations
- Configure TPM Platform Validation Profile For Native UEFI Firmware Configurations
- Configure TPM Platform Validation Profile (Windows Vista, Windows 7, Windows Server 2008, Windows Server 2008 R2)
- Configure Use Of Passwords For Operating System Drives
- Disallow Standard Users From Changing The PIN Or Password
- Enforce Drive Encryption Type On Operating System Drives
- Enable User Of BitLocker Authentication Requiring Preboot Keyboard Input On Slates
- Require Additional Authentication At Startup
- Reset Platform Validation Data After BitLocker Recovery

Removable Data Drive policies

- Allow Access To BitLocker-Protected Removable Data Drives From Earlier Versions Of Windows
- Choose How BitLocker-Protected Removable Drives Can Be Recovered
- Configure Use Of Hardware-Based Encryption For Removable Data Drives

- Configure Use Of Passwords For Removable Data Drives
- Configure Use Of Smart Cards On Removable Data Drives
- Control Use Of BitLocker On Removable Drives
- Deny Write Access To Removable Drives Not Protected By BitLocker
- Enforce Drive Encryption Type On Removable Data Drives

Active Directory includes TPM and BitLocker recovery extensions for Server objects. For TPM, the extensions define a single property of the Server object, called ms-TPM-OwnerInformation. When the TPM is initialized or when the owner password is changed, the hash of the TPM ownership password can be stored as a value of the ms-TPM-OwnerInformation attribute on the related Server object. For BitLocker, these extensions define Recovery objects as child objects of Server objects and are used to store recovery passwords and associate them with specific BitLocker-encrypted volumes.

By default, Windows Server 2016 stores the full TPM owner authorization, the TPM administrative delegation blob, and the TPM user delegation in the registry. Because of this change, you no longer have to save this information separately to Active Directory for backup and recovery purposes. For more information, see the "TPM Management and Policies" section earlier in this chapter.

To ensure that BitLocker recovery information is always available, you can configure Group Policy to save recovery information in Active Directory as follows:

- With Choose How BitLocker-Protected Fixed Drives Can Be Recovered, enable the policy and accept the default options to allow data recovery agents and save the recovery information in Active Directory.
- With Choose How BitLocker-Protected Operating System Drives Can Be Recovered, enable the policy and accept the default options to allow data recovery agents and save the recovery information in Active Directory.
- With Choose How BitLocker-Protected Removable Drives Can Be Recovered, enable the policy and accept the default options to allow data recovery agents, and then save the recovery information in Active Directory.

> **REAL WORLD** For Federal Information Processing Standard (FIPS) compliance, you cannot create or save BitLocker recovery passwords. Instead, you need to configure Windows to create recovery keys. The FIPS setting is located in the Security Policy Editor at Local Policies\Security Options\System Cryptography: Use FIPS Compliant Algorithms For Encryption, Hashing, And Signing.

To configure BitLocker to use recovery keys, enable the security option System Cryptography: Use FIPS Compliant Algorithms For Encryption, Hashing, And Signing in local Group Policy or Active Directory–based Group Policy as appropriate. With this setting enabled, users can only generate recovery keys.

Managing BitLocker Drive Encryption

You can configure and enable BitLocker Drive Encryption on both system volumes and data volumes. When you encrypt system volumes, you must unlock the server at startup, typically by using a TPM and network unlock when connected to the domain in addition to a TPM, a startup key, a startup PIN, or any required or optional combination of these. To enforce the strictest and highest security possible, use all three authentication methods.

In the current implementation of BitLocker, you do not have to encrypt a server's system volume prior to encrypting a server's data volumes. When you use encrypted data volumes, the operating system mounts BitLocker data volumes as it would any other volume, but it requires either a password or a smart card with a valid certificate to unlock the drive.

The encryption key for a protected data volume is created and stored independently from the system volume and all other protected data volumes. To allow the operating system to mount encrypted volumes, the key chain protecting the data volume is stored in an encrypted state on the operating system volume. If the operating system enters Recovery mode, the data volumes are not unlocked until the operating system is out of Recovery mode.

Setting up BitLocker Drive Encryption requires these steps:

1. Partitioning a server's hard disks appropriately and installing the operating system (if you are configuring a new server). Windows Setup partitions the drives for you automatically. However, the volume where BitLocker data is stored must always be the active, system volume.
2. Initializing and configuring a server's TPM (if applicable).
3. Turning on the BitLocker Drive Encryption feature (as necessary).

4. Checking firmware to ensure that the server is set to start first from the disk containing the active, system partition and the boot partition, not from USB or CD/DVD drives (applicable only when you encrypt system volumes).

5. Turning on and configuring BitLocker Drive Encryption.

> **NOTE** When you are using a Microsoft account on a non-domain-joined server, you have an additional save option. You can save the recovery key to the Windows Live SkyDrive. The user's SkyDrive account will then contain a BitLocker folder with a separate file for each saved recovery key.

After you've turned on and configured BitLocker encryption, you can use several techniques to maintain the environment and perform recovery.

Preparing for BitLocker Drive Encryption

As discussed previously, BitLocker Drive Encryption can be used in a TPM or a non-TPM configuration. Either configuration requires some preliminary work before you can turn on and configure BitLocker Drive Encryption.

You can determine the readiness status of a server by accessing the BitLocker Drive Encryption console. In Control Panel, click System And Security, and then click BitLocker Drive Encryption. If the system isn't properly configured, you'll receive an error message. Note the following:

- If you get an error message related to TPM on a server with a compatible TPM, refer to the "Enabling TPM in Firmware" section earlier in this chapter to learn more about TPM states and enabling TPM in firmware.
- If you get an error message related to TPM on a server with an incompatible TPM or no TPM, you need to change the server's Group Policy settings so that you can turn on BitLocker Drive Encryption without a TPM.

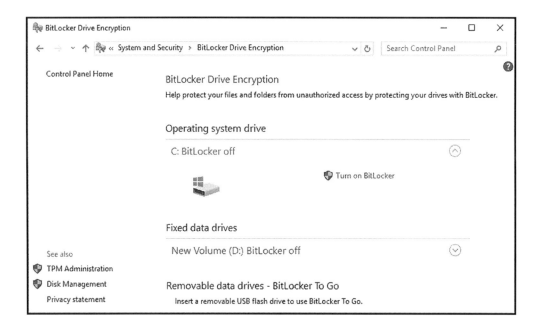

You can configure policy settings for BitLocker encryption in local Group Policy or in Active Directory–based Group Policy. In local policy, you apply the settings to the server's local GPO. For domain policy, you apply the settings to a Group Policy object processed by the server. While you are working with domain policy, you can also specify requirements for servers with a TPM.

To configure the way BitLocker can be used with or without a TPM, follow these steps:

1. Open the appropriate GPO for editing in the Group Policy Management Editor.

2. In the Administrative Templates policies for Computer Configuration under Windows Components\BitLocker Drive Encryption\Operating System Drives, double-click the Require Additional Authentication At Startup setting.

> **IMPORTANT** There are several versions of this policy and they are specific to the operating system. Configure the version or versions of this policy that are appropriate for your working environment and the servers to which the policy will be applied. The options for each related policy are slightly different because the TPM features supported are slightly different for each.

3. In the Require Additional Authentication At Startup dialog box define the policy setting by selecting Enabled.

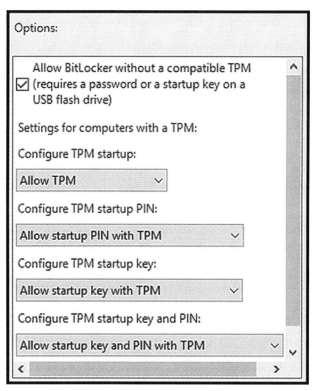

4. Do one of the following:

- If you want to allow BitLocker to be used without a compatible TPM, select the Allow BitLocker Without A Compatible TPM check box. This changes the policy setting so that you can use BitLocker encryption with a password or startup key on a server without a TPM.
- If you want to require BitLocker to be used with a TPM, clear the Allow BitLocker Without A Compatible TPM check box. This changes the policy setting so that you can use BitLocker encryption on a server with a TPM by using a startup PIN, a startup key, or both.

5. On a server with a compatible TPM, several authentication methods can be used at startup to provide added protection for encrypted data. These authentication methods can be allowed or required. The methods available depend on the operating system specific version of the policy with which you are working. Use the following guidelines to help you configure the options:

- If you want to allow TPM to be used at startup, set Configure TPM Startup to Allow TPM and use Do Not Allow for all other settings.
- If you want to require TPM to be used at startup, set Configure TPM Startup to Require TPM and use Do Not Allow for all other settings.
- If you want to use TPM only with a startup key, set Configure TPM Startup to Allow or Require TPM as appropriate and then set Configure TPM Startup Key to Allow or

Require Startup Key with TPM as appropriate. Use Do Not Allow for all other settings.

- If you want to use TPM only with a startup PIN, set Configure TPM Startup to Allow or Require TPM as appropriate and then set Configure TPM Startup PIN to Allow or Require Startup PIN with TPM as appropriate. Use Do Not Allow for all other settings.
- If you want to use TPM only with a startup key and PIN, set Configure TPM Startup to Allow or Require TPM and then set Configure TPM Startup Key And Pin to Allow or Require Startup Key and PIN with TPM. Use Do Not Allow for all other settings.
- If you want to allow TPM with any other authentication method, set allow options to allow.

6. Click OK to save your settings. This policy is enforced the next time Group Policy is applied.

7. Close the Group Policy Management Editor. To apply Group Policy immediately to the server you are logged on to, enter **gpupdate.exe /force** in the Apps Search box, and then press Enter.

Servers that have a startup key or a startup PIN also have a recovery password or certificate. The recovery password or certificate is required in the event any of the following occur:

- Changes are made to the system startup information
- The encrypted drive must be moved to another server
- The user is unable to provide the appropriate startup key or PIN

The recovery password or certificate should be managed and stored separately from the startup key or startup PIN. Although users are given the startup key or startup PIN, administrators should be the only ones with the recovery password or certificate. As an administrator, you need the recovery password or certificate to unlock the encrypted data on the volume if BitLocker enters a locked state. Generally, unless you use a common data-recovery agent, the recovery password or certificate is unique to this particular BitLocker encryption. This means you cannot use it to recover encrypted data from any other BitLocker-encrypted volume—even from other BitLocker-encrypted volumes on the same server. To increase security, you should store startup keys and recovery data apart from the server.

When BitLocker is installed, the BitLocker Drive Encryption console is available in Control Panel. Your configuration options for BitLocker depend on whether the server has a TPM and on how you've configured Group Policy.

Enabling BitLocker on Nonsystem Volumes

Encrypting a nonsystem volume protects the data stored on the volume. Any volume formatted with FAT, FAT32, exFAT, NTFS or ReFS can be encrypted with BitLocker. The length of time it takes to encrypt a drive depends on the amount of data to encrypt, the processing power of the server, and the level of activity on the server.

Before you enable BitLocker, you should configure the appropriate Fixed Data Drive policies and settings in Group Policy, and then wait for Group Policy to be refreshed. If you don't do this and you enable BitLocker, you might need to turn BitLocker off, and then turn BitLocker back on because certain state and management flags are set when you turn on BitLocker. To ensure that you can recover an encrypted volume, you should allow data-recovery agents and store recovery information in Active Directory.

To enable BitLocker encryption on a nonsystem volume, follow these steps:

1. In File Explorer, right-click the data volume, and then click Turn On BitLocker. BitLocker then verifies that your server meets its requirements and then initializes the drive.

> **NOTE** If BitLocker is already enabled, the Manage BitLocker option is displayed instead of Turn On BitLocker.

2. On the Choose How You Want To Unlock This Drive page, choose one or more of the following options, and then click Next:

- **Use A Password To Unlock The Drive** Select this option if you want the user to be prompted for a password to unlock the drive. Passwords allow a drive to be unlocked in any location and to be shared with other people.
- **Use My Smart Card To Unlock The Drive** Select this option if you want the user to use a smart card and enter the smart card PIN to unlock the drive. Because this feature requires a smart card reader, it's typically used to unlock a drive in the workplace and not for drives that might be used outside the workplace.

> **NOTE** When you click Next, the wizard generates a recovery key. You can use the key to unlock the drive if BitLocker detects a condition that prevents it from unlocking the drive during boot. Note that you should save the key on removable media or on a network share. You can't store the key on the encrypted volume or the root directory of a fixed drive.

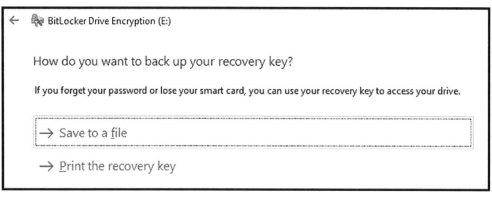

BitLocker Drive Encryption (E:)

Choose how you want to unlock this drive

☑ Use a password to unlock the drive

Passwords should contain uppercase and lowercase letters, numbers, spaces, and symbols.

Enter your password | •••••••••

Reenter your password | ••••••••••

☐ Use my smart card to unlock the drive

You'll need to insert your smart card. The smart card PIN will be required when you unlock the drive.

3. On the How Do You Want To Back Up Your Recovery Key? page, choose a save location for the recovery key, preferably a USB flash drive, other removable media or a network location.

BitLocker Drive Encryption (E:)

How do you want to back up your recovery key?

If you forget your password or lose your smart card, you can use your recovery key to access your drive.

→ Save to a file

→ Print the recovery key

4. You can now print the recovery key if you want to, such as for storage in your office safe. When you have finished, click Next.

5. If allowed in Group Policy, you can elect to encrypt used disk space only or the entire drive, and then click Next. Encrypting the used disk space only is faster than encrypting an entire volume. It's also the recommended option for newer servers and drives (except in high-security environments).

```
← 🔑 BitLocker Drive Encryption (E:)

Choose how much of your drive to encrypt

If you're setting up BitLocker on a new drive or a new PC, you only need to encrypt the part of the drive
that's currently being used. BitLocker encrypts new data automatically as you add it.

If you're enabling BitLocker on a PC or drive that's already in use, consider encrypting the entire drive.
Encrypting the entire drive ensures that all data is protected–even data that you deleted but that might still
contain retrievable info.

○ Encrypt used disk space only (faster and best for new PCs and drives)

◉ Encrypt entire drive (slower but best for PCs and drives already in use)
```

6. Choose the encryption mode. Windows Server 2016 and Windows 10 support standard AES encryption as well as enhanced XTS-AES encryption in 128-bit and 256-bit configurations. As earlier releases of Windows do not support the new XTS-AES option, you should only use this option if you the encrypted drive won't be used with earlier releases of Windows or Windows Server.

```
← 🔑 BitLocker Drive Encryption (E:)

Choose which encryption mode to use

Windows 10 (Version 1511) introduces a new disk encryption mode (XTS-AES). This mode provides
additional integrity support, but it is not compatible with older versions of Windows.

If this is a removable drive that you're going to use on older version of Windows, you should choose
Compatible mode.

If this is a fixed drive or if this drive will only be used on devices running at least Windows 10 (Version 1511)
or later, you should choose the new encryption mode

◉ New encryption mode (best for fixed drives on this device)

○ Compatible mode (best for drives that can be moved from this device)
```

7. On the Are You Ready To Encrypt This Drive? page, click Start Encrypting. How long the encryption process takes depends on the amount of data being encrypted and other factors.

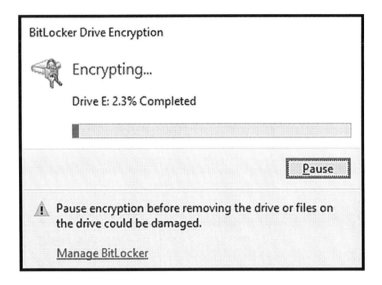

As the encryption process can be paused and resumed, you can shut down the server before the drive is completely encrypted and the encryption of the drive will resume when you restart the server. The encryption state is maintained in the event of a power loss as well.

Enabling BitLocker on USB Flash Drives

Encrypting USB flash drives protects the data stored on the volume. Any USB flash drive formatted with FAT, FAT32, exFAT, or NTFS can be encrypted with BitLocker. The length of time it takes to encrypt a drive depends on the size of the drive, the processing power of the server, and the level of activity on the server.

Before you enable BitLocker, you should configure the appropriate Removable Data Drives policies and settings in Group Policy and then wait for Group Policy to be refreshed. If you don't do this and you enable BitLocker, you might need to turn BitLocker off and then turn BitLocker back on because certain state and management flags are set when you turn on BitLocker.

To be sure that you can recover an encrypted volume, you should allow data-recovery agents and store recovery information in Active Directory. If you use a flash drive with earlier versions of Windows, the Allow Access To BitLocker-Protected Removable Data Drives From Earlier Versions Of Windows policy can ensure that you have access to the USB flash drive on other operating systems and servers. Unlocked drives are read-only.

To enable BitLocker encryption on a USB flash drive, follow these steps:

1. Insert the USB flash drive. In File Explorer, right-click the USB flash drive, and then click Turn On BitLocker. BitLocker then verifies that your server meets its requirements and then initializes the drive.

2. On the Choose How You Want To Unlock This Drive page, choose one or more of the following options, and then click Next:

- **Use A Password To Unlock This Drive** Select this option if you want the user to be prompted for a password to unlock the drive. Passwords allow a drive to be unlocked in any location and to be shared with other people.
- **Use My Smart Card To Unlock The Drive** Select this option if you want the user to use a smart card and enter the smart card PIN to unlock the drive. Because this feature requires a smart card reader, it's typically used to unlock a drive in the workplace and not for drives that might be used outside the workplace.

← 🔐 BitLocker Drive Encryption (G:)

Choose how you want to unlock this drive

☑ Use a password to unlock the drive
   Passwords should contain uppercase and lowercase letters, numbers, spaces, and symbols.

   Enter your password | •••••••••
   Reenter your password | •••••••••

☐ Use my smart card to unlock the drive
   You'll need to insert your smart card. The smart card PIN will be required when you unlock the drive.

---

3. On the How Do You Want To Back Up Your Recovery Key? page, click Save The Recovery Key To A File.

4. In the Save BitLocker Recovery Key As dialog box, choose a save location, and then click Save. As a best practice, you should save the recovery key to a network location or USB drive rather than the server to which the key belongs.

5. You can now print the recovery key if you want to, such as for storage in your office safe. When you have finished, click Next.

6. If allowed in Group Policy, you can elect to encrypt used disk space only or the entire drive, and then click Next. Encrypting the used disk space only is faster than encrypting an entire volume. It's also the recommended option for newer servers and drives (except in high-security environments).

7. Choose the encryption mode. Windows Server 2016 and Windows 10 support standard AES encryption as well as enhanced XTS-AES encryption in 128-bit and 256-bit configurations. As earlier releases of Windows do not support the new XTS-AES option, you should only use this option if you the encrypted drive won't be used with earlier releases of Windows or Windows Server.

8. On the Are You Ready To Encrypt This Drive? page, click Start Encrypting. Be sure to pause encryption before removing the drive and then resume to complete the encryption. Do not otherwise remove the USB flash drive until the encryption process is complete. How long the encryption process takes depends on the amount of data to encrypt and other factors.

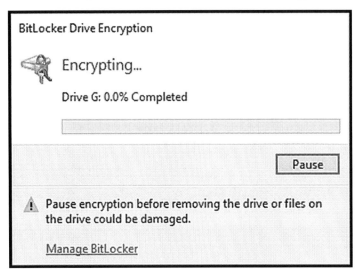

The encryption process does the following:

1. It adds an Autorun.inf file, the BitLocker To Go reader, and a Read Me.txt file to the USB flash drive.

2. It creates a virtual volume with the encrypted contents of the drive.

3. It encrypts the virtual volume to protect it. USB flash drive encryption takes approximately 6 to 10 minutes per gigabyte to complete. The encryption process can be paused and resumed, as long as you don't remove the drive.

When you insert an encrypted drive into a USB slot on a server running Windows Server 2016, a notification on the secure desktop is displayed. If the notification disappears before you can click it, right-click the drive in File Explorer and then select Unlock Drive.

Unlock drive H:
This drive is BitLocker-protected.

Click the notification to display the BitLocker dialog box. This dialog box is also displayed on the secure desktop.

BitLocker (H:)

Enter password to unlock this drive.

Fewer options

Enter recovery key

☐ Automatically unlock on this PC

Unlock

When you are prompted, enter the password. Optionally, click More Options to expand the dialog box so that you select Automatically Unlock On This Server to save the password in an encrypted file on the server's system volume. Finally, click Unlock to unlock the drive so that you can use it.

If you forget or lose the password for the drive but have the recovery key, click More Options, and then click Enter Recovery Key. Enter the 48-digit recovery key, and then click Unlock. This key is stored in the XML-formatted recovery key file as plain text.

Enabling BitLocker on System Volumes

Before you can encrypt a system volume, you should remove all bootable media from a server's CD/DVD drives, in addition to all USB flash drives. You should also back up critical files and data. You can then enable BitLocker encryption on the system volume by completing the following steps:

1. In File Explorer, right-click the system volume, and then click Turn On BitLocker. Windows checks the server and the drive to ensure that BitLocker can be enabled. If so, you'll see a prompt warning you that turning on BitLocker deletes any previously created restore points for the system volume. Click Yes to continue.

2. BitLocker Drive Encryption will then initialize the system volume, perform preliminary checks of the volume and also ensure the server meets requirements for using the feature. The system volume must be formatted with NTFS. When the preliminary checks are completed, click Next.

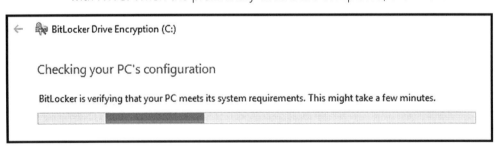

3. BitLocker warns you that a new system drive will be created. Click Next. As part of preparing the drive, BitLocker must create a new, unencrypted partition for the files required to start the operating system. This establishes the new system drive, which does not have a drive letter. The original

partition containing the other operating system files and your data will then be encrypted.

← ⚙ BitLocker Drive Encryption (C:)

Preparing your drive for BitLocker

An existing drive or unallocated free space on the hard drive will be used to turn on BitLocker.

⌃ Details

A new system drive will be created from free space on drive C:. The new drive will not have a drive letter.

← ⚙ BitLocker Drive Encryption (C:)

Preparing your drive for BitLocker

Do not turn off or restart your computer until this process has been completed.

✓ Shrinking drive C:
Creating new system drive
Preparing drive for BitLocker

Status:

NOTE If BitLocker is already enabled, the Manage BitLocker option is displayed instead of Turn On BitLocker. As part of the setup, Windows prepares the required BitLocker partition, if necessary. If Windows RE is in this partition, Windows moves Windows RE to the system volume and then uses this additional partition for BitLocker.

NOTE If the server doesn't have a TPM, the Allow BitLocker Without A Compatible TPM option must be enabled for operating system volumes in the Require Additional Authentication At Startup policy.

4. Once the first phase of drive preparation is complete, you'll be prompted to restart the server. If there is a problem moving the Windows RE to the system volume, you'll be notified of this and should consider creating a recovery drive containing a backup of the system files once the server restarts.

5. BitLocker setup resumes automatically. When you are ready to continue, click Next. You can now configure BitLocker startup preferences. Continue as discussed in the separate procedures that follow. If the server doesn't have a TPM, your options will be different. You'll be able to create a password to

unlock the drive, or you can insert a USB flash drive and store the startup key on the flash drive.

When a server has a TPM, you can use BitLocker to provide basic integrity checks of the volume without requiring any additional keys. In this configuration, BitLocker protects the system volume by encrypting it. This configuration does the following:

* Grants access to the volume to users who can log on to the operating system
* Prevents those who have physical access to the server from booting to an alternative operating system to gain access to the data on the volume
* Allows the server to be used with or without a TPM for additional boot security
* Does not require a password or a smart card with a PIN

To use BitLocker without any additional keys, follow these steps:

1. On the Choose How To Unlock Your Drive At Startup page, click Let BitLocker Automatically Unlock My Drive.

2. On the How Do You Want To Back Up Your Recovery Key? page, click Save To A File.

3. In the Save BitLocker Recovery Key As dialog box, choose the location of your USB flash drive or an appropriate network share, and then click Save. Do not use a USB flash drive that is BitLocker-encrypted.

4. You can now optionally save the recovery key to another location, print the recovery key, or both. Click an option, and then follow the wizard steps to set the location for saving or printing the recovery key. When you have finished, click Next.

5. If allowed in Group Policy, you can elect to encrypt used disk space only or the entire drive, and then click Next. Encrypting the used disk space only is faster than encrypting an entire volume. It's also the recommended option for newer servers and drives (except in high-security environments).

6. On the Encrypt The Drive page, click Start Encrypting. How long the encryption process takes depends on the amount of data to encrypt and other factors.

To enhance security, you can require additional authentication at startup. This configuration does the following:

* Grants access to the volume only to users who can provide a valid key
* Prevents those who have physical access to the server from booting to an alternative operating system to gain access to the data on the volume

- Allows the server to be used with or without a TPM for additional boot security
- Requires a password or a smart card with a PIN
- Optionally uses network unlock to unlock the volume when the server joined to and connected to the domain

You can enable BitLocker encryption for use with a startup key by following these steps:

1. Insert a USB flash drive in the server (if one is not already there). Do not use a USB flash drive that is BitLocker-encrypted.

2. On the Choose How To Unlock Your Drive At Startup page, click the Insert A USB Flash Drive option.

3. On the Back Up Your Startup Key page, click the USB flash drive, and then click Save.

4. Next, you need to save the recovery key. Because you should not store the recovery key and the startup key on the same medium, remove the USB flash drive and insert a second USB flash drive.

> **NOTE** The startup key is different from the recovery key. If you create a startup key, this key is required to start the server. The recovery key is required to unlock the server if BitLocker enters Recovery mode, which might happen if BitLocker suspects the server has been tampered with while the server was offline.

5. On the How Do You Want To Back Up Your Recovery Key? page, click Save To A File.

6. In the Save BitLocker Recovery Key As dialog box, choose the location of your USB flash drive, and then click Save. Do not remove the USB drive with the recovery key.

7. You can now optionally save the recovery key to a network folder, print the recovery key, or both. Click an option, and then follow the wizard's steps to set the location for saving or printing the recovery key. When you have finished, click Next.

8. If allowed in Group Policy, you can elect to encrypt used disk space only or the entire drive, and then click Next. Encrypting the used disk space only is faster than encrypting an entire volume. It's also the recommended option for newer servers and drives (except in high-security environments).

9. On the Encrypt The Volume page, confirm that Run BitLocker System Check is selected, and then click Continue.

10. Confirm that you want to restart the server by clicking Restart Now. The server restarts, and BitLocker ensures that the server is BitLocker-compatible and ready for encryption. If the server is not ready for encryption, you will get an error and need to resolve the error status before you can complete this procedure. If the server is ready for encryption, the Encryption In Progress status bar is displayed. You can monitor the status of the disk volume encryption by pointing to the BitLocker Drive Encryption icon in the notification area. By double-clicking this icon, you can open the Encrypting dialog box and monitor the encryption process more closely. You also have the option to pause the encryption process. Volume encryption takes approximately 1 minute per gigabyte to complete.

By completing this procedure, you have encrypted the operating system volume and created a recovery key unique to that volume. The next time you turn on your server, either the USB flash drive with the startup key must be plugged into a USB port on the server or the server must be connected to the domain network and using network unlock. If the USB flash drive is required for startup and you do not have the USB flash drive containing your startup key, you will need to use Recovery mode and supply the recovery key to gain access to the data.

You can enable BitLocker encryption for use with a startup PIN by following these steps:

1. On the Choose How To Unlock Your Drive At Startup page, select the Enter A PIN option.

2. On the Enter A PIN page, enter and confirm the PIN. The PIN can be any number you choose and must be 4 to 20 digits in length. The PIN is stored on the server.

3. Insert a USB flash drive on which you want to save the recovery key, and then click Set PIN. Do not use a USB flash drive that is BitLocker-encrypted.

4. Continue with steps 5-9 in the previous procedure.

When the encryption process is complete, you have encrypted the entire volume and created a recovery key unique to this volume. If you created a PIN or a startup key, you are required to use the PIN or startup key to start the server (or the server must be connected to the domain network and using network unlock). Otherwise, you will observe no change to the server unless the TPM changes or cannot be accessed, or if someone tries to modify the disk while the operating system is offline. In this case, the server enters Recovery mode, and you need to enter the recovery key to unlock the server.

Managing and Troubleshooting BitLocker

You can determine whether a system volume, data volume, or inserted removable drive uses BitLocker by clicking System And Security in Control Panel, and then double-clicking BitLocker Drive Encryption. You'll find the status of BitLocker on each volume.

The BitLocker Drive Encryption service must be started for BitLocker to work properly. Usually, this service is configured for manual startup and runs under the LocalSystem account.

To use smart cards with BitLocker, the Smart Card service must be started. Typically, this service is configured for manual startup and runs under the LocalService account.

After you create a startup key or PIN and a recovery key for a server, you can create duplicates of the startup key, startup PIN, or recovery key as necessary for backup or replacement purposes by using the options on the BitLocker Drive Encryption page in Control Panel.

> **NOTE** With fixed data and operating system drives, another way to access this page is to right-click the volume in File Explorer, and then click Manage BitLocker. If BitLocker is turned off, the Turn On BitLocker option is displayed instead.

The management options provided depend on the type of volume with which you are working and the encryption settings you choose. The available options include the following:

- **Back Up Recovery Key** Enables you to save or print the recovery key. Click this option, and then follow the prompts.
- **Change Password** Allows you to change the encryption password. Click this option, enter the old password, and then enter and confirm the new password. Click Change Password.
- **Remove Password** Click this option to remove the encryption password requirement for unlocking the drive. You can do this only if another unlocking method is configured first.

- **Add Smart Card**   Enables you to add a smart card for unlocking the drive. Click this option, and then follow the prompts.
- **Remove Smart Card**   Click this option to remove the smart card requirement for unlocking the drive.
- **Change Smart Card**   Enables you to change the smart card used to unlock the drive. Click this option, and then follow the prompts.
- **Turn On Auto-Unlock**   Click this option to turn on automatic unlocking of the drive.
- **Turn Off Auto-Unlock**   Click this option to turn off automatic unlocking of the drive.
- **Turn Off BitLocker**   Click this option to turn off BitLocker and decrypt the drive.

Recovering Data Protected by BitLocker Drive Encryption

If you've configured BitLocker Drive Encryption and the server enters Recovery mode, you need to unlock the server. To unlock the server by using a recovery key stored on a USB flash drive, follow these steps:

1. Turn on the server. If the server is locked, the server opens the BitLocker Drive Encryption Recovery console.

2. When you are prompted, insert the USB flash drive that contains the recovery key, and then press Enter.

3. The server will unlock and reboot automatically. You do not need to enter the recovery key manually.

If you saved the recovery key file in a folder on another server or on removable media, you can use another server to open and validate the recovery key file. To locate the correct file, find Password ID on the recovery console displayed on the locked server and write down this number. The file containing the recovery key uses this Password ID as the file name. Open the file and locate the recovery key.

To unlock the server by typing the recovery key, follow these steps:

1. Turn on the server. If the server is locked, the BitLocker Drive Encryption Recovery console opens.

2. Type the recovery key, and then press Enter. The server will unlock and reboot automatically.

A server can become locked if a user tries to enter the recovery key but is repeatedly unsuccessful. In the recovery console, you can press Esc twice to exit the recovery prompt and turn off the server. A server might also become locked if an error related to TPM occurs or boot data is modified. In this case, the server halts very early in the boot process, before the operating system starts. At this point, the locked server might not be able to accept standard keyboard numbers. If that is the case, you must use the function keys to enter the recovery password. Here, the function keys F1–F9 represent the digits 1 through 9, and the F10 function key represents 0.

Disabling or Turning Off BitLocker Drive Encryption

When you need to make changes to TPM or make other changes to the system, you might first need to temporarily turn off BitLocker encryption on the system volume. You cannot temporarily turn off BitLocker encryption on data volumes; you can only decrypt data volumes.

To temporarily turn off BitLocker encryption on the system volume, follow these steps:

1. In Control Panel, click System And Security, and then double-click BitLocker Drive Encryption.
2. For the system volume, click Turn Off BitLocker Drive Encryption.
3. When prompted, click Disable BitLocker Drive Encryption.

    By completing this procedure, you have temporarily disabled BitLocker on the operating system volume.

To turn off BitLocker Drive Encryption and decrypt a data volume or USB drive, follow these steps:

1. In Control Panel, click System And Security, and then double-click BitLocker Drive Encryption.
2. For the appropriate volume, click Turn Off BitLocker Drive Encryption.
3. When prompted to confirm, click Turn Off BitLocker Drive Encryption.

Chapter 6. Using Storage Spaces

Storage Spaces provide the primary means for protecting critical data. Storage management and the ways that Windows Server works with disks have changed substantially since the introduction of Storage Spaces. Although traditional storage management techniques relate to physical drives located inside the server, many servers today use attached storage and virtual disks. Generally, when you work with internal fixed drives, you often need to perform advanced disk setup procedures, such as creating a volume set or setting up a redundant array of independent disks (RAID) array. Here, you create volumes or arrays that can span multiple drives and you know the exact physical layout of those drives.

On the other hand, when you work with attached storage, you might not know which actual physical disk or disks the volume you are working with resides on. Instead, you are presented with a virtual disk, also referred to as a logical unit number (LUN), which is a logical reference to a portion of the storage subsystem. Although the virtual disk can reside on one or more physical disks (spindles), the layout of the physical disks is controlled separately from the operating system (by the storage subsystem).

Standards-based, storage management approaches rely on the storage subsystem to manage the physical disk architecture and can be used with a server's internal, external or attached disks. When internal disks are used in this way, the internal disks—such as virtual disks on attached storage—are resources to be allocated by using standards-based approaches. This means you can create virtual disk volumes on the physical disks, add the physical disks to storage pools, and create Internet SCSI (iSCSI) virtual disks that can be targeted. You can also enable data deduplication on your virtual disks.

Standards-based storage management focuses on the storage volumes themselves rather than the underlying physical layout, relying on hardware to handle the architecture particulars for data redundancy and the portions of disks that are presented as usable disks. This means the layout of the physical disks is controlled by the storage subsystem instead of by the operating system.

Getting Started with Storage Spaces

With Storage Spaces and other standards-based management approaches, the physical layout of disks (spindles) is abstracted, so a "disk" can be a logical reference to a portion of a storage subsystem (a virtual disk) or an actual physical disk. This means a disk simply becomes a unit of storage and volumes can be created to allocate space within disks for file systems.

Taking this concept a few steps further, you can pool available space on disks so that units of storage (virtual disks) can be allocated from this pool on an as-needed basis. These units of storage, in turn, are apportioned with volumes to allocate space and create usable file systems.

Technically, the pooled storage is referred to as a *storage pool* and the virtual disks created within the pool are referred to as *storages spaces*. Given a set of "disks," you can create a single storage pool by allocating all the disks to the pool or create multiple storage pools by allocating disks separately to each pool.

> **REAL WORLD**   When you throw storage subsystems into the mix, it's really a three-layered architecture. In Layer 1, the layout of the physical disks is controlled by the storage subsystem. The storage system likely will use some form of RAID to ensure that data is redundant and recoverable in case of failure. In Layer 2, the virtual disks created by the arrays are made available to servers. The servers simply see the disks as storage that can be allocated. Windows Server can apply software-level RAID or other redundancy approaches to help protect against failure. In Layer 3, the server creates volumes on the virtual disks, and these volumes provide the usable file systems for file and data storage.

Grouping Disks into Storage Pools

When you are working with File And Storage Services, you can group available physical disks into storage pools so that you can create virtual disks from available capacity. Each virtual disk you create is a storage space. Storage Spaces are made available through the Storage Services role service, which is automatically installed on every server running Windows Server 2016.

To integrate Storage Spaces with standards-based storage management frameworks, you'll want to add the Windows Standards-Based Storage Management feature to your file servers. When a server is configured with the File Services And Storage role, the Windows Standards-Based Storage Management feature adds components and updates Server Manager with the options for working with standards-based volumes. You might also want to do the following:

- Add the Data Deduplication role service if you want to enable data deduplication. Data deduplication works with volumes up to 64 TB and file sizes up to 1 TB.
- Add the iSCSI Target Server and iSCSI Target Storage Provider role services if you want the server to host iSCSI virtual disks.

After you configure your servers as appropriate for your environment, you can select the File And Storage Services node in Server Manager to work with your storage volumes, and additional options will be available as well. The Servers subnode lists file servers that have been configured for standards-based management.

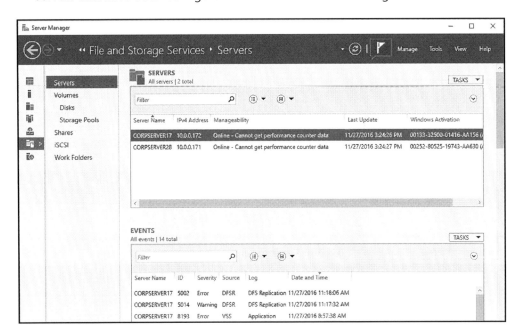

The Volumes subnode lists allocated storage on each server according to how volumes are provisioned and how much free space is available. Volumes are listed regardless of whether the underlying disks are physical or virtual. Right-click a volume to display management options, including the following:

- **Configure Data Deduplication**   Allows you to enable and configure data deduplication for NTFS volumes. If the feature is enabled, you can then use this option to disable data deduplication as well.

- **Delete Volume**   Allows you to delete the volume. The space that was used is then marked as unallocated on the related disk.
- **Extend Volume**   Allows you to extend the volume to unallocated space of the related disk.
- **Format**   Allows you to create a new file system on the volume that overwrites the existing volume.
- **Manage Drive Letter And Access Paths**   Allows you to change the drive letter or access path associated with the volume.
- **New iSCSI Virtual Disk**   Allows you to create a new iSCSI virtual disk that is stored on the volume.
- **New Share**   Allows you to create new Server Message Block (SMB) or Network File System (NFS) shares on the volume.
- **Properties**   Displays information about the volume type, file system, health, capacity, used space, and free space. You can also use this option to set the volume label.
- **Repair File System Errors**   Allows you to repair errors detected during an online scan of the file system.
- **Scan File System For Errors**   Allows you to perform an online scan of the file system. Although Windows attempts to repair any errors that are found, some errors can be corrected only by using a repair procedure.

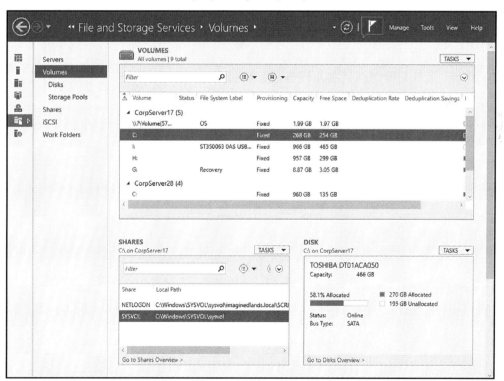

The Disks subnode lists the disks available to each server according to total capacity, unallocated space, partition style, subsystem, and bus type. Server Manager attempts to differentiate between physical disks and virtual disks by showing the virtual disk label (if one was provided) and the originating storage subsystem. Right-click a disk to display management options, including the following:

- **Bring Online** Enables you to take an offline disk and make it available for use.
- **Take Offline** Enables you to take a disk offline so that it can no longer be used.
- **Reset Disk** Enables you to completely reset the disk, which deletes all volumes on the disk and removes all available data on the disk.
- **New Volume** Enables you to create a new volume on the disk.

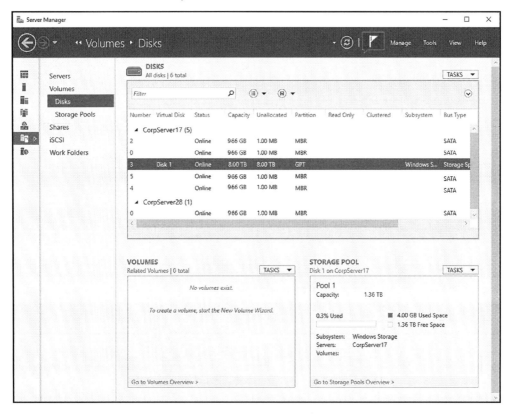

In Server Manager, you can work with storage pools and allocate space by selecting the File And Storage Services node, and then selecting the related Storage Pools subnode. The Storage Pools subnode lists the available storage pools, the virtual disks created within storage pools, and the available physical disks. Keep in mind that what's presented as physical disks might actually be LUNs (virtual disks) from a storage subsystem.

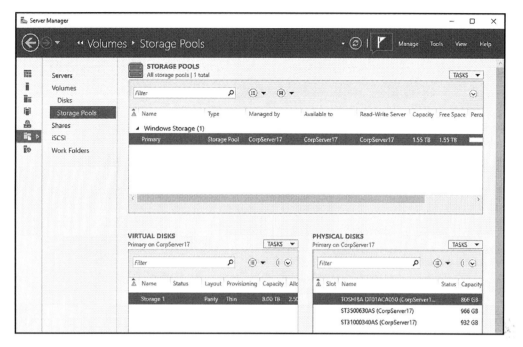

Storage Pool Options, Versions and Features

Working with storage pools is a multistep process:

1. You create storage pools to pool available space on one or more disks.

2. You allocate space from this pool to create one or more virtual disks.

3. You create one or more volumes on each virtual disk to allocate storage for file systems.

The version of Storage Spaces that ships with Windows Server 2016 is different from the version that ships with earlier releases of Windows Server. If you have any questions about which version of Storage Spaces is being used, complete the following steps to check the version:

1. In Server Manager, select the File And Storage Services node and then select the Storage Pools node.

2. Right-click the storage pool you want to examine and then select Properties.

3. In the Properties dialog box, the storage pool version is listed on the General tab.

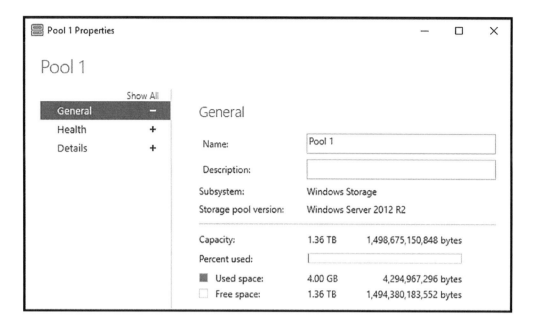

You also can use this technique to check capacity, total used space and available space. By default, Storage Space alerts you when storage is approaching capacity and when a storage space reaches 70 percent of the total provisioned size. When you get such an alert, you should consider allocating additional storage.

> **NOTE** The Health tab provides details about the operational status of the storage pool. If you are using a storage pool from an earlier version of Windows Server, you'll see a warning status and the storage pool will be listed as having a degraded operational status. This status simply means the storage pool cannot use any of the new functionality of the current Storage Spaces version. While in a degraded state, the storage pool continues to operate normally and can be used with servers running the specified version of Windows Server as well as Windows Server 2016.

You can upgrade the version of Storage Spaces being used by a storage pool by right-clicking a storage pool, and then selecting Upgrade Storage Pool Version. As the warning prompt states, the version upgrade cannot be reversed once completed.

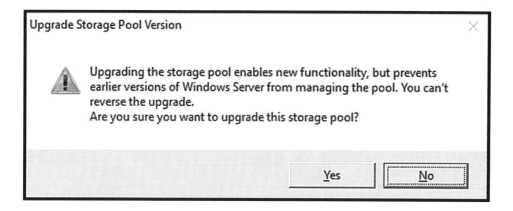

Upgrade Storage Pool Version ✕

⚠ Upgrading the storage pool enables new functionality, but prevents earlier versions of Windows Server from managing the pool. You can't reverse the upgrade.
Are you sure you want to upgrade this storage pool?

[Yes] [No]

The Windows Server 2016 version of Storage Spaces does the following:

- Supports using tiered storage when you combine hard disk drives and solid state drives in a storage pool. With storage tiers, the most frequently used files are moved from hard disk storage to solid state storage to improve performance.
- Supports using local storage and removes the need for shared SAS fabric. This allows a server to use the network as the storage fabric and take advantage of the improvements provided with SMB3 and SMB Direct. Microsoft calls this feature Storage Spaces Direct.
- Supports block-level synchronous or asynchronous replication between servers using SMB3 as the transport. Microsoft calls this feature Storage Replica.
- Supports storage spaces that have dual parity, and parity and dual parity spaces on failover clusters. With dual parity, storage spaces are protected against two simultaneous drive failures.
- Supports automatic rebuild of storage spaces from storage pool free space instead of having to use hot spares to recover from drive failures. Here, instead of writing a copy of data that was on a failed disk to a hot spare, the parity or mirrored data is copied to multiple drives in the pool to achieve the previous level of resiliency automatically. As a result, you don't need to specifically allocate hot spares in storage pools, provided that a sufficient number of drives is assigned to the pool to allow for automatic resiliency recovery.
- Supports storage tiers to automatically move frequently used files from slower physical disks to faster Solid State Drive (SSD) storage. This feature is applicable only when a storage space has a combination of SSD storage and hard disk drive (HDD) storage. Additionally, the storage type must be set as fixed, the volumes created on virtual disks must be the same size as the virtual disk, and enough free space must be available to accommodate the preference. For fine-grained management, use the Set-FileStorageTier cmdlet to assign files to standard physical drive storage or faster SSD storage.
- Supports write-back caching when a storage pool uses SSD storage. Write-back cache buffers small random writes to SSD storage before later writing the data to

HDD storage. Buffering writes in this way helps to protect against data loss in the event of power failures. For write-back cache to work properly, storage spaces with simple volumes must have at least one SSD, storage spaces with two-way mirroring or single-parity must have at least two SSDs, and storage spaces with three-way mirroring or dual parity must have at least three SSDs. When these requirements are met, the volumes automatically will use a 1-GB write-back cache by default. You can designate SSDs that should be used for write-back caching by setting the usage as Journal (the default in this configuration). If enough SSDs are not configured for journaling, the write-back cache size is set to 0 (meaning write-back caching will not be used). The only exception is for parity spaces, which will then have the write-back cache size set to 32 MB.

If you have any question about the size of the write-back cache, complete the following steps to check the cache size:

1. Right-click the virtual disk you want to examine, and then select Properties.

2. In the Properties dialog box, select Details in the left pane, and then choose WriteCacheSize on the Property selection list.

You also can use this technique to check allocated size, status, provisioned size, provision type, redundancy type, and more.

Creating Storage Pools

Storage pools allow you to pool available space on disks so that units of storage (virtual disks) can be allocated from this pool. To create a storage pool, you must have at least one unused disk and a storage subsystem to manage it. This storage subsystem can be the one included with the Storage Spaces feature or a subsystem associated with attached storage.

Using Drives and Volumes in a Storage Pool

When a computer has extra drives in addition to the drive on which Windows is installed, you can allocate one or more of the additional drives to a storage pool. However, keep in mind that if you use a formatted drive with a storage pool, Windows permanently deletes all the files on that drive. Additionally, it's important to point out that physical disks with the MBR partition style are converted automatically to the GPT partition style when you add them to a storage pool and create volumes on them.

Each physical disk allocated to the pool can be handled in one of three ways:

- As a data store that is available for use
- As a data store that can be manually allocated for use
- As a hot spare in case a disk in the pool fails or is removed from the subsystem

Types of volumes you can create are as follows:

- **Simple Volumes**   Creates a simple volume by writing one copy of your data to one or more drives. With simple volumes, there is no redundancy and no associated overhead. As an example, you can create a single volume that spans two 2-TB drives, making 4 TB of storage available. However, because there is no resiliency, a failure of any drive in a simple volume causes the entire volume to fail.
- **Two-way mirrors**   Creates a mirrored set by writing two copies of a computer's data, helping to protect against a single drive failure. Two-way mirrors require at least two drives. With two-way mirrors, there is a 1/2 (50 percent) overhead for redundancy with two drives. As an example, you could allocate two 2-TB drives as a two-way mirror, giving you 2 TB of mirrored storage.
- **Parity volumes**   Creates a volume that uses disk striping with parity, helping to provide fault tolerance with less overhead than mirroring. Parity volumes require at least three drives. With parity volumes there is a 1/3 (33.33 percent) overhead for redundancy with three drives. As an example, you could allocate three 2-TB drives as a parity volume, giving you 4 TB of protected storage.
- **Dual parity volumes**   Creates a volume that uses disk striping with two sets of parity data, helping to protect against two simultaneous drive failures while requiring less overhead than three-way mirroring. Dual parity volumes require at least seven drives.

- **Three-way mirrors** Creates a mirrored set by writing three copies of a computer's data and by using disk striping with mirroring, helping to protect against two simultaneous drive failures. Although three-way mirrors do not have a penalty for read operations, they do have a performance penalty for write operations because of the overhead associated with having to write data to three separate disks. This overhead can be mitigated by using multiple drive controllers. Ideally, you'll want to ensure that at least three drive controllers are used. Three-way mirrors require at least five drives.

If you are familiar with RAID 6, you are familiar with dual parity volumes. Although dual parity does not have a penalty for read operations, it does have a performance penalty for write operations because of the overhead associated with calculating and writing dual parity values. With standard dual parity volumes, the usable capacity of dual parity volumes is calculated as the sum of the number of volumes minus two times the size of the smallest volume in the array or (N -2) X MinimumVolumeSize. For example, with 7 volumes and the smallest volume size of 1TB, the usable capacity typically is 5 TB [calculated as (7 - 2) * 1 TB = 5 TB].

Although logically it would seem that you need at least six drives to have three mirrored copies of data, mathematically you need only five. Why? If you want three copies of your data, you need at least 15 logical units of storage to create those three copies. Divide 15 by 3 to come up with the number of disks required, and the answer is that you need 5 disks. Thus, Storage Spaces uses 1/3 of each disk to store original data and 2/3 of each disk to store copies of data. Following this, a three-way mirror with five volumes has a 2/3 (66.66 percent) overhead for redundancy. Or put another way, you could allocate five 3-TB drives as a three-way mirror, giving you 5 TB of mirrored storage (and 10 TB of overhead).

With single parity volumes, data is written out horizontally with parity calculated for each row of data. Dual parity differs from single parity in that row data is not only stored horizontally, it is also stored diagonally. If a single disk fails or a read error from a bad bit or block error occurs, the data is re-created by using only the horizontal row parity data (just as in single parity volumes). In the case of a multiple drive issue, the horizontal and diagonal row data are used for recovery.

To understand how dual parity typically works, consider the following simplified example:

Each horizontal row of data has a parity value, the sum of which is stored on the parity disk for that row (and calculated by using an exclusive OR). Each horizontal parity stripe misses one and only one disk. If the parity value is 2, 3, 1, and 4 on disks 0, 1, 2, and 3 respectively, the parity sum stored on the disk 4 (the parity disk for this row) is 10 (2 + 3 + 1 + 4 = 10). If disk 0 were to have a problem, the parity value for the row on this disk could be restored by subtracting the remaining horizontal values from the horizontal parity sum (10 − 3 − 1 − 4 = 2).

The second set of parity data is written diagonally (meaning in different data rows on different disks). Each diagonal row of data has a diagonal parity value, the sum of which is stored on the diagonal parity disk for that row (and calculated by using an exclusive OR). Each diagonal parity stripe misses two disks: one disk in which the diagonal parity sum is stored and one disk that is omitted from the diagonal parity striping. Additionally, the diagonal parity sum includes a data row from the horizontal row parity as part of its diagonal parity sum.

If the diagonal parity value is 1, 4, 3, and 7 on disks 1, 2, 3, and 4 respectively (with four associated horizontal rows), the diagonal parity sum stored on disk 5 (the diagonal parity disk for this row) is 15 (4 + 1 + 3 + 7 = 15) and the omitted disk is disk 0. If disk 2 and disk 4 were to have a problem, the diagonal parity value for the row can be used to restore both of the lost values. The missing diagonal value is restored first by subtracting the remaining diagonal values from the diagonal parity sum. The missing horizontal value is restored next by subtracting the remaining horizontal values for the subject row from the horizontal parity sum for that row.

NOTE Keep in mind that dual parity as implemented in Storage Spaces uses 7 disks and the previous example was simplified. Although parity striping with 7 disks works differently than discussed in this example, the basic approach uses horizontal and vertical stripes.

Creating a Storage Pool

You can create a storage pool by completing the following steps:

1. In Server Manager, select the File And Storage Services node, and then select the related Storage Pools subnode.

2. Select Tasks in the Storage Pools panel, and then select New Storage Pool. This starts the New Storage Pool Wizard. If the wizard displays the Before You Begin page, read the Welcome text, and then select Next.

3. On the Specify A Storage Pool Name And Subsystem page, enter a name and description of the storage pool, and then select the primordial pool with

which you want to work. (A *primordial pool* is simply a group of disks managed by and available to a specific server via a storage subsystem.) Select Next.

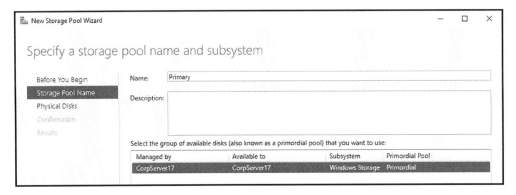

> **TIP**   Select the primordial pool for the server you want to associate the pool with and allocate storage for. For example, if you are configuring storage for CorpServer38, select the primordial pool that is available to CorpServer38.

4.   On the Select Physical Disks For The Storage Pool page, select the unused physical disks that should be part of the storage pool, and then specify the type of allocation for each disk. A storage pool must have more than one disk to use the mirroring and parity features available to protect data in case of error or failure. When setting the Allocation value, keep the following in mind:

- Choose Automatic to allocate the disk to the pool and make it available for use as needed.
- Choose Manual to allocate the disk to the pool but not allow it to be used until it is manually allocated.
- Choose Hot Spare to allocate the disk to the pool as a spare disk that is made available for use if another disk in the pool fails or is removed from the subsystem.

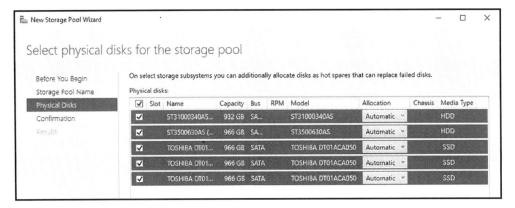

> **_TIP_** Storage tiers allow you to configure Storage Pools that automatically move frequently used files to the fastest storage available. Generally, this means files are moved from hard disk drives to solid state drives as appropriate. Tiered storage is only available when a storage pool has a mix of hard disk drives and solid state drives. Specifically, the storage pool must have at least one automatically added physical disk of each media type.

5. When you are ready to continue, select Next. After you confirm your selections, select Create. The wizard tracks the progress of the pool creation. When the wizard finishes creating the pool, the View Results page will be updated to reflect this. Review the details to ensure that all phases were completed successfully, and then select Close.

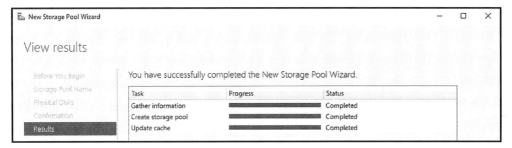

If any portion of the configuration failed, note the reason for the failure and take corrective actions as appropriate before repeating this procedure.

- If one of the physical disks is currently formatted with a volume, you'll get the following error:

  Could not create storage pool. One of the physical disks specified is not supported by this operation.

  This error occurs because physical disks that you want to add to a storage pool cannot contain existing volumes. To resolve the problem, you'll need to repeat the procedure and select a different physical disk, or remove any existing volumes on the physical disk, repeat the procedure, and then select the disk again. Keep in mind that deleting a volume permanently erases all data it contains.

- If one of the physical disks is unavailable after being selected, you'll see the error:

  Could not create storage pool. One or more parameter values passed to the method were invalid.

  This error occurs because a physical disk that was available when you started the New Storage Pool Wizard has become unavailable or is offline. To resolve the problem, you'll need to a) repeat the procedure and select a different physical disk, or b) bring the physical disk online or otherwise make it available for use, repeat the procedure, and then select the disk again.

> **NOTE** External storage can become unavailable for a variety of reasons. For example, an external connected cable might have been disconnected or a LUN previously allocated to the server might have been reallocated by a storage administrator.

Creating Virtual Disks and Volumes

After you create a storage pool, you can allocate space from the pool to virtual disks that are available to your servers. You can then create volumes on the disks to enable data storage.

Creating a Virtual Disk in a Storage Space

Each physical disk allocated to the pool can be handled in one of three ways:

- As a data store that is available for use
- As a data store that can be manually allocated for use
- As a hot spare in case a disk in the pool fails or is removed from the subsystem

When a storage pool has a single disk, your only option for allocating space on that disk is to create virtual disks with a simple layout. A simple layout does not protect against disk failure. If a storage pool has multiple disks, you have these additional layout options:

- **Mirror** With a mirror layout, data is duplicated on disks by using a mirroring technique similar to what I discussed previously in this chapter. However, the mirroring technique is more sophisticated in that data is mirrored onto two or three disks at a time. Like standard mirroring, this approach has its advantages and disadvantages. If a storage space has two or three disks, you are fully protected against a single disk failure, and if a storage space has five or more disks, you are fully protected against two simultaneous disk failures. The disadvantage is that mirroring reduces capacity by up to 50 percent. For example, if you mirror two 1-TB disks, the usable space is 1 TB.
- **Parity** With a parity layout, data and parity information are striped across physical disks by using a striping-with-parity technique similar to what I discussed previously in this chapter. Like standard striping with parity, this approach has its advantages and disadvantages. You need at least three disks to fully protect yourself against a single disk failure. You lose some capacity to the striping, but not as much as with mirroring.

You can create a virtual disk in a storage pool by completing the following steps:

1. In Server Manager, select the File And Storage Services node, and then select the related Storage Pools subnode.

2. Select Tasks in the Virtual Disks panel, and then select New Virtual Disk. This starts the New Virtual Disk Wizard. If the wizard displays the Before You Begin page, read the Welcome text, and then select Next.

3. On the Storage Pool page, select the storage pool in which you want to create the virtual disk, and then select Next. Each available storage pool is listed according to the server it is managed by and available to. Make sure the pool has enough free space to create the virtual disk.

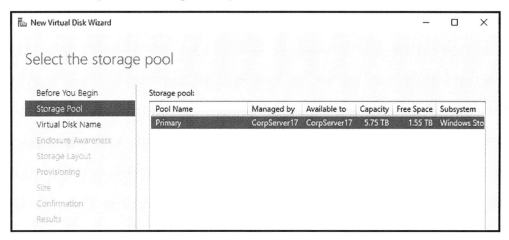

TIP Select the storage pool for the server you want to associate the virtual disk with and allocate storage from. For example, if you are configuring storage for CorpServer38, select a storage pool that is available to CorpServer38.

4. On the Specify The Virtual Disk Name page, enter a name and description for the virtual disk. If you are using a combination of SSD storage and HDD storage, use the check box provided to specify whether you want to create storage tiers. With storage tiers, the most frequently accessed files are automatically moved from slower HDD to faster SSD storage. This option is not applicable when the server has only HDD or SSD storage. To continue, select Next.

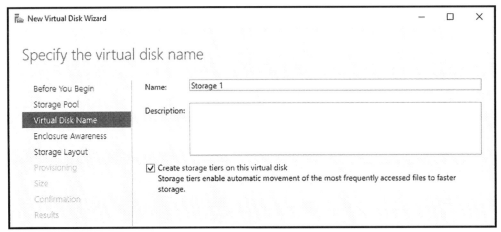

5. If you allocated storage from 3 or more different enclosures using the automatic option, you can enable enclosure awareness on the Specify Enclosure Awareness page. With enclosure awareness, copies of your data are stored on separate enclosures to help protect your data if an entire enclosure fails.

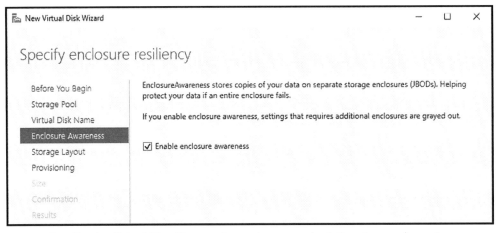

6. On the Select The Storage Layout page, select the storage layout as appropriate for your reliability and redundancy requirements. The simple layout is the only option for storage pools that contain a single disk. If the underlying storage pool has multiple disks, you can choose a simple layout, a mirror layout, or a parity layout. Select Next.

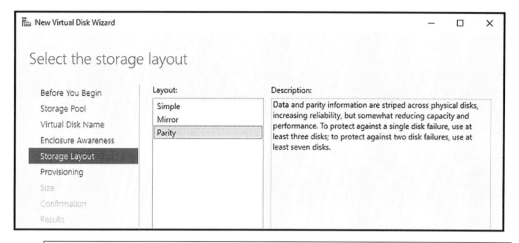

REAL WORLD   If there aren't enough available disks to implement the storage layout, you'll get the error: The storage pool does not contain enough physical disks to support the selected storage layout. Select a different layout or repeat this procedure and select a different storage pool to work with initially.

Keep in mind the storage pool might have one or more disks allocated as hot spares. Hot spares are made available automatically to recover from disk failure when you use mirroring or parity volumes—and cannot otherwise be used. To force Windows to use a hot spare, you can remove the hot spare from the storage pool by right-clicking it and selecting Remove, and then adding the drive back to the storage pool as an automatically allocated disk by right-clicking the storage pool and selecting Add Physical Drive. Unfortunately, doing so might cause a storage pool created with a hot spare to report that it is in an Unhealthy state. If you subsequently try to add the drive again in any capacity, you'll get an error stating "Error adding task: The storage pool could not complete the operation because its configuration is read-only." The storage pool is not, in fact, in a read-only state. If the storage pool were in a read-only state you could enter the following command at an administrator PowerShell prompt to clear this state:

Get-Storagepool "PoolName" | Set-Storagepool -IsReadonly $false

However, entering this command likely will not resolve the problem. To clear this error, I needed to reset Storage Spaces and the related subsystem. You might find it easier to simply restart the server. After you reset or restart the server, the storage pool will transition from an error state (where a red circle with an 'x' is showing) to a warning state (where a yellow triangle with an '!' is showing). You can then remove the physical disk from the storage pool by right-clicking it and selecting Remove. Afterward, you will be able to add the physical disk as an automatically-allocated disk by right-clicking the storage pool and selecting Add Physical Drive.

7. On the Specify The Provisioning Type page, select the provisioning type. Storage can be provisioned in a thin disk or a fixed disk. With thin-disk provisioning, the volume uses space from the storage pool as needed, up to the volume size. With fixed provisioning, the volume has a fixed size and uses space from the storage pool equal to the volume size. Select Next.

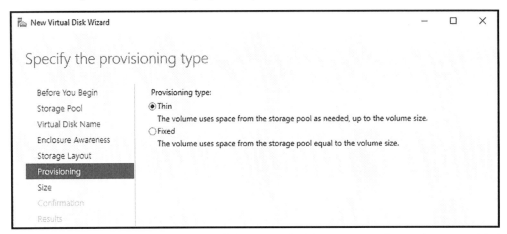

8. On the Specify The Size Of The Virtual Disk page, use the options provided to set the size of the virtual disk. With fixed provisioning, selecting Maximum Size ensures that the disk is created and sized with the maximum space possible given the available space. For example, if you use a 2-TB disk and a 1.5-TB disk with a mirrored layout, a 1.5-TB fixed disk will be created as this is the maximum mirrored size possible.

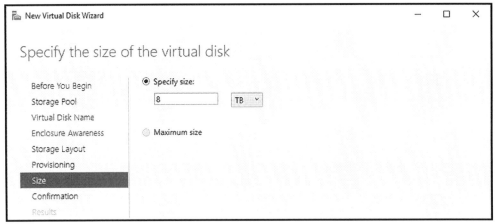

9. When you are ready to continue, select Next. After you confirm your selections, select Create. The wizard tracks the progress of the disk creation. When the wizard finishes creating the disk, the View Results page will be updated to reflect this. Review the details to ensure that all phases were completed successfully. If any portion of the configuration failed, note the

reason for the failure and take corrective actions as appropriate before repeating this procedure.

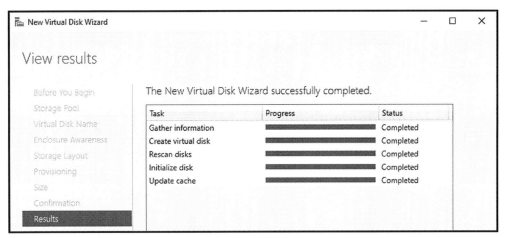

10. When you select Close, the New Volume Wizard should start automatically. Use the wizard to create a volume on the disk as discussed in the following section.

Creating a Standard Volume

Standard volumes can be created on any physical or virtual disk available. You use the same technique regardless of how the disk is presented to the server. This allows you to create standard volumes on a server's internal disks, on virtual disks in a storage subsystem available to a server, and on virtual iSCSI disks available to a server. If you add the data deduplication feature to a server, you can enable data deduplication for standard volumes created for that server.

You can create a standard volume by completing the following steps:

1. Start the New Volume Wizard. If you just created a storage space, the New Volume Wizard might start automatically. If it did not, do one of the following:

   ▪ On the Disks subnode, all available disks are listed in the Disks panel. Select the disk with which you want to work, and then under Tasks, select New Volume.
   ▪ On the Storage Pools subnode, all available virtual disks are listed in the Virtual Disks panel. Select the disk with which you want to work, and then under Tasks, select New Volume.

2. On the Select The Server And Disk page, select the server for which you are provisioning storage, select the disk where the volume should be created,

and then select Next. If you just created a storage space and then New Volume Wizard started automatically, the related server and disk are selected automatically and you simply need to select Next.

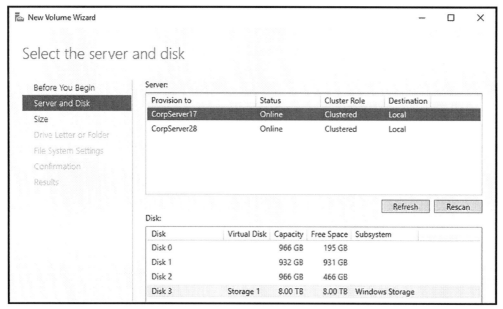

3. On the Specify The Size Of The Volume page, use the options provided to set the volume size. By default, the volume size is set to the maximum available on the related disk. Select Next.

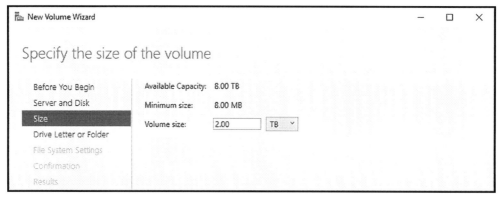

4. On the Assign To A Drive Letter Or Folder page, specify whether you want to assign a drive letter or path to the volume, and then select Next. You use these options as follows:

▪ **Drive Letter** To assign a drive letter, choose this option, and then select an available drive letter in the list provided.

- **The Following Folder**   To assign a drive path, choose this option, and then enter the path to an existing folder on an NTFS drive, or select Browse to search for or create a folder.
- **Don't Assign To A Drive Letter Or Drive Path**   To create the volume without assigning a drive letter or path, choose this option. You can assign a drive letter or path later if necessary.

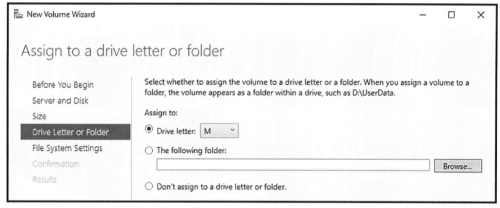

5. On the Select File System Settings page, specify how the volume should be formatted by using the following options:

- **File System**   Sets the file system type, such as NTFS or ReFS.
- **Allocation Unit Size**   Sets the cluster size for the file system. This is the basic unit in which disk space is allocated. The default allocation unit size is based on the volume's size and is set dynamically prior to formatting. To override this feature, you can set the allocation unit size to a specific value.
- **Volume Label**   Sets a text label for the partition. This label is the partition's volume name.

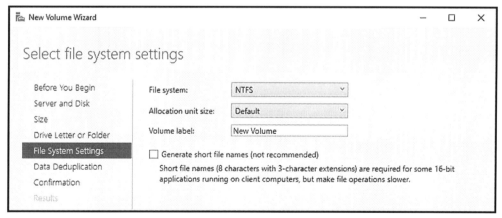

6. If you elected to create an NTFS volume and added data deduplication to the server, you can enable and configure data deduplication. When you are ready to continue, select Next.

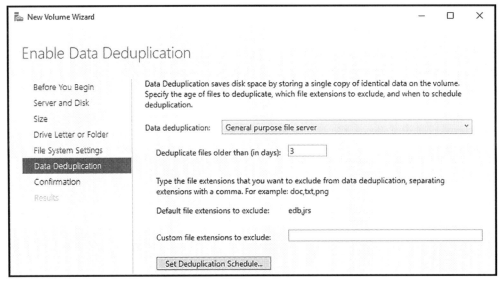

7. After you confirm your selections, select Create. The wizard tracks the progress of the volume creation. When the wizard finishes creating the volume, the View Results page will be updated to reflect this. Review the details to ensure that all phases were completed successfully. If any portion of the configuration failed, note the reason for the failure and take corrective actions as appropriate before repeating this procedure.

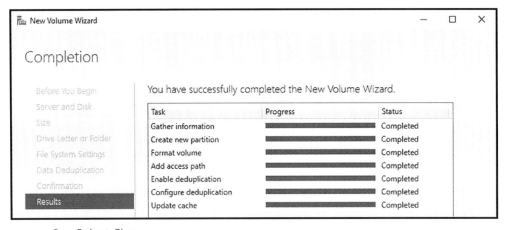

8. Select Close.

> **REAL WORLD** In the Registry under HKLM\SYSTEM\CurrentControlSet\Control\FileSystem, the NtfsDisableLastAccessUpdate and RefsDisableLastAccessUpdate values control whether NTFS and ReFS update the last-access timestamp on each directory when it lists directories on a volume. If you notice that a busy server with a large number of directories isn't very responsive when you list directories, this could be because the filesystem log buffer in physical memory is getting filled with timestamp update records. To prevent this, you can set the

> value to 1. When the value is set to 1, the filesystem does not update the last-access timestamp, and it does not record time stamp updates in the file system log. Otherwise, when the value is set to 0 (the default), the filesystem updates the last-access timestamp on each directory it detects, and it records each time change in the filesystem log.

Troubleshooting Storage Spaces

Typical problems creating storage spaces and allocating storage were discussed previously. You also might find that a physical disk that should be available for use isn't available. With the Storage Pools node selected in Server Manager, you can add a physical disk that has been detected but isn't listed as available by selecting Tasks on the Physical Disks panel, and then selecting Add Physical Disk. Next, in the Add Physical Disk dialog box, select the physical disk, and then select OK. Alternatively, if the physical disk has not been detected by the storage system, select Tasks on the Storage Pools panel, and then select Rescan Storage.

Other problems you might experience with storage spaces relate to drive failures and a loss of resiliency. When a storage space uses two-way mirroring, three-way mirroring, parity, or dual parity, you can recover resiliency by reconnecting a disconnected drive or replacing a failed drive. When a storage space uses a simple volume and drives were disconnected, you can recover the volume by reconnecting the drives.

Selecting the notification icon for Action Center displays the related notifications. If there is a problem with storage spaces, Action Center updates the related notification panel in the desktop notification area with a message stating "Check Storage Spaces for issues." To open Server Manager, select the notification icon, and then select the link provided. In Server Manager, you'll need to select the File And Storage Services node, and then select Storage Pools to get the relevant error and warning icons.

To view errors and warnings for storage pools, right-click the storage pool with the error or warning icon, and then select Properties. In the Properties dialog box, select Health in the left pane to display the health status and operational status in the main pane. For example, you might find that the health status is listed as Warning and the operation status is listed as Degraded. Degraded is a status you'll get when there is a loss of redundancy.

To view errors and warnings for virtual disks and their associated physical disks, right-click the virtual disk with the error or warning icon, and then select Properties. In the Properties dialog box, select Health in the left pane to display the health status and operational status in the main pane. Note the storage layout and the physical disks in use as well. If there is a problem with a physical disk, such as a loss of communication, this status will be displayed. You'll get a Loss of Communication status when a physical disk is missing, failed, or disconnected.

When storage spaces use external drives, a missing drive might be a common problem you encounter. In this case, users can continue to work and redundancy will be restored when you reconnect the drive. On the other hand, if a drive failed, you'll need to complete the following steps to restore redundancy:

1. Physically remove the failed drive. If the drive is connected internally, you'll need to shut down and unplug the computer before you can remove the drive; otherwise, simply disconnect an externally connected drive.

2. Physically add or connect a replacement drive. Next, add the drive to the storage space by doing the following:

   On the Storage Spaces panel, right-click the storage space you want to configure, and then select Add Physical Drive.

   In the Add Physical Disk dialog box, select the drive that should be allocated to the storage pool.

   When you select OK, Windows Server will prepare the drive and allocate it to the storage pool.

3. At this point, the failed drive should be listed as "Retired." Remove the failed drive from the storage space by selecting the related Remove Disk option, and then confirm that you want to remove the drive by selecting Yes when prompted.

Windows Server restores redundancy by copying data as necessary to the new disk. During this process, the status of the storage space normally is listed as "Repairing." You'll also see a value depicting how much of the repair task is completed. When this value reaches 100 percent, the repair is complete.

Chapter 7. Using RAID

Although Storage Spaces are preferred for protecting critical data volumes, Windows Server 2016 continues to support traditional software-based RAID for system volumes and other volumes. You can use RAID technology to span volumes and add fault tolerance. With RAID, you increase data integrity and availability by creating redundant copies of the data. You can also use RAID to improve your disks' performance.

Different implementations of RAID technology are available, and these implementations are described in terms of levels. Each RAID level offers different features. Windows Server 2016 supports RAID levels 0, 1, and 5:

- **RAID 0 (Disk striping)**   Two or more volumes, each on a separate drive, are configured as a striped set. Data is broken into blocks, called *stripes*, and then written sequentially to all drives in the striped set.
- **RAID 1 (Disk mirroring)**   Two volumes on two drives are configured identically. Data is written to both drives. If one drive fails, no data loss occurs because the other drive contains the data. (This level doesn't include disk striping.)
- **RAID 5 (Disk striping with parity)**   Uses three or more volumes, each on a separate drive, to create a striped set with parity error checking. In the case of failure, data can be recovered.

You can use RAID-0 to improve the performance of your drives, and you use RAID-1 and RAID-5 to provide fault tolerance for data. In addition to redundancy, RAID 1 offers better write performance than disk striping with parity. RAID 5 offers fault tolerance with less overhead than mirroring and better read performance than disk mirroring.

Implementing RAID

Windows Server 2016 supports disk mirroring, disk striping, and disk striping with parity. Implementing these RAID techniques is discussed in the sections that follow.

The most common RAID levels in use on servers running Windows Server 2016 are level 1 (disk mirroring), and level 5 (disk striping with parity). With respect to upfront costs, disk mirroring is the least expensive way to increase data protection with redundancy. Here, you use two identically sized volumes on two different drives to create a redundant data set. If one of the drives fails, you can still obtain the data from the other drive.

On the other hand, disk striping with parity requires more disks—a minimum of three—but offers fault tolerance with less overhead than disk mirroring. If any of the drives fail, you can recover the data by combining blocks of data on the remaining disks with a parity record. Parity is a method of error checking that uses an exclusive OR operation to create a checksum for each block of data written to the disk. This checksum is used to recover data in case of failure.

> **REAL WORLD**   Although it's true that the upfront costs for mirroring should be less than the upfront costs for disk striping with parity, the actual cost per gigabyte might be higher with disk mirroring. With disk mirroring, you have an overhead of 50 percent. For example, if you mirror two 750-gigabyte (GB) drives (a total storage space of 1500 GB), the usable space is only 750 GB. With disk striping with parity, on the other hand, you have an overhead of around 33 percent. For example, if you create a RAID-5 set by using three 500-GB drives (a total storage space of 1500 GB), the usable space (with one-third lost for overhead) is 1000 GB.

Implementing RAID-0: Disk Striping

RAID level 0 is disk striping. With disk striping, two or more volumes—each on a separate drive—are configured as a striped set. Data written to the striped set is broken into blocks called *stripes*. These stripes are written sequentially to all drives in the striped set. You can place volumes for a striped set on up to 32 drives, but in most circumstances sets with 2 to 5 volumes offer the best performance improvements. Beyond this, the performance improvement decreases significantly.

The major advantage of disk striping is speed. Data can be accessed on multiple disks by using multiple drive heads, which improves performance considerably. However, this performance boost comes with a price tag. As with volume sets, if any hard disk drive in the striped set fails, the striped set can no longer be used, which essentially means that all data in the striped set is lost. You need to re-create the striped set and restore the data from backups.

> **CAUTION**   The boot and system volumes shouldn't be part of a striped set. Don't use disk striping with these volumes.

When you create striped sets, you should use volumes that are approximately the same size. Disk Management bases the overall size of the striped set on the smallest volume size. Specifically, the maximum size of the striped set is a multiple of the smallest volume size. For example, if you want to create a three-volume striped set but the smallest volume is 20 GB, the maximum size for the striped set is 60 GB even if the other two values are 2-TB each.

You can maximize performance of the striped set in a couple of ways:

- Use disks that are on separate disk controllers. This allows the system to simultaneously access the drives.
- Don't use the disks containing the striped set for other purposes. This allows the disk to dedicate its time to the striped set.

You can create a striped set by following these steps:

1. In Disk Management's Graphical View, right-click an area marked Unallocated on a dynamic disk, and then click New Striped Volume. This starts the New Striped Volume Wizard. Read the Welcome page, and then click Next.

2. Select the disks that you want to be part of the striped set, and then size the volume segments on those disks. You need at least two dynamic disks to create a striped volume.

3. Available disks are shown in the Available list. If necessary, select a disk in this list, and then click Add to add the disk to the Selected list. If you make a mistake, you can remove disks from the Selected list by selecting the disk, and then clicking Remove.

> **CAUTION** The disk wizards in Windows Server 2016 show both basic and dynamic disks with available disk space. If you add space from a basic disk, the wizard converts the disk to a dynamic disk before creating the volume set. Before clicking Yes to continue, be sure you really want to do this because it can affect how the disk is used by the operating system.

4. Select a disk in the Selected list, and then specify the size of the volume on the disk in the Select The Amount Of Space In MB box. The Maximum Available Space In MB box shows you the largest area of free space available on the disk. The Total Volume Size In Megabytes box shows you the total disk space selected for use with the volume. Click Next.

> **TIP** Although you can size a volume set any way you want, consider how you'll use volume sets on the system. Simple and spanned volumes aren't fault tolerant; rather than creating one monstrous volume with all the available free

space, you might want to create several smaller volumes to help ensure that losing one volume doesn't mean losing all your data.

5. Specify whether you want to assign a drive letter or path to the volume, and then click Next. You use the available options as follows:

- **Assign The Following Drive Letter**   To assign a drive letter, choose this option, and then select an available drive letter in the list provided.
- **Mount In The Following Empty NTFS Folder**   To assign a drive path, choose this option, and then type the path to an existing folder on an NTFS drive, or click Browse to search for or create a folder.
- **Do Not Assign A Drive Letter Or Drive Path**   To create the volume without assigning a drive letter or path, choose this option. You can assign a drive letter or path later if necessary.

6. Specify whether the volume should be formatted. If you elect to format the volume, set the following formatting options:

- **File System**   Specifies the file system type, such as NTFS or ReFS.
- **Allocation Unit Size**   Specifies the cluster size for the file system. This is the basic unit in which disk space is allocated. The default allocation unit size is based on the volume's size and is set dynamically prior to formatting. Although you can't change the default size if you select ReFS, you can set the allocation unit size to a specific value with other formats. If you use a lot of small files, you might want to use a smaller cluster size, such as 512 or 1024 bytes. With these settings, small files use less disk space.
- **Volume Label**   Specifies a text label for the partition. This label is the partition's volume name.
- **Perform A Quick Format**   Tells Windows to format without checking the partition for errors. With large partitions, this option can save you a few minutes. However, it's more prudent to check for errors, which allows Disk Management to mark bad sectors on the disk and lock them out.

7. Click Next, and then click Finish.

After you create a striped volume, you can use the volume as you would any other volume. You can't extend a striped set after it's created; therefore, you should carefully consider the setup before you implement it.

Implementing RAID-1: Disk Mirroring

RAID level 1 is disk mirroring. With disk mirroring, you use identically sized volumes on two different drives to create a redundant data set. The drives are written with identical sets of information, and if one of the drives fails, you can still obtain the data from the other drive.

Disk mirroring offers about the same fault tolerance as disk striping with parity. Because mirrored disks don't need to write parity information, they can offer better write performance in most circumstances. However, disk striping with parity usually offers better read performance because read operations are spread over multiple drives.

The major drawback to disk mirroring is that it effectively cuts the amount of storage space in half. For example, to mirror a 500-GB drive, you need another 500-GB drive. That means you use 1000 GB of space to store 500 GB of information.

> **TIP** If possible, you should mirror boot and system volumes. Mirroring these volumes ensures that you are able to boot the server in case of a single drive failure.

As with disk striping, you'll often want the mirrored disks to be on separate disk controllers to provide increased protection against failure of the disk controller. If one of the disk controllers fails, the disk on the other controller is still available. Technically, when you use two separate disk controllers to duplicate data, you're using a technique known as *disk duplexing*. The figure that follows shows difference between the two techniques. Where disk mirroring typically uses a single drive controller, disk duplexing uses two drive controllers; otherwise, the two techniques are essentially the same.

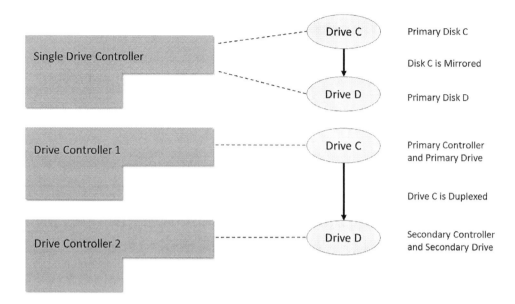

If one of the mirrored drives in a set fails, disk operations can continue. Here, when users read and write data, the data is written to the remaining disk. You need to break the mirror before you can fix it. To learn how, see "Managing RAID and Recovering From Failures" later in this chapter.

Creating a Mirror Set in Disk Management

You create a mirror set by following these steps:

1. In Disk Management's Graphical View, right-click an area marked Unallocated on a dynamic disk, and then click New Mirrored Volume. This starts the New Mirrored Volume Wizard. Read the Welcome page, and then click Next.

2. Create the volume as described in "Implementing RAID-0: Disk Striping" earlier in this chapter. The key difference when creating the mirror set is that you must create two identically sized volumes, and these volumes must be on separate dynamic drives. You won't be able to continue past the Select Disks window until you select the two disks with which you want to work.

Like other RAID techniques, mirroring is transparent to users. Users see the mirrored set as a single drive they can access and use like any other drive.

> **NOTE** The status of a normal mirror is Healthy. During the creation of a mirror, you'll get a status of Resynching, which tells you that Disk Management is creating the mirror.

Mirroring an Existing Volume

Rather than create a new mirrored volume, you can use an existing volume to create a mirrored set. To do this, the volume you want to mirror must be a simple volume, and you must have an area of unallocated space on a second drive of equal or larger size than the existing volume.

In Disk Management, you mirror an existing volume by following these steps:

1. Right-click the simple volume you want to mirror, and then click Add Mirror. This displays the Add Mirror dialog box.
2. In the Disks list, select a location for the mirror, and then click Add Mirror. Windows Server 2016 begins the mirror creation process. In Disk Management, you'll get a status of Resynching on both volumes. The disk on which the mirrored volume is being created has a warning icon.

Implementing RAID-5: Disk Striping with Parity

RAID level 5 is disk striping with parity. With this technique, you need a minimum of three hard disk drives to set up fault tolerance. Disk Management sizes the volumes on these drives identically.

RAID-5 distributes data and parity data sequentially across the disks in the array. Fault tolerance ensures that the failure of a single drive won't bring down the entire drive set. Instead, the set continues to function with disk operations directed at the remaining volumes in the set.

To allow for fault tolerance, RAID-5 writes parity checksums with the blocks of data. If any of the drives in the striped set fails, you can use the parity information to recover the data. (This process, called *regenerating the striped set*, is covered in "Managing RAID and Recovering From Failures" later in the chapter.) If two disks fail, however, the parity information isn't sufficient to recover the data, and you need to rebuild the striped set from backup.

Creating a Striped Set with Parity in Disk Management

In Disk Management, you can create a striped set with parity by following these steps:

1. In Disk Management's Graphical View, right-click an area marked Unallocated on a dynamic disk, and then click New RAID-5 Volume. This starts the New RAID-5 Volume Wizard. Read the Welcome page, and then click Next.

2. Create the volume as described previously in "Implementing RAID-0: Disk Striping." The key difference when creating a striped set with parity is that you must select free space on three separate dynamic drives.

After you create a striped set with parity (RAID-5), users can use the set just like they would a normal drive. Keep in mind that you can't extend a striped set with parity after you create it; therefore, you should carefully consider the setup before you implement it.

Managing RAID and Recovering From Failures

Managing mirrored drives and striped sets is somewhat different from managing other drive volumes, especially when it comes to recovering from failure. The techniques you use to manage RAID arrays and to recover from failure are covered in this section.

Breaking a Mirrored Set

You might want to break a mirror for two reasons:

- If one of the mirrored drives in a set fails, disk operations can continue. When users read and write data, these operations use the remaining disk. At some point, however, you need to fix the mirror, and to do this you must first break the mirror, replace the failed drive, and then reestablish the mirror.
- If you no longer want to mirror your drives, you might also want to break a mirror. This allows you to use the disk space for other purposes.

> **BEST PRACTICES**   Although breaking a mirror doesn't delete the data in the set, you should always back up the data before you perform this procedure to ensure that if you have problems, you can recover your data.

In Disk Management, you can break a mirrored set by following these steps:

1. Right-click one of the volumes in the mirrored set, and then click Break Mirrored Volume.

2. Confirm that you want to break the mirror by clicking Yes. If the volume is in use, you'll get another warning dialog box. Confirm that it's okay to continue by clicking Yes.

Windows Server 2016 breaks the mirror, creating two independent volumes.

Resynchronizing and Repairing a Mirrored Set

Windows Server 2016 automatically synchronizes mirrored volumes on dynamic drives; however, data on mirrored drives can become out of sync. For example, if one of the drives goes offline, data is written only to the drive that's online.

You can resynchronize and repair mirrored sets, but you must rebuild the set by using disks with the same partition style—either master boot record (MBR) or GUID partition table (GPT). You need to get both drives in the mirrored set online. The mirrored set's status should read Failed Redundancy. The corrective action you take depends on the failed volume's status:

* If the status is Missing or Offline, be sure that the drive has power and is connected properly. Then start Disk Management, right-click the failed volume, and click Reactivate Volume. The drive status should change to Regenerating and then to Healthy. If the volume doesn't return to the Healthy status, right-click the volume, and then click Resynchronize Mirror.
* If the status is Online (Errors), right-click the failed volume, and then click Reactivate Volume. The drive status should change to Regenerating and then to Healthy. If the volume doesn't return to the Healthy status, right-click the volume, and then click Resynchronize Mirror.
* If one of the drives shows a status of Unreadable, you might need to rescan the drives on the system by choosing Rescan Disks from Disk Management's Action menu. If the drive status doesn't change, you might need to reboot the computer.
* If one of the drives still won't come back online, right-click the failed volume, and then click Remove Mirror. Next, right-click the remaining volume in the original mirror, and then click Add Mirror. You now need to mirror the volume on an unallocated area of free space. If you don't have free space, you need to create space by deleting other volumes or replacing the failed drive.

Repairing a Mirrored System Volume to Enable Boot

The failure of a mirrored drive might prevent your system from starting Typically, this happens when you're mirroring the system or boot volume, or both, and the primary mirror drive has failed. In previous versions of the Windows operating system, you often had to go through several procedures to get the system back up and running.

With Windows Server 2016, the failure of a primary mirror is usually much easier to resolve.

When you mirror a system volume, the operating system should add an entry to the system's boot manager that allows you to start to the secondary mirror. Resolving a primary mirror failure is much easier with this entry in the boot manager file than without it because all you need to do is select the entry to start to the secondary mirror. If you mirror the boot volume and a secondary mirror entry is not created for you, you can modify the boot entries in the boot manager to create one by using the BCD Editor (Bcdedit.exe).

If a system fails to start to the primary system volume, restart the system and select the Windows Server 2016—Secondary Plex option for the operating system you want to start. The system should start normally. After you successfully start the system to the secondary drive, you can schedule the maintenance necessary to rebuild the mirror as described in the following steps:

1. Shut down the system, and replace the failed volume or add a hard disk drive. Then restart the system.

2. Break the mirror set, and then re-create the mirror on the drive you replaced, which is usually drive 0. Right-click the remaining volume that was part of the original mirror, and then click Add Mirror. Next, follow the technique in "Mirroring an Existing Volume" earlier in the chapter.

3. If you want the primary mirror to be on the drive you added or replaced, use Disk Management to break the mirror again. Be sure that the primary drive in the original mirror set has the drive letter that was previously assigned to the complete mirror. If it doesn't, assign the appropriate drive letter.

4. Right-click the original system volume, and then click Add Mirror. Now re-create the mirror.

5. Check the boot entries in the boot manager and use the BCD Editor to ensure that the original system volume is used during startup.

Removing a Mirrored Set

Using Disk Management, you can remove one of the volumes from a mirrored set. When you do this, all data on the removed mirror is deleted and the space it used is marked as Unallocated.

To remove a mirror, follow these steps:

1. In Disk Management, right-click one of the volumes in the mirrored set, and then click Remove Mirror to display the Remove Mirror dialog box.
2. In the Remove Mirror dialog box, select the disk from which to remove the mirror.
3. Confirm the action when prompted. All data on the removed mirror is deleted.

Repairing a Striped Set Without Parity

A striped set without parity doesn't have fault tolerance. If a drive that's part of a striped set fails, the entire striped set is unusable. Before you try to restore the striped set, you should repair or replace the failed drive. Then you need to re-create the striped set and recover the data contained on the striped set from backup.

Regenerating a Striped Set with Parity

With RAID-5, you can recover the striped set with parity if a single drive fails. You'll know that a striped set with parity drive has failed because the set's status changes to Failed Redundancy and the individual volume's status changes to Missing, Offline, or Online (Errors).

You can repair RAID-5 disks, but you must rebuild the set by using disks with the same partition style—either MBR or GPT. You need to get all drives in the RAID-5 set online. The set's status should read Failed Redundancy. The corrective action you take depends on the failed volume's status:

- If the status is Missing or Offline, make sure the drive has power and is connected properly. Then start Disk Management, right-click the failed volume, and select Reactivate Volume. The drive's status should change to Regenerating and then to Healthy. If the drive's status doesn't return to Healthy, right-click the volume and select Regenerate Parity.
- If the status is Online (Errors), right-click the failed volume, and select Reactivate Volume. The drive's status should change to Regenerating and then to Healthy. If the drive's status doesn't return to Healthy, right-click the volume and select Regenerate Parity.
- If one of the drives shows as Unreadable, you might need to rescan the drives on the system by choosing Rescan Disks from Disk Management's Action menu. If the drive status doesn't change, you might need to restart the computer.

- If one of the drives still won't come back online, you need to repair the failed region of the RAID-5 set. Right-click the failed volume, and then select Remove Volume. You now need to select an unallocated space on a separate dynamic disk for the RAID-5 set. This space must be at least as large as the region to repair, and it can't be on a drive that the RAID-5 set is already using. If you don't have enough space, the Repair Volume command is unavailable, and you need to free space by deleting other volumes or by replacing the failed drive.

> **BEST PRACTICES**   If possible, you should back up the data before you perform this procedure to ensure that if you have problems, you can recover your data.

Chapter 8. Maintaining Partitions and Drives

Disk Management provides many features to manage existing partitions and drives. Use these options to assign drive letters, delete partitions, set the active partition, and more. In addition, Windows Server 2016 provides other utilities to carry out common tasks such as converting a volume to NTFS, checking a drive for errors, and cleaning up unused disk space. These options and tools are discussed in this chapter.

Drive Maintenance Essentials

As part of routine maintenance, you may need to assign drive letters and paths or perform other tasks, such as changing drive labels. You may also need to resize or delete partitions.

Assigning Drive Letters and Paths

You can assign drives one drive letter and one or more drive paths, provided that the drive paths are mounted on NTFS drives. Drives don't have to be assigned a drive letter or path. A drive with no designators is considered to be unmounted, and you can mount it by assigning a drive letter or path at a later date. You need to unmount a drive before moving it to another computer.

To manage drive letters and paths, right-click the drive you want to configure in Disk Management, and then click Change Drive Letter And Paths. You can now do the following:

- **Add a drive path**   Click Add, select Mount In The Following Empty NTFS Folder, and then type the path to an existing folder, or click Browse to search for or create a folder.
- **Remove a drive path**   Select the drive path to remove, click Remove, and then click Yes.
- **Assign a drive letter**   Click Add, select Assign The Following Drive Letter, and then choose an available letter to assign to the drive.
- **Change the drive letter**   Select the current drive letter, and then click Change. Select Assign The Following Drive Letter, and then choose a different letter to assign to the drive.
- **Remove a drive letter**   Select the current drive letter, click Remove, and then click Yes.

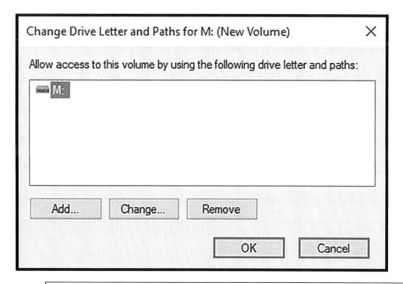

Changing or Deleting the Volume Label

The volume label is a text descriptor for a drive. With FAT, the volume label can be up to 11 characters and can include spaces. With NTFS and ReFS, the volume label can be up to 32 characters. Additionally, although FAT doesn't allow you to use some special characters—including * / \ [ ] : ; | = , . + " ? < >—NTFS and ReFS do allow you to use these special characters.

Because the volume label is displayed when the drive is accessed in various Windows Server 2016 utilities, including File Explorer, it can provide information about a drive's contents. You can change or delete a volume label by using Disk Management or File Explorer.

Using Disk Management, you can change or delete a label by following these steps:

1. Right-click the partition, and then click Properties.
2. On the General tab of the Properties dialog box, enter a new label for the volume in the Label text box or delete the existing label. Click OK.

Using File Explorer, you can change or delete a label by following these steps:

1. Right-click the drive icon, and then click Properties.

2. On the General tab of the Properties dialog box, enter a new label for the volume in the Label text box or delete the existing label. Click OK.

Resizing Partitions and Volumes

With Windows Server 2016, you can extend and shrink both basic and dynamic disks using Disk Management, DiskPart, or PowerShell. In extending a volume, you convert areas of unallocated space and add them to the existing volume. For spanned volumes on dynamic disks, the space can come from any available dynamic disk, not only from those on which the volume was originally created. Thus, you can combine areas of free space on multiple dynamic disks and use those areas to increase the size of an existing volume.

> **CAUTION**   Before you try to extend a volume, be aware of several limitations. You cannot shrink or extend volumes that use traditional software RAID. Although you can extend simple and spanned volumes formatted with NTFS or ReFS, you can't extend striped volumes, volumes that aren't formatted, or volumes that are formatted with FAT. Additionally, you can't extend a system or boot volume, regardless of its configuration.

You can shrink a simple volume or a spanned volume by following these steps:

1. In Disk Management, right-click the volume you want to shrink, and then click Shrink Volume. This option is available only if the volume meets the previously discussed criteria.

2. In the box provided in the Shrink dialog box, enter the amount of space to shrink.

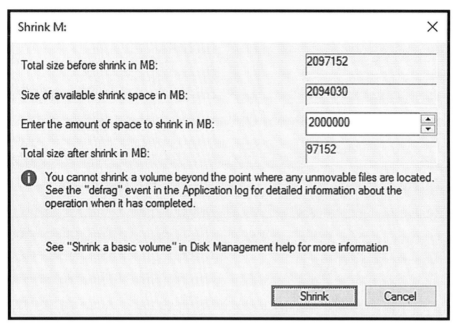

Shrink M:

Total size before shrink in MB:	2097152
Size of available shrink space in MB:	2094030
Enter the amount of space to shrink in MB:	2000000
Total size after shrink in MB:	97152

ⓘ You cannot shrink a volume beyond the point where any unmovable files are located. See the "defrag" event in the Application log for detailed information about the operation when it has completed.

See "Shrink a basic volume" in Disk Management help for more information

[Shrink] [Cancel]

The Shrink dialog box provides the following information:

* **Total Size Before Shrink In MB**   Lists the total capacity of the volume in megabytes. This is the formatted size of the volume.
* **Size Of Available Shrink Space In MB**   Lists the maximum amount by which the volume can be shrunk. This doesn't represent the total amount of free space on the volume; rather, it represents the amount of space that can be removed, not including any data reserved for the master file table, volume snapshots, page files, and temporary files.
* **Enter The Amount Of Space To Shrink In MB**   Lists the total amount of space that will be removed from the volume. The initial value defaults to the maximum amount of space that can be removed from the volume. For optimal drive performance, you'll want to ensure that the drive has at least 10 percent of free space after the shrink operation.
* **Total Size After Shrink In MB**   Lists what the total capacity of the volume will be (in megabytes) after the shrink. This is the new formatted size of the volume.

   3.   Click Shrink to shrink the volume.

You can extend a simple volume or a spanned volume by following these steps:

   1.   In Disk Management, right-click the volume you want to extend, and then click Extend Volume. This option is available only if the volume meets the previously discussed criteria and free space is available on one or more of the system's dynamic disks.

2. In the Extend Volume Wizard, read the introductory message, and then click Next.

3. On the Select Disks page, select the disk or disks from which you want to allocate free space. Any disks currently being used by the volume are automatically selected. By default, all remaining free space on those disks is selected for use.

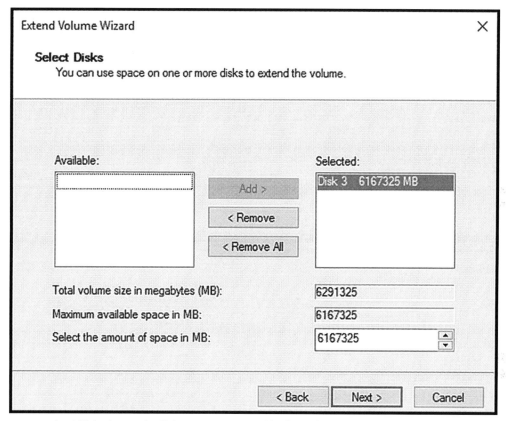

4. With dynamic disks, you can specify the additional space you want to use on other disks by performing the following tasks:

- Click the disk, and then click Add to add the disk to the Selected list.
- Select each disk in the Selected list, and then, in the Select The Amount Of Space In MB list, specify the amount of unallocated space to use on the selected disk.

5. Click Next, confirm your options, and then click Finish.

Deleting Partitions and Drives

To change the configuration of a drive that's fully allocated, you might need to delete existing partitions and logical drives. Deleting a partition or a drive removes the associated file system, and all data in the file system is lost. Before you delete a partition or a drive, you should back up any files and directories that the partition or drive contains.

> **NOTE** To protect the integrity of the system, you can't delete the system or boot partition. However, Windows Server 2016 does let you delete the active partition or volume if it is not designated as boot or system. Always check to be sure that the partition or volume you are deleting doesn't contain important data or files.

You can delete a primary partition, volume, or logical drive by following these steps:

1. In Disk Management, right-click the partition, volume, or drive you want to delete, and then click Explore. Using File Explorer, move all the data to another volume or verify an existing backup to ensure that the data was properly saved.

2. In Disk Management, right-click the partition, volume, or drive again, and then click the related Delete option.

3. Confirm that you want to delete the selected item by clicking Yes.

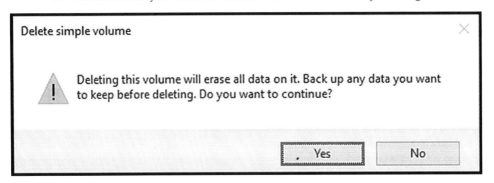

The steps for deleting an extended partition differ slightly from those for deleting a primary partition or a logical drive. To delete an extended partition, follow these steps:

1. Delete all the logical drives on the partition following the steps listed in the previous procedure.

2. Select the extended partition area itself and delete it.

Converting a Volume to NTFS

Windows Server 2016 provides a utility for converting FAT volumes to NTFS. This utility, Convert (Convert.exe), is located in the %SystemRoot% folder. When you convert a volume by using this tool, the file and directory structure is preserved and no data is lost. Keep in mind, however, that Windows Server 2016 doesn't provide a utility for converting NTFS to FAT. The only way to go from NTFS to FAT is to delete the partition by following the steps listed in the previous section, and then re-create the partition as a FAT volume.

Understanding the Convert Utility Syntax

Convert is run at the command prompt. If you want to convert a drive, use the following syntax:

```
convert volume /FS:NTFS
```

Here *volume* is the drive letter followed by a colon, drive path, or volume name. For example, if you want to convert the D drive to NTFS, use the following command:

```
convert D: /FS:NTFS
```

If the volume has a label, you are prompted to enter the volume label for the drive, but you are not prompted if the disk doesn't have a label.

The complete syntax for Convert is shown here:

```
convert volume /FS:NTFS [/V] [/X] [/CvtArea:filename] [/NoSecurity]
```

The options and switches for Convert are used as follows:

- **volume**   Sets the volume with which to work, such as G:.
- ***/FS:NTFS***   Converts to NTFS
- ***/V***   Sets verbose mode
- ***/X***   Forces the volume to dismount before the conversion (if necessary)
- ***/CvtArea: filename***   Sets the name of a contiguous file in the root directory to be a placeholder for NTFS system files
- ***/NoSecurity***   Removes all security attributes, and makes all files and directories accessible to the group Everyone

The following sample statement uses Convert:

```
convert C: /FS:NTFS /V
```

Using the Convert Utility

Before you use the Convert utility, determine whether the partition is being used as the active boot partition or a system partition containing the operating system. You can convert the active boot partition to NTFS. Doing so requires that the system gain exclusive access to this partition, which can be obtained only during startup. Thus, if you try to convert the active boot partition to NTFS, Windows Server 2016 displays a prompt asking if you want to schedule the drive to be converted the next time the system starts. If you click Yes, you can restart the system to begin the conversion process.

> **TIP**   Often, you will need to restart a system several times to completely convert the active boot partition. Don't panic. Let the system proceed with the conversion.

Before the Convert utility actually converts a drive to NTFS, the utility checks whether the drive has enough free space to perform the conversion. Generally, Convert needs a block of free space that's roughly equal to 25 percent of the total space used on the drive. For example, if the drive stores 200 GB of data, Convert needs about 50 GB of free space. If the drive doesn't have enough free space, Convert aborts and tells you that you need to free up some space. On the other hand, if the drive has enough free space, Convert initiates the conversion. Be patient. The conversion process takes several minutes (longer for large drives). Don't access files or applications on the drive while the conversion is in progress.

You can use the */CvtArea* option to improve performance on the volume so that space for the master file table (MFT) is reserved. This option helps to prevent fragmentation of the MFT. How? Over time, the MFT might grow larger than the space allocated to it. The operating system must then expand the MFT into other areas of the disk. Although the Optimize Drives utility can defragment the MFT, it cannot move the first section of the MFT, and it is very unlikely that there will be space after the MFT because this will be filled by file data.

To help prevent fragmentation in some cases, you might want to reserve more space than the default (12.5 percent of the partition or volume size). For example, you might want to increase the MFT size if the volume will have many small or average-size files rather than a few large files. To specify the amount of space to reserve, you can use FSUtil to create a placeholder file equal in size to that of the MFT you want to create. You can then convert the volume to NTFS and specify the name of the placeholder file to use with the /CvtArea option.

In the following example, you use FSUtil to create a 1.5-GB (1,500,000,000 bytes) placeholder file named Temp.txt:

```
fsutil file createnew c:\temp.txt 1500000000
```

To use this placeholder file for the MFT when converting drive C to NTFS, you would then type the following command:

```
convert c: /fs:ntfs /cvtarea:temp.txt
```

Notice that the placeholder file is created on the partition or volume that is being converted. During the conversion process, the file is overwritten with NTFS metadata and any unused space in the file is reserved for future use by the MFT.

Repairing Disks

Windows Server 2016 includes feature enhancements that reduce the amount of manual maintenance you must perform on disk drives. The following enhancements have the most impact on the way you work with disks:

- Transactional NTFS
- Self-healing NTFS

Transactional NTFS allows file operations on an NTFS volume to be performed transactionally, which means programs can use a transaction to group sets of file and registry operations so that all of them succeed or none of them succeed. While a transaction is active, changes are not visible outside the transaction. Changes are committed and written fully to disk only when a transaction is completed successfully. If a transaction fails or is incomplete, the program rolls back the transactional work to restore the file system to the state it was in prior to the transaction.

REAL WORLD Resilient File System (ReFS) takes the transactional and self-healing features of NTFS a few steps further. With ReFS, several background processes are used to maintain disk integrity automatically. The scrubber process checks the disk for inconsistencies and errors. If any are found, a repair process localizes the problems and performs automatic online correction. In the rare case that a physical drive has bad sectors that are causing the problem, ReFS uses a salvage process to mark the bad sectors and remove them from the file system—and all while the volume is online.

Transactions that span multiple volumes are coordinated by the Kernel Transaction Manager (KTM). The KTM supports independent recovery of volumes if a transaction fails. The local resource manager for a volume maintains a separate transaction log and is responsible for maintaining threads for transactions separate from threads that perform the file work.

Traditionally, you had to use the Check Disk tool to fix errors and inconsistencies in NTFS volumes on a disk. Because this process can disrupt the availability of Windows systems, Windows Server 2016 uses self-healing NTFS to protect file systems without requiring you to use separate maintenance tools to fix problems. Because much of the self-healing process is enabled and performed automatically, you might need to perform volume maintenance manually only when you are notified by the operating system that a problem cannot be corrected automatically. If such an error occurs, Windows Server 2016 notifies you about the problem and provides possible solutions.

Self-healing NTFS has many advantages over Check Disk, including the following:

* Check Disk must have exclusive access to volumes, which means system and boot volumes can be checked only when the operating system starts up. On the other hand, with self-healing NTFS, the file system is always available and does not need to be corrected offline (in most cases).
* Self-healing NTFS attempts to preserve as much data as possible if corruption occurs and reduces failed file system mounting that previously could occur if a volume was known to have errors or inconsistencies. During restart, self-healing NTFS repairs the volume immediately so that it can be mounted.
* Self-healing NTFS reports changes made to the volume during repair through existing Chkdsk.exe mechanisms, directory notifications, and update sequence number (USN) journal entries. This feature also allows authorized users and administrators to monitor repair operations through Verification, Waiting For Repair Completion, and Progress Status messages.

- Self-healing NTFS can recover a volume if the boot sector is readable but does not identify an NTFS volume. In this case, you must run an offline tool that repairs the boot sector, and then allow self-healing NTFS to initiate recovery.

Although self-healing NTFS is a terrific enhancement, at times you might want to (or might have to) manually check the integrity of a disk. In these cases, you can use Check Disk (Chkdsk.exe) to check for and (optionally) repair problems found on FAT, FAT32, exFAT, and NTFS volumes.

> **IMPORTANT** Because ReFS is self-correcting, you do not need to use Check Disk to check ReFS volumes for errors. However, it's important to point out that ReFS as originally released did not efficiently correct corruption on parity spaces. With Windows Server 2016, this deficiency has been corrected. ReFS automatically corrects corruption on parity spaces when integrity streams are enabled to detect corrupt data. When corruption is detected, ReFS examines the data copies that the parity spaces contain and then uses the correct version of the data to correct the problem. As ReFS now supports concurrent I/O requests to the same file, the performance of integrity streams also has been improved.

Although Check Disk can check for and correct many types of errors, the utility primarily looks for inconsistencies in the file system and its related metadata. One of the ways Check Disk locates errors is by comparing the volume bitmap to the disk sectors assigned to files in the file system. Beyond this, the usefulness of Check Disk is rather limited. For example, Check Disk can't repair corrupted data within files that appear to be structurally intact.

As part of automated maintenance, Windows Server 2016 performs a proactive scan of NTFS volumes. As with other automated maintenance, Windows scans disks using Check Disk at 2:00 A.M. if the computer is running on AC power and the operating system is idle. Otherwise, Windows scans disks the next time the computer is running on AC power and the operating system is idle. Although automated maintenance triggers the disk scan, the process of calling and managing Check Disk is handled by a separate task. In Task Scheduler, you'll find the ProactiveScan task in the scheduler library under Microsoft\Windows\Chkdsk, and you can get detailed run details by reviewing the information provided on the task's History tab.

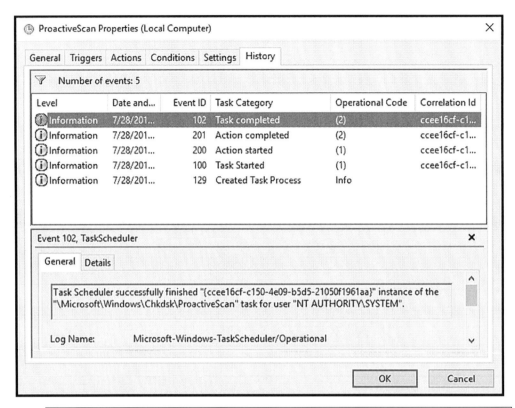

Level	Date and...	Event ID	Task Category	Operational Code	Correlation Id
Information	7/28/201...	102	Task completed	(2)	ccee16cf-c1...
Information	7/28/201...	201	Action completed	(2)	ccee16cf-c1...
Information	7/28/201...	200	Action started	(1)	ccee16cf-c1...
Information	7/28/201...	100	Task Started	(1)	ccee16cf-c1...
Information	7/28/201...	129	Created Task Process	Info	

> **REAL WORLD**   Automatic Maintenance is built on the Windows Diagnostics framework. By default, Windows periodically performs routine maintenance at 2:00 A.M. if the computer is running on AC power and the operating system is idle. Otherwise, maintenance will start the next time the computer is running on AC power and the operating system is idle. Because maintenance runs only when the operating system is idle, maintenance is allowed to run in the background for up to three days. This allows Windows to complete complex maintenance tasks automatically. Maintenance tasks include software updates, security scanning, system diagnostics, checking disks, and disk optimization. You can change the run time for automated maintenance by opening Action Center, expanding the Maintenance panel, selecting Change Maintenance Settings, and then selecting a new run schedule.

Checking Disks Manually

With Windows Server 2016, Check Disk performs enhanced scan and repair automatically, instead of using the legacy scan and repair available with earlier releases of Windows. Here, when you use Check Disk with NTFS volumes, Check Disk performs an online scan and analysis of the disk for errors. Check Disk writes information about any detected corruptions in the $corrupt system file. If the volume is in use, detected corruptions can be repaired by taking the volume offline temporarily; however, unmounting the volume for the repair invalidates all open file handles. With the boot/system volume, the repairs are performed the next time you start the computer.

Storing the corruption information and then repairing the volume while it is dismounted enables Windows to rapidly repair volumes. You can also keep using the disk while a scan is being performed. Typically, offline repair takes only a few seconds, compared to what otherwise would have been hours for very large volumes using the legacy scan and repair technique.

> **NOTE**   FAT, FAT32, and exFAT do not support the enhanced features. When you use Check Disk with FAT, FAT32, or exFAT, Windows Server 2016 uses the legacy scan and repair process. This means the scan and repair process typically requires taking the volume offline and preventing it from being used. You can't use Check Disk with ReFS.

You can run Check Disk from the command prompt or within other utilities. At a command prompt, you can test the integrity of the E drive by entering the following command:

```
chkdsk /scan E:
```

Check Disk then performs an analysis of the disk and returns a status message regarding any problems it encounters. Check Disk won't repair problems, however, unless you specify further options. To repair errors on drive E, use this command:

```
chkdsk /spotfix E:
```

Fixing the volume requires exclusive access to the volume. The way this works depends on the type of volume:

* For nonsystem volumes, you'll get a prompt asking whether you would like to force a dismount of the volume for the repair. In this case, you can enter **Y** to proceed or **N** to cancel the dismount. If you cancel the dismount, you'll get the prompt asking whether you would like to schedule the volume for the repair the next time the computer is started. In this case, you can enter **Y** to schedule the repair or **N** to cancel the repair.
* For system volumes, you'll get a prompt asking whether you would like to schedule the volume for the repair the next time the computer is started. In this case, you can enter **Y** to schedule the repair or **N** to cancel the repair.

You can't run Check Disk with both the *scan* and *spotfix* options because the scan and repair tasks are now independent of each other.

The complete syntax for Check Disk is as follows:

```
CHKDSK [volume[[path]filename]] [/F] [/V] [/R] [/X] [/I] [/C] [/B]
  [/L[:size]] [/scan] [/forceofflinefix] [/perf] [/spotfix]
  [/sdcleanup] [/offlinescanandfix]
```

The options and switches for Check Disk are used as follows:

* **volume**   Sets the volume with which to work.
* **[path]filename**   FAT only. It specifies files to check for fragmentation.
* **/B**   Reevaluates bad clusters on the volume (NTFS only; implies /R).
* **/C**   NTFS only. It skips the checking of cycles within the folder structure.
* **/F**   Fixes errors on the disk by using the offline (legacy) scan and fix behavior.
* **/I**   NTFS only. It performs a minimum check of index entries.
* **/L:size**   NTFS only. It changes the log file size.
* **/R**   Locates bad sectors, and recovers readable information (implies /F).
* **/V**   On FAT, it displays the full path and name of every file on the disk. On NTFS, it displays cleanup messages, if there are any.
* **/X**   Forces the volume to dismount first if necessary (implies /F).

For NTFS volumes, Check Disk supports these enhanced options:

* **/forceofflinefix**   Must be used with *scan*. It bypasses all online repair and queues errors for offline repair.
* **/offlinescanandfix**   Performs an offline scan and fix of the volume.
* **/perf**   Performs the scan as fast as possible by using more system resources.
* **/scan**   Performs an online scan of the volume (the default). Errors detected during the scan are added to the $corrupt system file.
* **/sdcleanup**   Cleans up unneeded security descriptor data. It implies /F (with legacy scan and repair).
* **/spotfix**   Allows certain types of errors to be repaired online (the default).

Running Check Disk Interactively

You can run Check Disk interactively by following these steps:

1. In File Explorer or Disk Management, right-click the drive, and then click Properties.

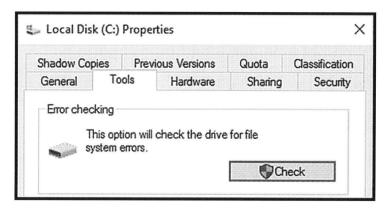

2. On the Tools tab of the Properties dialog box, click Check. This displays the Error Checking dialog box.

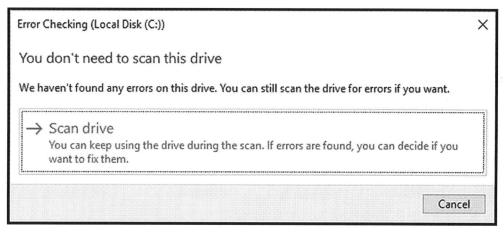

3. Click Scan Drive to start the scan. If no errors are found, Windows confirms this; otherwise,. if errors are found, you'll be prompted with additional options. As with checking disks at a prompt, the way this works depends on whether you are working with a system or nonsystem volume.

NOTE For FAT, FAT32, and exFAT volumes, Windows uses the legacy Check Disk. You click Scan And Repair Drive to start the scan. If the scan finds errors, you might need to restart the computer to repair them.

Analyzing and Optimizing Disks

Any time you add files to or remove files from a drive, the data on the drive can become fragmented. When a drive is fragmented, large files can't be written to a single continuous area on the disk. As a result, the operating system must write the file to several smaller areas on the disk, which means more time is spent reading the file from the disk. To reduce fragmentation, Windows Server 2016 can manually or automatically analyze and optimize disks by using the Optimize Drives utility.

With manual optimization, Optimize Drives performs an online analysis of volumes, and then reports the percentage of fragmentation. If defragmentation is needed, you can then elect to perform online defragmentation. System and boot volumes can be defragmented online as well, and Optimize Drives can be used with FAT, FAT32, exFAT, NTFS, and ReFS volumes.

You can manually analyze and optimize a disk by following these steps:

1. In File Explorer or Disk Management, right-click the drive, and then click Properties.

2. On the Tools tab, click Optimize. In the Optimize Drives dialog box, select a disk, and then click Analyze. Optimize Drives then analyzes the disk to determine whether it needs to be defragmented. If so, it recommends that you defragment at this point.

3. If a disk needs to be defragmented, select the disk, and then click Optimize.

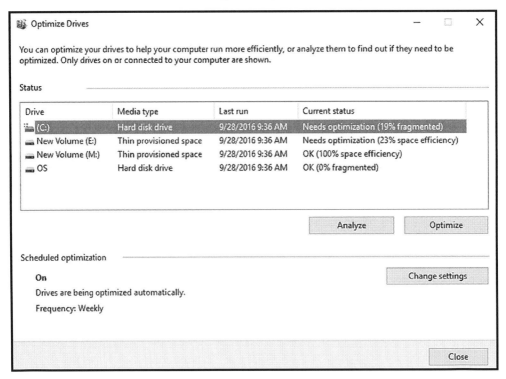

Automatic analysis and optimization of disks can occur while the disks are online, so long as the computer is on AC power and the operating system is running but otherwise idle. By default, disk optimization is a weekly task rather than a daily task—and there's a good reason for this. Normally, you need only to periodically optimize a server's disks, and optimization once a week is sufficient in most cases. Note, however, that although nonsystem disks can be rapidly analyzed and optimized, it can take significantly longer to optimize system disks online.

You can control the approximate start time for the analysis and optimization of disks by changing the automated maintenance start time. Windows Server also notifies you if three consecutive runs are missed. All internal drives and certain external drives are optimized automatically as part of the regular schedule, as are new drives you connect to the server.

> **NOTE** Windows Server 2016 automatically performs cyclic pickup defragmentation. With this feature, when a scheduled defragmentation pass is stopped and rerun, the computer automatically picks up where it left off or starts with the next unfinished volume in line to be defragmented.

You can configure and manage automated defragmentation by following these steps:

1. In Computer Management, select the Storage node and then the Disk Management node. Right-click a drive, and then click Properties.
2. On the Tools tab, click Optimize. This displays the Optimize Drives dialog box.
3. If you want to change how optimization works, click Change Settings. To cancel automated defragmentation, clear the Run On A Schedule check box. To enable automated defragmentation, select Run On A Schedule.

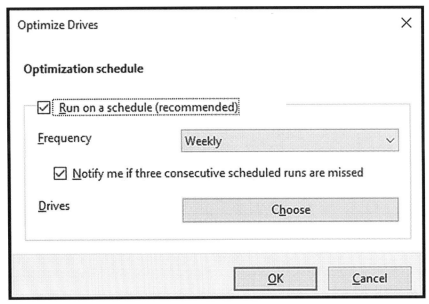

4. The default run frequency is set as shown. In the Frequency list, you can choose Daily, Weekly, or Monthly as the run schedule. If you don't want to be notified about missed runs, clear the Notify Me check box.

5. If you want to manage which disks are defragmented, click Choose, and then select the volumes to defragment. By default, all disks installed within or connected to the computer are defragmented, and any new disks are defragmented automatically as well. Select the check boxes for disks that should be defragmented automatically, and clear the check boxes for disks that should not be defragmented automatically. Click OK to save your settings.

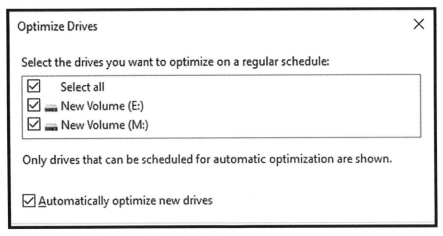

6. Click OK, and then click Close.

Chapter 9. Implementing File Sharing

The Server Message Block (SMB) protocol is the primary file sharing protocol used by computers running Microsoft Windows. When folders are shared over a network, an SMB client reads and writes to files and requests services from computers hosting SMB-shared folders. With SMB, Windows Server 2016 supports standard file sharing and public folder sharing. Standard file sharing enables remote users to access network resources such as files, folders, and drives. When you share a folder or a drive, you make all its files and subfolders available to a specified set of users. Because you don't need to move files from their current location, standard file sharing is also referred to as *in-place file sharing*.

You can enable standard file sharing on disks formatted with FAT, FAT32, exFAT, NTFS, or Resilient File System (ReFS). One set of permissions apply to disks formatted with exFAT, FAT, or FAT32. These permissions are called *share permissions*. Two sets of permissions apply to disks formatted with NTFS or ReFS: *NTFS permissions* (also referred to as *access permissions*) and *share permissions*. Having two sets of permissions enables you to determine precisely who has access to shared files and the level of access assigned. With either NTFS permissions or share permissions, you do not need to move the files you are sharing.

Working with SMB

SMB was designed to enable clients and servers to negotiate and then use the highest version supported by both the client attempting to connect an SMB share and the server hosting the share. At the time of this writing, the current version of SMB is version 3.11, which is supported by Windows 10 and Windows Server 2016. Thus, when a Windows 10 computer connects to an SMB share hosted on a server running Windows Server 2016, SMB 3.11 is the version used for the SMB session.

SMB Essentials

Standard (in-place) file sharing allows remote users to access files, folders, and drives over the network. When you share a folder or a drive, you make all its files and subfolders available to a specified set of users. Share permissions and access permissions together enable you to control who has access to shared files and the level of access assigned. You do not need to move the files you are sharing.

With standard file sharing, local users don't have automatic access to any data stored on a computer. You control local access to files and folders by using the security settings on the local disk. Windows Server 2016 adds layers of security through compound identities, claims-based access controls, and central access policies. With both Windows 10 and Windows Server 2016, you can assign claims-based access controls to file and folder resources on NTFS and ReFS volumes. Users are granted access to file and folder resources, either directly with access permissions and share permissions or indirectly with claims-based access controls and central access policies.

The earliest implementation of SMB was called CIFS, which was introduced with Windows NT 4.0, followed by SMB 1.0, which was used by all versions of Windows from Windows 2000 to Windows Server 2003 R2. In Windows Server 2016, support for CIFS and SMB 1.0 is an optional feature that must be enabled. Because CIFS and SMB 1.0 are outdated, perform poorly, and are less secure than their predecessors, SMB 1.0/CIFS File Sharing Support should not be enabled unless required.

You can enter **Get-SmbConnection** at an administrator PowerShell prompt to determine the version of SMB a client has negotiated with a file server. In the command output, the version is listed in the Dialect column, as shown in the following sample output:

```
ServerName   ShareName   UserName        Credential        Dialect   NumOpens
----------   ---------   --------        ----------        -------   --------
Server36     IPC$        TVPRESS\williams TVPRESS\williams  3.11       0
Server36     PrimaryData TVPRESS\williams TVPRESS\williams  3.11      14
```

SMB Encryption and Bandwidth Limits

Both Windows 10 and Windows Server 2016 support SMB 3.0. (They have an SMB 3.0 client.) SMB 3.0 makes it possible to encrypt data being transferred over the network. You can enable SMB encryption for shares configured on NTFS and ReFS volumes. SMB encryption works only when the computer requesting data from an SMB-based share (either a standard file share or a DFS share) and the server supplying the data support SMB 3.0.

If you add the SMB Bandwidth Limit feature to a server, you can use Windows PowerShell to define bandwidth limits for three categories of file transfers:

- **Default**   Standard file transfers
- **VirtualMachine**   File transfers related to virtual machines
- **LiveMigration**   File transfers related to live migration

The cmdlet you use to set limits is Set-SMBBandwidthLimit. The basic syntax is:

```
Set-SMBBandwidthLimit –Category Category –BytesPerSecond Limit
```

Where Category sets the type of transfers to limit and Limit sets the maximum number of bytes per second that the server can send for the specified traffic category. Add KB, MB or GB to define a limit in kilobytes, megabytes or gigabytes as shown in these examples:

```
Set-SMBBandwidthLimit –Category Default –BytesPerSecond 1 GB
Set-SMBBandwidthLimit –Category VirtualMachine –BytesPerSecond 100 MB
Set-SMBBandwidthLimit –Category LiveMigration –BytesPerSecond 900 KB
```

SMB Replication

Windows Server 2016 also supports server to server storage replication over SMB. Here, domain-joined servers, each with separate storage, synchronously or asynchronously replicate data to ensure critical data is always protected. The storage can be local SCSI/SATA, Just a Bunch of Disks (JBOD) SAS, iSCSI target or fibre channel SAN but must be available only to each of the servers with no shared access. Although both hard disk drives and solid state drives can be used for data drives, SSDs are recommended for log drives.

You enable replication by installing the Storage Replica feature, configuring storage and then establishing a replication partnership using Windows PowerShell. Storage on each server must be configured with two virtual disks: one for data and one for logs. The data disks and log disks must be identically sized and the underlying physical disks must have the same sector size.

The virtual disks can be created using Storage Spaces, either in a mirrored or parity configuration. They also can be created as volumes on disks protected with software or hardware RAID.

> **NOTE** As neither disk should contain system or boot files, you can't replicate the operating system volume or volumes containing page files or dump files. Before setting up a replication partnership, you can use Test-SRTopology to ensure your servers and environment meet all of the requirements.

The cmdlet you use to establish replication partnerships is New-SRPartnership. The basic syntax is:

```
New-SRPartnership -SourceComputerName ComputerName -SourceRGName RGName
-SourceVolumeName Drive -SourceLogVolumeName Drive -DestinationComputerName
ComputerName -DestinationRGName RGName -DestinationVolumeName Drive
-DestinationLogVolumeName Drive
```

Here, you specify the source and destination servers and assign each a replication group name while also specifying the source data volume, the source log volume, the destination data volume and the destination log volume, such as:

```
New-SRPartnership -SourceComputerName FileServer23 -SourceRGName SR01
-SourceVolumeName g: -SourceLogVolumeName h: -DestinationComputerName
FileServer87 -DestinationRGName SR02 -DestinationVolumeName s:
-DestinationLogVolumeName t:
```

The replication group name is used to get information about and work with the storage replica. When replication is being configured, the destination volumes are and their drive letters or mount points are dismounted. This ensures the destination volumes are protected and otherwise inaccessible while replication is active.

You can get information about replication using Get-SRGroup, Get-SRPartnership and Get-SRGroup replicas. These commands also help you track the status of replication. As related events also are recorded in the event logs, you can use the following command to monitor related events as well:

```
Get-WinEvent -ProviderName Microsoft-Windows-StorageReplica
```

You can use Set-SRPartnership to modify the replication settings. To stop replication, you must remove the replication partnership and related groups as shown in this example:

```
Get-SRPartnership | Remove-SRPartnership
Get-SRGroup | Remove-SRGroup
```

Storage Replica is designed to replace DFS replication, as it is much simpler to set up and manage. However, storage replication does have its limitations:

- Storage Replica only allows one-to-one replication between designated volumes. If you want to replicate multiple volumes between servers, you must configure multiple replication partnerships.
- Storage Replica doesn't allow users to access the replicated data on the destination server while replication is active. You must stop replication if you want users to be able to access the replicated data on the destination server.

Public Folder Sharing

Windows Server 2016 supports public folder sharing in addition to in-place file sharing. Public folder sharing is designed to enable users to share files and folders from a single location. With public folder sharing, you copy or move files you want to share to a computer's %SystemDrive%\Users\Public folder. You can access public folders in File Explorer by double-clicking the system drive, and then accessing the Users\Public folder.

The Public folder has several subfolders you can use to help organize public files:

- **Public Desktop**   Used for shared desktop items. Any files and program shortcuts placed in the Public Desktop folder appear on the desktop of all users who log on to the computer (and to all network users if network access has been granted to the Public folder).
- **Public Documents, Public Music, Public Pictures, Public Videos**   Used for shared document and media files. All files placed in one of these subfolders are available to all users who log on to the computer (and to all network users if network access has been granted to the Public folder).
- **Public Downloads**   Used for shared downloads. Any downloads placed in the Public Downloads subfolder are available to all users who log on to the computer (and to all network users if network access has been granted to the Public folder).

> **NOTE** By default, the Public Desktop folder is hidden from view. If hidden items aren't being displayed in File Explorer, click View, and then select Hidden Items.

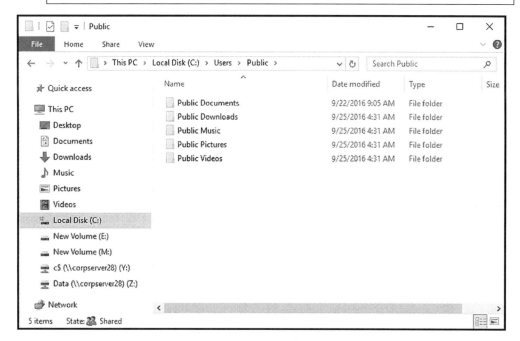

By default, anyone with a user account and password on a computer can access that computer's Public folder. When you copy or move files to the Public folder, access permissions are changed to match that of the Public folder, and some additional permissions are added as well.

You can change the default Public folder sharing configuration in two key ways:

- Allow users logged on to the computer to view and manage public files but restrict network users from accessing public files. When you configure this option, the implicit groups Interactive, Batch, and Service are granted special permissions on public files and public folders.
- Allow users with network access to view and manage public files. This allows network users to open, change, create, and delete public files. When you configure this option, the implicit group Everyone is granted Full Control permission to public files and public folders.

Windows Server 2016 can use either or both sharing models at any time. However, standard file sharing offers more security and better protection than public folder sharing, and increasing security is essential to protecting your organization's data.

With standard file sharing, share permissions are used only when a user attempts to access a file or folder from a different computer on the network. Access permissions are always used, whether the user is logged on to the console or is using a remote system to access a file or folder over the network. When data is accessed remotely, first the share permissions are applied, and then the access permissions are applied.

You can configure the basic file sharing settings for a server by using Advanced Sharing Settings in Network And Sharing Center. Separate options are provided for network discovery, file and printer sharing, and public folder sharing.

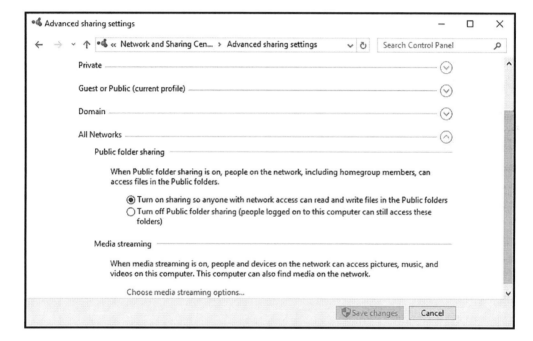

You can manage a computer's sharing configuration by following these steps:

1. In Control Panel, click View Network Status And Tasks under the Network And Internet heading to open Network And Sharing Center.

2. In Network And Sharing Center, click Change Advanced Sharing Settings in the left pane. Select the network profile for the network on which you want to enable file and printer sharing. Typically, this will be the Domain profile.

3. Standard file and printer sharing controls network access to shared resources. To configure standard file sharing, do one of the following:

▪ Select Turn On File And Printer Sharing to enable file sharing.
▪ Select Turn Off File And Printer Sharing to disable file sharing.

4. Public folder sharing controls access to a computer's Public folder. To configure public folder sharing, expand the All Networks panel by clicking the related expand button. On the Public Folder Sharing panel, choose one of the following options:

▪ **Turn On Sharing So Anyone With Network Access Can Read And Write Files In The Public Folders**   Enables public folder sharing by granting access to the Public folder and all public data to anyone who can access the computer over the network. Windows Firewall settings might prevent external access.

▪ **Turn Off Public Folder Sharing**   Disables public folder sharing, preventing local network access to the Public folder. Anyone who logs on locally to your computer can still access the Public folder and its files.

5. Click Save Changes.

Configuring Standard File Sharing

You use shares to control access for remote users. Permissions on shared folders have no effect on users who log on locally to a server or to a workstation that has shared folders.

Viewing Existing Shares

You can use both Computer Management and Server Manager to work with shares. You also can view current shares on a computer by entering **net share** at a command prompt or by entering **get-smbshare** at a PowerShell prompt.

TIP   The get-smbshare cmdlet is only one of many cmdlets associated with the smbshare module. To get a list of other cmdlets available for working with SMB shares, enter **get-command –module smbshare** at a PowerShell prompt.

NOTE   Computer Management, net share, and get-smbshare display information about SMB-based shares, including standard SMB folder shares, hidden SMB folder shares (those ending with the $ suffix), and SMB folders shared by using Distributed File System (DFS). Server Manager displays information about standard SMB folder shares, SMB folders shared by using DFS, and folders shared by using Network File System (NFS). Server Manager does not display information about hidden SMB folder shares.

In Computer Management, you can view the shared folders on a local or remote computer by following these steps:

1. To connect to a remote computer (you're connected to the local computer by default), right-click the Computer Management node, and then click Connect To Another Computer. Choose Another Computer, enter the name or IP address of the computer to which you want to connect, and then click OK.

2. In the console tree, expand System Tools, expand Shared Folders, and then select Shares. The current shares on the system are displayed.

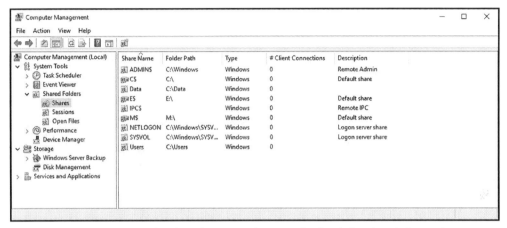

3. The columns for the Shares node provide the following information:

- **Share Name**   Name of the shared folder.
- **Folder Path**   Complete path to the folder on the local system.
- **Type**   What kind of computers can use the share. This normally shows as Windows because SMB shares are for Windows-based computers.
- **# Client Connections**   Number of clients currently accessing the share.
- **Description**   Description of the share.

In Server Manager, you can view the shared folders on a local or remote computer by following these steps:

1. Select the File And Storage Services node, and then select the related Shares subnode.

2. The Shares subnode provides information about shares on each file server that has been added for management. The columns for the Shares subnode provide the following information:

- **Share**   Name of the shared folder.
- **Local Path**   Complete path to the folder on the local system.
- **Protocol**   What protocol the share uses, either SMB or NFS.
- **Cluster Role**   If the server sharing the folder is part of a cluster, the cluster role is shown here. Otherwise, the cluster role is listed as None.

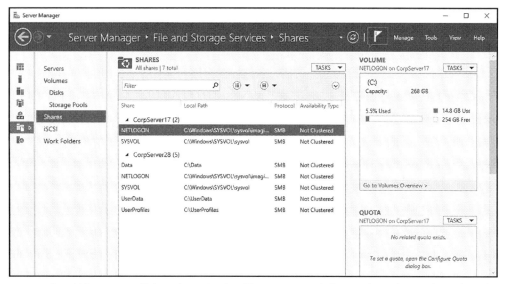

3. When you click a share in the Shares pane, information about the related volume is displayed in the Volume pane.

> **REAL WORLD**   NFS is the file sharing protocol used by UNIX-based systems, which includes computers running Apple OS X. As discussed in "Configuring NFS sharing" later in this chapter, you can enable support for NFS by installing the Server For NFS role service as part of the file server configuration.

Creating Shares in Computer Management

Windows Server 2016 provides several ways to share folders. You can share local folders by using File Explorer, and you can share local and remote folders by using Computer Management or Server Manager.

When you create a share with Computer Management, you can configure its share permissions and offline settings. When you create a share with Server Manager, you can provision all aspects of sharing, including NTFS permissions, encrypted data access, offline settings for caching, and share permissions. Normally, you create shares on NTFS volumes because NTFS offers the most robust solution.

In Computer Management, you share a folder by following these steps:

1. Right-click Shares, and then click New Share. This starts the Create A Shared Folder Wizard. Click Next.

2. In the Folder Path text box, enter the local file path to the folder you want to share, such as **E:\Reports**. If you don't know the full path, click Browse, use the Browse For Folder dialog box to find the folder you want to share, and then click OK. Click Next.

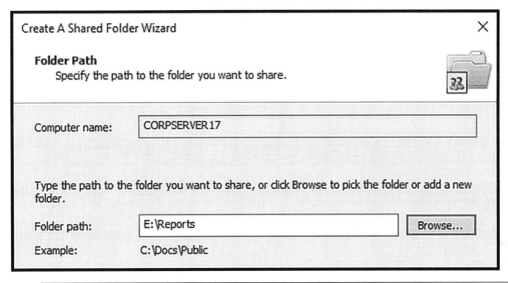

TIP   If the file path you specified doesn't exist, the wizard can create it for you. Click Yes when prompted to create the necessary folder or folders.

3. In the Share Name text box, enter a name for the share. This is the name of the folder to which users will connect. Share names must be unique for each system.

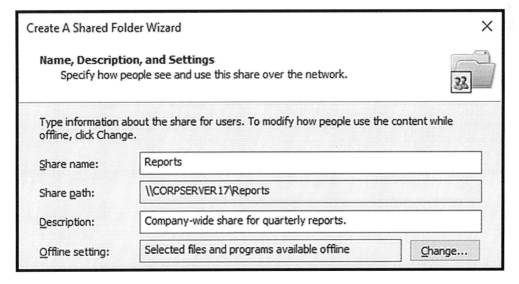

TIP If you want to hide a share from users (which means that they won't be able to view the shared resource when they try to browse to it in File Explorer or at the command line), enter a dollar sign (**$**) as the last character of the shared resource name. For example, you could create a share called PrivEngData$, which would be hidden from File Explorer, NET VIEW, and other similar utilities. Users can still connect to the share and access its data if they've been granted access permission and they know the share's name. Note that the **$** must be typed as part of the share name when mapping to the shared resource.

4. If you want to, enter a description of the share in the Description text box. When you view shares on a particular computer, the description is displayed in Computer Management.

5. By default, the share is configured so that only files and programs that users specify are available for offline use. Normally, this is the option you want to use because this option also enables users to take advantage of the new Always Offline feature. If you want to use different offline file settings, click Change, select the appropriate options in the Offline Settings dialog box, and then click OK. The offline availability settings available include the following:

* **Only The Files And Programs That Users Specify Are Available Offline** Select this option if you want client computers to cache only the files and programs that users specify for offline use. Optionally, if the BranchCache For Network Files role service is installed on the file server, select Enable BranchCache to enable computers in a branch office to cache files that are downloaded from the shared folder, and then securely share the files to other computers in the branch office.

* **No Files Or Programs From The Shared Folder Are Available Offline** Select this option if you don't want cached copies of the files and programs in the share to be available on client computers for offline use.

* **All Files And Programs That Users Open From The Shared Folder Are Automatically Available Offline** Select this option if you want client computers to automatically cache all files and programs that users open from the share. Optionally, select Optimize For Performance to run cached program files from the local cache instead of the shared folder on the server.

Offline Settings ✕

You can choose which files and programs, if any, are available to users who are offline.

⦿ Only the files and programs that users specify are available offline

☐ Enable BranchCache

◯ No files or programs from the shared folder are available offline

◯ All files and programs that users open from the shared folder are automatically available offline

☐ Optimize for performance

6. Click Next, and then set basic permissions for the share. You'll find helpful pointers in "Managing Share Permissions" later in the chapter. The available options are as follows:

- **All Users Have Read-Only Access**   Gives users access to view files and read data. They can't create, modify, or delete files and folders.
- **Administrators Have Full Access; Other Users Have Read-Only Access**   Gives administrators complete control over the share. Full access allows administrators to create, modify, and delete files and folders. On an NTFS volume or partition, it also gives administrators the right to change permissions and to take ownership of files and folders. Other users can view files and read data; however, they can't create, modify, or delete files and folders.
- **Administrators Have Full Access; Other Users Have No Access**   Gives administrators complete control over the share, but prevents other users from accessing the share.
- **Customize Permissions**   Allows you to configure access for specific users and groups, which is usually the best technique to use. Setting share permissions is discussed fully in "Managing Share Permissions."

7. When you click Finish, the wizard creates the share and displays a status report, which should state "Sharing Was Successful." If an error is displayed instead, note the error and take corrective action as appropriate before repeating this procedure to create the share. Click Finish.

Individual folders can have multiple shares. Each share can have a different name and a different set of access permissions. To create additional shares on an existing share, simply follow the preceding steps for creating a share with these changes:

* In step 3, when you name the share, make sure that you use a different name.
* In step 4, when you add a description for the share, use a description that explains what the share is used for and how it's different from the other shares for the same folder.

Creating Shares in Server Manager

In Server Manager, you share a folder by following these steps:

1. The Shares subnode of the File And Storage Services node shows existing shares for file servers that have been added for management. In the Shares pane, click Tasks, and then click New Share to start the New Share Wizard.

2. Choose one of the available file share profiles, and then click Next. The New Share Wizard has the following file share profiles:

* **SMB Share—Quick**   A basic profile for creating SMB file shares that allows you to configure the settings and permissions of the shares.

- **SMB Share—Advanced** An advanced profile for creating SMB file shares that allows you to configure the settings, permissions, management properties, and NTFS quota profile (if applicable) of the shares.
- **SMB Share—Applications** A custom profile for creating SMB file shares with settings appropriate for Hyper-V, certain databases, and other server applications. It's essentially the same as the quick profile, but it doesn't allow you to enable access-based enumeration or offline caching.

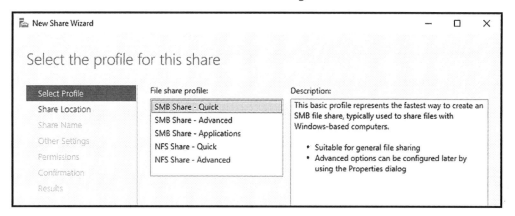

NOTE If you are using the Server For NFS role service, options are available for creating NFS shares as well.

REAL WORLD SMB 3 includes enhancements for server-based applications. These enhancements improve performance for small random reads and writes, which are common with server-based applications, such as Microsoft SQL Server OLTP. With SMB 3, packets use large Maximum Transmission Units (MTUs) as well, which enhance performance for large, sequential data transfers, such as those used for deploying and copying virtual hard disks (VHDs) over the network, database backup and restore over the network, and SQL Server data warehouse transactions over the network.

3. On the Select The Server And Path For This Share page, select the server on which you want the share to be created. Only file servers you've added for management are available.

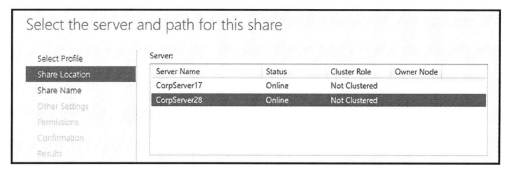

4. Select the volume on which you want the share to be created. By default, Server Manager creates the file share as a new folder in the \Shares directory on the selected volume. To override this, choose the Type A Custom Path option, and then either enter the share path, such as C:\CorpData, or click Browse to use the Select Folder dialog box to select the share path. When you are ready to continue, click Next.

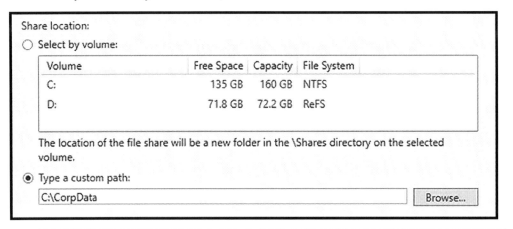

NOTE If you use a custom path, the folder path on the designated drive doesn't have to already be created. The folder path will be created as part of the set up process.

5. On the Specify Share Name page, enter a name for the share. This is the name of the folder to which users will connect. Share names must be unique for each system.

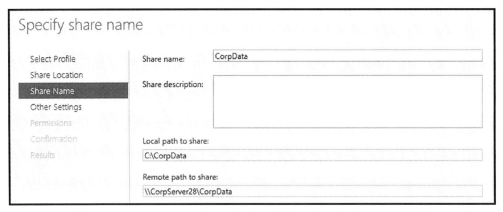

6. If you want to, enter a description of the share in the Description text box. When you view shares on a particular computer, the description is displayed in Computer Management.

7. Note the local and remote paths to the share. These paths are set based on the share location and share name you specified. When you are ready to continue, click Next.

8. If you used a custom path and the folder hasn't been created yet, you are prompted to create path. Click OK.

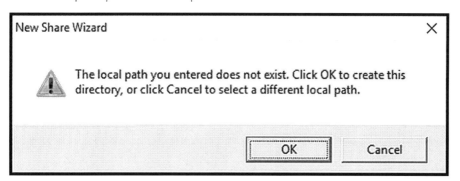

New Share Wizard   ✕

⚠ The local path you entered does not exist. Click OK to create this directory, or click Cancel to select a different local path.

OK   Cancel

9. On the Configure Share Settings page, use the following options to configure the way the share is used:

- **Enable Access-Based Enumeration** Configures permissions so that when users browse the folder, only files and folders a user has been granted at least Read access to are displayed. If a user doesn't have at least Read (or equivalent) permission for a file or folder within the shared folder, that file or folder is hidden from view. (This option is dimmed if you are creating an SMB share optimized for applications.)
- **Allow Caching Of Share** Configures the share to cache only the files and programs that users specify for offline use. Although you can later edit the share properties and change the offline files' availability settings, you normally want to select this option because it allows users to take advantage of the new Always Offline feature. Optionally, if the BranchCache For Network Files role service is installed on the file server, select Enable BranchCache to enable computers in a branch office to cache files that are downloaded from the shared folder and then securely share the files to other computers in the branch office. (This option is dimmed if you are creating an SMB share optimized for applications.)
- **Encrypt Data Access** Configures the share to use SMB encryption, which protects file data from eavesdropping while being transferred over the network. This option is useful on untrusted networks.

10. On the Specify Permissions To Control Access page, the default permissions assigned to the share are listed. By default, the special group Everyone is granted the Full Control share permission and the underlying folder permissions are as listed. To change share, folder, or both permissions, click Customize Permissions, and then use the Advanced Security Settings dialog box to configure the required permissions. Setting share permissions is

discussed fully in "Managing Share Permissions" later in this chapter. Setting folder permissions is discussed fully in "File and Folder Permissions" in Chapter 11 "Managing Permissions and Auditing."

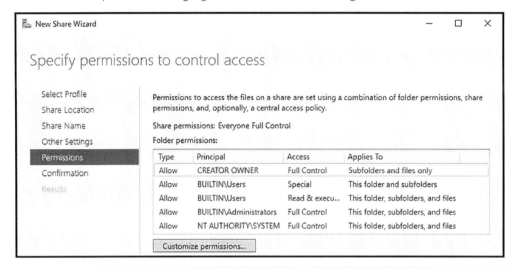

> **NOTE** If the share will be used for Hyper-V, you might need to enable constrained delegation for remote management of the Hyper-V host.

11. If you are using the advanced profile, optionally set the folder management properties, and then click Next. These properties specify the purpose of the folder and the type of data stored in it so that data management policies, such as classification rules, can then use these properties.

12. If you are using the advanced profile, optionally apply a quota based on a template to the folder, and then click Next. You can select only quota templates that have already been created. For more information, see "Managing Disk Quota Templates" in Chapter 12.

13. On the Confirm Selections page, review your selections. When you click Create, the wizard creates the share, configures it, and sets permissions. The status should state, "The share was successfully created." If an error is displayed instead, note the error and take corrective action as appropriate before repeating this procedure to create the share. Click Close.

Changing Share Settings

When you create a share, you can configure many basic and advanced settings, including those for access-based enumeration, encrypted data access, offline settings for caching, and management properties. In Server Manager, you can modify these settings by following these steps:

1. The Shares subnode of the File And Storage Services node shows existing shares for file servers that have been added for management. Right-click the share with which you want to work, and then click Properties.

2. In the Properties dialog box, you have several options panels that can be accessed by using controls in the left pane. You can expand the panels one by one or click Show All to expand all the panels at the same time.

3. Use the options provided to modify the settings as necessary, and then click OK. The options available are the same whether you use the basic, advanced, or applications profile to create the shared folder.

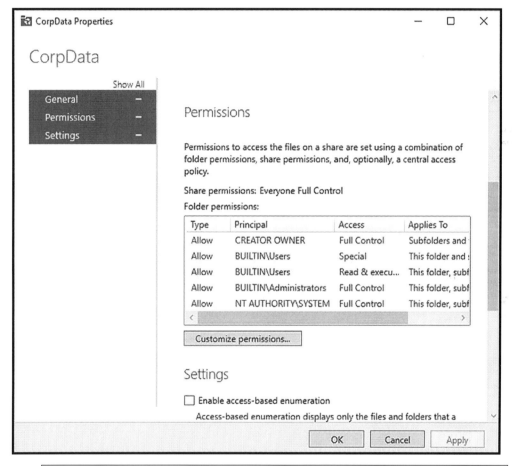

> **TIP** If you're creating a share for general use and general access, you can publish the shared resource in Active Directory. Publishing the resource in Active Directory makes finding the share easier for users; however, this option is not available in Server Manager. To publish a share in Active Directory, right-click the share in Computer Management, and then click Properties. On the Publish tab, select the Publish This Share In Active Directory check box, add an optional description and owner information, and then click OK.

Managing Share Permissions

Share permissions set the maximum allowable actions available within a shared folder. By default, when you create a share, everyone with access to the network has Read access to the share's contents. This is an important security change—in previous editions of Windows Server, the default permission was Full Control.

With NTFS and ReFS volumes, you can use file and folder permissions and ownership, in addition to share permissions, to further constrain actions within the share. With FAT volumes, share permissions control only access.

Understanding the Various Share Permissions

From the most restrictive to the least restrictive, the share permissions available are as follows:

* **No Access**   No permissions are granted for the share.
* **Read**   Users can do the following:

* View file and subfolder names
* Access the subfolders in the share
* Read file data and attributes
* Run program files

* **Change**   Users have Read permission and the ability to do the following:

* Create files and subfolders
* Modify files
* Change attributes on files and subfolders
* Delete files and subfolders

* **Full Control**   Users have Read and Change permissions, in addition to the following capabilities on NTFS volumes:

* Change file and folder permissions
* Take ownership of files and folders

You can assign share permissions to users and groups. You can even assign permissions to implicit groups. For details on implicit groups, see Chapter 7, "Accounts: The Essentials" in *Windows Server 2016: Essentials for Administration* (Stanek & Associates, 2016.

Viewing and Configuring Share Permissions

You can view and configure share permissions in Computer Management or Server Manager. To view and configure share permissions in Computer Management, follow these steps:

1. In Computer Management, connect to the computer on which the share is created. In the console tree, expand System Tools, expand Shared Folders, and then select Shares.

2. Right-click the share with which you want to work, and then click Properties.

3. In the Properties dialog box, click the Share Permissions tab. You can now view the users and groups that have access to the share and the type of access they have.

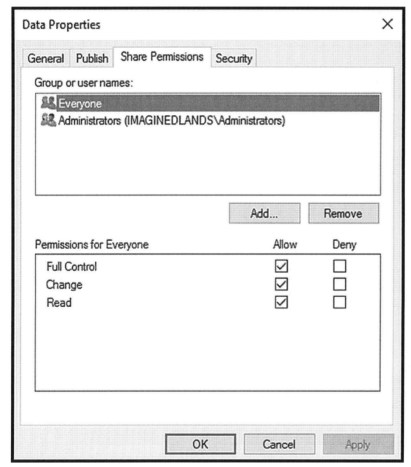

4. Users or groups that already have access to the share are listed in the Group Or User Names list. You can remove permissions for these users and groups

by selecting the user or group you want to remove, and then clicking Remove. You can change permissions for these users and groups by selecting the user or group you want to change and then allowing or denying access permissions in the Permissions list.

5. To add permissions for another user or group, click Add. This opens the Select Users, Computers, Service Accounts, Or Groups dialog box.

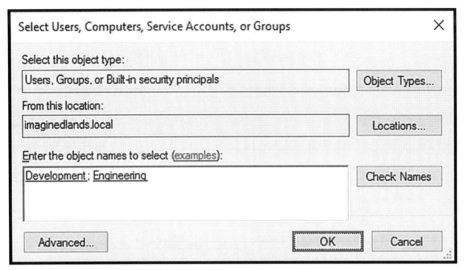

6. Enter the name of a user, computer, or group in the current domain, and then click Check Names. This produces one of the following results:

■ If a single match is found, the dialog box is automatically updated and the entry is underlined.

■ If no matches are found, you either entered an incorrect name part or you're working with an incorrect location. Modify the name and try again, or click Locations to select a new location.

■ If multiple matches are found, select the name or names you want to use, and then click OK. To assign permissions to other users, computers, or groups, enter a semicolon (;) and then repeat this step.

> **NOTE** The Locations button enables you to access account names in other domains. Click Locations to find a list of the current domains, trusted domains, and other resources you can access. Because of the transitive trusts in Windows Server, you can usually access all the domains in the domain tree or forest.

7. Click OK. The users and groups are added to the Group Or User Names list for the share.

8. Configure access permissions for each user, computer, and group by selecting an account name and then allowing or denying access permissions.

Keep in mind that you're setting the maximum allowable permissions for a particular account.

9. Click OK. To assign additional security permissions for NTFS, see "File and Folder Permissions" in Chapter 11.

> **IMPORTANT** Keep in mind that you can select the opposite permission to override an inherited permission. Note also that Deny normally overrides Allow, so if you explicitly deny permission to a user or group for a child folder or file, this permission should be denied to that user or group of users.

To view and configure share permissions in Server Manager, follow these steps:

1. The Shares subnode of the File And Storage Services node shows existing shares for file servers that have been added for management.

2. Right-click the share with which you want to work, and then click Properties.

3. In the Properties dialog box, click the Permissions in the left pane. You can now view the users and groups that have access to the share and the type of access they have.

4. To change share, folder, or both permissions, click Customize Permissions. Next, select the Share tab in the Advanced Security Settings dialog box.

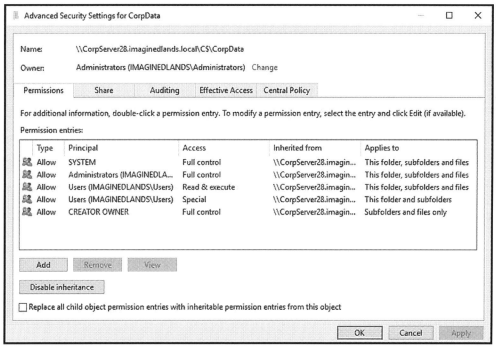

5. Users or groups that already have access to the share are listed in the Permission Entries list. Although you can't modify inherited permissions, you

can block inheritance by clicking Disable Inheritance and then either converting the inherited permissions to explicit permissions that can be managed or removing all inherited permissions.

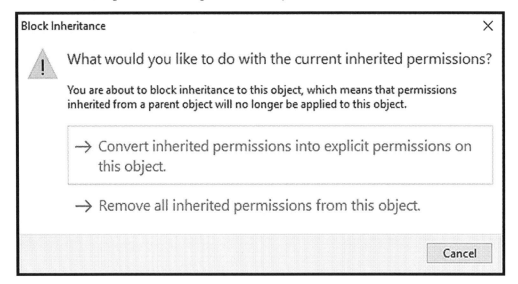

While you are working with the Advanced Security Settings For... dialog box you can manage permissions in a variety of ways. You can change, remove or add non-inherited permissions. To change permissions for users and groups, double-click the user or group you want to work with, and then use the Permissions For... dialog box to manage the permissions. To remove permissions for users or groups, select the user or group by clicking it and then click Remove.

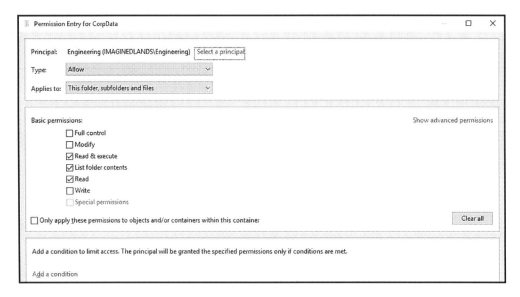

To add permissions for another user or group, click Add. This opens the Permission Entry dialog box. Next, click Select A Principal to display the Select User, Computer, Service Account Or Group dialog box. Enter the name of a user or a group account. Be sure to reference the user account name rather than the user's full name. Only one name can be entered at a time.

Click Check Names. If a single match is found for each entry, the dialog box is automatically updated, and the entry is underlined. Otherwise, you'll get an additional dialog box. If no matches are found, you either entered the name incorrectly or you're working with an incorrect location. Modify the name in the Name Not Found dialog box and try again, or click Locations to select a new location. When multiple matches are found, in the Multiple Names Found dialog box, select the name you want to use, and then click OK twice.

The user and group is added as the Principal, and the Permission Entry dialog box is updated to show this. Use the Type list to specify whether you are configuring allowed or denied permissions, and then select the permissions you want to allow or deny. Click OK to return to the Advanced Security Settings dialog box. You can assign additional security permissions for NTFS as discussed in "File and Folder Permissions" in Chapter 11.

Connecting to Network Drives

Users can connect to a network drive and to shared resources available on the network. This connection is shown as a network drive that users can access like any other drive on their systems.

> **NOTE** When users connect to network drives, they're subject not only to the permissions set for the shared resources, but also to Windows Server 2016 file and folder permissions. Differences in these permission sets are usually the reason users might not be able to access a particular file or subfolder within the network drive.

Mapping a Network Drive

In Windows Server 2016, you connect to a network drive by mapping to it using NET USE and New-PsDrive. The syntax for NET USE isthe following syntax:

```
net use DeviceName \\ComputerName\ShareName
```

DeviceName specifies the drive letter or an asterisk (*) to use the next available drive letter, and *ComputerName\ShareName* is the UNC path to the share, such as either of the following:

```
net use g: \\ROMEO\DOCS
```

or

```
net use * \\ROMEO\DOCS
```

> **NOTE** To ensure that the mapped drive is available each time the user logs on, make the mapping persistent by adding the */Persistent:Yes* option.

The syntax for New-PsDrive is:

```
New-PsDrive –Name DriveLetter –Root \\ServerName\ShareName
-PsProvider FileSystem
```

Where *DriveLetter* is the driver letter to use and *ServerName* is the DNS name or IP address of the server hosting the share and *ShareName* is the name of the share, such as:

```
New-PsDrive –Name g: -Root \\CorpServer21\CorpData
-PsProvider FileSystem
```

> **NOTE** To ensure that the mapped drive is available each time the user logs on, add the –Persist parameter.

If the client computer is running Windows 10, you can map network drives by completing the following steps:

1. When you open File Explorer, the This PC node should be opened by default. If you have an open Explorer window and This PC is not the selected node, select the leftmost option button in the address list, and then select This PC.

2. Next, click the Map Network Drive button in the Computer panel, and then click Map Network Drive.

3. Use the Drive list to select a free drive letter to use, and then click the Browse button to the right of the Folder list. In the Browse For Folder dialog box,

expand the network folders until you can select the name of the workgroup or the domain with which you want to work.

4. When you expand the name of a computer in a workgroup or a domain, you'll get a list of shared folders. Select the shared folder with which you want to work, and then click OK.

5. Select Reconnect At Logon if you want Windows to connect to the shared folder automatically at the start of each session.

6. Click Finish. If the currently logged-on user doesn't have appropriate access permissions for the share, select Connect Using Different Credentials, and then click Finish. After you click Finish, you can enter the user name and password of the account with which you want to connect to the shared folder. Enter the user name in Domain\Username format, such as **Cpandl\Williams**. Before clicking OK, select Remember My Credentials if you want the credentials to be saved. Otherwise, you'll need to provide credentials in the future.

Disconnecting a Network Drive

In Windows Server 2016, you disconnect to a network drive using NET USE and Remove-PsDrive. The syntax for NET USE is:

```
net use DeviceName /delete
```

DeviceName specifies the network drive to remove, such as:

```
net use g: /delete
```

The syntax for Remove-PsDrive is:

```
Remove-PsDrive -Name DriveLetter
```

Where *DriveLetter* is the network drive to remove, such as:

```
Remove-PsDrive -Name g:
```

> **NOTE** If the network drive has open connections, you can force remove the network drive using –Force parameter.

In File Explorer, you can disconnect a network drive by following these steps:

1. When you open File Explorer, the This PC node should be opened by default. If you have an open Explorer window and This PC is not the selected node, select the leftmost option button in the address list, and then select This PC.

2. Under Network Location, right-click the network drive icon, and then click Disconnect.

Managing Existing Shares

As an administrator, you often have to manage shared folders. This section covers the common administrative tasks of managing shares.

Understanding Special Shares

When you install Windows Server, the operating system creates special shares automatically. These shares are known as *administrative shares* and *hidden shares*, and they are designed to help make system administration easier. You can't set access permissions on automatically created special shares; Windows Server assigns access permissions. You can create your own hidden shares by adding the $ symbol as the last character of the share name.

You can delete special shares temporarily if you're certain the shares aren't needed; however, the shares are re-created automatically the next time the operating system starts. To permanently disable the administrative shares, change the following registry values to 0 (zero):

* HKEY_LOCAL_MACHINE\SYSTEM\CurrentControlSet\Services\lanmanserver\parameters\AutoShareServer
* HKEY_LOCAL_MACHINE\SYSTEM\CurrentControlSet\Services\lanmanserver\parameters\AutoShareWks

Which special shares are available depends on your system configuration. A list of special shares you might find and how they're used follows:

* **ADMIN$**   A share used during remote administration of a system. It provides access to the operating system %SystemRoot%. On workstations and servers, administrators and backup operators can access these shares. On domain controllers, server operators also have access.
* **FAX$**   Supports network faxes. Used by fax clients when sending faxes.

- **IPC$** Supports named pipes during remote interprocess communications (IPC) access. Used by programs when performing remote administration and when viewing shared resources.
- **NETLOGON** Supports the Net Logon service. Used by the Net Logon service when processing domain logon requests. Everyone has Read access.
- **PRINT$** Supports shared printer resources by providing access to printer drivers. Used by shared printers. Everyone has Read access. Administrators, server operators, and printer operators have Full Control.
- **SYSVOL** Supports Active Directory. Used to store data and objects for Active Directory.
- ***Driveletter$*** A share that allows administrators to connect to a drive's root folder. These shares are shown as C$, D$, E$, and so on. On workstations and servers, administrators and backup operators can access these shares. On domain controllers, server operators also have access.

Connecting to Special Shares

Most special shares end with the $ symbol. Although these shares aren't displayed in File Explorer, administrators and certain operators can connect to them (except for NETLOGON and SYSVOL). If your current logon account has appropriate permissions, you can connect directly to a special share or any standard share simply by typing the UNC path for the share in File Explorer's address box. The basic syntax is:

\\ServerName\ShareName

Where *ServerName* is the DNS name or IP address of the server and *ShareName* is the name of the share. In the following example, you connect to the D$ share on CorpServer34:

\\CorpServer34\D$

If you always want the drive to be listed as a network location in This PC or need to specify credentials, you can connect to a special share by following these steps:

1. When you open File Explorer, the This PC node should be opened by default. If you have an open Explorer window and This PC is not the selected node, select the leftmost option button in the address list, and then select This PC.

2. Next, click the Map Network Drive button on the Computer panel, and then click Map Network Drive. This displays the Map Network Drive dialog box.

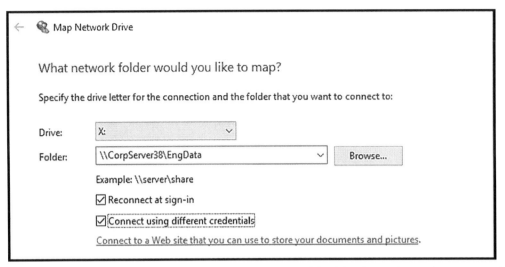

What network folder would you like to map?

Specify the drive letter for the connection and the folder that you want to connect to:

Drive: **X:**

Folder: **\\CorpServer38\EngData**   **Browse...**

Example: \\server\share

☑ Reconnect at sign-in

☑ Connect using different credentials

Connect to a Web site that you can use to store your documents and pictures.

3. In the Drive list, select a free drive letter. This drive letter is used to access the special share.

4. In the Folder text box, enter the Universal Naming Convention (UNC) path to the share. For example, to access the C$ share on a server called Twiddle, you would use the path \\TWIDDLE\C$.

5. The Reconnect At Sign-In check box is selected automatically to ensure that the network drive is connected each time you log on. If you need to access the share only during the current logon session, clear this check box.

6. If you need to connect to the share using different user credentials, select the Connect Using Different Credentials check box.

7. Click Finish. If you are connecting using different credentials, enter the user name and password when prompted. Enter the user name in Domain\Username format, such as **Imaginedlands\Williams**. Before clicking OK, select Remember My Credentials if you want the credentials to be saved. Otherwise, you'll need to provide credentials in the future.

After you connect to a special share, you can access it as you would any other drive. Because special shares are protected, you don't have to worry about ordinary users accessing these shares. The first time you connect to the share, you might be prompted for a user name and password. If you are prompted, provide that information.

Viewing User and Computer Sessions

You can use Computer Management to track all connections to shared resources on a Windows Server 2016 system. Whenever a user or computer connects to a shared resource, Windows Server 2016 lists a connection in the Sessions node.

To view connections to shared resources, enter **net session** at an administrator command prompt or Get-SMBSession at an administrator PowerShell prompt. You also can follow these steps:

1. In Computer Management, connect to the computer on which you created the shared resource.
2. In the console tree, expand System Tools, expand Shared Folders, and then select Sessions. You can now view connections to shares for users and computers.

The columns for the Sessions node provide the following important information about user and computer connections:

* **User** The names of users or computers connected to shared resources. Computer names are shown with a $ suffix to differentiate them from users.
* **Computer** The name of the computer being used.
* **Type** The type of network connection being used.
* **# Open Files** The number of files with which the user is actively working. For more detailed information, access the Open Files node.
* **Connected Time** The time that has elapsed since the connection was established.
* **Idle Time** The time that has elapsed since the connection was last used.
* **Guest** Whether the user is logged on as a guest.

As shown in the following example, the output of Get-SMBSession provides the session ID, client computer name, client user name and the number of open files for each session:

```
SessionId     ClientComputerName    ClientUserName    NumOpens

---------     ------------------    --------------    --------

834295421326  10.0.0.60             TVPRESS\williams    21
```

Managing Sessions and Shares

Managing sessions and shares is a common administrative task. Before you shut down a server or an application running on a server, you might want to disconnect users from shared resources. You might also need to disconnect users when you plan to change access permissions or delete a share entirely. Another reason to disconnect users is to break locks on files. You disconnect users from shared resources by ending the related user sessions.

Ending Individual Sessions

To disconnect individual users from shared resources, enter **net session** *computername* **/delete** at an administrator command prompt or Close-SMBSession at –ComputerName *computername* an elevated PowerShell prompt. In both instances, *computername* is the DNS name or IP address of computer from which the session originates. You also can disconnect users by following these steps:

1. In Computer Management, connect to the computer on which you created the share.
2. In the console tree, expand System Tools, expand Shared Folders, and then select Sessions.
3. Right-click the user sessions you want to end, and then click Close Session.
4. Click Yes to confirm the action.

Ending All Sessions

To disconnect all users from shared resources, follow these steps:

1. In Computer Management, connect to the computer on which you created the share.
2. In the console tree, expand System Tools, expand Shared Folders, and then right-click Sessions.
3. Click Disconnect All Sessions, and then click Yes to confirm the action.

> **NOTE** Keep in mind that you're disconnecting users from shared resources, not from the domain. You can use only logon hours and Group Policy to force users to log off after they've logged on to the domain. Thus, disconnecting users doesn't log them off the network. It simply disconnects them from the shared resource.

To disconnect individual users from shared resources, enter **net session** *computername* **/delete** at an administrator command prompt or Close-SMBSession at –ComputerName *computername* an elevated PowerShell prompt. In both instances, *computername* is the DNS name or IP address of computer from which the session originates. You also can disconnect users by following these steps:

You also can use Windows PowerShell to disconnect multiple users from a shared resource. The key here is to ensure you only close the sessions you want to close. Consider the following example:

```
ForEach-Object ($Session in (Get-SMBSession)) {
Close-SMBSession –force}
```

This example uses a ForEach loop to get all active SMB sessions and then close each SMB session in turn. Thus, if you enter this example at an administrator PowerShell prompt, you will disconnect all users from all shared resources.

To close all connections only for a specific share, you must create a ForEach loop that only examines the connections for that share, such as:

```
ForEach-Object ($Session in (Get-SMBShare CorpData |
Get-SMBSession)) {Close-SMBSession –force}
```

This example uses a ForEach loop to get all active SMB sessions for the CorpData share and then close each of those sessions in turn. Thus, if you enter this example at an administrator PowerShell prompt, you only disconnect users from the CorpData share.

Managing Open Resources

Any time users connect to shares, the individual file and object resources they are working with are displayed in the Open Files node. The Open Files node might show the files the user has open but isn't currently editing.

You can access the Open Files node by following these steps:

1. In Computer Management, connect to the computer on which you created the share.

2. In the console tree, expand System Tools, expand Shared Folders, and then select Open Files. This displays the Open Files node, which provides the following information about resource usage:

- **Open File**   The file or folder path to the open file on the local system. The path might also be a named pipe, such as \PIPE\spools, which is used for printer spooling.
- **Accessed By**   The name of the user accessing the file.
- **Type**   The type of network connection being used.
- **# Locks**   The number of locks on the resource.
- **Open Mode**   The access mode used when the resource was opened, such as read, write, or write+read.

You also can use Get-SMBOpenFile to list open files. As shown in the following example, Get-SMBOpenFile provides the file ID, session ID, path, share relative path, client computer name, and client user name for each open file:

```
FileId      SessionId   Path  ShareRelativePath ClientComputerName ClientUserName
------      ---------   ----  ----------------- ------------------ --------------
601295424973 601295421497 C:\PrimaryData\    10.0.0.60      TVPRESS\williams
601295425045 601295421577 C:\Windows\SYSVOL tvp... 10.0.0.60 TVPRESS\CORPPC29$
```

Closing an Open File

To close an open file on a computer's shares, follow these steps:

1. In Computer Management, connect to the computer with which you want to work.

2. In the console tree, expand System Tools, expand Shared Folders, and then select Open Files.

3. Right-click the open file you want to close, and then click Close Open File.

4. Click Yes to confirm the action.

You also can use Close-SMBOpenFile to close open files. When you close a file, you use the –FileID parameter to specify the identifier for the file to close, such as:

```
Close-SMBOpenFile –FileID 601295424973
```

Add the –Force parameter to force close the file if needed. However, if the file has been modified by a user, any changes to the file could be lost.

Closing All Open Files

To close all open files on a computer's shares, follow these steps:

1. In Computer Management, connect to the computer on which the share is created.
2. In the console tree, expand System Tools, expand Shared Folders, and then right-click Open Files.
3. Click Disconnect All Open Files, and then click Yes to confirm the action.

You also can use Windows PowerShell to close all open files on a computer's share. The key here is to ensure you only close the files you want to close. Consider the following example:

```
ForEach-Object ($Session in (Get-SMBOpenFile)) {
Close-SMBOpenFile -force}
```

This example uses a ForEach loop to get all open SMB files and then close each SMB file in turn. Thus, if you enter this example at an administrator PowerShell prompt, you will close all open files for all shared resources.

To close open files on a specific share, you must create a ForEach loop that only examines the open files for that share, such as:

```
ForEach-Object ($Session in (Get-SMBShare CorpData |
Get-SMBOpenFile)) {Close-SMBOpenFile -force}
```

This example uses a ForEach loop to get all open SMB files for the CorpData share and then close each of those files in turn. Thus, if you enter this example at an administrator PowerShell prompt, you only close open files for the CorpData share.

Stopping File and Folder Sharing

To stop sharing a folder, follow these steps:

1. Do one of the following:

* In Server Manager, select the share you want to manage on the Shares subnode of the File And Storage Services node.

- In Computer Management, connect to the computer on which you created the share, and then access the Shares node.

2. Right-click the share you want to remove, click Stop Sharing, and then click Yes to confirm the action.

> **CAUTION** You should never delete a folder containing shares without first stopping the shares. If you fail to stop the shares, Windows Server 2016 attempts to reestablish the shares the next time the computer is started, and the resulting error is logged in the system event log.

Configuring NFS Sharing

To enable NFS sharing, you can install Server For NFS as a role service on a file server. Server For NFS provides a file sharing solution for enterprises with mixed Windows, OS X, and UNIX environments, allowing users to transfer files between Windows Server 2016, OS X, and UNIX operating systems by using the NFS protocol.

You can configure NFS sharing using either File Explorer or Server Manager. In File Explorer, follow these steps to enable and configure NFS sharing:

1. Right-click the share you want to manage, and then click Properties to display a Properties dialog box for the share.
2. On the NFS Sharing tab, click Manage NFS Sharing.
3. In the NFS Advanced Sharing dialog box, select the Share This Folder check box.
4. In the Share Name text box, enter a name for the share. This is the name of the folder to which UNIX users will connect. NFS share names must be unique for each system and can be the same as those used for standard file sharing.
5. ANSI is the default encoding for text associated with directory listings and file names. If your UNIX computers use a different default encoding, you can choose that encoding in the Encoding list.

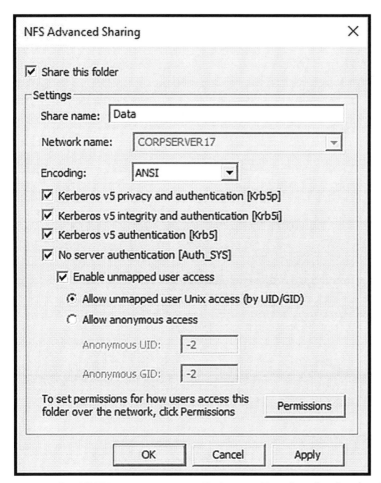

NFS Advanced Sharing

☑ Share this folder

Settings

Share name: Data

Network name: CORPSERVER17

Encoding: ANSI

☑ Kerberos v5 privacy and authentication [Krb5p]
☑ Kerberos v5 integrity and authentication [Krb5i]
☑ Kerberos v5 authentication [Krb5]
☑ No server authentication [Auth_SYS]

  ☑ Enable unmapped user access

    ● Allow unmapped user Unix access (by UID/GID)

    ○ Allow anonymous access

      Anonymous UID: -2

      Anonymous GID: -2

To set permissions for how users access this folder over the network, click Permissions   [Permissions]

[OK] [Cancel] [Apply]

6. UNIX computers use Kerberos v5 authentication by default. Typically, you want to allow Kerberos integrity and authentication in addition to standard Kerberos authentication. Select the check boxes for the authentication mechanisms you want to use. Clear the check boxes for those you don't want to use.

7. The share can be configured so that no server authentication is required. If you want to require server authentication, select the No Server Authentication check box, and then choose additional options as appropriate. Unmapped user access can be allowed and enabled. If you want to allow anonymous access to the NFS share, select the Allow Anonymous Access option, and then enter the anonymous user UID and anonymous group GID.

8. For UNIX computers, you configure access primarily based on the computer names (also referred to as *host names*). By default, no UNIX computers have access to the NFS share. If you want to grant read-only or read/write permissions, click Permissions, set the permissions you want to use in the

NFS Share Permissions dialog box, and then click OK. You can configure no access, read-only access, or read/write access by client computer name and client computer groups.

9. Click OK twice to close the open dialog boxes and save your settings.

In File Explorer, you can disable NFS sharing by following these steps:

1. Right-click the share you want to manage, and then click Properties. This displays a Properties dialog box for the share.

2. On the NFS Sharing tab, click Manage NFS Sharing.

3. In the NFS Advanced Sharing dialog box, clear the Share This Folder check box, and then click OK twice.

With Server Manager, you can configure NFS permissions as part of the initial share configuration when you are provisioning a share. On the Shares subnode of the File And Storage Services node, you can create an NFS share by following these steps:

1. In the Shares pane, click Tasks, and then click New Share to start the New Share Wizard. Choose NFS Share—Quick or NFS Share—-Advanced as the share profile, and then click Next.

2. Specify the share name and location as you would for an SMB share.

3. On the Specify Authentication Methods page, configure Kerberos v5 Authentication and No Server Authentication. The options provided are similar to those discussed previously in this section.

4. On the Specify Share Permissions page, configure access for UNIX hosts. Hosts can be set for no access, read-only access, or read/write access to the share.

5. On the Specify Permissions To Control Access, optionally set NTFS permissions for the share.

6. On the Confirm Selections page, review your selections. When you click Create, the wizard creates the share, configures it, and sets permissions. The status should state, "The share was successfully created." If an error is displayed instead, note the error and take corrective action. However, because typical errors relate to configuring host access, you probably won't need to repeat this procedure to create the share. Instead, you might need to modify only the share permissions. Click Close.

Chapter 10. Using Shadow Copies and Work Folders

Shadow Copies and Work Folders are extensions to file sharing. Any time your organization uses shared folders, you should consider creating shadow copies of these shared folders as well. Shadow copies are point-in-time backups of data files that users can access directly in shared folders.

Point-in-time backups can save you and the other administrators in your organization a lot of work, especially if you routinely have to retrieve lost, overwritten, or corrupted data files from backups. The normal procedure for retrieving shadow copies is to use the Previous Versions or Shadow Copy client. Windows Server 2016 includes a feature enhancement that enables you to revert an entire (nonsystem) volume to a previous shadow copy state.

Although the standard approach to sharing files requires a computer that is joined and connected to a domain, synced sharing does not. With sync shares, users can use an Internet or corporate network connection to sync data to their devices from folders located on enterprise servers. You implement synced sharing by using Work Folders.

Work Folders is a feature that you can add to servers running Windows Server 2016 or later. Work Folders use a client-server architecture. A Work Folders client is natively integrated into Windows 10 and is also available for iPad and other devices.

Using Shadow Copies

You can create shadow copies only on NTFS volumes. You use the Shadow Copy feature to create automatic backups of the files in shared folders on a per-volume basis. For example, on a file server that has three NTFS volumes, each containing shared folders, you need to configure this feature for each volume separately.

If you enable this feature in its default configuration, shadow copies are created twice each weekday (Monday–Friday) at 7:00 A.M. and 12:00 P.M. You need at least 300 megabytes (MB) of free space to create the first shadow copy on a volume. The total disk space used beyond this depends on the amount of data in the volume's shared folders. You can restrict the total amount of disk space used by Shadow Copy by setting the allowable maximum size of the point-in-time backups.

Creating Shadow Copies

When shadow copies are enabled on a disk, you configure and view current Shadow Copy settings via the disk's Properties dialog box. In File Explorer or Computer Management, right-click the icon for the disk with which you want to work, click Properties, and then click the Shadow Copies tab. The Select A Volume panel shows the following:

- **Volume**   The volume label of NTFS volumes on the selected disk drive
- **Next Run Time**   The status of Shadow Copy as Disabled, or the next time a shadow copy of the volume will be created
- **Shares**   The number of shared folders on the volume
- **Used**   The amount of disk space used by Shadow Copy

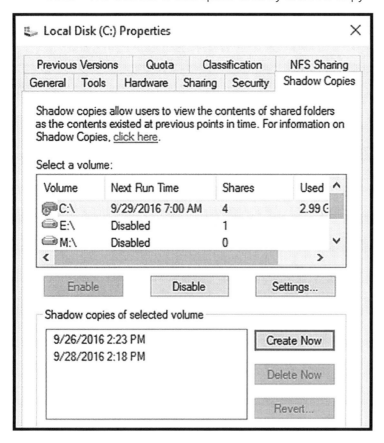

Individual shadow copies of the currently selected volume are listed in the Shadow Copies Of Selected Volume panel by date and time.

Disks have the Shadow Copies tab only when shadow copies are enabled. To enable shadow copies on a disk and create the first shadow copy, follow these steps:

1. In Computer Management, right-click the Disk Management node, point to All Tasks, and then click Configure Shadow Copies.

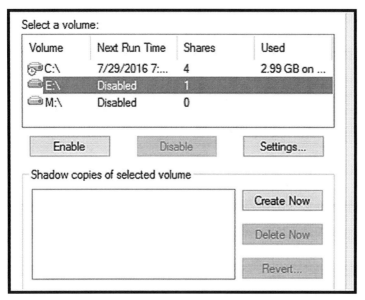

2. In the Shadow Copies dialog box, volumes listed with a Disabled status in the Next Run Time column haven't been configured to use shadow copies. Select a disabled volume by clicking it.

3. Click Settings. In the Settings dialog box, click Details to display information about the total and free disk space on the selected volume. Then close this dialog box by clicking OK. Next, configure the maximum size of all shadow copies for this volume. For maximum size, you can set an exact limit or specify that there is no size limit. Typically, the default maximum size is approximately 10% of the total disk space available.

4. In the Settings dialog box, click Schedule. As discussed previously, two default schedules are defined. If you want to change the default schedule, select a schedule in the Schedule list and then change its configuration using the options provided. Click OK to close the Schedule dialog box, then click OK to close the Settings dialog box.

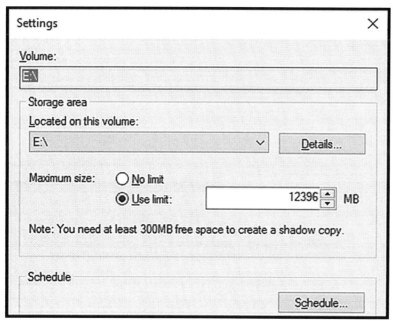

5. After you configure the volume for shadow copying, click Enable if necessary. When prompted to confirm this action, click Yes. Enabling shadow copying creates the first shadow copy and sets the schedule for later shadow copies. Click OK to close the Shadow Copies dialog box.

> **NOTE** If you create a run schedule when configuring the Shadow Copy settings, shadow copying is enabled automatically for the volume when you click OK to close the Settings dialog box. However, the first shadow copy won't be created until the next scheduled run time. If you want to create a shadow copy of the volume now, select the volume and then click Create Now.

Once you've enabled shadows copies on a disk, the copies are created automatically according to the schedule defined. You can create a shadow copy at any time by following these steps:

1. In Computer Management, right-click the Disk Management node, point to All Tasks, and then click Configure Shadow Copies.

2. In the Shadow Copies dialog box, select the volume with which you want to work by clicking it.

3. Click Create Now.

Restoring a Shadow Copy

Users working on client computers access shadow copies of individual shared folders by using the Previous Versions or Shadow Copy client. The best way to access shadow copies on a client computer is to follow these steps:

1. In File Explorer, right-click the share for which you want to access previous file versions, click Properties, and then click the Previous Versions tab.

2. On the Previous Versions tab, select the folder version with which you want to work. Each folder has a date and time stamp. Click the button corresponding to the action you want to perform:

- Click Open to open the shadow copy in File Explorer.
- Click Copy to display the Copy Items dialog box, which lets you copy the snapshot image of the folder to the location you specify.
- Click Restore to roll back the shared folder to its state at the time of the snapshot image you selected.

Reverting an Entire Volume

Windows Server 2016 features a shadow copy enhancement that enables you to revert an entire volume to the state it was in when a particular shadow copy was created. Because volumes containing operating system files can't be reverted, the volume you want to revert must not be a system volume. The same goes for volumes on a cluster shared disk.

To revert an entire volume to a previous state, follow these steps:

1. In Computer Management, right-click Disk Management, point to All Tasks, and then click Configure Shadow Copies.

2. On the Shadow Copies tab, select the volume with which you want to work in the Select A Volume list.

3. Individual shadow copies of the currently selected volume are listed by date and time in the Shadow Copies Of Selected Volume panel. Select the shadow copy with the date and time stamp to which you want to revert, and then click Revert.

4. To confirm this action, select the Check Here If You Want To Revert This Volume check box, and then click Revert Now. Click OK to close the Shadow Copies dialog box.

Deleting Shadow Copies

Each point-in-time backup is maintained separately. You can delete individual shadow copies of a volume as necessary, and this recovers the disk space used by the shadow copies.

To delete a shadow copy, follow these steps:

1. In Computer Management, right-click Disk Management, point to All Tasks, and then click Configure Shadow Copies.

2. On the Shadow Copies tab, select the volume with which you want to work in the Select A Volume list.

3. Individual shadow copies of the currently selected volume are listed by date and time in the Shadow Copies Of Selected Volume panel. Select the shadow copy you want to delete, and then click Delete Now. Click Yes to confirm the action.

Disabling Shadow Copies

If you no longer want to maintain shadow copies of a volume, you can disable the Shadow Copy feature. Disabling this feature turns off the scheduling of automated point-in-time backups and removes any existing shadow copies.

To disable shadow copies of a volume, follow these steps:

1. In Computer Management, right-click Disk Management, point to All Tasks, and then click Configure Shadow Copies.

2. On the Shadow Copies tab, select the volume with which you want to work in the Select A Volume list, and then click Disable.

3. When prompted, confirm the action by clicking Yes. Click OK to close the Shadow Copies dialog box.

Configuring Synced Sharing

Although the standard approach to sharing files requires a computer that is joined and connected to a domain, synced sharing does not. With sync shares, users can use an Internet or corporate network connection to sync data to their devices from folders located on enterprise servers. You implement synced sharing by using Work Folders.

Work Folders is a feature that you can add to servers running Windows Server 2016. Work Folders use a client-server architecture. A Work Folders client is natively integrated into Windows 10 and is also available for iPad and other devices.

Getting Started with Work Folders

You deploy Work Folders in the enterprise by performing these procedures:

1. Add the Work Folders role to servers that you want to host sync shares.
2. Use Group Policy to enable discovery of Work Folders.
3. Create sync shares on your sync servers and optionally, enable SMB access to sync shares.
4. Configure clients to access Work Folders.

NOTE Group Policy is discussed in detail in Chapter 13. For detailed information about configuring Group Policy to enable discovery of Work Folders, see "Automatically Configuring Work Folders," in that chapter.

Work Folders use a remote web gateway configured as part of the IIS hostable web core. When users access a sync share via a URL provided by an administrator and configured in Group Policy, a user folder is created as a subfolder of the sync share and this subfolder is where the user's data is stored. The folder naming format for the user-specific folder is set when you create a sync share. The folder can be named by using only the user alias portion of the user's logon name or the full logon name in alias@domain format. The format you choose primarily depends on the level of compatibility required. Using the full logon name eliminates potential conflicts when users from different domains have identical user aliases, but this format is not compatible with redirected folders.

To maintain compatibility with redirected folders, you should configure sync folders to use aliases. However, in enterprises with multiple domains, the drawback to this approach is that there could be conflicts between identical user aliases in different domains. Although the automatically configured permissions for a user folder would prevent amyh from the imaginedlands.com domain from accessing a user folder created for amyh from the pocket-consultant.com domain, the conflict would cause problems. If there was an existing folder for amyh from the imaginedlands.com domain, the server would not be able to create a user folder for amyh from the pocket-consultant.com.

With Work Folders, you have several important options during initial setup. You can encrypt files in Work Folders on client devices and ensure that the screens on client devices lock automatically and require an access password. Encryption is implemented by using the Encrypting File System (EFS). EFS encrypts files with an enterprise encryption key rather than an encryption key generated by the client device. The enterprise encryption key is specific to the enterprise ID of the user (which by default is the primary SMTP address of the user). Having an enterprise encryption key that is separate from a client's standard encryption key is important to ensure that encrypted personal files and encrypted work files are managed separately.

When files are encrypted, administrators can use a selective wipe to remove enterprise files from a client device. The selective wipe simply removes the enterprise encryption key and thus renders the work files unreadable. Selective wipe does not affect any encrypted personal files. As the work files remain encrypted, there's no need to actually delete the work files from the client device. That said, you could run Disk Optimizer on the drive where the work files were stored. During optimization, Disk Optimizer should then overwrite the sectors where the work files were stored. Selective wipe only works when you've enabled the encryption option on Work Folders.

Although encryption is one way to protect enterprise data, another way is to configure client devices to lock screens and require a password for access. The exact policy enforced requires:

* A minimum password length of 6 characters
* A maximum password retry of 10
* A screen that automatically locks in 15 minutes or less

If you enforce the use of automatic lock screens and passwords, any device that doesn't support these requirements is prevented from connecting to the Work Folder.

By default, sync shares are not available in the same way as standard file shares. Because of this, users can only access sync shares by using the Work Folders client. If you want to make sync shares available to users as standard file shares, you must enable SMB access. After you enable SMB access, users can access files stored in Work Folders by using syncing and by mapping network drives.

When a user makes changes to files in Work Folders, the changes might not be immediately apparent to others using the same Work Folders. For example, if a user deletes a file from a Work Folder by using SMB, other users accessing the Work Folder might still see the file as available. This inconsistency can occur because by default clients only poll the sync server every 10 minutes for SMB changes.

A sync server also uses a Work Folders client to check periodically for changes users have made using SMB; the default polling interval is 5 minutes. When the server identifies changes, the server relays the changes the next time a client syncs. Following this, you can determine that it could take up to 15 minutes for a change made using SMB to fully propagate.

> **REAL WORLD**   To minimize support issues related to Work Folders, you'll want to let readers know how the technology works. Specifically, you'll want to let readers know changes might not be immediately apparent and they'll need to be patient when waiting for changes to propagate.

You can specify how frequently the server checks for changes made locally on the server or through SMB by using the –MinimumChangeDetectionMins parameter of the Set-SyncServerSetting cmdlet. However, as the server must check the change information for each file stored in the sync share, you need to be careful that you don't configure a server to try to detect changes too frequently. A server that checks for changes too frequently can become overloaded. Remember, change detection uses more resources as the number of files stored in the sync share increases.

If you deploy roles and features that require a full version of the Web (IIS) role, you might find that these roles and features or the Work Folders feature itself don't work together. A conflict can occur because the full version of the Web (IIS) role has a Default Web Site that uses port 80 for HTTP communications and port 443 for secure HTTP communications. For example, running Windows Essentials Experience and Work Folders together on the same server requires a special configuration. Typically, you need to change the ports used by Windows Essentials Experience so that they don't conflict with the ports used by Work Folders.

To enable detailed logging of Work Folders, you can enable and configure the Audit Object Access policy setting for a Group Policy Object (GPO) processed by the server. You'll find this setting in the Administrative Templates for Computer Configuration under Windows Settings\Security Settings\Local Policies Audit Policies. After you enable Audit Object Access, add an audit entry for the specific folders you want to audit. In File Explorer, right-click a folder you want to audit, and then select Properties. In the Properties dialog box, on the Security tab, select Advanced. In the Advanced Security Settings dialog box, use the options on the Auditing tab to configure auditing.

Creating Sync Shares and Enabling SMB Access

You create a sync share to identify a local folder on a sync server that will be synchronized and accessible to domain users via the Work Folders client. As sync shares are mapped to local paths on sync servers, I recommend that you create any folders that you want to use before creating sync shares. This will make it easier to select the exact folders with which you want to work. For details on adding the Work Folders role and configure Work Folders in Group Policy, see "Automatically Configuring Work Folders" in Chapter 13 "Using Group Policy for Administration."

To create a sync share, complete the following steps:

1. In Server Manager, select File And Storage Services, and then select Work Folders. On the Work Folders panel, select Tasks, and then select New Sync Share to open the New Sync Share Wizard. If the Before You Begin page is displayed, click Next.

2. On the Select The Server And Path page, select the server with which you want to work. Keep in mind that only servers that have the Work Folders role installed are available for selection.

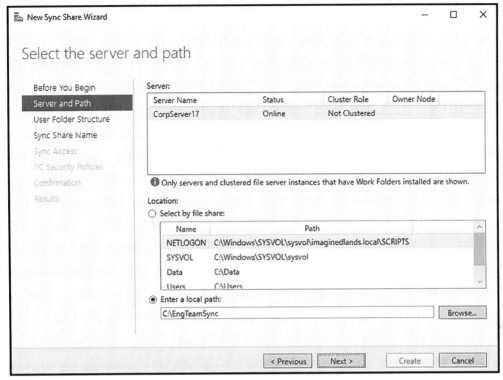

3. When configuring sync shares, you have several options. You can:

- Add syncing to an existing file share by choosing the Select By File Share option, and then selecting the file share that should also be synced.
- Add syncing to an existing local folder by choosing Enter A Local Path, selecting Browse, and then using the Select Folder dialog box to locate and chose the folder to sync.
- Add syncing to a new local folder by choosing Enter A Local Path, and then entering the path to use.

4. When you are ready to continue, click Next. If you specified a new folder location, you are prompted to confirm whether you want to create this folder. Select OK to create the folder and continue.

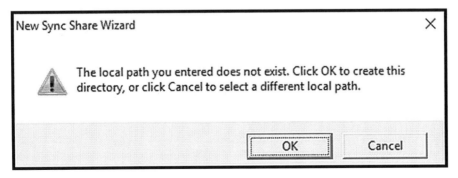

5. On the Specify The Structure For User Folders page, choose a folder naming format for the subfolders where user data is stored. To use only the user alias portion of the user's logon name for naming user folders, choose User Alias. To use the full logon name for naming user folders, choose User alias@domain.

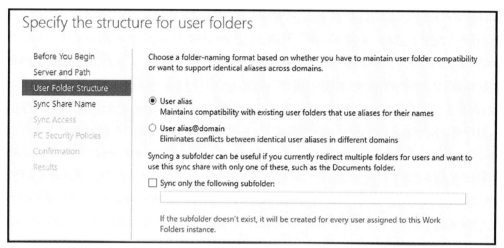

6. By default, all folders and files stored under the user folder are synced automatically. If you'd prefer that only a specific folder is synced, select the Sync Only The Following Folder check box, and then enter the name of the folder, such as Documents. Click Next to continue

7. On the Enter The Sync Share Name page, enter a share name and description before clicking Next to continue.

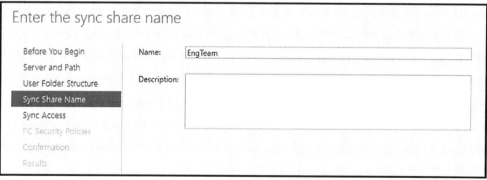

8. On the Grant Sync Access To Groups page, use the options provided to specify the users and groups that should be able to access the sync share. To add a user or group, click Add, and then use the Select User Or Group dialog box to specify the user or group that should have access to the sync share.

> **SECURITY ALERT** Any users and groups you specify will be granted
> permissions on the base folder that allows the users and groups to create
> folders and access files in their folders. Specifically, Creator/Owner is granted
> Full Control on subfolders and files only. The users and groups are granted
> List Folder/Read Data, Create Folders/Append Data, Traverse Folder/Execute
> File, Read/Write attributes on the base folder. Local System is granted Full
> Control of the base folder, subfolders, and files. Administrator is granted Read
> permission on the base folder.

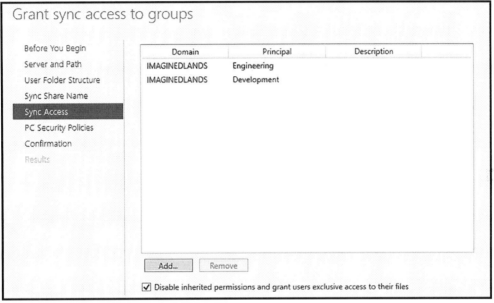

9. By default, inherited permissions are disabled and users have exclusive access
   to their user folders. Because of this, only the user who stores a file has
   access to this file on the share. If the base folder for the share has
   permissions that you want to be applied to user folders, such as those that
   would grant administrators access to user folders, clear the Disable Inherited
   Permissions check box. When you are ready to continue, click Next.

10. On the Specify Security Policies page, you have two options. You can select
    Encrypt Work Folders to encrypt files in Work Folders on client devices. You
    can select Automatically Lock Screen And Require A Password to ensure that
    the screens on client devices lock automatically and require a password for
    access.

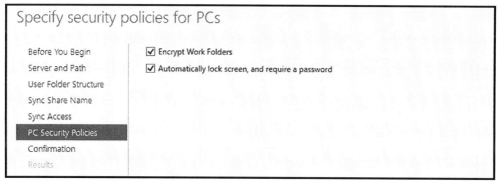

Specify security policies for PCs

Before You Begin
Server and Path
User Folder Structure
Sync Share Name
Sync Access
PC Security Policies
Confirmation
Results

☑ Encrypt Work Folders
☑ Automatically lock screen, and require a password

11. Click Next to continue, and then confirm your selections. Select Create to create the sync share. If the wizard is unable to create the sync share, you'll get an error and will need to note the error and take appropriate corrective action. A common error you might get occurs when the server hosts both Work Folders (which use the hostable web core) and the full Web (IIS) role. Before you can crate sync shares, you'll need to modify the ports used so they do not conflict or install Work Folders on a server that doesn't have the full Web (IIS) role.

12. If you did not select an existing file share during set up and want to enable the sync share for SMB access, open File Explorer. In File Explorer, right-click the folder, select Share With, and then select Specific People. Finally, configure file sharing as discussed earlier in this chapter.

Accessing Work Folders on Clients

Users with a domain user account can access Work Folders from a client device over the Internet or over the corporate network. You can configure Work Folder Access for a user by completing the following steps:

1. In Control Panel, click System And Security, and then select Work Folders. On the Manage Work Folders page, click Set Up Work Folders.

2. On the Enter Your Work Email Address page, enter the user email address, such as **amyh@imaginedlands.com**, and then click Next. If the client device is joined to the domain, you will not be prompted for the user's credentials. Otherwise, you are prompted for the user's credentials. After the user enters her credentials, you can select Remember My Credentials to store the user's credentials for future use, and then click OK to continue.

3. On the Introducing Work Folders page, note where the work files for the user will be stored. By default, work files are stored in a user profile subfolder called Work Folders. For example, the work files for Amyh would be stored under %SystemDrive%\Users\Amyh\WorkFolders. To store work files in

another location, click Change and then use the options provided to specify a new save location for work files. When you are ready to continue, click Next.

4. On the Security Policies page, review the security policies that will be applied, and then have the user select the I Accept These Policies On My PC check box. You will not be able to continue if you do not select this check box.

5. Select Set Up Work Folders to create Work Folders on the client device.

After you configure Work Folders for initial use on a client device, the user can access Work Folders in File Explorer. When a user opens File Explorer, the This PC node should be opened by default. If so, the user simply needs to double-click Work Folders to view work files. If a user has an open Explorer window and This PC is not the selected node, she simply needs to click the leftmost option button in the address list, and then click This PC.

As the user works with files, the changes the user makes trigger sync actions with the server. If the user doesn't change any files locally for an extended period of time, the client connects to the server every 10 minutes to determine whether there are changes to sync.

Chapter 11. Managing Permissions and Auditing

Data is the heart of any enterprise and few aspects of administration are more important than ensuring that data is protected. Although file and folder permissions protects important resources by restricting access, protecting enterprise data isn't just about file and folder permissions. To secure enterprise data appropriately, you need a firm understanding of object management, ownership, inheritance, and auditing. To help ensure that enterprise data is manageable, you also need to know how to implement quotas that restrict the amount of data that can be stored on servers.

Object Management, Ownership, and Inheritance

Windows Server 2016 takes an object-based approach to describing resources and managing permissions. Objects that describe resources are defined on NTFS volumes and in Active Directory Domain Services (AD DS). With NTFS volumes, you can set permissions for files and folders. With Active Directory, you can set permissions for other types of objects, such as users, computers, and groups. You can use these permissions to control access with precision.

Objects and Object Managers

Whether defined on an NTFS volume or in Active Directory, each type of object has an object manager and primary management tools. The object manager controls object settings and permissions. The primary management tools are the tools of choice for working with the object. Objects, their managers, and management tools are summarized in Table 9-1.

TABLE 9-1 Windows Server 2016 objects

OBJECT TYPE	OBJECT MANAGER	MANAGEMENT TOOL
Files and folders	NTFS	File Explorer
Printers	Print spooler	Printers in Control Panel

OBJECT TYPE	OBJECT MANAGER	MANAGEMENT TOOL
Registry keys	Windows registry	Registry Editor
Services	Service controllers	Security Configuration Tool Set
Shares	Server service	File Explorer, Computer Management, Share And Storage Management

Object Ownership and Transfer

It's important to understand the concept of object ownership. In Windows Server 2016, the object owner isn't necessarily the object's creator; instead, the object owner is the person who has direct control over the object. Object owners can grant access permissions and give other users permission to take ownership of the object.

As an administrator, you can take ownership of objects on the network to ensure that you can't be locked out of files, folders, printers, and other resources. After you take ownership of files, however, you can't return ownership to the original owner (in most cases). This prevents administrators from accessing files and then trying to hide the fact.

The way ownership is assigned initially depends on the location of the resource being created. In most cases, the Administrators group is listed as the current owner, and the object's actual creator is listed as a person who can take ownership.

Ownership can be transferred in several ways:

- If the Administrators group is initially assigned as the owner, the creator of the object can take ownership, if she does this before someone else takes ownership.
- The current owner can grant the Take Ownership permission to other users, allowing those users to take ownership of the object.
- An administrator can take ownership of an object, if the object is under his administrative control.

To take ownership of an object, follow these steps:

1. Open the management tool for the object. For example, if you want to work with files and folders, start File Explorer.

2. Right-click the object you want to take ownership of, and then click Properties. In the Properties dialog box, click the Security tab.

3. On the Security tab, click Advanced to display the Advanced Security Settings dialog box where the current owner is listed under the file or folder name.

4. Click Change. Use the options in the Select User, Computer, Service Account, Or Group dialog box to select the new owner.

5. Click OK twice when you have finished.

> **TIP** If you're taking ownership of a folder, you can take ownership of all subfolders and files within the folder by selecting the Replace Owner On Subcontainers And Objects check box. This option also works with objects that contain other objects, in which case you would take ownership of all child objects.

Object Inheritance

Objects are defined by using a parent-child structure. A parent object is a top-level object, and a child object is an object defined below a parent object in the hierarchy. For example, the folder C:\ is the parent of the folders C:\Data and C:\Backups. Any subfolders created in C:\Data or C:\Backups are children of these folders and grandchildren of C:\.

Child objects can inherit permissions from parent objects; in fact, all Windows Server 2016 objects are created with inheritance enabled by default. This means that child objects automatically inherit the permissions of the parent; therefore, the parent object permissions control access to the child object. If you want to change permissions on a child object, you must do one of the following:

- Edit the permissions of the parent object.
- Stop inheriting permissions from the parent object, and then assign permissions to the child object.
- Select the opposite permission to override the inherited permission. For example, if the parent allows the permission, you would deny it on the child object.

To stop inheriting permissions from a parent object, follow these steps:

1. Open the management tool for the object. For example, if you want to work with files and folders, start File Explorer.

2. Right-click the object with which you want to work, and then click Properties. In the Properties dialog box, click the Security tab.

3. Click Advanced to display the Advanced Security Settings dialog box.

4. On the Permissions tab, click Change Permissions to display an editable version of the Permissions tab.

5. On the Permissions tab, you'll see a Disable Inheritance button if inheritance currently is enabled. Click Disable Inheritance.

6. You can now either convert the inherited permissions to explicit permissions or remove all inherited permissions and apply only the permissions that you explicitly set on the folder or file.

Keep in mind that if you remove the inherited permissions and no other permissions are assigned, everyone but the owner of the resource is denied access. This effectively locks out everyone except the owner of a folder or file; however, administrators still have the right to take ownership of the resource regardless of the permissions. Thus, if an administrator is locked out of a file or a folder and truly needs access, she can take ownership and then have unrestricted access.

To start inheriting permissions from a parent object, follow these steps:

1. Open the management tool for the object. For example, if you want to work with files and folders, start File Explorer.

2. Right-click the object with which you want to work, and then click Properties. In the Properties dialog box, click the Security tab.

3. Click Advanced to display the Advanced Security Settings dialog box.

4. On the Permissions tab, click Enable Inheritance, and then click OK. Note that the Enable Inheritance button is available only if permission inheritance currently is disabled.

File and Folder Permissions

NTFS permissions are always evaluated when a file is accessed. On NTFS and ReFS volumes, you can set security permissions on files and folders to grant or deny access to the files and folders. Because Windows Server 2016 adds new layers of security, NTFS permissions now encompass the following:

- Basic permissions
- Claims-based permissions
- Special permissions

You can view NTFS permissions for files and folders by following these steps:

1. In File Explorer, right-click the file or folder with which you want to work, and then click Properties. In the Properties dialog box, click the Security tab.

2. In the Group Or User Names list, select the user, computer, or group whose permissions you want to view. If the permissions are not available (dimmed), the permissions are inherited from a parent object.

Shared folders have both share permissions and NTFS permissions. You can view the underlying NTFS permissions for shared folders by following these steps:

1. In Server Manager, the Shares subnode of the File And Storage Services node shows existing shares for file servers that have been added for management.

2. Right-click the folder with which you want to work, and then click Properties to display a Properties dialog box.

3. When you click Permissions in the left pane, the current share permissions and NTFS permissions are shown in the main pane.

4. To get more information, click Customize Permissions to open the Advanced Security Settings dialog box.

On file servers running Windows Server 2016, you can also use central access policies to precisely define the specific attributes that users and devices must have to access resources.

Understanding File and Folder Permissions

The basic permissions you can assign to files and folders are summarized in the list that follows. File permissions include Full Control, Modify, Read & Execute, Read, and Write. Folder permissions include Full Control, Modify, Read & Execute, List Folder Contents, Read, and Write.

- **Read** For folders, permits viewing and listing files and subfolders. For files, permits viewing or accessing a file's contents.
- **Write** For folders, permits adding files and subfolders. For files, permits writing to a file.

* **Read & Execute**   For folders, does not permit viewing the contents of files. You can list file and folder names, but you can't open files to read, nor can you execute files if that execute requires opening the file (as in a batch or PS1 file). Inherited by files and folders. For files, permits viewing and accessing a file's contents in addition to executing a file.
* **List Folder Contents**   For folders, permits viewing and listing file names and subfolder names in addition to executing files; inherited by folders only. Not applicable to files.
* **Modify**   For folders, permits reading and writing of files and subfolders; allows deletion of the folder. For files, permits reading and writing of a file; allows deletion of a file.
* **Full Control**   For folders, permits reading, writing, changing, and deleting files and subfolders. For files, permits reading, writing, changing, and deleting a file.

Any time you work with file and folder permissions, you should keep the following in mind:

* Read is the only permission needed to run scripts. Execute permission doesn't matter.
* Read access is required to access a shortcut and its target.
* Giving a user permission to write to a file but not to delete it doesn't prevent the user from deleting the file's contents.
* If a user has full control over a folder, the user can delete files in the folder regardless of the permission on the files.

The basic permissions are created by combining special permissions in logical groups. By using advanced permission settings, you can assign these special permissions individually, if necessary. As you study the special permissions, keep the following in mind:

* By default, if no access is specifically granted or denied, the user is denied access. Further, if a permission has been explicitly denied, the deny will override any permission grant.
* Actions that users can perform are based on the sum of all the permissions assigned to the user and to all the groups of which the user is a member. For example, if the user GeorgeJ has Read access and is a member of the group Techies, which has Change access, GeorgeJ will have Change access. If Techies is a member of Administrators, which has Full Control, GeorgeJ will have complete control over the file. However, if GeorgeJ has been explicitly denied a permission, the deny will override any grant.

As you work with special permissions, keep in mind that when you create files and folders, these files and folders inherit certain permission settings from parent objects. These permission settings are shown as the default permissions.

Setting Basic File and Folder Permissions

To set basic NTFS permissions for files and folders, follow these steps:

1. In File Explorer, right-click the file or folder with which you want to work, and then click Properties. In the Properties dialog box, click the Security tab.

2. Click Edit to display an editable version of the Security tab.

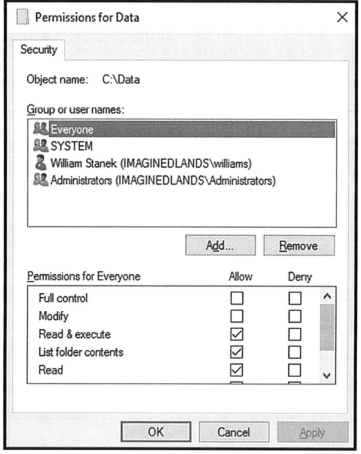

3. Users or groups that already have access to the file or folder are listed in the Group Or User Names list. You can change permissions for these users and groups by selecting the user or group you want to change and then granting or denying access permissions in the Permissions list box.

> **TIP** Inherited permissions are shaded (dimmed). If you want to override an inherited permission, select the opposite permission.

4. To set access permissions for additional users, computers, or groups, click Add to display the Select Users, Computers, Service Accounts, Or Groups dialog box.

5. Enter the name of a user, computer, or group in the current domain, and then click Check Names. One of the following actions occurs:

- If a single match is found, the dialog box is updated and the entry is underlined.
- If no matches are found, you entered an incorrect name part or are working with an incorrect location. Modify the name and try again, or click Locations to select a new location.
- If multiple matches are found, select the name or names you want to use, and then click OK. To add more users, computers, or groups, enter a semicolon (;), and then repeat this step.

> **NOTE** The Locations button allows you to access account names in other domains. Click Locations to view a list of the current domain, trusted domains, and other resources you can access. Because of the transitive trusts in Windows Server 2016, you can usually access all the domains in the domain tree or forest.

6. In the Group Or User Names list, select the user, computer, or group you want to configure, and in the check boxes in the Permissions list, allow or deny permissions. Repeat for other users, computers, or groups.

7. Click OK.

Because shared folders also have NTFS permissions, you might want to set basic NTFS permissions by using Server Manager. To do this, follow these steps:

1. In Server Manager, select File and Storage Services, select the server you want to work with, and then Select Shares.

2. Right-click the folder with which you want to work, and then click Properties to display a Properties dialog box.

3. When you click Permissions in the left pane, the current share permissions and NTFS permissions are shown in the main pane.

4. Click Customize Permissions to open the Advanced Security Settings dialog box with the Permissions tab selected.

5. Users or groups that already have access to the file or folder are listed under Permission Entries. Use the options provided to view, edit, add, or remove permissions for users and groups.

Setting Special Permissions on Files and Folders

To set special NTFS permissions for files and folders, follow these steps:

1. In File Explorer, right-click the file or folder with which you want to work, and then click Properties.

2. In the Properties dialog box, select the Security tab, and then click Advanced to display the Advanced Security Settings dialog box. Before you can modify permissions, you must click Change Permissions. The permissions are presented much as they are on the Security tab. The key differences are that you see individual allow or deny permission sets, whether permissions are inherited and where they are from, and the resources to which the permissions apply.

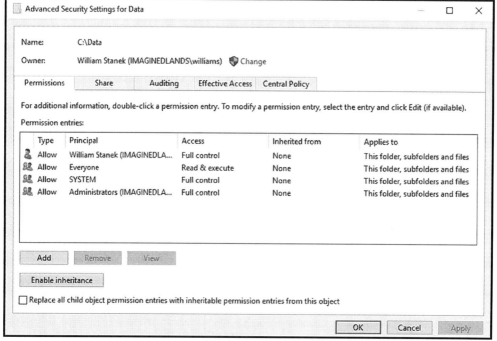

3. If a user or group already has permissions set for the file or folder (and those permissions are not being inherited), you can modify the special permissions by selecting the user or group, and then clicking Edit. Afterward, skip steps 4–7, and then follow the rest of the steps in this procedure.

4. To add special permissions for a user or group, click Add to display the Permission Entry dialog box. Click Select A Principal to display the Select User, Computer, Service Account, Or Group dialog box.

5. Enter the name of a user or a group account. Be sure to reference the user account name rather than the user's full name. Only one name can be entered at a time.

6. Click Check Names. If a single match is found for each entry, the dialog box is automatically updated and the entry is underlined; otherwise, you'll get an additional dialog box. If no matches are found, you either entered the name incorrectly, or you're working with an incorrect location. Modify the name in the Name Not Found dialog box and try again, or click Locations to select a new location. When multiple matches are found, in the Multiple Names Found dialog box, select the name you want to use, and then click OK.

7. Click OK. The user and group are added as the Principal, and the Permission Entry dialog box is updated to show this.

8. When you are editing permissions, only basic permissions are listed by default. Click Show Advanced Permissions to display the special permissions.

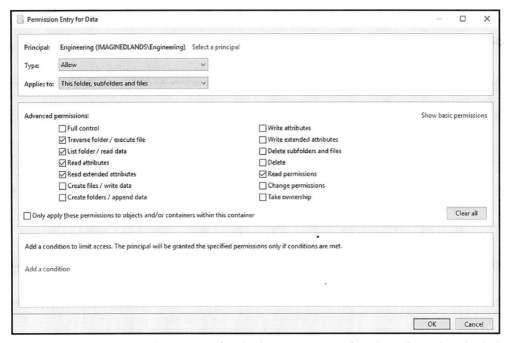

9. Use the Type list to specify whether you are configuring allowed or denied special permissions, and then select the special permissions you want to allow or deny. If any permissions are dimmed (unavailable), they are inherited from a parent folder.

NOTE You allow and deny special permissions separately. Therefore, if you want to both allow and deny special permissions, you need to configure the allowed permissions, and then repeat this procedure starting with step 1 to configure the denied permissions.

10. If the options in the Applies To list are available, choose the appropriate option to ensure that the permissions are properly inherited. The options include the following:

- **This Folder Only**   The permissions apply only to the currently selected folder.
- **This Folder, Subfolders And Files**   The permissions apply to this folder, any subfolders of this folder, and any files in any of these folders.
- **This Folder And Subfolders**   The permissions apply to this folder and any subfolders of this folder. They do not apply to any files in any of these folders.
- **This Folder And Files**   The permissions apply to this folder and any files in this folder. They do not apply to any subfolders of this folder.
- **Subfolders And Files Only**   The permissions apply to any subfolders of this folder and any files in any of these folders. They do not apply to this folder itself.
- **Subfolders Only**   The permissions apply to any subfolders of this folder but not to the folder itself or any files in any of these folders.
- **Files Only**   The permissions apply to any files in this folder and any files in subfolders of this folder. They do not apply to this folder itself or to subfolders.

11. When you have finished configuring permissions, click OK.

Because shared folders also have NTFS permissions, you might want to set special NTFS permissions by using Server Manager. To do this, follow these steps:

1. In Server Manager, select File And Storage Services, select the server you want to work with, and then select Shares. Next, right-click the folder with which you want to work, and then click Properties to display a Properties dialog box.

2. When you click Permissions in the left pane, the current share permissions and NTFS permissions are shown in the main pane.

3. Click Customize Permissions to open the Advanced Security Settings dialog box with the Permissions tab selected.

4. Users or groups that already have access to the file or folder are listed under Permission Entries. Use the options provided to view, edit, add, or remove permissions for users and groups. When you are editing or adding permissions in the Permission Entry dialog box, follow steps 8-11 of the previous procedure to display and work with special permissions.

Setting Claims-Based Permissions

Claims-based access controls use compound identities that incorporate not only the groups of which a user and the user's computer is a member, but also claim types, which are assertions about objects based on Active Directory attributes, and resource properties, which classify objects and describe their attributes. When resources are remotely accessed, claims-based access controls and central access policies rely on Kerberos with Armoring for authentication of computer device claims. Kerberos with Armoring improves domain security by allowing domain-joined clients and domain controllers to communicate over secure, encrypted channels.

You use claims-based permissions to fine-tune access by defining conditions that limit access as part of a resource's advanced security permissions. Typically, these conditions add device claims or user claims to the access controls. User claims identify users; device claims identify devices. For example, you could define claim types based on business category and country code. The Active Directory attributes are businessCategory and countryCode, respectively. By using these claim types, you could then fine-tune access to ensure that only users, devices, or both that belong to specific business categories and have certain country codes are granted access to a resource. You could also define a resource property called Project to help fine-tune access even more.

> **MORE INFO**   With central access policies, you define central access rules in Active Directory and those rules are applied dynamically throughout the enterprise. Central access rules use conditional expressions that require you to determine the resource properties, claim types, and/or security groups required for the policy, in addition to the servers to which the policy should be applied.

Before you can define and apply claim conditions to a computer's files and folders, a claims-based policy must be enabled. For computers that are not joined to the domain, you can do this by enabling and configuring the KDC Support For Claims, Compound Authentication And Kerberos Armoring policy in the Administrative Templates policies for Computer Configuration under System\KDC. The policy must be configured to use one of the following modes:

- **Supported**   Domain controllers support claims, compound identities, and Kerberos armoring. Client computers that don't support Kerberos with Armoring can be authenticated.
- **Always Provide Claims**   This mode is the same as the Supported mode, but domain controllers always return claims for accounts.
- **Fail Unarmored Authentication Requests**   Kerberos with Armoring is mandatory. Client computers that don't support Kerberos with Armoring cannot be authenticated.

The Kerberos Client Support For Claims, Compound Authentication And Kerberos Armoring policy controls whether the Kerberos client running on Windows 10 and Windows Server 2016 requests claims and compound authentication. The policy must be enabled for compatible Kerberos clients to request claims and compound authentication for Dynamic Access Control and Kerberos armoring. You'll find this policy in the Administrative Templates policies for Computer Configuration under System\Kerberos.

For application throughout a domain, a claims-based policy should be enabled for all domain controllers in a domain to ensure consistent application. Because of this, you typically enable and configure this policy through the Default Domain Controllers Group Policy Object (GPO), or the highest GPO linked to the domain controller's organizational unit (OU).

After you've enabled and configured the claims-based policy, you can define claim conditions by completing these steps:

1. In File Explorer, right-click the file or folder with which you want to work, and then click Properties. In the Properties dialog box, select the Security tab, and then click Advanced to display the Advanced Security Settings dialog box.

2. If the user or group already has permissions set for the file or folder, you can edit their existing permissions. Here, click the user with which you want to work, click Edit, and then skip steps 3–6.

3. Click Add to display the Permission Entry dialog box. Click Select A Principal to display the Select User, Computer, Service Account, Or Group dialog box.

4. Enter the name of a user or a group account. Be sure to reference the user account name rather than the user's full name. Only one name can be entered at a time.

5. Click Check Names. If a single match is found for each entry, the dialog box is automatically updated and the entry is underlined. Otherwise, you'll get an additional dialog box. If no matches are found, you either entered the name incorrectly or you're working with an incorrect location. Modify the name in the Name Not Found dialog box and try again, or click Locations to select a new location. When multiple matches are found, in the Multiple Names Found dialog box, select the name you want to use and then click OK.

6. Click OK. The user and group are added as the Principal. Click Add A Condition.

7. Use the options provided to define the condition or conditions that must be met to grant access. With users and groups, set basic claims based on group membership, previously defined claim types, or both. With resource properties, define conditions for property values.

8. When you have finished configuring conditions, click OK.

Because shared folders also have NTFS permissions, you might want to set claims-based permissions by using Server Manager. To do this, follow these steps:

1. In Server Manager, select File and Storage Services, select the server you want to work with, and then Select Shares.

2. Right-click the folder with which you want to work, and then click Properties to display a Properties dialog box.

3. When you click Permissions in the left pane, the current share permissions and NTFS permissions are shown in the main pane.

4. Click Customize Permissions to open the Advanced Security Settings dialog box with the Permissions tab selected.

5. Users or groups that already have access to the file or folder are listed under Permission Entries. Use the options provided to view, edit, add, or remove permissions for users and groups. When you are editing or adding permissions in the Permission Entry dialog box, you can add conditions just as I discussed in steps 6 to 8 of the previous procedure.

Auditing System Resources

Auditing is the best way to track what's happening on your Windows Server 2016 systems. You can use auditing to collect information related to resource usage such as file access, system logons, and system configuration changes. Any time an action occurs that you've configured for auditing, the action is written to the system's security log, where it's stored for your review. The security log is accessible from Event Viewer.

> **NOTE** For most auditing changes, you need to be logged on using an account that's a member of the Administrators group or you need to be granted the Manage Auditing And Security Log right in Group Policy.

Setting Auditing Policies

Auditing policies are essential to help ensure the security and integrity of your systems. Just about every computer system on the network should be configured with some type of security logging. You configure auditing policies for individual computers with local Group Policy and for all computers in domains with Active Directory–based Group Policy. Through Group Policy, you can set auditing policies for an entire site, a domain, or an organizational unit. You can also set policies for an individual workstation or server.

After you access the GPO with which you want to work, you can set auditing policies by following these steps:

1. In the Group Policy Management Editor, access the Audit Policy node by working your way down the console tree. Expand Computer Configuration, Policies, Windows Settings, Security Settings, and Local Policies, and then select Audit Policy.

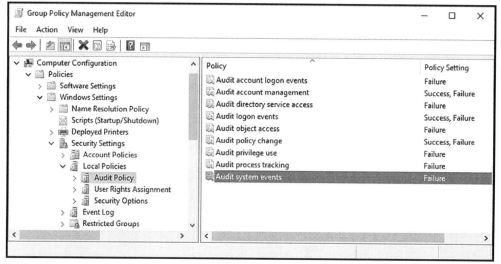

2. The auditing options are as follows:

- **Audit Account Logon Events**   Tracks events related to user logon and logoff.
- **Audit Account Management**   Tracks account management by means of Active Directory Users And Computers. Events are generated any time user, computer, or group accounts are created, modified, or deleted.
- **Audit Directory Service Access**   Tracks access to Active Directory. Events are generated any time users or computers access the directory.

- **Audit Logon Events**   Tracks events related to user logon, logoff, and remote connections to network systems.
- **Audit Object Access**   Tracks system resource usage for files, directories, shares, printers, and Active Directory objects.
- **Audit Policy Change**   Tracks changes to user rights, auditing, and trust relationships.
- **Audit Privilege Use**   Tracks the use of user rights and privileges, such as the right to back up files and directories.

> **NOTE**   The Audit Privilege Use policy doesn't track system access-related events, such as the use of the right to log on interactively or the right to access the computer from the network. You track these events with logon and logoff auditing.

- **Audit Process Tracking**   Tracks system processes and the resources they use.
- **Audit System Events**   Tracks system startup, shutdown, and restart, in addition to actions that affect system security or the security log.

   3. To configure an auditing policy, double-click its entry, or right-click the entry, and then click Properties.

   4. In the dialog box that is displayed, select the Define These Policy Settings check box, and then select either the Success check box, the Failure check box, or both. Success logs successful events, such as successful logon attempts. Failure logs failed events, such as failed logon attempts.

   5. Click OK.

When auditing is enabled, the security event log will reflect the following:

- Event IDs of 560 and 562 detailing user audits
- Event IDs of 592 and 593 detailing process audits

Auditing Files and Folders

If you configure a GPO to enable the Audit Object Access option, you can set the level of auditing for individual folders and files. This enables you to control precisely how folder and file usage is tracked. Auditing of this type is available only on NTFS volumes.

You can configure file and folder auditing by following these steps:

   1. In File Explorer, right-click the file or folder to be audited, and then click Properties.

2. Click the Security tab, and then click Advanced to display the Advanced Security Settings dialog box.

3. On the Auditing tab, click Continue. You can now view and manage auditing settings.

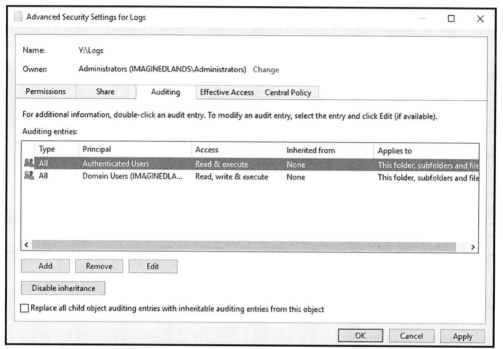

4. The Auditing Entries list shows the users, groups, or computers whose actions you want to audit. To remove an account, select the account in the Auditing Entries list, and then click Remove.

5. To configure auditing for additional users, computers, or groups, click Add. This displays the Select Users, Computers, Service Accounts, Or Groups dialog box.

6. Enter the name of a user, computer, or group in the current domain, and then click Check Names. If a single match is found, the dialog box is automatically updated and the entry is underlined; otherwise, you'll get an additional dialog box. If no matches are found, you either entered the name incorrectly or you're working with an incorrect location. Modify the name in the Name Not Found dialog box and try again, or click Locations to select a new location. When multiple matches are found, in the Multiple Names Found dialog box, select the name you want to use, and then click OK.

7. Click OK. The user and group are added, and the Principal and the Auditing Entry dialog box are updated to show this. Only basic permissions are listed

by default. If you want to work with advanced permissions, click Show Advanced Permissions to display the special permissions.

8. As necessary, use the Applies To list to specify where objects are audited. If you are working with a folder and want to replace the auditing entries on all child objects of this folder (and not on the folder itself), select Only Apply These Settings To Objects And/Or Containers Within This Container.

   Keep in mind that the Applies To list lets you specify the locations *where* you want the auditing settings to apply. The Only Apply These Settings To Objects And/Or Containers Within This Container check box controls *how* auditing settings are applied. When this check box is selected, auditing settings on the parent object replace settings on child objects. When this check box is cleared, auditing settings on the parent are merged with existing settings on child objects.

9. Use the Type list to specify whether you are configuring auditing for success, failure, or both, and then specify which actions should be audited. Success logs successful events, such as successful file reads. Failure logs failed events, such as failed file deletions. The events you can audit are the same as the special permissions, except that you can't audit the synchronizing of offline files and folders. For essential files and folders, you'll typically want to track the following:

* Write Attributes—Successful
* Write Extended Attributes—Successful
* Delete Subfolders And Files—Successful
* Delete—Successful
* Change Permissions—Successful

> **TIP**   If you want to audit actions for all users, use the special group Everyone; otherwise, select the specific user groups, users, or both that you want to audit.

10. If you're using claims-based policies and want to limit the scope of the auditing entry, you can add claims-based conditions to the auditing entry. For example, if all corporate computers are members of the Domain Computers group, you might want to closely audit access by devices that aren't members of this group.

11. When you have finished configuring auditing, click OK. Repeat this process to audit other users, groups, or computers.

Auditing the Registry

If you configure a GPO to enable the Audit Object Access option, you can set the level of auditing for keys within the registry. This enables you to track when key values are set, when subkeys are created, and when keys are deleted.

You can configure registry auditing by following these steps:

1. Open the Registry Editor. At a command prompt, enter **regedit**; or enter **regedit.exe** in the Search box, and then press Enter.

2. Browse to a key you want to audit. On the Edit menu, select Permissions.

3. In the Permissions dialog box, click Advanced. In the Advanced Security Settings dialog box, click the Auditing tab.

4. Click Add to display the Auditing Entry dialog box. Click Select A Principal to display the Select User, Computer, Service Account, Or Group dialog box.

5. In the Select User, Computer, Service Account, Or Group dialog box, enter **Everyone**, click Check Names, and then click OK.

6. In the Auditing Entry dialog box, only basic permissions are listed by default. Click Show Advanced Permissions to display the special permissions.

7. Use the Applies To list to specify how the auditing entry is to be applied.

8. Use the Type list to specify whether you are configuring auditing for success, failure, or both, and then specify which actions should be audited. Typically, you'll want to track the following advanced permissions:

- Set Value—Successful and Failed
- Create Subkey—Successful and Failed
- Delete—Successful and Failed

9. Click OK three times to close all open dialog boxes and apply the auditing settings.

Auditing Active Directory Objects

If you configure a GPO to enable the Audit Directory Service Access option, you can set the level of auditing for Active Directory objects so that you can control precisely how object usage is tracked.

To configure object auditing, follow these steps:

1. In Active Directory Users And Computers, ensure that Advanced Features is selected on the View menu, and then access the container for the object.

2. Double-click the object to be audited to open the related Properties dialog box.

3. Click the Security tab, and then click Advanced.

4. In the Advanced Settings dialog box, click the Auditing tab. The Auditing Entries list shows the users, groups, or computers whose actions you are auditing currently (if any). To remove an account, select the account in the Auditing Entries list, and then click Remove.

5. To add specific accounts, click Add to display the Auditing Entry dialog box. Click Select A Principal to display the Select User, Computer, Service Account, Or Group dialog box.

6. Enter the name of a user, computer, or group in the current domain, and then click Check Names. If a single match is found, the dialog box is automatically updated and the entry is underlined; otherwise, you'll get an additional dialog box. If no matches are found, you either entered the name incorrectly or you're working with an incorrect location. Modify the name in the Name Not Found dialog box and try again, or click Locations to select a new location. When multiple matches are found, in the Multiple Names Found dialog box, select the name you want to use, and then click OK.

7. Click OK to return to the Auditing Entry dialog box. Use the Applies To list to specify how the auditing entry is to be applied.

8. Use the Type list to specify whether you are configuring auditing for success, failure, or both, and then specify which actions should be audited. Success logs successful events, such as a successful attempt to modify an object's permissions. Failed logs failed events, such as a failed attempt to modify an object's owner.

9. Click OK. Repeat this process to audit other users, groups, or computers.

Chapter 12. Configuring Disk Quotas

Windows Server 2016 supports two mutually exclusive types of disk quotas:

- **NTFS disk quotas** NTFS disk quotas are supported on all editions of Windows Server 2016 and enable you to manage disk space usage by users. You configure quotas on a per-volume basis. Although users who exceed limits get warnings, administrators are notified primarily through the event logs.
- **Resource Manager disk quotas** Resource Manager disk quotas are supported on all editions of Windows Server 2016, allowing you to manage disk space usage by folder, by file type, and by volume. Users who are approaching or have exceeded a limit can be automatically notified by email. The notification system also allows for notifying administrators by email, triggering incident reporting, running commands, and logging related events.

Regardless of the quota system being used, you can configure quotas only for NTFS volumes. You can't create quotas for FAT, FAT32, or ReFS volumes.

Using NTFS Disk Quotas

Administrators use NTFS disk quotas to manage disk space usage for critical volumes, such as those that provide corporate data shares or user data shares. When you enable NTFS disk quotas, you can configure two values:

- **Disk quota limit** Sets the upper boundary for space usage, which you can use to prevent users from writing additional information to a volume, to log events regarding the user exceeding the limit, or both.
- **Disk quota warning** Warns users and logs warning events when users are getting close to their disk quota limit.

> **TIP** You can set disk quotas but not enforce them, and you might be wondering why you'd want to do this. Sometimes you want to track disk space usage on a per-user basis and know when users have exceeded some predefined limit, but instead of denying them additional disk space, you log an event in the application log to track the overage. You can then send out warning messages or figure out other ways to reduce the space usage.

NTFS disk quotas apply only to end users and not to administrators. Administrators can't be denied disk space even if they exceed enforced disk quota limits.

Understanding NTFS Disk Quotas

In a typical environment, you restrict disk space usage in megabytes (MB) or gigabytes (GB). For example, on a corporate data share used by multiple users in a department, you might want to limit disk space usage from 20 to 100 GB. For a user data share, you might want to set the level much lower, such as from 5 to 20 GB, which restricts the user from creating large amounts of personal data. Often you'll set the disk quota warning as a percentage of the disk quota limit. For example, you might set the warning from 90 to 95 percent of the disk quota limit.

Because NTFS disk quotas are tracked on a per-volume, per-user basis, disk space used by one user doesn't affect the disk quotas for other users. Thus, if one user exceeds his limit, any restrictions applied to this user don't apply to other users. For example, if a user exceeds a 5-GB disk quota limit and the volume is configured to prevent writing over the limit, the user can no longer write data to the volume. Users can, however, remove files and folders from the volume to free up disk space. They can also move files and folders to a compressed area on the volume, which might free up space, or they can elect to compress the files themselves. Moving files to a different location on the volume doesn't affect the quota restriction. The amount of file space is the same unless the user moves uncompressed files and folders to a folder with compression. In any case, the restriction on a single user doesn't affect other users' ability to write to the volume (as long as there's free space on the volume).

You can enable NTFS disk quotas on the following:

- **Local volumes**   To manage disk quotas on local volumes, you work with the local disk itself. When you enable disk quotas on a local volume, the Windows system files are included in the volume usage for the user who installed those files. Sometimes this might cause the user to go over the disk quota limit so to prevent this, you might want to set a higher limit on a local workstation volume.
- **Remote volumes**   To manage disk quotas on remote volumes, you must share the root directory for the volume, and then set the disk quota on the volume. Remember, you set quotas on a per-volume basis, so if a remote file server has separate volumes for different types of data—that is, a corporate data volume and a user data volume—these volumes have different quotas.

Only members of the Domain Admins group or the local system Administrators group can configure disk quotas. The first step in using quotas is to enable quotas in Group Policy, which you can do at two levels:

- **Local** Through local Group Policy, you can enable disk quotas for an individual computer.
- **Enterprise** Through Group Policy that applies to a site, a domain, or an organizational unit, you can enable disk quotas for groups of users and computers.

Having to keep track of disk quotas does cause some overhead on computers. This overhead is a function of the number of disk quotas being enforced, the total size of the volumes and their data, and the number of users to which the disk quotas apply.

Although on the surface disk quotas are tracked per user, behind the scenes Windows Server 2016 manages disk quotas according to security identifiers (SIDs). Because SIDs are tracked by disk quotas, you can safely modify user names without affecting the disk quota configuration. Tracking by SIDs does cause some additional overhead when viewing disk quota statistics for users because Windows Server 2016 must correlate SIDs to user account names so that the account names can be displayed in dialog boxes. This means contacting the local user manager and the Active Directory domain controller as necessary.

After Windows Server 2016 looks up names, it caches them to a local file so that they can be available immediately the next time they're needed. The query cache is infrequently updated—if you notice a discrepancy between what's displayed and what's configured, you need to refresh the information. Usually, this means choosing Refresh from the View menu or pressing F5 in the current window.

When you apply disk quotas, you need to be particularly careful in the way you enforce quotas, especially with respect to system accounts, service accounts, or other special purpose accounts. Improper application of disk quotas to these types of accounts can cause serious problems that are difficult to diagnose and resolve. Enforcing quotas on the System, NetworkService, and LocalService accounts could prevent the computer from completing important operating system tasks. As an example, if these accounts reach their enforced quota limit, you would not be able to apply changes to Group Policy because the Group Policy client runs within a Local-System context by default and would not be able to write to the system disk. If the service can't write to the system disk, Group Policy changes cannot be made, and being unable to change Group Policy could have all sorts of unexpected consequences because you would be stuck with the previously configured settings. For example, you would be unable to disable or modify the quota settings through Group Policy.

In this scenario, where service contexts have reached an enforced quota limit, any other configuration settings that use these service contexts and require making changes to files on disk would likely also fail. For example, you would be unable to complete the installation or removal of roles, role services, and features. This would leave the server in a state in which Server Manager always includes a warning that you need to restart the computer to complete configuration tasks, but restarting the computer would not resolve these issues.

To address this problem, you need to edit the disk quota entries for the system disk, raise the enforced limits on the service accounts, and then restart the computer. Restarting the computer triggers the finalization tasks and enables the computer to complete any configuration tasks stuck in a pending status. Because the Group Policy client service could process changes and write them to the system disk, changes to Group Policy would then be applied as well.

Enabling Quotas Through Group Policy

The best way to configure NTFS disk quotas is through Group Policy. When you configure disk quotas through local policy or through unit, domain, and site policy, you define general policies that are set automatically when you enable quota management on individual volumes. Thus, rather than having to configure each volume separately, you can use the same set of rules and apply them in turn to each volume you want to manage.

Policies that control NTFS disk quotas are applied at the system level. You access these policies through the Administrative Templates for Computer Configuration under System\Disk Quotas. The available policies are:

- **Apply Policy To Removable Media**   Determines whether quota policies apply to NTFS volumes on removable media. If you don't enable this policy, quota limits apply only to fixed media drives.
- **Enable Disk Quotas**   Turns disk quotas on or off for all NTFS volumes of the computer, and prevents users from changing the setting.

- **Enforce Disk Quota Limit**   Specifies whether quota limits are enforced. If quotas are enforced, users will be denied disk space if they exceed the quota. This overrides settings on the Quota tab on the NTFS volume.
- **Log Event When Quota Limit Exceeded**   Determines whether an event is logged when users reach their limit, and prevents users from changing their logging options.
- **Log Event When Quota Warning Level Exceeded**   Determines whether an event is logged when users reach the warning level.
- **Specify Default Quota Limit And Warning Level**   Sets a default quota limit and warning level for all users. This setting overrides other settings and affects only new users.

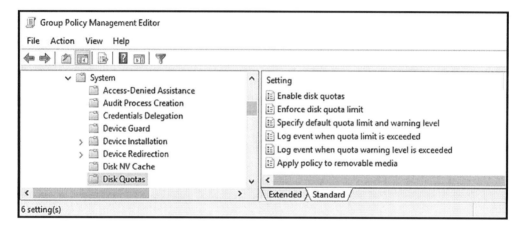

Whenever you work with quota limits, you should use a standard set of policies on all systems; however, you typically, won't want to enable all the policies. Instead, you'll selectively enable policies and then use the standard NTFS features to control quotas on various volumes. If you want to enable quota limits, follow these steps:

1. In the Group Policy Management Console, open the appropriate Group Policy Object for editing or access local policy on the server with which you want to work.

2. In the policy editor, access the Disk Quotas node by expanding System, and then selecting Disk Quotas in the Administrative Templates for Computer Configuration.

3. Double-click Enable Disk Quotas. Select Enabled, and then click OK.

4. Double-click Enforce Disk Quota Limit. If you want to enforce disk quotas on all NTFS volumes residing on this computer, click Enabled. Otherwise, click Disabled, and then set specific limits on a per-volume basis. Click OK.

5. Double-click Specify Default Quota Limit And Warning Level. In the dialog
    box shown, select Enabled.

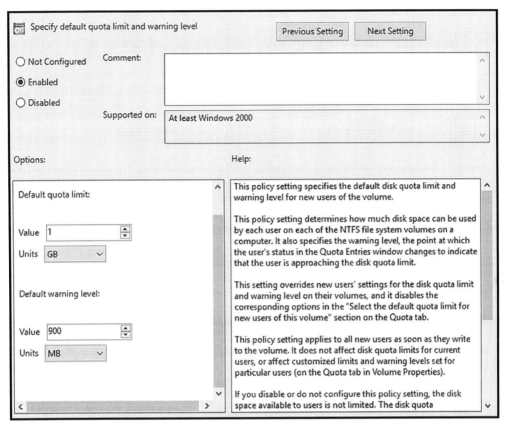

6. Under Default Quota Limit, set a default limit that's applied to users when
    they first write to the quota-enabled volume. The limit doesn't apply to
    current users or affect current limits in place. On a corporate share, such as a
    share used by members of a project team, a good limit is between 5 and 10
    GB. Of course, this depends on the size of the data files that the users
    routinely work with, the number of users, and the size of the disk volume.
    Graphic designers and data engineers might need much more disk space.

7. To set a warning limit, scroll down in the Options window. A good warning
    limit is about 90 percent of the default quota limit, which means that if you
    set the default quota limit to 10 GB, you should set the warning limit to 9 GB.
    Click OK.

8. Double-click Log Event When Quota Limit Exceeded. Select Enabled so that
    limit events are recorded in the application log, and then click OK.

9. Double-click Log Event When Quota Warning Level Exceeded. Select Enabled
    so that warning events are recorded in the application log, and then click OK.

10. Double-click Apply Policy To Removable Media. Select Disabled so that the quota limits apply only to fixed media volumes on the computer, and then click OK.

> **TIP** To ensure that the policies are enforced immediately, access the System\Group Policy node in the Administrative Templates for Computer Configuration, and then double-click Configure Disk Quota Policy Processing. Select Enabled, and then select the Process Even If The Group Policy Objects Have Not Changed check box. Click OK.

Enabling Quotas Through Disk Properties

You can set NTFS disk quotas on a per-volume basis. Only NTFS volumes can have disk quotas. After you configure the appropriate group policies, you can use Computer Management to set disk quotas for local and remote volumes.

> **NOTE** If you use the Enforce Disk Quota Limit policy setting to enforce quotas, users are denied disk space if they exceed the quota. This overrides settings on the Quota tab on the NTFS volume.

If you aren't using quotas enforced by policy and want to enable NTFS disk quotas on an NTFS volume, follow these steps:

1. Using Volume List view or Graphical View in Disk Management, right-click the volume with which you want to work, and then click Properties.

2. On the Quota tab, select Show Quota Settings.

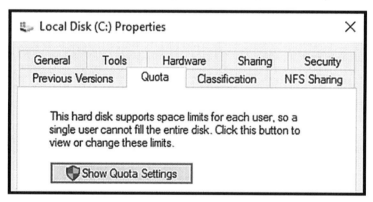

3. Select the Enable Quota Management check box. If you already set quota management values through Group Policy, the options are unavailable and you can't change them. You must modify options through Group Policy instead.

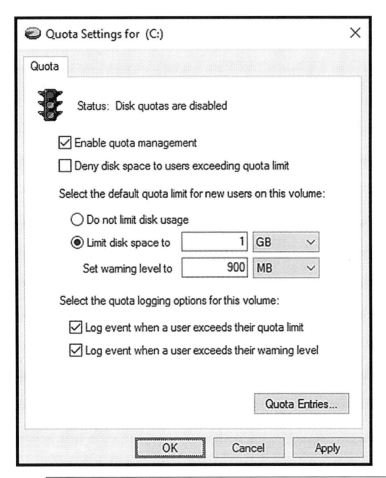

Quota Settings for (C:)   ✕

Quota

Status: Disk quotas are disabled

☑ Enable quota management

☐ Deny disk space to users exceeding quota limit

Select the default quota limit for new users on this volume:

○ Do not limit disk usage

⦿ Limit disk space to   1 | GB   ⌄

Set warning level to   900 | MB   ⌄

Select the quota logging options for this volume:

☑ Log event when a user exceeds their quota limit

☑ Log event when a user exceeds their warning level

Quota Entries...

OK   Cancel   Apply

BEST PRACTICES   Whenever you work with the Quota tab, pay particular
attention to the Status text and the associated traffic light icon. Both change
based on the state of quota management. If quotas aren't configured, the
traffic light icon shows a red light and the status is inactive or not configured. If
the operating system is working or updating the quotas, the traffic light icon
shows a yellow light and the status shows the activity being performed. If
quotas are configured, the traffic light icon shows a green light and the status
text states that the quota system is active.

4.   To set a default disk quota limit for all users, select Limit Disk Space To. In the
text boxes provided, set a limit in kilobytes, megabytes, gigabytes, terabytes,
petabytes, or exabytes. Then set the default warning limit in the Set Warning
Level To text boxes. Again, you'll usually want the disk quota warning limit to
be 90–95 percent of the disk quota limit.

TIP   Although the default quota limit and warning apply to all users, you can
configure different levels for individual users. You do this in the Quota Entries
dialog box. If you create many unique quota entries and don't want to re-create

them on a volume with similar characteristics and usage, you can export the quota entries and import them into a different volume.

5. To enforce the disk quota limit and prevent users from going over the limit, select the Deny Disk Space To Users Exceeding Quota Limit check box. Keep in mind that this creates an actual physical limitation for users (but not for administrators).

6. To configure logging when users exceed a warning limit or the quota limit, select the Log Event check boxes. Click OK to save your changes.

7. If the quota system isn't currently enabled, you'll get a prompt asking you to enable the quota system. Click OK so that Windows Server 2016 can rescan the volume and update disk usage statistics. Actions might be taken against users who exceed the current limit or warning levels. These actions can include preventing additional writing to the volume, notifying them the next time they access the volume, and logging applicable events to the application log.

Viewing Disk Quota Entries

Disk space usage is tracked on a per-user basis. When disk quotas are enabled, each user storing data on a volume has an entry in the disk quota file. This entry is updated periodically to show the current disk space used, the applicable quota limit, the applicable warning level, and the percentage of allowable space being used. As an administrator, you can modify disk quota entries to set different limits and warning levels for particular users. You can also create disk quota entries for users who haven't yet saved data on a volume. The key reason for creating entries is to ensure that when a user does make use of a volume, the user has an appropriate limit and warning level.

To view the current disk quota entries for a volume, follow these steps:

1. Using Volume List view or Graphical View in Disk Management, right-click the volume with which you want to work, and then click Properties.

2. On the Quota tab, select Show Quota Settings. Next, click Quota Entries in the Quota Settings dialog box. This displays the Quota Entries dialog box.

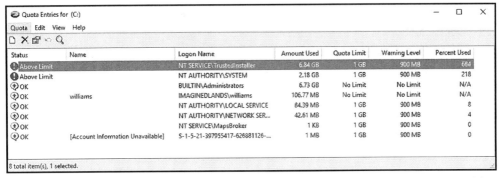

Quota Entries for (C:)

Quota | Edit | View | Help

Status	Name	Logon Name	Amount Used	Quota Limit	Warning Level	Percent Used
Above Limit		NT SERVICE\TrustedInstaller	6.84 GB	1 GB	900 MB	684
Above Limit		NT AUTHORITY\SYSTEM	2.18 GB	1 GB	900 MB	218
OK		BUILTIN\Administrators	6.73 GB	No Limit	No Limit	N/A
OK	williams	IMAGINEDLANDS\williams	106.77 MB	No Limit	No Limit	N/A
OK		NT AUTHORITY\LOCAL SERVICE	84.39 MB	1 GB	900 MB	8
OK		NT AUTHORITY\NETWORK SER...	42.61 MB	1 GB	900 MB	4
OK		NT SERVICE\MapsBroker	1 KB	1 GB	900 MB	0
OK	[Account Information Unavailable]	S-1-5-21-397955417-626881126-...	1 MB	1 GB	900 MB	0

8 total item(s), 1 selected.

3. Each quota entry is listed according to a status, which is meant to quickly depict whether a user has gone over a limit. A status of OK means the user is working within the quota boundaries. Any other status usually means the user has reached the warning level or the quota limit.

Creating Disk Quota Entries

You can create disk quota entries for users who haven't yet saved data on a volume. This enables you to set custom limits and warning levels for a particular user. You usually use this feature when a user frequently stores more information than other users and you want to allow the user to go over the normal limit or when you want to set a specific limit for administrators. As you might recall, administrators aren't subject to disk quota limits, so if you want to enforce limits for individual administrators, you must create disk quota entries for each administrator you want to limit.

> **REAL WORLD** You shouldn't create individual disk quota entries haphazardly. You need to track individual entries carefully. Ideally, you should keep a log that details any individual entries so that other administrators understand the policies in place and how those policies are applied. When you modify the base rules for quotas on a volume, you should reexamine individual entries to see whether they're still applicable or need to be updated as well. I've found that certain types of users are exceptions more often than not, and that it's sometimes better to put different classes of users on different volumes and then apply disk quotas to each volume. In this way, each class or category of user has a quota limit that's appropriate for its members' typical usage, and you have fewer (perhaps no) exceptions. For example, you might use separate volumes for executives, managers, and standard users, or you might have separate volumes for management, graphic designers, engineers, and all other users.

To create a quota entry on a volume, follow these steps:

1. Using Volume List view or Graphical View in Disk Management, right-click the volume with which you want to work, and then click Properties.

2. On the Quota tab, select Show Quota Settings. Next, click Quota Entries in the Quota Settings dialog box. This displays the Quota Entries dialog box. Current quota entries for all users are listed. To refresh the listing, press F5 or choose Refresh from the View menu.

3. If the user doesn't have an existing entry on the volume, you can create it by choosing New Quota Entry from the Quota menu. This opens the Select Users dialog box.

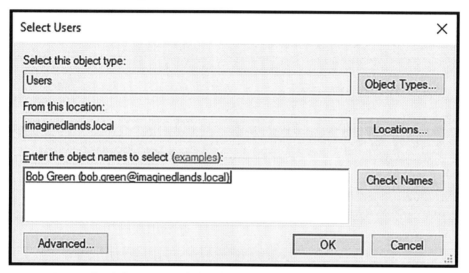

4. In the Select Users dialog box, enter the name of a user you want to use in the Enter The Object Names To Select text box, and then click Check Names. If a match is found, select the account you want to use, and then click OK. If no matches are found, update the name you entered and try searching again. Repeat this step as necessary, and then click OK. You also can enter user names separated by semicolons to apply the same quota to multiple users at the same time.

5. After you select a user, the Add New Quota Entry dialog box is displayed. You have two options. You can remove all quota restrictions for this user by selecting Do Not Limit Disk Usage, or you can set a specific limit and warning level by selecting Limit Disk Space To and then entering the appropriate values. Click OK.

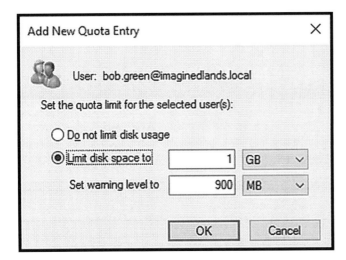

Deleting Disk Quota Entries

When you've created disk quota entries on a volume and a user no longer needs to use the volume, you can delete the associated disk quota entry. When you delete a disk quota entry, all files owned by the user are collected and displayed in a dialog box so that you can permanently delete the files, take ownership of the files, or move the files to a folder on a different volume.

To delete a disk quota entry for a user and manage the user's remaining files on the volume, follow these steps:

1. Using Volume List view or Graphical View in Disk Management, right-click the volume with which you want to work, and then click Properties.

2. On the Quota tab, select Show Quota Settings. Next, click Quota Entries in the Quota Settings dialog box. This displays the Quota Entries dialog box. Current quota entries for all users are listed. To refresh the listing, press F5 or choose Refresh from the View menu.

3. Select the disk quota entry you want to delete, and then press Delete, or choose Delete Quota Entry from the Quota menu. You can select multiple entries by using the Shift and Ctrl keys.

4. When prompted to confirm the action, click Yes to display the Disk Quota dialog box with a list of current files owned by the selected user or users.

5. In the List Files Owned By list, display files for a user whose quota entry you're deleting. You must now specify how the files for the user are to be handled. You can handle each file separately by selecting individual files and

then choosing an appropriate option, or you can select multiple files by using the Shift and Ctrl keys. The following options are available:

- **Permanently Delete Files**   Select the files to delete, and then press Delete. When prompted to confirm the action, click Yes.
- **Take Ownership Of Files**   Select the files you want to take ownership of, and then click Take Ownership Of Files.
- **Move Files To**   Select the files you want to move, and then enter the path to a folder on a different volume. If you don't know the path you want to use, click Browse to display the Browse For Folder dialog box. When you find the folder, click Move.

6. Click Close when you have finished managing the files. If you've appropriately handled all user files, the disk quota entries will be deleted.

Exporting and Importing NTFS Disk Quota Settings

Rather than re-creating custom disk quota entries on individual volumes, you can export the settings from a source volume, and then import the settings to another volume. You must format both volumes by using NTFS. To export and then import disk quota entries, follow these steps:

1. Using Volume List view or Graphical View in Disk Management, right-click the volume with which you want to work, and then click Properties.

2. On the Quota tab, select Show Quota Settings. Next, click Quota Entries in the Quota Settings dialog box. This displays the Quota Entries dialog box.

3. Current quota entries for all users are listed. To refresh the listing, press F5 or choose Refresh from the View menu.

4. Select Export from the Quota menu to display the Export Quota Settings dialog box. Choose the save location for the file containing the quota settings, and then enter a name for the file in the File Name text box. Click Save.

> **NOTE**   If you save the settings file to a mapped drive on the target volume, you'll have an easier time importing the settings. Quota files are usually small, so you don't need to worry about disk space usage.

5. On the Quota menu, click Close to exit the Quota Entries dialog box.

6. Right-click Computer Management in the console tree, and then click Connect To Another Computer. In the Select Computer dialog box, choose the computer containing the target volume. The target volume is the one on which you want to use the exported settings.

7. As explained previously, open the Properties dialog box for the target volume. Then click Quota Entries on the Quota tab to display the Quota Entries dialog box for the target volume.

8. Click Import on the Quota menu. In the Import Quota Settings dialog box, select the quota settings file you saved previously. Click Open.

9. If the volume had previous quota entries, you are given the choice to replace existing entries or keep existing entries. When prompted about a conflict, click Yes to replace an existing entry, or click No to keep the existing entry. To apply the option to replace or keep existing entries to all entries on the volume, select the Do This For All Quota Entries check box prior to clicking Yes or No.

Disabling NTFS Disk Quotas

When disk quotas are managed in Group Policy, you'll need to edit the appropriate policy object or objects to disable disk quotas:

1. In the Group Policy Management Console, open the appropriate Group Policy Object for editing or access local policy on the server with which you want to work.

2. In the policy editor, access the Disk Quotas node by expanding System, and then selecting Disk Quotas in the Administrative Templates for Computer Configuration.

3. Double-click Enable Disk Quotas. Select Disabled or Not Configured as appropriate, and then click OK.

4. Double-click Enforce Disk Quota Limit. Select Disabled or Not Configured as appropriate, and then click OK.

5. Double-click Specify Default Quota Limit And Warning Level. Select Disabled or Not Configured as appropriate, and then click OK.

6. Double-click Log Event When Quota Limit Exceeded. Select Disabled or Not Configured as appropriate, and then click OK.

7. Double-click Log Event When Quota Warning Level Exceeded. Select Disabled or Not Configured as appropriate, and then click OK.

Otherwise, you can disable quotas for individual users or all users on per-volume basis. When you disable quotas for a particular user, the user is no longer subject to the quota restrictions but disk quotas are still tracked for other users. When you disable quotas on a volume, quota tracking and management are completely removed. To disable quotas for a particular user, follow the technique outlined earlier in the chapter in "Viewing Disk Quota Entries." To disable quota tracking and management on a particular volume, follow these steps:

1. Using Volume List view or Graphical View in Disk Management, right-click the volume with which you want to work, and then click Properties.

2. On the Quota tab, select Show Quota Settings. This displays the Quota Settings dialog box.

3. Clear the Enable Quota Management check box. Click OK. When prompted to confirm, click OK.

> **IMPORTANT** Disabling quota tracking doesn't delete existing quota entries on a volume. If you later enable quota management, the previously created quota entries will be available and will be enforced.

Resource Manager Disk Quotas

Windows Server 2016 supports an enhanced quota management system called *Resource Manager disk quotas*. By using Resource Manager disk quotas, you can manage disk space usage by folder and by volume.

> **TIP** Because you manage Resource Manager disk quotas separately from NTFS disk quotas, you can configure a single volume to use both quota systems; however, it's recommended that you use one quota system or the other. Alternatively, if you've already configured NTFS disk quotas, you might want to continue by using NTFS disk quotas on a per-volume basis and supplement this quota management with Resource Manager disk quotas for important folders.

Understanding Resource Manager Disk Quotas

If you want to use Resource Manager disk quotas on a server, you must add the File Server Resource Manager role service. This role service is part of the File And Storage Services role.

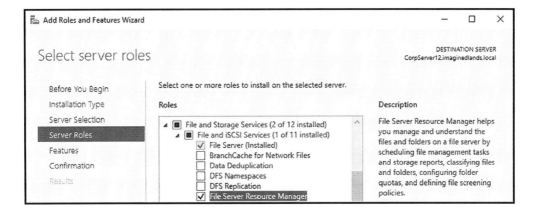

When you're working with Windows Server 2016, Resource Manager disk quotas are another tool you can use to manage disk usage. You can configure Resource Manager disk quotas on a per-volume or per-folder basis. You can set disk quotas with a specific hard limit—meaning a limit can't be exceeded—or a soft limit, meaning a limit can be exceeded.

Generally, you should use hard limits when you want to prevent users from exceeding a specific disk-usage limitation. Use soft limits when you want to monitor usage and simply warn users who exceed or are about to exceed usage guidelines. All quotas have a quota path, which designates the base file path on the volume or folder to which the quota is applied. The quota applies to the designated volume or folder and all subfolders of the designated volume or folder. The particulars of how quotas work and how users are limited or warned are derived from a source template that defines the quota properties.

Windows Server 2016 includes several default templates including:

- **Templates with 100 MB, 2 GB, 5GB and 10 GB limits** Each of which has a designated hard limit and sends warnings to users as the limit is approached and exceeded.
- **Templates that monitor volume usage** Each of which has a soft limit, monitors volume usage, and warns when the limit is approached and exceeded.
- **Templates that monitor share usage** Each of which has a soft limit, monitors share usage, and warns when the limit is approached and exceeded.

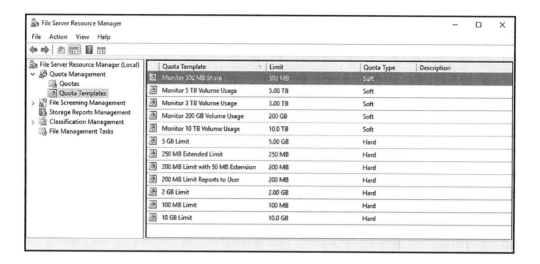

By using the File Server Resource Manager, you can easily define additional templates that would then be available whenever you define quotas, or you can set single-use custom quota properties when defining a quota.

Quota templates or custom properties define the following:

- **Limit**   The disk space usage limit
- **Quota type**   Hard or soft
- **Notification thresholds**   The types of notification that occur when usage reaches a specific percentage of the limit

Although each quota has a specific limit and type, you can define multiple notification thresholds as either a warning threshold or a limit threshold. Warning thresholds are considered to be any percentage of the limit that is less than 100 percent. Limit thresholds occur when the limit reached is 100 percent. For example, you could define warning thresholds that are triggered at 85 percent and 95 percent of the limit and a limit threshold that is triggered when 100 percent of the limit is reached.

Users who are approaching or have exceeded a limit can be automatically notified by email. The notification system also allows for notifying administrators by email, triggering incident reporting, running commands, and logging related events.

Managing Disk Quota Templates

You use disk quota templates to define quota properties, including the limit, quota type, and notification thresholds. In File Server Resource Manager, you can view the currently defined disk quota templates by expanding the Quota Management node, and then selecting Quota Templates. Variables that can be used for automatically generated messages and events include:

- **[Admin Email]** Inserts the email addresses of the administrators defined under the global options
- **[File Screen Path]** Inserts the local file path, such as C:\Data
- **[File Screen Remote Path]** Inserts the remote path, such as \\server\share
- **[File Screen System Path]** Inserts the canonical file path, such as \\?\VolumeGUID
- **[Server Domain]** Inserts the domain of the server on which the notification occurred
- **[Server]** Inserts the server on which the notification occurred
- **[Source File Owner]** Inserts the user name of the owner of the file/folder
- **[Source File Owner Email]** Inserts the email address of the owner of the file/folder
- **[Source File Path]** Inserts the source path of the file/folder

You can modify existing disk quota templates by following these steps:

1. In File Server Resource Manager, expand the Quota Management node, and then select Quota Templates.

   Currently defined disk quota templates are listed by name, limit, and quota type.

2. To modify disk quota template properties, double-click the disk quota template name. This displays a related Properties dialog box.

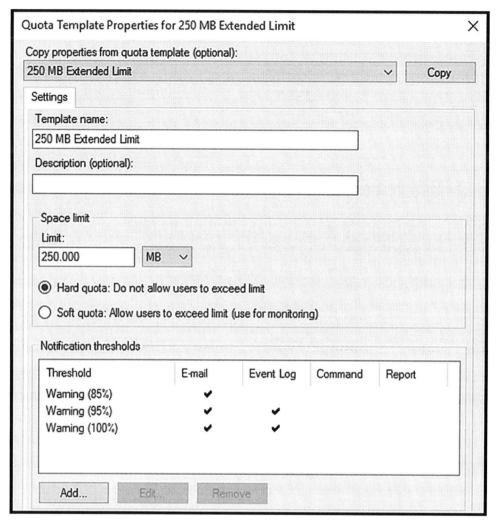

3. On the Settings tab, you can set the template name, limit, and quota type. Current notification thresholds are listed. To modify an existing threshold, select it and then click Edit. To define a new threshold, click Add.

4. When you have finished modifying the quota template, click OK to save the changes.

You can create a new disk quota template by following these steps:

1. In File Server Resource Manager, expand the Quota Management node, and then select Quota Templates.

2. On the Action menu or in the Actions pane, click Create Quota Template to display the Create Quota Template dialog box.

3. On the Settings tab, set the template name, limit, and quota type. You should create a limit threshold first, and then create additional warning thresholds as necessary. In the Limit list, enter the limit value and specify whether you are setting the limit in kilobytes, megabytes, gigabytes, or terabytes.

4. Click Add to add warning thresholds. In the Add Threshold dialog box, enter a percentage value under Generate Notifications When Usage Reaches (%). Warning thresholds are considered to be any percentage of the limit that is less than 100 percent. Limit thresholds occur when the limit reached is 100 percent.

5. On the E-Mail Message tab, you can configure notification as follows:

- To notify an administrator when the disk quota is triggered, select the Send E-Mail To The Following Administrators check box, and then enter the email address or addresses to use. Be sure to separate multiple email addresses with a semicolon. Use the value [Admin Email] to specify the default administrator as configured previously under the global options.
- To notify users, select the Send E-Mail To The User Who Exceeded The Threshold check box.
- Specify the contents of the notification message in the Subject and Message Body text boxes.

6. On the Event Log tab, you can configure event logging. Select the Send Warning To Event Log check box to enable logging, and then specify the text of the log entry in the Log Entry text box.

7. On the Command tab, you can optionally specify a command or script to run, arguments to pass in to the command or script, and a working directory. The default the security context for commands is Local Service, which grants standard user access to local resources but denies access to network resources. If the command requires access to both local and network resources, you can run the command as Network Service.

8. On the Report tab, select the Generate Reports check box to enable incident reporting, and then select the types of reports to generate. Incident reports are stored under %SystemDrive%\StorageReports\Incident by default, and they can also be sent to designated administrators. Use the value [Admin Email] to specify the default administrator as configured previously under the global options.

9. Repeat steps 5–7 to define additional notification thresholds.

10. Click OK when you have finished creating the template.

Creating Resource Manager Disk Quotas

You use disk quotas to designate file paths that have specific usage limits. In File Server Resource Manager, you can view current disk quotas by expanding the Quota Management node, and then selecting Quotas. Before you define disk quotas, you should specify screening file groups and disk quota templates that you will use, as discussed in "Managing Disk Quota Templates" earlier in this chapter.

After you define the necessary file groups and disk quota templates, you can create a disk quota by following these steps:

1. In File Server Resource Manager, expand the Quota Management node, and then select Quotas.

2. Click Create Quota on the Action menu or in the Actions pane.

3. In the Create Quota dialog box, set the local computer path for the quota by clicking Browse and then by using the Browse For Folder dialog box to select the path, such as C:\Data. Click OK.

4. In the Derive Properties From This Quota Template list, choose the disk quota template that defines the quota properties you want to use.

5. Click Create.

Chapter 13. Using Group Policy for Administration

You can use Group Policy to manage users and computers in many different ways. In this chapter, I'll describe some specific management areas, including the following:

- Folder redirection
- Computer and user scripts
- Software deployment
- Work Folders options
- Computer and user certificate enrollment
- Automatic update settings

Managing Automatic Updates in Group Policy

Automatic Updates help you keep the operating system up to date. Although you can configure Automatic Updates on a per-computer basis, you'll typically want to configure this feature for all users and computers that process a GPO—this is a much more efficient management technique.

Note that by default, Windows 10 and Windows Server 2016 use Windows Update to download Windows Components in addition to binaries for roles, role services, and features. If the Windows diagnostics framework detects that a Windows component needs to be repaired, Windows uses Windows Update to download the component. If an administrator is trying to install a role, role service, or feature and the payload is missing, Windows uses Windows Update to download the related binaries.

Configuring Automatic Updates

When you manage Automatic Updates through Group Policy, you can set the update configuration to any of the following options:

- **Auto Download And Schedule The Install** Updates are automatically downloaded and installed according to a schedule you specify. When updates have been downloaded, the operating system notifies the user so that she can review the updates that are scheduled to be installed. The user can install the updates at that time or wait for the scheduled installation time.
- **Auto Download And Notify For Install** The operating system retrieves all updates as they become available, and then prompts the user when they're ready to be installed. The user can then accept or reject the updates. Accepted updates

are installed. Rejected updates aren't installed but remain on the system, where they can be installed at a later date.

- **Notify For Download And Notify For Install**   The operating system notifies the user before retrieving any updates. If a user elects to download the updates, the user still has the opportunity to accept or reject them. Accepted updates are installed. Rejected updates aren't installed but remain on the system, where they can be installed at a later date.

- **Allow Local Admin To Choose Setting**   Allows the local administrator to configure Automatic Updates on a per-computer basis. Note that if you use any other setting, local users and administrators are unable to change settings for Automatic Updates.

You can configure Automatic Updates in Group Policy by following these steps:

1. In the GPMC, right-click the GPO with which you want to work, and then click Edit.

2. In the policy editor, access Windows Components\Windows Update in the Administrative Templates policies for Computer Configuration.

3. Double-click Configure Automatic Updates. In the Properties dialog box, you can now enable or disable Group Policy management of Automatic Updates. To enable management of Automatic Updates, select Enabled. To disable management of Automatic Updates, select Disabled, click OK, and then skip the remaining steps.

4. Choose an update configuration from the options in the Configure Automatic Updating list. On Windows 8 and later as well as Windows Server 2012 and later, updates can be automatically installed during the scheduled maintenance window by selecting the Install During Automatic Maintenance check box.

5. If you select Auto Download And Schedule The Install, you can schedule the installation day and time by using the lists provided. Click OK to save your settings.

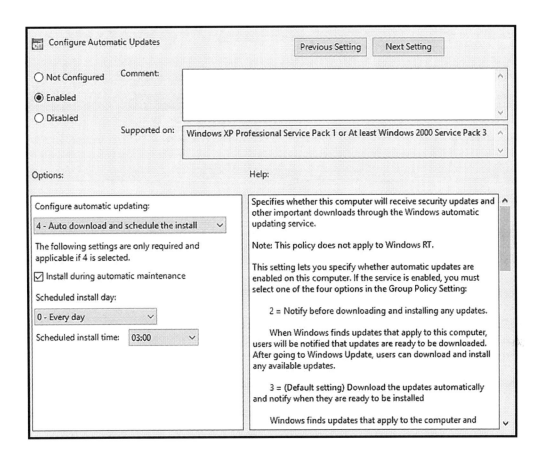

By default, Windows Update runs daily at 3:00 a.m. as part of other automatic maintenance and uses the computer's power management features to wake the computer from hibernation or sleep at the scheduled update time and then install updates. Generally, this wake-up-and-install process will occur whether the computer is on battery or AC power.

If a restart is required to finalize updates applied as part of automatic maintenance and there is an active user session, Windows caches the credentials of the user currently logged on to the console and then restarts the computer automatically. After the restart, Windows uses the cached credentials to sign in as this user. Next, Windows restarts applications that were running previously, and then locks the session using the Secure Desktop. If BitLocker is enabled, the entire process is protected by BitLocker encryption as well.

The maintenance process does not need a user to be logged on. The maintenance process runs whether a user is logged on or not. If no user is logged on when scheduled maintenance begins and a restart is required, Windows restarts the computer without caching credentials or storing information about running applications. When Windows restarts, Windows does not log on as any user.

Because Windows automatically wakes computers to perform automatic maintenance and updates, you'll also want to carefully consider the power options that are applied. Unless a power plan is configured to turn off the display and put the computer to sleep, the computer may remain powered on for many hours after automatic maintenance and updates.

Optimizing Automatic Updates

By default, current releases of Windows and Windows Server schedule a restart if required to complete updates. This restart occurs at the scheduled install time during the maintenance window. If you want important updates to be installed quicker, follow these steps:

1. In the GPMC, right-click the GPO with which you want to work, and then click Edit.

2. In the policy editor, access Windows Components\Windows Update in the Administrative Templates policies for Computer Configuration.

3. Double-click Always Automatically Restart At The Scheduled Time. In the Properties dialog box, select Enabled to allow a restart timer to be used to ensure important updates are installed.

4. Set a restart timer value. The restart timer always begins immediately after Windows Update installs important updates and can be configured to start with any value from 15 to 180 minutes. Then when the timer runs out, the computer is restarted.

5. Click OK.

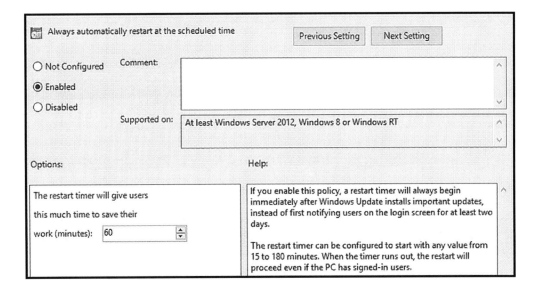

Updates for Windows 10 and Windows Server 2016 include changes that upgrade the operating system as well as update components and features. On critical systems you might not want these types of updates or any others to be installed immediately. Instead, you may want to delay updates or defer upgrades to ensure they can be tested first by following these steps:

1. In the GPMC, right-click the GPO with which you want to work, and then click Edit.

2. In the policy editor, access Windows Components\Windows Update in the Administrative Templates policies for Computer Configuration.

3. Double-click Defer Upgrades And Updates. In the Properties dialog box, select Enabled.

4. Specify how long upgrades should be deferred with a value between 1 and 8 months. If you enter a value of 0, upgrades will not be deferred.

5. Specify how long updates should be deferred with a value between 1 and 4 weeks. If you enter a value of 0, updates will not be deferred.

6. Click OK.

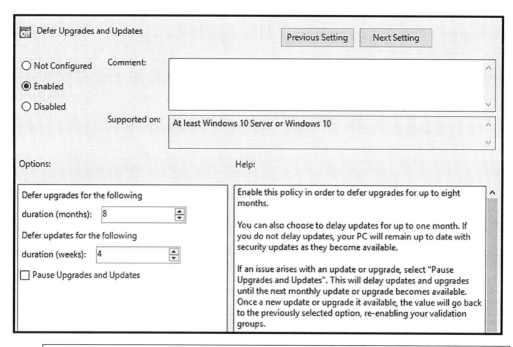

Defer Upgrades and Updates

Previous Setting   Next Setting

○ Not Configured   Comment:
◉ Enabled
○ Disabled

Supported on: At least Windows 10 Server or Windows 10

Options: Help:

Defer upgrades for the following   Enable this policy in order to defer upgrades for up to eight
                                            months.
duration (months):   8
                                            You can also choose to delay updates for up to one month. If
Defer updates for the following   you do not delay updates, your PC will remain up to date with
                                            security updates as they become available.
duration (weeks):   4
                                            If an issue arises with an update or upgrade, select "Pause
☐ Pause Upgrades and Updates   Upgrades and Updates". This will delay updates and upgrades
                                            until the next monthly update or upgrade becomes available.
                                            Once a new update or upgrade it available, the value will go back
                                            to the previously selected option, re-enabling your validation
                                            groups.

> **TIP**   Defer Upgrades And Updates policy can also be used to pause
> upgrades and updates until the next monthly update or upgrade becomes
> available. Use this option if a problem occurs and you need to temporarily
> delay applying updates or upgrades. The Pause option will clear automatically
> when a new update or upgrade becomes available. Note also that the settings
> of this policy are ignored if Specify Intranet Microsoft Update Service Location
> policy is enabled.

Using Intranet Update Service Locations

Computers running Windows 10 get updates from other PCs on the local network or the Internet and send parts of previously downloaded updates to other PCs. Computers running other versions of Windows and all versions of Windows Server get their updates through the Automatic Update process. On networks with hundreds or thousands of computers, either approach can use a considerable amount of network bandwidth, and having all the computers check for updates and install them over the Internet doesn't make sense.

Instead, computers running Windows 10 can be configured so that they don't share updates or get updates from PCs on the Internet and like other computers, they also can be configured to get updates from a dedicated update server on your network. The designated update server must run Windows Server Update Services (WSUS), be configured as a web server running IIS, and be able to handle the additional workload, which might be considerable on a large network during peak usage times. Additionally, the update server must have access to the external network on port 80. The use of a firewall or proxy server on this port shouldn't present any problems.

The update process also tracks configuration information and statistics for each computer. This information is necessary for the update process to work properly, and it can be stored on a separate statistics server (an internal server running IIS) or on the update server itself.

To specify an internal update server, follow these steps:

1. After you install and configure an update server, open the GPO with which you want to work for editing. In the policy editor, access Windows Components\Windows Update in the Administrative Templates policies for Computer Configuration.

2. Double-click Specify Intranet Microsoft Update Service Location. In the Properties dialog box, select Enabled.

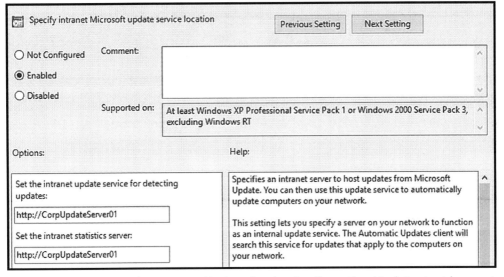

3. In the Set The Intranet Update Service For Detecting Updates text box, enter the URL of the update server. In most cases, this is http://*servername*, such as *http://CorpUpdateServer01*.

4. Enter the URL of the statistics server in the Set The Intranet Statistics Server text box. This doesn't have to be a separate server; you can specify the update server in this text box.

> **NOTE** If you want a single server to handle both updates and statistics, enter the same URL in both boxes. Otherwise, if you want a different server for updates and statistics, enter the URL for each server in the appropriate box.

5. Click OK. After the applicable GPO is refreshed, systems running appropriate versions of Windows will look to the update server for updates. You'll want to monitor the update and statistics servers closely for several days or weeks to ensure that everything is working properly. Directories and files will be created on the update and statistics servers.

User and Computer Script Management

You can configure four types of scripts with Windows Server:

- **Computer Startup** Executed during startup
- **Computer Shutdown** Executed prior to shutdown
- **User Logon** Executed when a user logs on
- **User Logoff** Executed when a user logs off

Windows supports scripts written as command-shell batch scripts ending with the .bat or .cmd extension or scripts that use the Windows Script Host (WSH). WSH is a feature of Windows Server that enables you to use scripts written in a scripting language, such as VBScript, without needing to insert the script into a webpage. To provide a multipurpose scripting environment, WSH relies on scripting engines. A scripting engine is the component that defines the core syntax and structure of a particular scripting language. Windows Server ships with scripting engines for VBScript and JScript. Other scripting engines are also available.

Current Windows operating systems also support Windows PowerShell scripts. When Windows PowerShell is installed on computers that process a particular GPO, you can use Windows PowerShell scripts in much the same way as you use other scripts. You have the option of running Windows PowerShell scripts before or after other types of scripts.

Assigning Computer Startup and Shutdown Scripts

Computer startup and shutdown scripts are assigned as part of a GPO; as a result, all computers that are members of the site, domain, or organizational unit—or all three—execute scripts automatically when they're started or shut down.

To assign a computer startup or shutdown script, follow these steps:

1. In File Explorer, open the folder containing the script or scripts you want to use.

2. In the GPMC, right-click the GPO for the site, domain, or organizational unit with which you want to work, and then click Edit to open the policy editor for the GPO.

3. In the Computer Configuration\Policies node, double-click the Windows Settings folder, and then click Scripts.

4. To work with startup scripts, right-click Startup, and then click Properties. To work with shutdown scripts, right-click Shutdown and select Properties.

5. On the Scripts tab, you can manage command-shell batch scripts ending with the .bat or .cmd extension and scripts that use the Windows Script Host. On the PowerShell Scripts tab, you can manage Windows PowerShell scripts. When working with either tab, click Show Files.

6. Copy the files in the open File Explorer window, and then paste them into the window that opened when you clicked Show Files.

7. Click Add to open the Add A Script dialog box and assign a script. In the Script Name text box, enter the name of the script you copied to the -Machine\Scripts\Startup or the Machine\Scripts\Shutdown folder for the related policy. In the Script Parameters text box, enter any parameters to pass to the script. Repeat this step to add other scripts.

8. During startup or shutdown, scripts are executed in the order in which they're listed in the Properties dialog box. On the Scripts tab, use the Up and Down buttons to reorder scripts as necessary. Do the same on the PowerShell Scripts tab. On the PowerShell Scripts tab, you can also use the selection list to specify whether Windows PowerShell scripts should run before or after other types of scripts.

9. If you want to edit the script name or parameters later, select the script in the Script For list, and then click Edit. To delete a script, select the script in the Script For list, and click Remove.

10. To save your changes, click OK.

Assigning User Logon and Logoff Scripts

You can assign user scripts in one of the three following ways:

- You can assign logon and logoff scripts as part of a GPO; and as a result, all users who are members of the site, domain, or organizational unit—or all three—execute scripts automatically when they log on or log off.
- You can also assign logon scripts individually through the Active Directory Users And Computers console, which enables you to assign a separate logon script to each user or group.
- You can also assign individual logon scripts as scheduled tasks by using the Scheduled Task Wizard.

To assign a logon or logoff script in a GPO, follow these steps:

1. In File Explorer, open the folder containing the script or scripts you want to use.

2. In the GPMC, right-click the GPO for the site, domain, or organizational unit with which you want to work, and then click Edit to open the policy editor for the GPO.

3. Double-click the Windows Settings folder in the User Configuration\Policies node, and then click Scripts.

4. To work with logon scripts, right-click Logon, and then click Properties. To work with logoff scripts, right-click Logoff, and then click Properties.

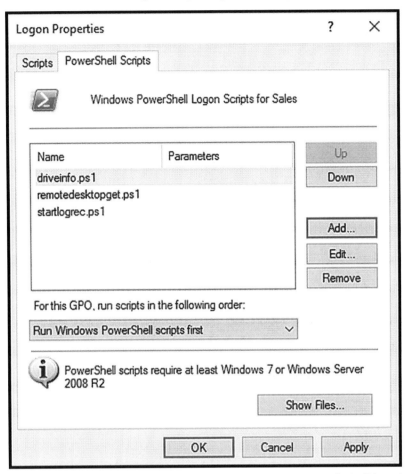

5. On the Scripts tab, you can manage command-shell batch scripts ending with the .bat or .cmd extension and scripts that use the Windows Script Host. On the PowerShell Scripts tab, you can manage Windows PowerShell scripts. When working with either tab, click Show Files.

6. Copy the files in the open File Explorer window, and then paste them into the window that opened when you clicked Show Files.

7. Click Add to open the Add A Script dialog box and assign a script. In the Script Name text box, enter the name of the script you copied to the User\Scripts\Logon or the User\Scripts\Logoff folder for the related policy. In the Script Parameter text box, enter any parameters to pass to the script. Repeat this step to add other scripts.

8. During logon or logoff, scripts are executed in the order in which they're listed in the Properties dialog box. On the Scripts tab, use the Up and Down

buttons to reorder scripts as necessary. Do the same on the PowerShell Scripts tab, on which you can also use the selection list to specify whether Windows PowerShell scripts should run before or after other types of scripts.

9. If you want to edit the script name or parameters later, select the script in the Script For list, and then click Edit. To delete a script, select the script in the Script For list, and then click Remove.

10. To save your changes, click OK.

Centrally Managing Special Folders

You can centrally manage special folders used by Windows Server through folder redirection. You do this by redirecting special folders to a central network location instead of using multiple default locations on each computer. For current releases of Windows, the special folders you can manage are AppData (Roaming), Desktop, Start Menu, Documents, Pictures, Music, Videos, Favorites, Contacts, Downloads, Links, Searches, and Saved Games.

Note that even though current releases of Windows store personal folders in slightly different ways, you manage the folders in the same way within Group Policy.

You have two general options for redirection. You can redirect a special folder to the same network location for all users, or you can designate locations based on user membership in security groups. In either case, you should make sure that the network location you plan to use is available as a network share. See Chapter 9, "Implementing File Sharing," for details on sharing data on a network.

By default, users can redirect folders no matter which computer they're using within the domain. Windows 10 and Windows Server 2016 enable you to modify this behavior by specifying from which computers a user can access roaming profiles and redirected folders. You do this by designating certain computers as primary computers, and then configuring domain policy to restrict the downloading of profiles, redirected folders, or both to primary computers. For more information, see Chapter 11, "Managing Computers, Users and Groups" in *Windows Server 2016: Essentials for Administration* (Stanek & Associates, 2016).

Redirecting a Special Folder to a Single Location

You can redirect a special folder to a single location by following these steps:

1. In the Group Policy Management Console (GPMC), right-click the Group Policy object (GPO) for the site, domain, or organizational unit with which you want to work, and then click Edit to open the policy editor for the GPO.

> **NOTE**   If you'd rather create a new GPO, right-click the site, domain or organizational unit and then select Create A GPO… And Link It Here. In the New GPO dialog box, enter a name for the GPO and then select OK.

2. In the policy editor, expand the following nodes: User Configuration, Policies, Windows Settings, and Folder Redirection.

3. Under Folder Redirection, right-click the special folder with which you want to work, such as AppData(Roaming), and then click Properties.

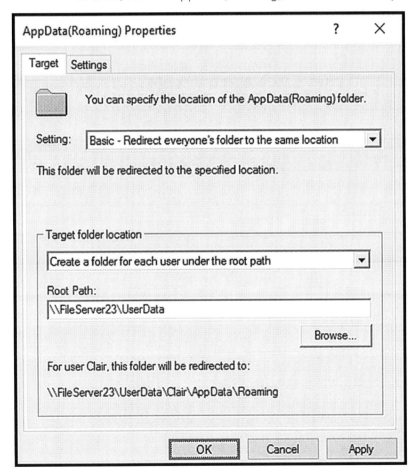

4. In the Setting list on the Target tab, choose Basic—Redirect Everyone's Folder To The Same Location.

5. Under Target Folder Location, you have several options depending on the folder with which you're working, and those options include the following:

- **Redirect To The User's Home Directory**   If you select this option, the folder is redirected to a subdirectory within the user's home directory. You set the location of the user's home directory with the %HomeDrive% and %HomePath% environment variables.
- **Create A Folder For Each User Under The Root Path**   If you select this option, a folder is created for each user at the location you enter in the Root Path text box. The folder name is the user account name as specified by %UserName%. Thus, if you enter the root path value \\Zeta\UserDocuments, the folder for Williams will be located at \\Zeta\UserDocuments\Williams.
- **Redirect To The Following Location**   If you select this option, the folder is redirected to the location you enter in the Root Path text box. Here, you typically want to use an environment variable to customize the folder location for each user. For example, you could use the root path value \\Zeta\UserData\%UserName%\docs.
- **Redirect To The Local Userprofile Location**   If you select this option, the folder is redirected to a subdirectory within the user profile directory. You set the location of the user profile with the %UserProfile% variable.

> **IMPORTANT**   When specifying the root path, be sure to specify the UNC path for the server and not a local path. The basic syntax for a UNC path is \\ServerName\ShareName, such as \\CorpServer38\CorpData.

6. Click the Settings tab, configure the following additional options, and then click OK to complete the process:

- **Grant The User Exclusive Rights To**   Gives users full rights to access their data in the special folder.
- **Move The Contents Of *FolderName* To The New Location**   Moves the data in the special folders from the individual systems on the network to the central folder or folders.
- **Also Apply Redirection Policy To**   Applies the redirection policy to previous releases of Windows as well.

Redirecting a Special Folder Based on Group Membership

You can redirect a special folder based on group membership by following these steps:

1. In the GPMC, right-click the GPO for the site, domain, or organizational unit with which you want to work, and then click Edit to open the policy editor for the GPO.

2. In the policy editor, expand the following nodes: User Configuration, Policies, Windows Settings, and Folder Redirection.

3. Under Folder Redirection, right-click the special folder with which you want to work, such as AppData(Roaming), and then click Properties.

4. In the Setting list on the Target tab, choose Advanced – Specify Locations For Various User Groups. A Security Group Membership panel is added to the Properties dialog box.

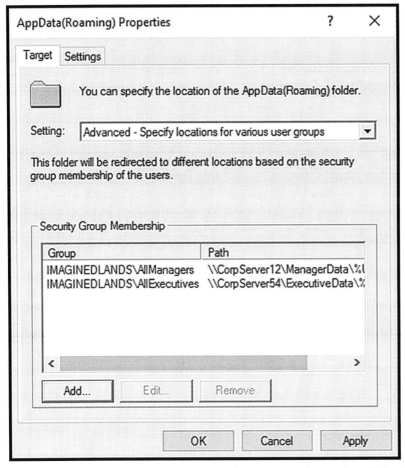

5. Click Add to open the Specify Group And Location dialog box. Or select a group entry, and then click Edit to modify its settings.

6. In the Security Group Membership text box, enter the name of the security group for which you want to configure redirection, or click Browse to find a security group to add.

7. As with basic redirection, the options available depend on the folder with which you're working and include the following:

- **Redirect To The User's Home Directory**   If you select this option, the folder is redirected to a subdirectory within the user's home directory. You set the location of the user's home directory with the %HomeDrive% and %HomePath% environment variables.
- **Create A Folder For Each User Under The Root Path**   If you select this option, a folder is created for each user at the location you enter in the Root Path text box. The folder name is the user account name as specified by %UserName%. Thus, if you enter the root path value \\Zeta\UserDocuments, the folder for Williams will be located at \\Zeta\UserDocuments\Williams.
- **Redirect To The Following Location**   If you select this option, the folder is redirected to the location you enter in the Root Path text box. Here, you typically want to use an environment variable to customize the folder location for each user. For example, you could use the root path value \\Zeta\UserData\%UserName%\docs.
- **Redirect To The Local Userprofile Location**   If you select this option, the folder is redirected to a subdirectory within the user profile directory. You set the location of the user profile with the %UserProfile% variable.

8. Click OK. Repeat steps 5–7 for other groups you want to configure.

9. When you're done creating group entries, click the Settings tab, configure the following additional options, and then click OK to complete the process:

- **Grant The User Exclusive Rights To**   Gives users full rights to access their data in the special folder.
- **Move The Contents Of *FolderName* To The New Location**   Moves the data in the special folders from the individual systems on the network to the central folder or folders.
- **Also Apply Redirection Policy To**   Applies the redirection policy to early releases of Windows as well.

Removing Redirection

Sometimes you might want to remove redirection from a particular special folder. You remove redirection by following these steps:

1. In the GPMC, right-click the GPO for the site, domain, or organizational unit with which you want to work, and then click Edit to open the policy editor for the GPO.

2. In the policy editor, expand the following nodes: User Configuration, Policies, Windows Settings, and Folder Redirection.

3. Under Folder Redirection, right-click the special folder with which you want to work, and then click Properties.

4. Click the Settings tab, and then make sure that an appropriate Policy Removal option is selected. The following two options are available:

- **Leave The Folder In The New Location When Policy Is Removed** When you select this option, the folder and its contents remain at the redirected location and current users are still permitted to access the folder and its contents at this location.
- **Redirect The Folder Back To The Local Userprofile Location When Policy Is Removed** When you select this option, the folder and its contents are copied back to the original location; however, the contents aren't deleted from the previous location.

5. If you changed the Policy Removal option, click Apply, and then click the Target tab. Otherwise, just click the Target tab.

6. To remove all redirection definitions for the special folder, choose Not Configured in the Setting list.

7. To remove redirection for a particular security group, select the security group in the Security Group Membership panel, and then click Remove. Click OK.

Deploying Software Through Group Policy

Group Policy includes basic functionality, called Software Installation policy, for deploying software. Although Software Installation policy is not designed to replace enterprise solutions such as System Center, you can use it to automate the deployment and maintenance of software in just about any size organization if your computers are running the Windows operating system.

Getting to Know Software Installation Policy

In Group Policy, you can deploy software on a per-computer or per-user basis. Per-computer applications are available to all users of a computer and configured under

Computer Configuration\Policies\Software Settings\Software Installation. Per-user applications are available to individual users and configured under User Configuration\Policies\Software Settings\Software Installation.

You deploy software in three key ways:

- **Computer assignment** Assigns the software to client computers so that it is installed when the computer starts. This technique requires no user intervention, but it does require a restart to install the software. Installed software is then available to all users on the computer.
- **User assignment** Assigns the software to users so that it is installed when a user logs on. This technique requires no user intervention, but it does require the user to log on to install or advertise the software. The software is associated with the user only and not the computer.
- **User publishing** Publishes the software so that users can install it manually through Programs And Features. This technique requires the user to explicitly install software or activate installation. The software is associated with the user only.

When you use user assignment or user publishing, you can advertise the software so that a computer can install the software when it is first used. With advertisements, the software can be installed automatically in the following situations:

- When a user accesses a document that requires the software
- When a user opens a shortcut to the application
- When another application requires a component of the software

When you configure Software Installation policy, you should generally not use existing GPOs. Instead, you should create GPOs that configure software installation, and then link those GPOs to the appropriate containers in Group Policy. When you use this approach, it's much easier to redeploy software and apply updates.

After you create a GPO for your software deployment, you should set up a distribution point. A distribution point is a shared folder that is available to the computers and users to which you are deploying software. With basic applications, you prepare the distribution point by copying the installer package file and all required application files to the share and configuring permissions so that these files can be accessed. With other applications, you may need to prepare the distribution point by performing an administrative installation to the share. The advantage of an administrative installation is that the software can be updated and redeployed through Software Installation policy.

You can update applications deployed through Software Installation policy by using an update or service pack or by deploying a new version of the application. Each task is performed in a slightly different way.

Deploying Software Throughout Your Organization

Software Installation policy uses either Windows Installer Packages (.msi) or ZAW Down-Level Application Packages (.zap). When you use computer assignment, user assignment, or user publishing, you can deploy software by using Windows Installer Packages. When you use user publishing, you can deploy software by using either Windows Installer Packages or ZAW Down-Level Application Packages. With either technique, you must set file permissions on the installer package so that the appropriate computer and user accounts have read access.

Because Software Installation policy is applied only during foreground processing of policy settings, per-computer application deployments are processed at startup and per-user application deployments are processed at logon. You can customize installation by using transform (.mst) files. Transform files modify the installation process according to the settings you defined for specific computers and users.

You can deploy software by following these steps:

1. In the GPMC, right-click the GPO you want to use for the deployment, and then click Edit.

2. In the policy editor, open Computer Configuration\Policies\Software Settings\Software Installation or User Configuration\Policies\Software Settings\Software Installation as appropriate for the type of software deployment.

3. Right-click Software Installation. On the shortcut menu, click New, and then click Package.

4. In the Open dialog box, go to the network share where your package is located, click the package to select it, and then click Open.

> **NOTE** Windows Installer Packages (.msi) is selected by default in the Files Of Type list. If you are performing a user publishing deployment, you can also choose ZAW Down-Level Application Packages (.zap) as the file type.

5. In the Deploy Software dialog box, select one of the following deployment methods, and then click OK:

- **Published**   To publish the application without modifications
- **Assigned**   To assign the application without modifications
- **Advanced**   To deploy the application by using advanced configuration options

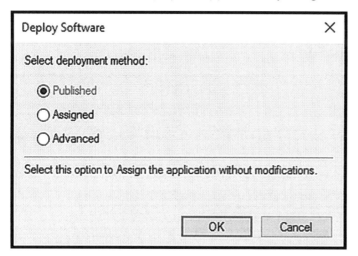

Configuring Software Deployment Options

You can view and set general options for a software package by following these steps:

1. In the GPMC, right-click the GPO you want to use for the deployment, and then click Edit.

2. In the policy editor, access Computer Configuration\Policies\Software Settings\Software Installation or User Configuration\Policies\Software Settings\Software Installation as appropriate for the type of software deployment.

3. Double-click the Software Installation package. In the Properties dialog box, review or modify software deployment options.

4. On the Deployment tab, you can change the deployment type and configure the following deployment and installation options:

- **Auto-Install This Application By File Extension Activation**   Advertises any file extensions associated with this package for install-on-first-use deployment. This option is selected by default.
- **Uninstall This Application When It Falls Out Of The Scope Of Management** Removes the application if it no longer applies to the user.

- **Do Not Display This Package In The Add/Remove Programs Control Panel** Prevents the application from appearing in Add/Remove Programs, which prevents a user from uninstalling an application.
- **Install This Application At Logon** Configures full installation—rather than advertisement—of an application when the user logs on. This option cannot be set when you publish a package for users.
- **Installation User Interface Options** Controls how the installation is performed. With the default setting, Maximum, the user gets all setup screens and messages during installation. With the Basic option, the user gets only error and completion messages during installation.

   5. Click OK.

Updating Deployed Software

When an application uses a Windows Installer package, you can apply an update or service pack to a deployed application by following these steps:

1. After you obtain an .msi file or .msp (security update) file containing the update or service pack to be applied, copy the .msi or .msp file and any new installation files to the folder containing the original .msi file. Overwrite any duplicate files as necessary.

2. In the GPMC, right-click the GPO you want to use for the deployment, and then click Edit.

3. In the policy editor, access Computer Configuration\Policies\Software Settings\Software Installation or User Configuration\Policies\Software Settings\Software Installation as appropriate for the type of software deployment.

4. Right-click the package with which you want to work. On the shortcut menu, click All Tasks, and then click Redeploy Application.

5. When prompted to confirm the action, click Yes. The application is then redeployed to all users and computers as appropriate for the GPO with which you are working.

When an application uses an Installer package that is not Windows-based, you can update a deployed application or apply a service pack by following these steps:

1. In the GPMC, right-click the GPO you want to use for the deployment, and then click Edit.

2. In the policy editor, access Computer Configuration\Policies\Software Settings\Software Installation or User Configuration\Policies\Software

Settings\Software Installation as appropriate for the type of software deployment.

3. Right-click the package. On the shortcut menu, click All Tasks, and then click Remove. Click OK to accept the default option of immediate removal.

4. Copy the new .zap file and all related files to a network share, and redeploy the application.

Upgrading Deployed Software

You can upgrade a previously deployed application to a new version by following these steps:

1. Obtain a Windows Installer file for the new software version, and copy it along with all required files to a network share. Alternatively, you can perform an administrative installation to the network share.

2. In the GPMC, right-click the GPO you want to use for the deployment, and then click Edit.

3. In the policy editor, access Computer Configuration\Policies\Software Settings\Software Installation or User Configuration\Policies\Software Settings\Software Installation as appropriate for the type of software deployment.

4. Right-click Software Installation. On the shortcut menu, click New, and then click Package. Create an assigned or published application by using the Windows Installer file for the new software version.

5. Right-click the upgrade package, and then click Properties. On the Upgrades tab, click Add. In the Add Upgrade Package dialog box, do one of the following:

- If the original application and the upgrade are in the current GPO, select Current Group Policy Object, and then select the previously deployed application in the Package To Upgrade list.
- If the original application and the upgrade are in different GPOs, select A Specific GPO, click Browse, and then select the GPO from the Browse For A Group Policy Object dialog box. Select the previously deployed application in the Package To Upgrade list.

6. Choose an upgrade option. If you want to replace the application with the new version, select Uninstall The Existing Package, Then Install The Upgrade Package. If you want to perform an in-place upgrade over the existing installation, select Package Can Upgrade Over The Existing Package.

7. Click OK to close the Add Upgrade Package dialog box. If you want to make this a required upgrade, select the Required Upgrade For Existing Packages check box, and then click OK to close the upgrade package's Properties dialog box.

Automatically Configuring Work Folders

Computers that are members of a workplace can access internal network resources, such as internal websites and business applications. Work Folders enable users to synchronize their corporate data to their devices and vice versa. Those devices can be joined to the corporate domain or a workplace. Devices access Work Folders via a remote web gateway running on Microsoft Internet Information Services (IIS).

To deploy Work Folders, you add the File And Storage Services \ Work Folders role to a file server, and then configure Work Folders by using Server Manager. Afterward, you can use policy settings to control related options, such as the server to which users can connect remotely and access Work Folders. You control the connection server in one of two ways:

- By specifying the exact URL of a file server hosting the Work Folders for the user, such as *https://server12.imaginedlands.com*.
- By specifying the URL used within your organization for Work Folders discovery, such as *https://workfolders.imaginedlands.com*.

REAL WORLD Clients use secure encrypted communications to connect to work folders as long as the file servers hosting the Work Folders have valid SSL certificates. When a device initiates an SSL connection, the server sends the certificate to the client. The client evaluates the certificate and continues only if the certificate is valid and can be trusted. If you configure a connection to an exact URL, the client can connect directly to the specified sever and synchronize data in Work Folders. The server's certificate must have a Common Name (CN) or a Subject Alternative Name (SAN) that matches the host header in the request. For example, if the client makes a request to https://server18.imaginedlands.com, the CN or SAN must be server18.imaginedlands.com.

In Group Policy, you specify the URL used within your organization for Work Folders discovery by using the Specify Work Folders Settings policy found under Administrative Templates policies for User Configuration\Windows Components\Work Folders. Any server configured with Work Folders acts as a discovery server by default. If you configure a discovery URL, a client connects to one of several servers, and the email address of the user is used to discover which specific server hosts the Work Folders for the client. The client is then connected to this server. Each discovery server will need to have a certificate with multiple Subject Alternative Names, which includes the server name and the discovery name. For example, if a client makes a request to *https://workfolders.imaginedlands.com* and connects to *FileServer87.imaginedlands.com*, the server's certificate must have a CN or SAN of *fileserver87.imaginedlands.com* and a SAN of *workfolders.imaginedlands.com*.

If you want to configure Work Folders in Group Policy, use the following technique:

1. Access Group Policy for the system, site, domain, or OU with which you want to work. Next, access the Work Folders node by using the Administrative Templates policies for User Configuration under Windows Components\Work Folders.

2. Double-click Specify Work Folders Settings, and then select Enabled.

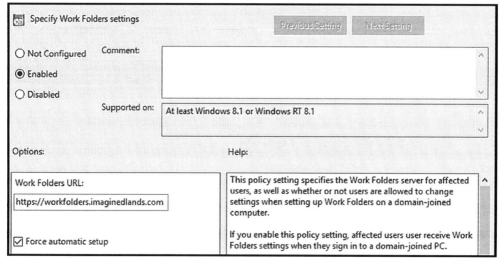

3. In the World Folders URL text box, enter the URL of the file server that hosts the Work Folders for the user or the URL used within your organization for Work Folders discovery.

4. If you want to prevent users from changing settings when setting up Work Folders, select Force Automatic Setup.

5. Click OK.

Automatically Enrolling Computer and User Certificates

A server designated as a certificate authority (CA) is responsible for issuing digital certificates and managing certificate revocation lists (CRLs). Servers running Windows Server can be configured as certificate authorities by installing Active Directory Certificate Services. Computers and users can use certificates for authentication and encryption.

In an enterprise configuration, enterprise CAs are used for automatic enrollment. This means authorized users and computers can request a certificate, and the certificate authority can automatically process the certificate request so that the users and computers can immediately install the certificate.

Group Policy controls the way automatic enrollment works. When you install enterprise CAs, automatic enrollment policies for users and computers are enabled automatically. The policy for computer certificate enrollment is Certificate Services Client—Auto-Enrollment Settings under Computer Configuration\Policies\Windows Settings\Security Settings\Public Key Policies. The policy for user certificate enrollment is Certificate Services Client—Auto-Enrollment under User Configuration\Policies\Windows Settings\Security Settings\Public Key Policies.

You can configure automatic enrollment by following these steps:

1. In the GPMC, right-click the GPO with which you want to work, and then click Edit.
2. In the policy editor, access User Configuration\Policies\Windows Settings\Security Settings\Public Key Policies or Computer Configuration\Policies\Windows Settings\Security Settings\Public Key Policies as appropriate for the type of policy you want to review.
3. Double-click Certificate Services Client—Auto-Enrollment. To disable automatic enrollment, select Disabled from the Configuration Model list, click OK, and then skip the remaining steps in this procedure. To enable automatic enrollment, select Enabled from the Configuration Model list.
4. To automatically renew expired certificates, update pending certificates, and remove revoked certificates, select the related check box.
5. To ensure that the latest version of certificate templates are requested and used, select the Update Certificates That Use Certificate Templates check box.

6. To notify users when a certificate is about to expire, specify when notifications are sent using the box provided. By default, notifications are sent when 10 percent of the certificate lifetime remains.

7. Click OK to save your settings.

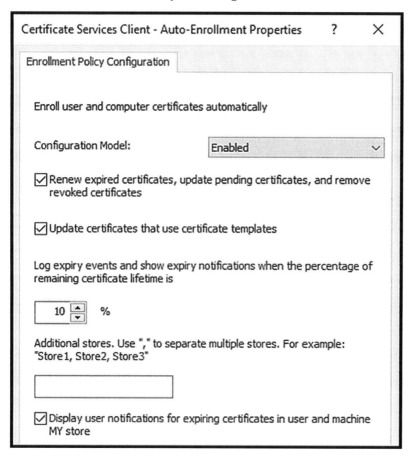

Chapter 14. Implementing Print Services

As an administrator, you need to take two main steps to enable users throughout a network to access print devices connected to Windows Server 2016. First, you need to set up a print server, and then you need to use the print server to share print devices on the network.

This chapter covers the essentials of setting up shared printing and describes how users access shared printing on the network. You'll also find advice on administering printers and troubleshooting printer problems, which is where we'll begin.

Managing the Print and Document Services Role

A print server provides a central location for sharing printers on a network. When many users require access to the same printers, you should configure print servers in the domain. In earlier releases of the Windows Server operating system, all servers were installed with basic print services. With Windows Server 2016, you must specifically configure a server to be a print server.

Using Print Devices

Two types of print devices are used on a network:

* **Local print device**   A print device that's physically attached to a user's computer and employed only by the user who's logged on to that computer.
* **Network print device**   A print device that's set up for remote access over the network. This can be a print device attached directly to a print server or a print device attached directly to the network through a network interface card (NIC).

> **NOTE**   The key difference between a local printer and a network printer is that a local printer isn't shared. You can easily make a local printer a network printer. To learn how to do this, see "Starting and Stopping Printer Sharing" in Chapter 15.

You install new network printers on print servers or as separate print devices attached to the network. A *print server* is a workstation or server configured to share one or more printers. These printers can be physically attached to the computer or connected to the network. The disadvantage of running a print server with a workstation operating system instead of a server operating system is the limited number of allowed connections. With Windows Server 2016, you don't have to worry about operating system–enforced connection limits.

You can configure any Windows Server 2016 system as a print server. The print server's primary job is to share print devices on the network and to handle print spooling. The main advantages of print servers are that printers have a centrally managed print queue and you don't have to install printer drivers on client systems.

You don't have to use a print server, however. You can connect users directly to a network-attached printer. When you do this, the network printer is handled much like a local printer attached directly to the user's computer. The key differences are that multiple users can connect to the printer and that each user has a different print queue. Each individual print queue is managed separately, which can make administration and problem resolution difficult.

Printing Essentials

An understanding of how printing works can go a long way when you're trying to troubleshoot printer problems. When you print documents, many processes, drivers, and devices work together to print the documents. If you use a printer connected to a print server, the key operations are as follows:

- **Printer driver** When you print a document in an application, your computer uses a printer driver to handle the printing process. If the print device is attached to your computer physically, the printer driver is accessed from a local disk drive. If the print device is located on a remote computer, the printer driver might be downloaded from the remote computer. The availability of printer drivers on the remote computer is configurable by operating system and chip architecture. If the computer can't obtain the latest printer driver, an administrator probably hasn't enabled the driver for the computer's operating system. For more information, see "Managing Printer Drivers" in Chapter 15.
- **Local print spool and print processor** The application from which you print uses the printer driver to translate the document into a file format that the selected print device can understand. Your computer then passes the document to the local print spooler. The local spooler in turn passes the document to a print processor, which creates the raw print data necessary for printing on the print device.
- **Print router and print spooler on the print server** The raw data is passed back to the local print spooler. If you're printing to a remote printer, the raw data is then routed to the print spooler on the print server. On Windows Server 2016 systems,

the printer router, Winspool.drv, handles the tasks of locating the remote printer, routing print jobs, and downloading printer drivers to the local system if necessary. If any of these tasks fails, the print router is usually the culprit. See "Solving spooling problems" and "Setting Printer Access Permissions" in Chapter 15 to learn about possible fixes for this problem. If these procedures don't work, you might want to replace or restore Winspool.drv.

> The main reason for downloading printer drivers to clients is to maintain a single location for installing driver updates. This way, instead of having to install a new driver on all the client systems, you install the driver on the print server and enable clients to download the new driver. For more information on working with printer drivers, see "Managing Printer Drivers" in Chapter 15.

- **Printer (print queue)**   The document goes from the print spooler to the printer stack—which in some operating systems is called the *print queue*—for the selected print device. When in the queue, the document is referred to as a *print job*—a task for the print spooler to handle. The length of time the document waits in the printer stack is based on its priority and position within the printer stack. For more information, see "Scheduling and Prioritizing Print Jobs" in Chapter 15.
- **Print monitor**   When the document reaches the top of the printer stack, the print monitor sends the document to the print device, where it's actually printed. If the printer is configured to notify users that the document has been printed, you get a confirmation message.

> The specific print monitor used by Windows Server 2016 depends on the print device configuration and type. You might also find monitors from the print device manufacturer. This dynamic-link library (DLL) is required to print to the print device. If it's corrupted or missing, you might need to reinstall it.

- **Print device**   The print device is the physical device that prints documents on paper. Common print device problems and display errors include Insert Paper Into Tray X, Low Toner, Out Of Paper, Out Of Toner or Out Of Ink, Paper Jam, and Printer Offline.

Group Policy can affect your ability to install and manage printers. If you're having problems and believe they're related to Group Policy, you should examine the key policies in the following locations:

- Computer Configuration\Administrative Templates\Printers
- User Configuration\Administrative Templates\Control Panel\Printers
- User Configuration\Administrative Templates\Start Menu And Taskbar

REAL WORLD   Windows Server 2016 is a 64-bit operating system and a print queue running on this operating system cannot function without a native 64-bit printer driver. Because of this, you should verify the availability of required 64-

bit print drivers before migrating print queues from servers running 32-bit operating systems to Windows Server 2016. Keep in mind that if your organization has older printers still in use, those printers might have third-party 32-bit drivers and there might not be 64-bit equivalents.

Configuring Print Servers

You configure a server as a print server by adding the Print and Document Services role and configuring this role to use one or more of the following role services:

- **Print Server**   Configures the server as a print server and installs the Print Management console. You can use the Print Management console to manage multiple printers and print servers, to migrate printers to and from other print servers, and to manage print jobs.
- **Line Printer Daemon (LPD) Service**   Enables UNIX-based computers or other computers using the Line Printer Remote (LPR) service to print to shared printers on the server.
- **Internet Printing**   Creates a website where authorized users can manage print jobs on the server. It also lets users who have Internet Printing Client installed to connect and print to shared printers on the server by using the Internet Printing Protocol (IPP). The default Internet address for Internet Printing is http://*ServerName*/Printers, where *ServerName* is a placeholder for the internal or external server name, such as http://PrintServer15/Printers or http://www.imaginedlands.com/Printers.
- **Distributed Scan Server**   Establishes the server as a scan server, which is used to run scan processes. Scan processes are rules that define scan settings and control delivery of scanned documents on your network. The Scan Management snap-in is installed when you install this role service. Scan Management enables you to manage Web Services on Devices (WSD)–enabled scanners, scan servers, and scan processes.

You can add the Print and Document Services role to a server by following these steps:

1. In Server Manager, click Manage, and then click Add Roles And Features, or select Add Roles And Features in the Quick Start pane. This starts the Add Roles And Features Wizard. If the wizard displays the Before You Begin page, read the Welcome text, and then select Next.

2. On the Installation Type page, Role-Based Or Feature-Based Installation is selected by default. Select Next.

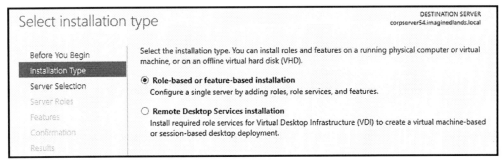

Select installation type

DESTINATION SERVER
corpserver54.imaginedlands.local

Before You Begin
Installation Type
Server Selection
Server Roles
Features
Confirmation
Results

Select the installation type. You can install roles and features on a running physical computer or virtual machine, or on an offline virtual hard disk (VHD).

⦿ **Role-based or feature-based installation**
Configure a single server by adding roles, role services, and features.

○ **Remote Desktop Services installation**
Install required role services for Virtual Desktop Infrastructure (VDI) to create a virtual machine-based or session-based desktop deployment.

3. On the Server Selection page, you can choose to install roles and features on running servers or virtual hard disks. Either select a server from the server pool or select a server from the server pool on which to mount a virtual hard disk (VHD). If you are adding roles and features to a VHD, click Browse, and then use the Browse For Virtual Hard Disks dialog box to locate the VHD. When you are ready to continue, select Next.

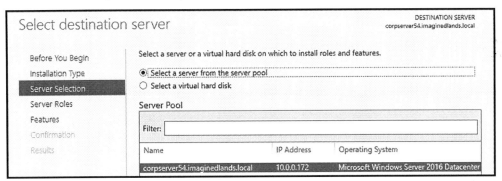

Select destination server

DESTINATION SERVER
corpserver54.imaginedlands.local

Before You Begin
Installation Type
Server Selection
Server Roles
Features
Confirmation
Results

Select a server or a virtual hard disk on which to install roles and features.

⦿ Select a server from the server pool
○ Select a virtual hard disk

Server Pool

Filter:

Name	IP Address	Operating System
corpserver54.imaginedlands.local	10.0.0.172	Microsoft Windows Server 2016 Datacenter

4. On the Select Roles page, select Print And Document Services. When you are ready to continue, select Next three times.

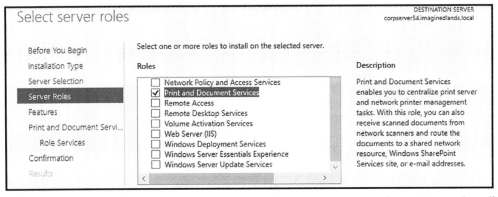

Select server roles

DESTINATION SERVER
corpserver54.imaginedlands.local

Before You Begin
Installation Type
Server Selection
Server Roles
Features
Print and Document Servi...
   Role Services
Confirmation
Results

Select one or more roles to install on the selected server.

Roles

- ☐ Network Policy and Access Services
- ☑ Print and Document Services
- ☐ Remote Access
- ☐ Remote Desktop Services
- ☐ Volume Activation Services
- ☐ Web Server (IIS)
- ☐ Windows Deployment Services
- ☐ Windows Server Essentials Experience
- ☐ Windows Server Update Services

Description

Print and Document Services enables you to centralize print server and network printer management tasks. With this role, you can also receive scanned documents from network scanners and route the documents to a shared network resource, Windows SharePoint Services site, or e-mail addresses.

5. On the Select Role Services page, select one or more role services to install. To allow for interoperability with UNIX, be sure to add LPD Service. Click Next.

6. When you install Internet Printing, you must also install Web Server (IIS) and some related components. You are prompted to automatically add the required role services. Select Add Features to continue.

Select role services

DESTINATION SERVER
corpserver54.imaginedlands.local

Before You Begin
Installation Type
Server Selection
Server Roles
Features
Print and Document Servi...
Role Services
Confirmation
Results

Select the role services to install for Print and Document Services

Role services

☑ Print Server
☐ Distributed Scan Server
☐ Internet Printing
☐ LPD Service

Description

Print Server includes the Print Management snap-in, which is used for managing multiple printers or print servers and migrating printers to and from other Windows print servers.

NOTE If the server on which you want to install the Print And Document Services role doesn't have all the required binary source files, the server gets the files via Windows Update by default or from a location specified in Group Policy. You also can specify an alternate path for the required source files by clicking the Specify An Alternate Source Path link, entering that alternate path in the box provided, and then clicking OK. For network shares, enter the UNC path to the share, such as \\CorpServer82\WinServer2012\. For mounted Windows images, enter the WIM path prefixed with *WIM:* and including the index of the image to use, such as WIM:\\CorpServer82\WinServer2012\install.wim:4.

7. After you review the installation options and save them as necessary, select Install to begin the installation process. The Installation Progress page tracks the progress of the installation. If you close the wizard, select the Notifications icon in Server Manager, and then select the link provided to reopen the wizard.

8. When Setup finishes installing the Print And Document Services role, the Installation Progress page will be updated to reflect this. Review the installation details to ensure that all phases of the installation were completed successfully.

9. When you install Distributed Scan Server, you'll get a notification that additional configuration is required. Select the link provided to open Scan Management, which you can use to specify scanners to manage. In Scan Management, expand the Scan Management node in the left pane, right-click the Managed Scanners node, and then select Manage to open the Add Or Remove Scanners dialog box. Use the Add Or Remove Scanners dialog box to identify the distributed scanners in your organization.

When you install Distributed Scan Server, a security group called Scan Operators is added to the Users container in Active Directory Domain Services (AD DS) for the current logon domain. Any users who need to manage the Distributed Scan service should be added to this group.

Enabling and Disabling File and Printer Sharing

File and printer sharing settings control access to file shares and printers that are attached to a computer. You can manage a computer's file and printer sharing configuration by following these steps:

1. In File Explorer, select Network in the left pane. On the toolbar in Network Explorer, select Network, and then select Network And Sharing Center.

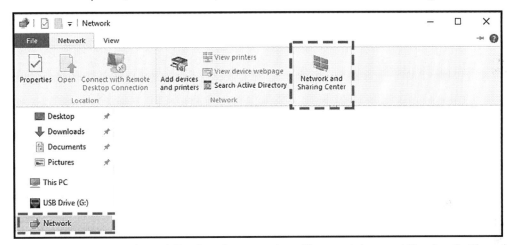

2. In Network And Sharing Center, select Change Advanced Sharing Settings in the left pane. Select the network profile for the network for which file and printer sharing should be enabled. Typically, this is the Domain profile.

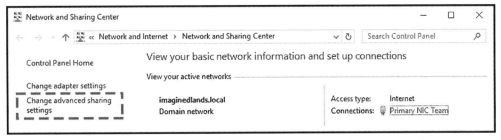

3. Standard file and printer sharing controls network access to shared resources. To configure standard file sharing, do one of the following:

   ▪ Select Turn On File And Printer Sharing to enable file and printer sharing.

* Select Turn Off File And Printer Sharing to disable file and printer sharing.

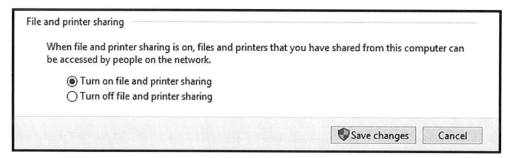

Getting Started with Print Management

Print Management should be your tool of choice for working with printers and print servers. After you install the Print and Document Services role, Print Management is available on the Tools menu in Server Manager as a stand-alone console. You can also add Print Management as a snap-in to any custom console you create.

By using Print Management, you can install, view, and manage the printers and Windows print servers in your organization. Print Management also displays the status of printers and print servers. When you expand a server-level node and select the Printers node, you get a list of printers the server is hosting. If you are accessing the selected print server by using a Remote Desktop connection, you might also find entries for printers being redirected from your logon computer. Redirected printers are listed clearly as such with a (redirected) suffix.

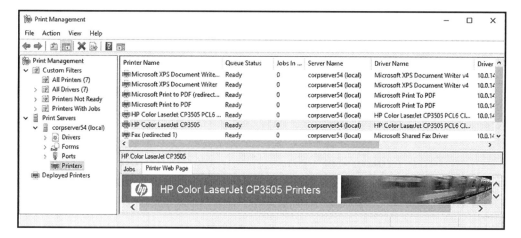

By default, Print Management enables you to manage local print servers. You can manage and monitor other print servers in the organization by adding them to the console. Additionally, to manage a remote print server, you must be a member of the local Administrators group on the print server or a member of the Domain Admins group in the domain of which the print server is a member.

When you select a print server's Printers node, the main pane lists the associated printer queues by printer name, queue status, number of jobs in a queue, and server name. If you right-click Printers, and then click Show Extended View, you can turn on Extended view. Extended view makes it easy to track the status of both printers and print jobs by displaying information about the status of a print job, its owner, the number of pages, the size of the job, when it was submitted, its port, and its priority.

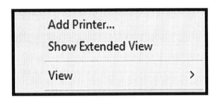

In addition, when a printer has a webpage, Extended view displays a Printer Web Page tab that lets you directly access the printer's webpage. This webpage provides details about the printer's status, its physical properties, and its configuration, and it sometimes allows remote administration.

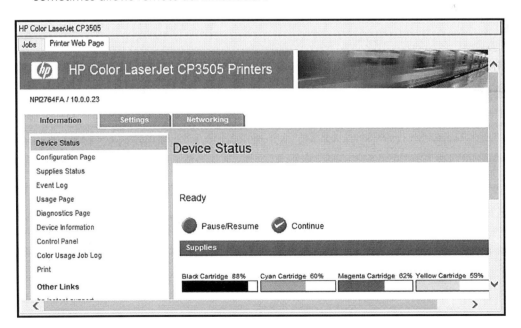

You can add print servers to Print Management by following these steps:

1. In Print Management, right-click the Print Servers node in the left pane, and then click Add/Remove Servers.

2. In the Add/Remove Servers dialog box, you'll find a list of the print servers you previously added.

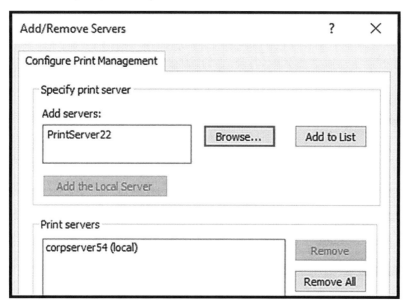

Do one of the following, and then click Add To List:

- In the Add Servers list, enter or paste the names of the print servers you want to add. Use commas to separate computer names.
- Click Browse to display the Select Print Server dialog box. Click the print server you want to use, and then click Select Server.

3. Repeat the previous step as necessary, and then click OK.

You can remove print servers from Print Management by following these steps:

1. In Print Management, right-click the Print Servers node in the left pane, and then click Add/Remove Servers.

2. In the Add/Remove Servers dialog box, you'll find a list of the print servers that are being monitored. Under Print Servers, select one or more servers, and then click Remove.

Installing Printers

The following sections examine techniques you can use to install printers. Windows Server 2016 makes it possible for you to install and manage printers anywhere on the network. To install or configure a new printer on Windows Server 2016, you must be a member of the Administrators, Print Operators, or Server Operators group. To connect to a printer and print documents, you must have the appropriate access permissions. See "Setting Printer Access Permissions" in Chapter 15 for details.

Using Autoinstall

Print Management can automatically detect all network printers located on the same subnet as the computer on which the console is running. After detection, Print Management can automatically install the appropriate printer drivers, set up print queues, and share the printers. To automatically install network printers and configure a print server, follow these steps:

1. Start Print Management by clicking Tools in Server Manager, and then clicking Print Management.

2. In Print Management, expand the Print Servers node by double-clicking it.

3. Right-click the entry for the local or remote server with which you want to work, and then click Add Printer to start the Network Printer Installation Wizard.

4. On the Print Installation page, select Search The Network For Printers, and then click Next.

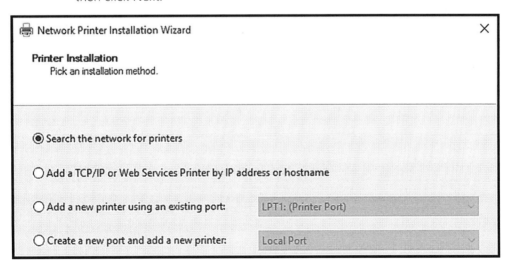

5. The wizard searches the local subnet for network printers. If printers are found, you'll get a list of printers by name and IP address. Click a printer to install, click Next, and then continue this procedure to install the automatically detected printer.

If a printer you want to use is not listed, you should ensure that the printer is powered on and is online and then repeat this procedure. If a printer you want to use is powered on and online but is not listed, see "Installing Network-Attached Print Devices" to complete the installation.

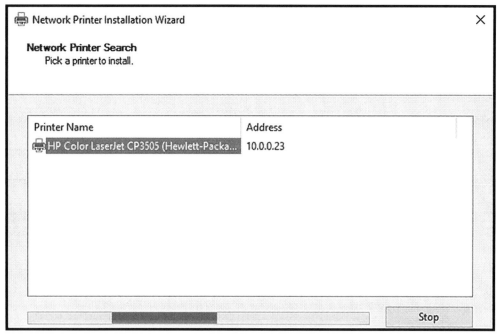

6. The wizard automatically detects the TCP/IP port configuration of the selected printer and then communicates with the print to obtain the information required to configure the printer. Afterward, the wizard sets the default name and share name of the printer. The printer is configured as a shared resource as well.

The printer name is the name you encounter when you work with the printer in Print Management. The share name is the name users view when they work with the printer.

Optionally, enter information in the Location and Comment text boxes that will help users locate and identify the printer. For example, you might want to specify the printer location as: Room 314 in Building 7.

Network Printer Installation Wizard ✕

Printer Name and Sharing Settings
You can give the printer a friendly name and specify whether other people can use the printer.

Printer Name:

> HP Color LaserJet CP3505

☑ Share this printer

Share Name:

> HP Color LaserJet CP3505 (Hewlett-Packard)

Location:

> Room 314 in Building 7.

Comment:

NOTE The printer name and share name can be up to 256 characters and can include spaces. In a large organization, you'll want the share name to be logical and helpful in locating the printer. For example, you might want to give the name Twelfth Floor NE to the printer that points to a print device in the northeast corner of the twelfth floor.

7. The next page lets you review the settings. When you're ready to complete the installation, click Next.

8. When you share a printer, Windows Server automatically makes drivers available so that users can download them when they first connect to the printer. The status page should confirm that printer driver and printer installation were successful. If there was a problem with the installation, note the errors provided. For example, someone might have powered off the printer while you were trying to configure it. If so, you'll need to power the printer back on and repeat this procedure.

9. If you'd like to print a test page on the printer, select the Print Test Page check box, and then click Finish. Otherwise, just click Finish.

10. By default, the printer share is not listed in Active Directory. Listing the printer share in Active Directory enables users to search for and find the printer more easily. If you want the printer share to be listed in Active Directory, select the Printers node in the left pane, right-click the printer in the main window, and then select List In Directory.

Open Printer Queue...
Pause Printing
List in Directory
Deploy with Group Policy...
Set Printing Defaults...
Manage Sharing...
Print Test Page
Enable Branch Office Direct Printing
Properties...

11. By default, print jobs are sent to the print server where they are rendered and then sent to the printer. You can change this behavior by using Branch Office Direct Printing. With Branch Office Direct Printing, print jobs are rendered on client computers and then sent directly to the printer. If you want to enable direct printing, select the Printers node in the left pane, right-click the printer in the main window, and then select Enable Branch Office Direct Printing.

Installing Physically-Attached Print Devices

Most physically attached print devices are connected to a computer directly through a USB cable. You can configure physically attached printers as local print devices or as network print devices. The key difference is that a local device is accessible only to users logged on to the computer and a network device is accessible to network users as a shared print device. Remember that the workstation or server you're logged on to becomes the print server for the device you're configuring. If the computer is sleeping or turned off, the printer will not be available.

You can install physically attached print devices locally by logging on to the print server you want to configure; you can install the print devices remotely through Remote Desktop. If you're configuring a local Plug and Play printer and are logged on to the print server, installing a print device is a snap. After the printer is installed, you need to configure it for use.

You can install and configure a print device by following these steps:

1. Power on the printer, and then connect the print device to the server by using the appropriate cable.

2. If Windows Server automatically detects the print device, Windows begins installing the device and the necessary drivers. If the necessary drivers aren't found, you might need to insert the printer's driver disc into the CD/DVD drive.

3. If Windows Server doesn't detect the print device automatically, you need to install the print device manually as described in the next set of instructions.

4. After you install the printer, you can configure the printer. In Print Management, expand the Print Servers node and the node for the server with which you want to work. When you select the Printers node for the server you are configuring, you'll find a list of available printers in the main pane. Right-click the printer you want to configure, and then click Manage Sharing. This displays the printer's Properties dialog box with the Sharing tab selected.

5. When you select the Share This Printer check box, Windows Server sets the default share name to the name of the printer. You can enter a different name for the printer share in the Share Name text box.

6. By default, the Render Print Jobs On Client Computers check box is selected, which configures the printer for Branch Office Direct Printing. With Branch Office Direct Printing, print jobs are rendered on client computers and then sent directly to the printer. If you want print jobs to be sent to the print server for rendering and then sent to the printer, clear the Render Print Jobs On Client Computers check box.

7. Listing the printer share in Active Directory enables users to search for and find the printer more easily. If you want the printer share to be listed in Active Directory, select the List In The Directory check box.

8. Click OK.

Sometimes Windows Server won't detect your printer. In this case, follow these steps to install the print device:

1. In Print Management, expand the Print Servers node and the node for the server with which you want to work.

2. Right-click the server's Printers node, and then click Add Printer to start the Network Printer Installation Wizard.

3. On the Printer Installation page, select Add A New Printer Using An Existing Port, and then choose the appropriate LPT, COM, or USB port. You can also

print to a file. If you do, Windows Server 2016 prompts users for a file name each time they print. Click Next.

4. On the Printer Driver page, choose one of the following options:

- If Windows detected the printer type on the selected port and a compatible driver was found automatically, a printer driver is listed that reflects the printer manufacturer and model and the Use The Printer Driver That The Wizard Selected option is selected by default. To accept this setting, click Next.
- If a compatible driver is not available and you want to choose an existing driver installed on the computer, select the Use An Existing Driver On The Computer option. After you choose the appropriate driver from the selection list, click Next.
- If a compatible driver is not available and you want to install a new driver, select Install A New Driver, and then click Next. You must now specify the print device manufacturer and model. This enables Windows Server 2016 to assign a printer driver to the print device. After you choose a print device manufacturer, choose a printer model.

REAL WORLD If the device manufacturer and model you're using aren't displayed in the list, click Windows Update. Windows will then connect to the Windows Update Web site to update the list of printers to show additional models. This automatic driver provisioning process can take several minutes. When the update process is complete, you should then be able to select your printer manufacturer and model. If you can't, download the driver from the manufacturer's website, and then extract the driver files. Click Have Disk. In the Install From Disk dialog box, click Browse. In the Locate File dialog box, locate the .inf driver file for the device, and then click Open.

NOTE If a driver for the specific printer model you're using isn't available, you often can select a generic driver or a driver for a similar print device. Consult the print device documentation for pointers.

---

5. Assign a name to the printer. This is the name that will be listed in Print Management.

6. Specify whether the printer is available to remote users. To create a printer accessible to remote users, select the Share This Printer option, and then enter a name for the shared resource. In a large organization you'll want the share name to be logical and helpful in locating the printer. For example, you could give the name Twelfth Floor NE to the printer that points to the print device in the northeast corner of the twelfth floor.

7. If you like, you can enter a location description and comment. This information can help users find a printer and determine its capabilities. Click Next.

8. The final page lets you review the settings. When you're ready to complete the installation, click Next.

9. After Windows installs the printer driver and configures the printer, you'll get a status page. Ensure that the driver and printer installation succeeded before continuing. If there were errors, you need to correct any problems and repeat this process. To test the printer, select Print Test Page, and then click Finish.

When the Network Printer Installation Wizard finishes installing the new printer, the Printers folder will have an additional icon with the name set the way you specified. You can change the printer properties and check printer status at any time. For more information, see "Configuring Printer Properties" in Chapter 15.

> **TIP** If you repeat this process, you can create additional printers for the same print device. All you need to do is change the printer name and share name. Having additional printers for a single print device makes it possible for you to set different properties to serve different needs. For example, you could have a high-priority printer for print jobs that need to be printed immediately and a low-priority printer for print jobs that aren't as urgent.

Installing Network-Attached Print Devices

A network-attached print device is attached directly to the network through a network adapter card or a wireless network card. Network-attached printers are configured as network print devices so that they're accessible to network users as shared print devices. Remember that the server on which you configure the print device becomes the print server for the device you're configuring.

Install a network-attached print device by following these steps:

1. In Print Management, expand the Print Servers node and the node for the server with which you want to work.

2. Right-click the server's Printers node, and then click Add Printer to start the Network Printer Installation Wizard.

3. On the Printer Installation page, select Add A TCP/IP Or Web Services Printer By IP Address Or Hostname, and then click Next.

4. On the Printer Address page, choose one of the following options in the Type Of Device list:

- **Autodetect** Choose this option if you are unsure of the printer device type. Windows Server will try to detect the type of device automatically.
- **TCP/IP Device** Choose this option if you are sure the printer is a TCP/IP device.
- **Web Services Printer** Choose this option if you are sure the printer is a Web Services for Devices (WSD) capable printer.

- **Web Services Secure Printer**   Choose this option if you are sure the printer supports WSD Secure Printing.

> **REAL WORLD**   With WSD Secure Printing, print servers can create a private secure channel to the print device on the network without the need for additional security technologies such as IPsec. However, users and computers that work with the secure printer must be members of an Active Directory domain. You use the domain settings to manage printer permissions and Active Directory Domain Services acts as the trust arbitrator between the print server and the printer.

5. Enter the host name or IP address for the printer, such as 192.168.1.90. With the Autodetect and TCP/IP Device options, the wizard sets the port name to the same value, but you can also choose to use a different value.

> **TIP**   The port name doesn't matter as long as it's unique on the server. If you're configuring multiple printers on the print server, be sure to record the port-to-printer mapping.

6. Click Next, and the wizard attempts to contact the printer and automatically configure the print device. If the wizard is unable to detect the print device, be sure that the following are true:

- You selected the correct type of print device.
- The print device is turned on and connected to the network.
- The printer is configured properly.
- You entered the correct IP address or printer name.

7. If the device type, IP address, or printer name is incorrect, click OK to close the warning dialog box. Next, click Back, and then reenter the required printer information.

8. On the Printer Driver page, choose one of the following options:

- If Windows detected the printer type on the selected port and a compatible driver was found automatically, a printer driver is listed that reflects the printer manufacturer and model and the Use The Printer Driver That The Wizard Selected option is selected by default. To accept this setting, click Next.
- If a compatible driver is not available and you want to choose an existing driver installed on the computer, select the Use An Existing Driver option. After you use the selection list to choose the appropriate driver, click Next.
- If a compatible driver is not available and you want to install a new driver, select Install A New Driver, and then click Next. Specify the print device manufacturer to enable Windows Server to assign a printer driver to the print device. After you choose a print device manufacturer, choose a printer model.

> **REAL WORLD**   If the device manufacturer and model you're using aren't displayed in the list, click Windows Update. Windows will then connect to the Windows Update Web site to update the list of printers to show additional models. This feature is part of the automatic driver provisioning feature. It can take several minutes to retrieve the updated list. You should then be able to select your printer manufacturer and model. If you can't, download the driver from the manufacturer's website, and then extract the driver files. Click Have Disk. In the Install From Disk dialog box, click Browse. In the Locate File dialog box, locate the .inf driver file for the device, and then click Open.

9. Assign a name to the printer. This is the name that will be listed in Print Management.

10. Specify whether the printer is available to remote users. To create a printer accessible to remote users, select the Share Name option, and then enter a name for the shared resource. In a large organization, you should use a share name that is logical and helpful in locating the printer. For example, Twelfth Floor NE would be a good name for the printer that points to the print device in the northeast corner of the twelfth floor.

11. If you like, you can enter a location description and comment. This information can help users find a printer and determine its capabilities. Click Next.

12. The final page lets you review the settings. When you're ready to complete the installation, click Next.

13. After Windows installs the printer driver and configures the printer, you'll get a status page. Ensure that the driver and printer installation succeeded before continuing. If there were errors, you need to correct any problems and repeat this process. To test the printer, select Print Test Page, and then click Finish. To install another printer, select Add Another Printer, and then click Finish.

14. By default, the printer share is not listed in Active Directory. Listing the printer share in Active Directory makes it possible for users to search for and find the printer more easily. If you want the printer share to be listed in Active Directory, select the Printers node in the left pane, right-click the printer in the main window, and then select List In Directory.

15. By default, print jobs are sent to the print server where they are rendered and then sent to the printer. You can change this behavior by using Branch Office Direct Printing. With Branch Office Direct Printing, print jobs are rendered on client computers and then sent directly to the printer. If you want to enable direct printing, select the Printers node in the left pane, right-click the printer in the main window, and then select Enable Branch Office Direct Printing.

When the Network Printer Installation Wizard finishes installing the new printer, the Printers folder will have an additional icon with the name set the way you specified. You can change the printer properties and check printer status at any time. For more information, see "Configuring Printer Properties" in Chapter 15.

> **TIP** If you repeat this process, you can create additional printers for the same print device. All you need to do is change the printer name and share name. Having additional printers for a single print device makes it possible for you to set different properties to serve different needs. For example, you could have a high-priority printer for print jobs that need to be printed immediately and a low-priority printer for print jobs that aren't as urgent.

Connecting to Network Printers

After you create a network printer, remote users can connect to it and use it much as they do any other printer. You need to set up a connection on a user-by-user basis or have users do this themselves. To create a connection to the printer on a Windows 7 system, follow these steps:

1. With the user logged on, click Start, and then click Devices And Printers. In Devices And Printers, click Add A Printer to start the Add Printer Wizard.

2. Select Add A Network, Wireless Or Bluetooth Printer. The wizard searches for available devices.

3. If the printer you want is listed in the Select A Printer list, click it, and then click Next.

4. If the printer you want is not listed in the Select A Printer list, click The Printer That I Want Isn't Listed. On the Find A Printer By Name Or TCP/IP Address page, do one of the following:

- To browse the network for shared printers, choose Find A Printer In The Directory, Based On Location Or Feature, and then click Next. Click the printer to use, and then click Select.
- To specify the printer to use by its share path, choose Select A Shared Printer By Name. Enter the UNC path to the shared printer, such as **\\PrintServer12\Twelfth Floor NE**, or the Web path to an Internet Printer, such as **http://PrintServer12/Printers/IPrinter52/.printer**.
- To specify a printer to use by TCP/IP address or host name, select Add A Printer Using A TCP/IP Address Or Hostname, and then click Next. Choose a device type, and then enter the host name or IP address for the printer, such as **192.168.1.90**. If you select the Autodetect or TCP/IP Device options, the wizard will set the port name to the same value, but you can also choose a different value. Click Next.

5. On the Type A Printer Name page, the printer name is set for you. You can accept the default name or enter a new name. Click Next to install the printer, and then click Finish. The user can now print to the network printer by selecting the printer in an application. The Device And Printers folder on the user's computer shows the new network printer as well.

To create a connection to the printer on a Windows 10 system, follow these steps:

1. Open the Settings app. On the home page, click Devices.

2. On the Printers & Scanners page, click Add A Printer Or Scanner. Settings will then attempt to detect the printer automatically.

   If the wizard finds the printer with which you want to work, click it in the list provided, follow the prompts, and skip the rest of the steps in this procedure. If the wizard doesn't find the printer, click The Printer That I Want Isn't Listed, and then complete the rest of this procedure.

3. In the Add Printer Wizard, click Add Bluetooth, Wireless Or Network Discoverable Printer.

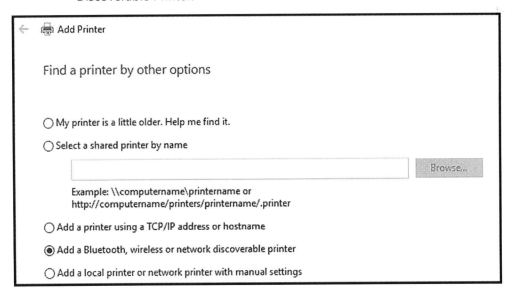

4. In the list of available printers, select the printer you want to use, and then click Next.

5. If prompted, install the printer driver on your computer. Complete the additional steps in the wizard, and then click Finish. You can confirm the printer is working by printing a test page.

If you have trouble connecting to the printer, try the following as part of troubleshooting:

- Be sure that a firewall isn't blocking connectivity to the printer. You might need to open a firewall port to enable access between the computer and the printer.
- Be sure the printer is turned on and connected to the same network as the computer. If your network consists of multiple subnets connected together, try to connect the printer to the same network subnet. You can determine the subnet by looking at the computer's IP address.
- Be sure the printer is configured to broadcast its presence on the network. Most network printers automatically do this.
- Be sure the printer has an IP address and proper network settings. With DHCP, network routers assign IP addresses automatically as printers connect to the network.

Managing Installed Printers

Once you've installed network printers, you'll need to perform a number of management tasks. This section looks at routine tasks, including those for deployment printer connections, configuring restrictions, moving printers, monitoring print services and resolving spooling problems.

Deploying Printer Connections

Connecting to printers is fairly easy, but you can make the process even easier by deploying printer connections through Group Policy. You can deploy printer connections to computers or users via the Group Policy objects (GPOs) that Windows applies. Deploy the connections to groups of users when you want users to be able to access the printers from any computer they log on to. Deploy the connections to groups of computers when you want all users of the computers to access the printers. For per-computer connections, Windows adds or removes printer connections when the computer starts. For per-user connections, Windows adds or removes printer connections when the user logs on.

To deploy printer connections to computers, you must follow these steps:

1. In Print Management, expand the Print Servers node and the node for the server with which you want to work.

2. Select the server's Printers node. In the main pane, right-click the printer you want to deploy, and then click Deploy With Group Policy. This displays the Deploy With Group Policy dialog box.

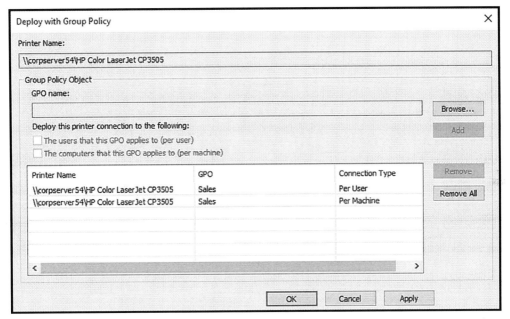

3. Click Browse. In the Browse For Group Policy Object dialog box, select the GPO to use, and then click OK.

4. Do one or both of the following:

- To deploy to the printer connection on a per-user basis, under Deploy This Printer Connection To The Following, select The Users That This GPO Applies To.
- To deploy to the printer connection on a per-computer basis, under Deploy This Printer Connection To The Following, select The Computers That This GPO Applies To.

5. Click Add to create a print connection entry.

6. Repeat steps 3–5 to deploy the printer connection to other GPOs.

7. Click OK to save the changes to the GPO. In the confirmation dialog box, ensure that all operations were completed successfully. If an error occurred, click Details to get more information about the error. The most common errors involve editing permissions for the GPO with which you are working. If

the account you are using doesn't have appropriate permissions, you need to use an account with additional privileges. Click OK.

Configuring Point and Print Restrictions

In Group Policy, thePoint And Print Restrictions setting controls security warnings and elevation prompts when users point and print and when drivers for printer connections need to be configured. This setting is found in the Administrative Templates for Computer Configuration under the Printers node.

The Point And Print Restrictions setting is used as follows:

* When enabled, clients can point and print to any server. You can configure Clients to show or hide warning and elevation prompts when users point and print and when a driver for an existing printer connection needs to be updated.
* When not configured, clients can point and print to any server in the forest. Clients also will not show a warning and elevation prompt when users point and print or when a driver for an existing printer connection needs to be updated.
* When disabled, clients can point and print to any server. Clients also will not show a warning and elevation prompt when users point and print or when a driver for an existing printer connection needs to be updated.

By default, Windows allows a user who is not a member of the local Administrators group to install only trustworthy printer drivers, such as those provided by Windows or in digitally signed printer driver packages. When you enable the Point And Print Restrictions setting, you also make it possible for users who are not members of the local Administrators group to install printer connections deployed in Group Policy that include additional or updated printer drivers that are not in the form of digitally signed printer driver packages. If you do not enable this setting, users might need to provide the credentials of a user account that belongs to the local Administrators group.

You can enable and configure the Point And Print Restrictions setting in Group Policy by following these steps:

1. In the Group Policy Management Console, right-click the GPO for the site, domain, or organizational unit with which you want to work, and then click Edit. This opens the policy editor for the GPO.

2. In the Group Policy Management Editor, expand the Administrative Templates for Computer Configuration, and then select the Printers node.

3. In the main pane, double-click Point And Print Restrictions.

4. In the Point And Print Restrictions dialog box, select Enabled.

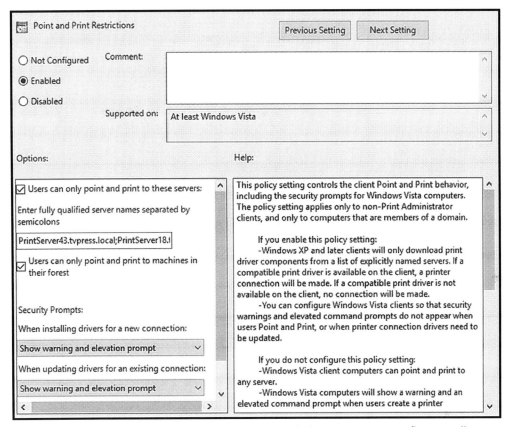

5. When you enable point and print restrictions, you can configure policy so that users can point and print only to a named list of servers. To enforce this restriction, select the related check box and enter a list of fully qualified server names separated by semicolons. To remove this restriction, clear the related check box.

6. When you enable point and print restrictions, you can configure policy so that users can point and print only to servers in their forest. To enforce this restriction, select the related check box. To remove this restriction, clear the related check box.

7. When you install drivers for a new connection, clients can show or not show a warning or elevation prompt. Use the related selection list to choose the option you want to use.

8. When you update drivers for an existing connection, clients can show or not show a warning or elevation prompt. Use the related selection list to choose the option you want to use.

9. Click OK to apply the configuration.

Moving Printers to a New Print Server

You can use the Printer Migration Wizard to move print queues, printer drivers, printer processors, and printer ports from one print server to another. This is an efficient way to consolidate multiple print servers or replace an older print server.

When you move printers, the server on which the printers are currently located is the source server, and the server to which you want to move the printers is the destination server. With this in mind, you can move printers to a new print server by following these steps:

1. In Print Management, right-click the source server, and then click Export Printers To A File. This starts the Printer Migration Wizard.

2. On the initial page, note the printer-related objects that will be exported, and then click Next.

3. On the Select The File Location page, click Browse. In the dialog box provided, select a save location for the printer migration file. After you enter a name for the file, click Save.

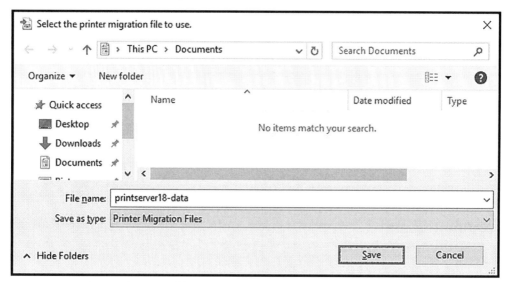

4. Printer migration files are saved with the .printerExport extension. Click Next to save the printer settings to this file.

5. If an error occurred during processing, click Open Event Viewer to review the events generated during the export process and then use the event entries to

determine what happened and possible actions to take to resolve the problem. When you have finished, exit the Event Viewer.

6. On the Exporting page, click Finish to exit the Printer Migration Wizard.

7. In Print Management, right-click the destination server, and then click Import Printers From A File. This launches the Printer Migration Wizard.

8. On the Select The File Location page, click Browse. In the dialog box provided select the printer migration file you created in steps 3 and 4, and then click Open.

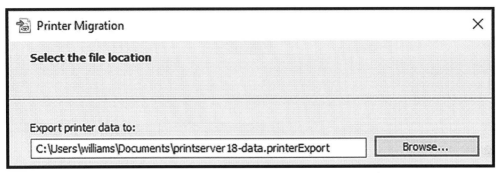

9. Click Next. Note the objects that will be imported, and then click Next. On the Select Import Options page, choose one of the following options in the Import Mode list:

- **Keep Existing Printers**   When you choose this option and existing printer queues have the same names as those you are importing, the wizard creates copies to ensure that the original printer queues and the imported printer queues are both available.
- **Overwrite Existing Printers**   When you choose this option and existing printer queues have the same names as those you are importing, the wizard overwrites the existing printer queues with the information from the printer queues you are importing.

10. On the Select Import Options page, choose one of the following options in the List In The Directory list:

- **List Printers That Were Previously Listed**   Choose this option to specify that only printers that were previously listed are listed in Active Directory.
- **List All Printers**   Choose this option to specify that all printers are listed in Active Directory.
- **Don't List Any Printers**   Choose this option to specify that no printers are listed in Active Directory.

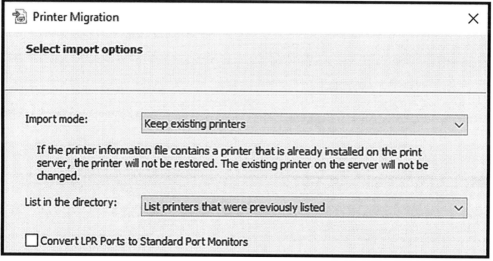

Printer Migration   ×

Select import options

Import mode: Keep existing printers   ⌄

If the printer information file contains a printer that is already installed on the print
server, the printer will not be restored. The existing printer on the server will not be
changed.

List in the directory: List printers that were previously listed   ⌄

☐ Convert LPR Ports to Standard Port Monitors

11. Click Next to begin the import process. If an error occurred during
    processing, click Open Event Viewer to review the events generated during
    the export process and then use the event entries to determine what
    happened and possible actions to take to resolve the problem. When you
    have finished, exit the Event Viewer.

12. On the Importing page, click Finish to exit the Printer Migration Wizard.

Monitoring Printers and Printer Queues

Printer filters display only the printers, printer queues, and printer drivers that meet
specific criteria. Through automated notification, you can use printer filters to
automate monitoring of printers.

In Print Management, you can view existing filters by expanding the Custom Filters
node. If you expand the Custom Filters node and then select a filter, the main pane
shows all printers or print drivers that match the filter criteria. Print Management
includes the following default printer filters:

- **All Printers**   Lists all printers associated with print servers that have been added
  to the console
- **All Drivers**   Lists all printer drivers associated with print servers that have been
  added to the console
- **Printers Not Ready**   Lists all printers that are not in a Ready state, such as those
  with errors
- **Printers With Jobs**   Lists all printers associated with print servers that have active
  or pending print jobs

You can create a new custom filter by follow these steps:

1. In Print Management, right-click the Custom Filters node, and then click Add New Printer Filter to start the New Printer Filter Wizard.

2. On the Printer Filter Name And Description page, enter a filter name and description. If you'd like the number of matching items to be displayed after the filter name, select the Display The Total Number Of Printers check box. Click Next.

3. On the Define A Filter page, define the filter by specifying the text box, condition, and value to match in the first row. If you want to further narrow the possible matches, define additional criteria in the second, third, and subsequent rows. Click Next when you are ready to continue.

NOTE When you use filters for monitoring and notification, you use the Queue Status text box the most. This text box enables you to receive a notification when a printer has a specific status. You can match the following status values: Attention Required, Busy, Deleting, Door Open, Error, Initializing, IO Active, Manual Feed Required, No Toner Ink, Not Available, Offline, Out of Memory, Out of Paper, Output Bin Full, Page Punt, Paper Jam, Paper Problem, Paused, Printing, Processing, Ready, Toner Ink Low, Waiting, and Warming Up

TIP When you are matching conditions in a filter, you can match an exact condition that does exist or one that does not exist. For example, if you want to be notified only of conditions that need attention, you can look for Queue Status conditions that are not exactly the following: Deleting, Initializing, IO Active, Printing, Processing, Waiting, Warming Up, and Ready.

---

4. On the Set Notifications (Optional) page, you can specify whether to send an email message, run a script, or take both actions when the specified criteria are met. Click Finish to complete the configuration.

You can modify an existing custom filter by following these steps:

1. In Print Management, expand the Custom Filters node. Select and then right-click the filter with which you want to work. On the shortcut menu, click Properties.

2. In the filter's Properties dialog box, use the options provided to manage the filter settings. This dialog box has the following three tabs:

- **General** Shows the name and description of the printer filter. Enter a new name and description as necessary.
- **Filter Criteria** Shows the filter criteria. Enter new filter criteria as necessary.

- **Notification** Shows the email and script options. Enter new email and script options as necessary.

Solving Spooling Problems

Windows Server 2016 uses the Print Spooler service to control the spooling of print jobs. If this service isn't running, print jobs can't be spooled. Use the Services console to check the status of the Print Spooler. Follow these steps to check and restart the Print Spooler service:

1. On the Tools menu in Server Manager, click Computer Management.

2. If you want to connect to a remote computer, right-click the Computer Management entry in the console tree, and then click Connect To Another Computer. You can now choose the system whose services you want to manage.

3. Expand the Services And Applications node, and then click Services.

4. Select the Print Spooler service. The Status should be Started. If it isn't, right-click Print Spooler, and then click Start. The Startup Type should be Automatic. If it isn't, double-click Print Spooler and set Startup Type to Automatic.

> **TIP** Spoolers can become corrupted. Symptoms of a corrupted spooler include a frozen printer or one that doesn't send jobs to the print device. Sometimes the print device might print pages of garbled data. In most of these cases, you can resolve the problem by stopping and starting the Print Spooler service. Other spooling problems might be related to permissions. See "Setting Printer Access Permissions" in Chapter 15.

Chapter 15. Configuring and Maintaining Print Services

Few things are as frustrating for users as when printing doesn't work properly. Users want to be able to click Print in an application and have the document print on a printer. They don't care how it all works; they just want it to work when they need it to. For this reason and others, you need to work behind the scenes to ensure print services operate smoothly. In this chapter, you'll learn how to work with print servers, printers, print queues and print jobs. Print server properties are managed separately from printer properties as are print queues and print jobs.

Configuring Print Server Properties

In Windows Server 2016, you control global settings for print servers by using print server properties. To access these properties, complete the following steps:

1. Open Print Management. In Server Manager, click Tools and then select Print Management.

2. Open the Print Server Properties dialog box. In Print Management, right-click the server entry for the print server with which you want to work, and then click Properties.

> **NOTE** If the print server isn't listed, you can add it in the Add/Remove Servers dialog box. To open the dialog box, right-click Print Servers, and then click Add/Remove Servers.

The sections that follow examine some of the print server properties that you can configure.

Locating the Spool Folder and Enabling Printing

The Spool folder holds a copy of all documents in the printer spool. By default, this folder is located at %SystemRoot%\System32\Spool\Printers. On the NTFS file system, all users who access a printer must have the following special permissions on this directory:

* Read Attributes
* Read Extended Attributes

- Create Files / Write Data
- Create Folders / Append Data

If users don't have these permissions, they won't be able to print documents.

If you're experiencing problems, check the permission on this directory by following these steps:

1. Access the Print Server Properties dialog box.

2. Click the Advanced tab. The location of the Spool folder is shown in the Spool Folder text box. Note this location.

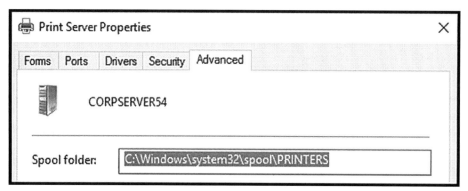

3. In File Explorer, open the properties dialog box for the Spool folder. For example, if the Spool folder is C:\Windows\System32\Spool\PRINTERS. Access C:\Windows\System32\Spool, right-click PRINTERS and then select Properties.

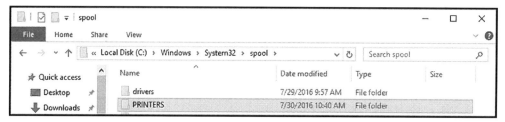

4. In the Properties dialog box, select the Security tab, and then click Advanced.

5. In the Advanced Security Settings dialog box, click the user or group whose permissions you want to verify and then click Edit.

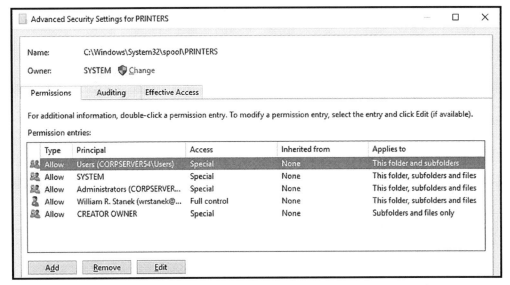

6. In the Permission Entry For dialog box, select Show Advanced Permissions. You'll then be able to verify that the permissions are set appropriately.

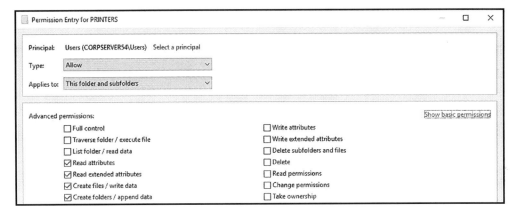

Managing High-Volume Printing

Printers used in corporate environments can print hundreds of documents daily or more. This high volume puts a heavy burden on print servers and can cause printing delays, document corruption, and other problems. To alleviate some of this burden, you should do the following:

- Use network-attached printers rather than directly attached printers. Network-attached printers use fewer system resources (namely CPU time) than do other printers.

- Use Branch Office Direct Printing to render print jobs on client computers, and then send the print jobs directly to a printer. Otherwise, print jobs are sent to the print server where they are rendered, and then sent to the printer.
- Dedicate the print server to handle print services only, such as with a virtual server. If the print server is handling other network duties, it might not be very responsive to print requests and management. To increase responsiveness, you can move other network duties to other servers.
- Move the Spool folder to a drive dedicated to printing. By default, the Spool folder is on the same file system as the operating system. To further improve disk input/output (I/O), use a drive that has a separate controller.

Enabling Print Job Error Notification

Print servers can beep to notify users when a remote document fails to print. By default, this feature is turned off because it can be annoying. If you want to activate or remove notification, access the Advanced tab of the Print Server Properties dialog box, and then select or clear the check box labeled Beep On Errors Of Remote Documents.

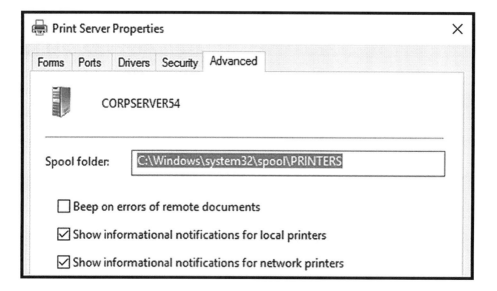

Managing Printer Drivers

In a Windows Server 2016 domain you should configure and update printer drivers only on your print servers. You don't need to update printer drivers on Windows clients. Instead, you configure the network printer to provide the drivers to client systems as necessary.

Updating a Printer Driver

You can update a printer's driver by following these steps:

1. In Print Management, double-click the Print Servers node, and then double-click the entry for the print server itself.

2. Select Printers. Right-click the printer with which you want to work and then select Properties.

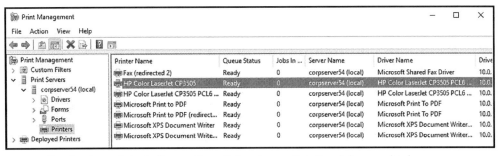

3. In the printer's Properties dialog box, click the Advanced tab.

4. In the Driver list, you can select the driver from a list of currently installed drivers. Use the Driver list to select a driver from a list of known drivers.

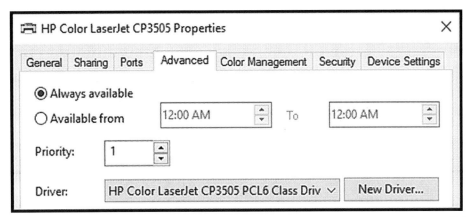

5. If the driver you need isn't listed or if you obtained a new driver, click New Driver to start the Add Printer Driver Wizard. Click Next.

6. Select the manufacturer and model of the print driver to install. Optionally, click Windows Update to see whether there are more drivers for the previously selected printer and processor. Here, Windows connects to the Windows Update Web site to update the list of printers to show additional models. This feature is part of the automatic driver provisioning feature. It can take several minutes to retrieve the updated list. You should then be able to select your printer manufacturer and model.

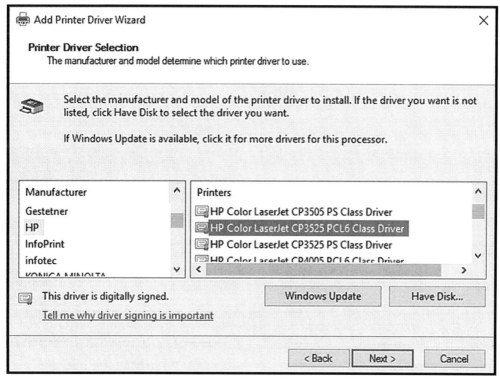

7. If the device manufacturer and model you're using aren't displayed in the list, choose Have Disk to install a new driver from a file or disc. In the Install From Disk dialog box, enter the folder path to the printer driver file or click Browse to find the printer driver file by using the Locate File dialog box. Click OK.

8. Click Next, and then click Finish.

Configuring Drivers for Clients

After you install a printer or change drivers, you might want to select the operating systems that should download the driver from the print server. By enabling clients to download the printer driver, you provide a single location for installing driver updates. This way, instead of having to install a new driver on all the client systems, you install the driver on the print server and enable clients to download the new driver.

You can enable clients to download the new driver by following these steps:

1. In Print Management, double-click the Print Servers node, and then double-click the entry for the print server itself.

2. Select Printers. Right-click the icon of the printer you want to configure, and then click Printer Properties.

3. Click the Sharing tab, and then click Additional Drivers.

4. In the Additional Drivers dialog box, select operating systems that can download the printer driver. As necessary, insert the Windows Server 2016 installation media, printer driver discs, or both for the selected operating systems. The Windows Server 2016 installation media has drivers for most Windows operating systems.

Configuring Printer Properties

In the sections that follow, I explain how to set commonly used printer properties. To open a printer's properties dialog box on a printer server, follow these steps:

1. In Print Management, expand the Print Servers node and the node for the server with which you want to work.

2. Select the server's Printers node. In the main pane, right-click the printer with which you want to work, and then click Properties. You can now set printer properties.

Adding Comments and Locations

To make it easier to determine which printer to use and when, you can add comments and location information for printers. Comments provide general information about the printer, such as the type of print device and who is responsible for it. Location describes the actual site of the print device. After set, applications can display these text boxes. For example, Microsoft Office Word displays this information in the Comment and Where text boxes when you select Print from the File menu.

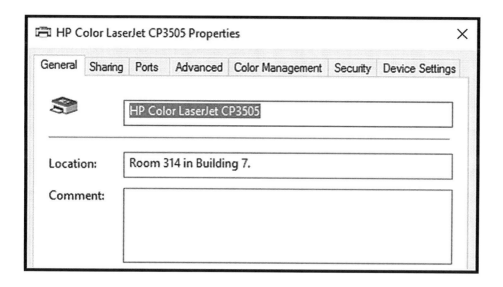

You can add comments and location information to a printer by using the text boxes on the General tab of the printer's Properties dialog box. Enter your comments in the Comment text box. Enter the printer location in the Location text box.

Listing Printers in Active Directory

Listing printers in Active Directory makes it easier for users to locate and install printers. You can list a printer in Active Directory by doing one of the following:

- Right-click the printer's name, and then click List In Directory.
- Open the printer's Properties dialog box, and then click the Sharing tab. Select the List In Directory check box, and then click OK.

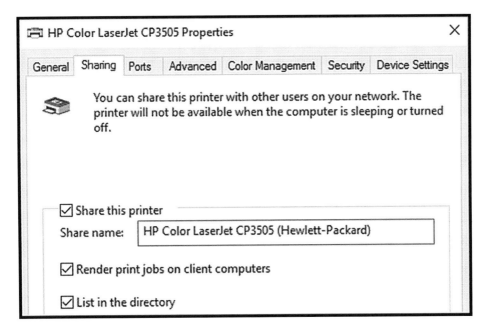

Setting Separator Pages and Print Device Modes

Separator pages have two uses on Windows Server 2016 systems:

- You can use them at the beginning of a print job to make it easier for users to find a document on a busy print device.
- You can use them to change the print device mode, such as whether the print device uses PostScript or Printer Control Language (PCL).

To set a separator page for a print device, follow these steps:

1. On the Advanced tab of the printer's Properties dialog box, click Separator Page. This opens the Separator Page dialog box.

2. When you work with a local server, click the Browse button in the Separator Page dialog box to open the %SystemRoot%\Windows\System32 folder for browsing. In this case, you can browse and select the separator page to use. In contrast, when you work with a remote server, the Browse button is typically not available, so you must enter the exact file name for the separator page.

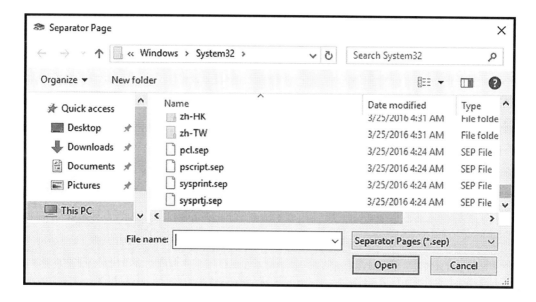

Typically, you'll want to use one of these available separator pages:

- **Pcl.sep**   Switches the print device to PCL mode and prints a separator page before each document
- **Pscript.sep**   Sets the print device to PostScript mode but doesn't print a separator page
- **Sysprint.sep**   Sets the print device to PostScript mode and prints a separator page before each document

> **NOTE**   Sysprintj.sep is an alternate version of Sysprint.sep. If fonts for Japanese are available and you want to use them, you can use Sysprintj.sep.

To stop using the separator page, open the Separator Page dialog box and remove the file name.

Changing the Printer Port

You can change the port used by a print device at any time by using the Properties dialog box for the printer you're configuring. Open the Properties dialog box, and then click the Ports tab.

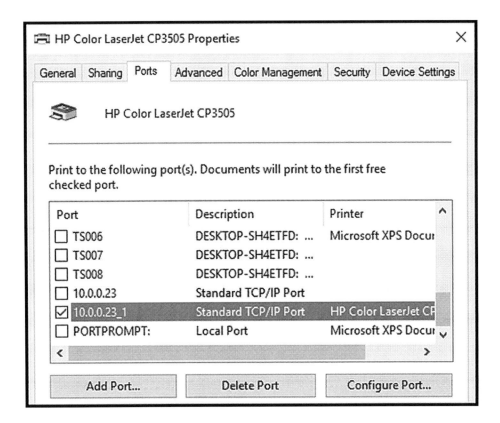

You can now add a port for printing by selecting its check box or remove a port by clearing its check box. To add a new port type, click Add Port. In the Printer Ports dialog box, select the port type, and then click New Port. Enter a valid port name, and then click OK. To remove a port permanently, select it, and then click Delete Port.

Starting and Stopping Printer Sharing

You set printer sharing in the Properties dialog box of the printer you're configuring. Right-click the icon of the printer you want to configure, and then click Manage Sharing. This opens the printer's Properties dialog box with the Sharing tab selected. You can use this tab to change the name of a network printer and to start sharing or stop sharing a printer. Printer sharing tasks that you can perform include the following:

- **Sharing a local printer (thus making it a network printer)**   To share a printer, select Share This Printer, and then specify a name for the shared resource in the Share Name text box. Click OK when you have finished.

- **Changing the shared name of a printer**   To change the shared name, just enter a new name in the Share Name text box, and then click OK.
- **Stopping the sharing of a printer**   To quit sharing a printer, clear the Share This Printer check box, and then click OK.

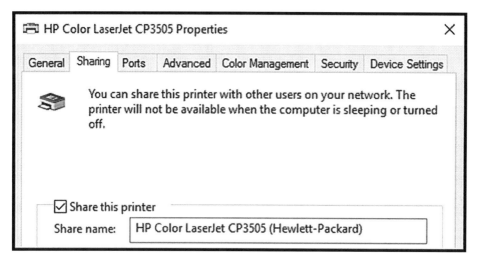

Setting Printer Access Permissions

Network printers are shared resources. As such, you can set access permissions for them. You set access permissions in the Properties dialog box of the printer you're configuring. Open the printer's Properties dialog box, and then click the Security tab. Permissions that you can grant or deny for printers are:

- **Print**   Allows you to print documents; pause, restart, resume, and cancel your own documents; and connect to printers.
- **Manage Documents**   Allows you to perform all Print permission tasks. Also allows you to control settings for print jobs and to pause, restart, and delete print jobs.
- **Manage This Printer**   Allows you to perform all Manage Documents tasks. Also allows you to share printers, change printer properties, change printer permissions, and delete printers.

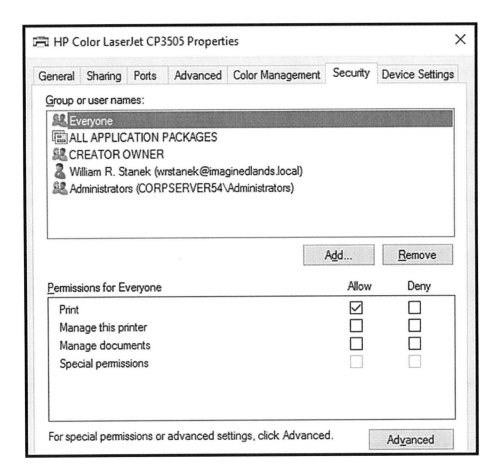

The default permissions are used for any new network printer you create. These settings are as follows:

- Members of the Administrators, Print Operators, and Server Operators groups have full control over printers by default. This makes it possible for you to administer a printer and its print jobs.
- The creator or owner of the document can manage his or her own document. This enables the person who printed a document to change its settings and to delete it.
- Everyone can print to the printer. This makes the printer accessible to all users on the network.

As with other permission sets, the basic permissions for printers are created by combining special permissions into logical groups. By using Advanced permission settings, you can assign these special permissions individually if necessary.

Setting Document Defaults

Document default settings are used only when you print from applications that are not based on Windows, such as when you print from the command prompt. You can set document defaults by following these steps:

1. Open the printer's Properties dialog box, and then click the General tab.
2. Click Preferences.
3. Use the text boxes on the tabs provided to configure the default settings for orientation, paper source, media, color and more.

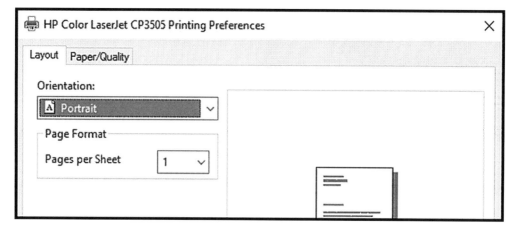

Scheduling and Prioritizing Print Jobs

You can use the Properties dialog box for the printer you're configuring to set default settings for print job priority and scheduling. Open the Properties dialog box, and then click the Advanced tab. You can now set the default schedule and priority settings.

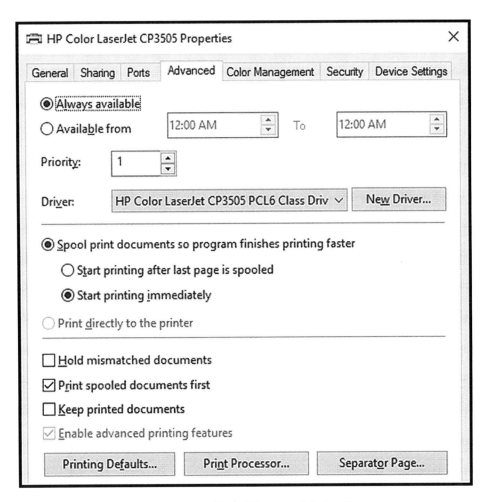

Scheduling Printer Availability and Priority

Printers are always available or available only during the hours specified. You set printer availability on the Advanced tab. Select Always Available to make the printer available at all times. Select Available From to set specific hours of operation.

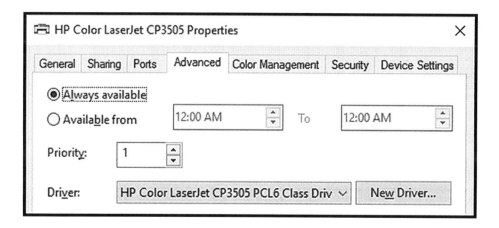

Use the Priority box on the Advanced tab to set the default priority for print jobs that are printed using the selected printer. Print jobs always print in order of priority. Jobs with higher priority print before jobs with lower priority. As a single physical printer could have multiple print queues, each with different priorities, you can use prioritization to ensure important documents are always printed before other documents.

Configuring Print Spooling

For print devices attached to the network, you usually want the printer to spool files rather than print files directly. Print spooling makes it possible to use a printer to manage print jobs.

- ◉ Spool print documents so program finishes printing faster
  - ○ Start printing after last page is spooled
  - ◉ Start printing immediately
- ○ Print directly to the printer

- ☐ Hold mismatched documents
- ☑ Print spooled documents first
- ☐ Keep printed documents
- ☑ Enable advanced printing features

| Printing Defaults... | Print Processor... | Separator Page... |

To enable spooling, use one of the following options on the Advanced tab:

- **Spool Print Documents So Program Finishes Printing Faster**   Select this option to spool print jobs.
- **Start Printing After Last Page Is Spooled**   Select this option if you want the entire document to be spooled before printing begins. This option ensures that the entire document makes it into the print queue before printing. If for some reason printing is canceled or not completed, the job won't be printed.
- **Start Printing Immediately**   Select this option if you want printing to begin immediately when the print device isn't already in use. This option is preferable when you want print jobs to be completed more quickly or when you want to ensure that the application returns control to users as soon as possible.

You can disable spooling by selecting the Print Directly To The Printer option. The following additional check boxes let you configure other spooling options:

- **Hold Mismatched Documents**   If you select this option, the spooler holds print jobs that don't match the setup for the print device. Selecting this option is a good idea if you frequently have to change printer form or tray assignments.
- **Print Spooled Documents First**   If you select this option, jobs that have completed spooling will print before jobs in the process of spooling, regardless of whether the spooling jobs have higher priority.
- **Keep Printed Documents**   Typically, documents are deleted from the queue after they're printed. To keep a copy of documents in the printer, select this option. Use this option if you're printing files that can't easily be re-created. In this way, you can reprint the document without having to re-create it. For details, see "Pausing, Resuming, and Restarting Document Printing" later in this chapter.
- **Enable Advanced Printing Features**   When you enable this option, you can use advanced printing options (if available), such as Page Order and Pages Per Sheet. If you note compatibility problems when using advanced options, you should disable the advanced printing features by clearing this check box.

Managing Print Jobs

You manage print jobs and printers by using the print queue window. If the printer is configured on your system, you can access the print queue window by using one of the following techniques:

- If the printer is configured on your system, you can manage the printer via Settings. On the Settings home page, select Devices. Under Printers & Scanners, click the icon of the printer with which you want to work and then select Open Queue.

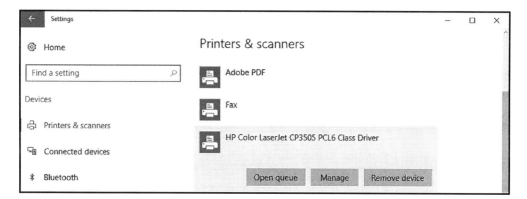

- In Print Management, double-click the Print Servers node, and then double-click the entry for the print server itself. Select Printers. Right-click the printer with which you want to work, and then click Open Printer Queue.

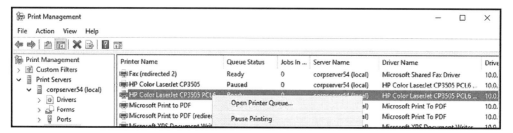

- In Print Management, right-click the Printers node, and then click Show Extended View. With the printer selected in the upper pane, the upper and lower panes in the main window provide functionality similar to that of the print management window.

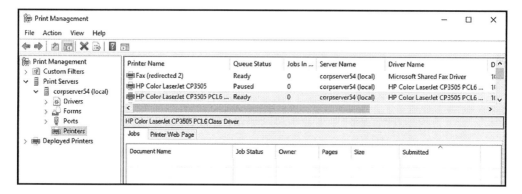

Viewing Printer Queues and Print Jobs

You can now manage print jobs and printers by using the print management window. The print management window shows information about documents in the printers. This information tells you the following:

- **Document Name**   The document file name, which can include the name of the application that printed it.
- **Status**   The status of the print job, which can include the document's status and the printer's status. Document status entries you'll find include Printing, Spooling, Paused, Deleting, and Restarting. Document status can be preceded by the printer status, such as Printer Off-Line.
- **Owner**   The document's owner.
- **Pages**   The number of pages in the document.
- **Size**   The document size in kilobytes or megabytes.
- **Submitted**   The time and date the print job was submitted.
- **Port**   The port used for printing, such as LPT1, COM3, File, or IP address (if applicable).

Pausing the Printer and Resuming Printing

Sometimes you need to pause a printer. You do this by using the print management window and selecting the Pause Printing option from the Printer menu. (A check mark indicates that the option is selected.) When you pause printing, the printer completes the current job and then puts all other jobs on hold.

To resume printing, select the Pause Printing option a second time. This should remove the check mark next to the option.

Emptying the Print Queue

You can use the print management window to empty the print queue and delete all its contents. To do this, choose Cancel All Documents from the Printer menu.

Pausing, Resuming, and Restarting Document Printing

You set the status of individual documents by using the Document menu in the print management window. To change the status of a document, right-click the document, and then use one of the following options on the shortcut menu to change the status of the print job.

- **Pause**   Puts the document on hold and lets other documents print
- **Resume**   Tells the printer to resume printing the document from where it left off
- **Restart**   Tells the printer to start printing the document again from the beginning

Removing Documents and Canceling Print Jobs

To remove a document from the printer or cancel a print job, select the document in the print management window. Right-click the document and click Cancel or press Delete.

> **NOTE** When you cancel a print job that's currently printing, the print device might continue to print part or all of the document. This occurs because most print devices cache documents in an internal buffer and the print device might continue to print the contents of this cache.

Checking Document Properties

Document properties can tell you many things about documents that are in the printer, such as the page source, orientation, and size. You can check the properties of a document in the printer by doing either of the following:

- Right-click the document in the print management window, and then click Properties.
- Double-click the document name in the print management window.

Setting Document Priority

Scheduling priority determines when documents print. Documents with higher priority print before documents with lower priority. You can set the priority of individual documents in the printer by following these steps:

1. Right-click the document in the print management window, and then click Properties.
2. On the General tab, use the Priority slider to change the document's priority. The lowest priority is 1 and the highest is 99.

Scheduling Document Printing

In a busy printing environment, you might need to schedule the printing of documents in the printer. For example, you might want large print jobs of low priority to print at night. To set the printing schedule, follow these steps:

1. Right-click the document in the print management window, and then click Properties.

2. On the General tab, select the Only From option, and then specify a time interval. The time interval you set determines when the job can print. For example, you can specify that the job can print only between midnight and 5:00 A.M.

Auditing Print Jobs

Windows Server 2016 lets you audit common printer tasks by following these steps:

1. Open the printer's Properties dialog box, and then click the Security tab.

2. Click Advanced to open the Advanced Security Settings dialog box.

NOTE Actions aren't audited by default. You must first enable auditing by establishing a group policy to audit the printer.

3. On the Auditing tab, add the names of users or groups you want to audit by using the Add button and remove names of users or groups by using the Remove button.

4. Select the events you want to audit by selecting the check boxes under the Successful and Failed headings, as appropriate.

5. Click OK.

Chapter 16. Implementing DHCP

You can use Dynamic Host Configuration Protocol (DHCP) to simplify administration of Active Directory domains, and in this chapter you'll learn how to do that. You use DHCP to dynamically assign TCP/IP configuration information to network clients. This not only saves time during system configuration, but also provides a centralized mechanism for updating the configuration. To enable DHCP on the network, you need to install and configure a DHCP server. This server is responsible for assigning the necessary network information.

Understanding DHCP

DHCP gives you centralized control over IP addressing and more. After DHCP is installed, you rely on the DHCP server to supply the basic information necessary for TCP/IP networking. This basic information can include the following: IP address, subnet mask, and default gateway; primary and secondary Domain Name System (DNS) servers; primary and secondary Windows Internet Name Service (WINS) servers; and the DNS domain name. DHCP servers can assign a dynamic IP version 4 (IPv4) address, a dynamic IP version 6 (IPv6) address, or both addresses to any of the network interface cards (NICs) on a computer.

Using Dynamic IPv4 Addressing and Configuration

A computer that uses dynamic IPv4 addressing and configuration is called a *DHCPv4 client*. When you start a DHCPv4 client, a 32-bit IPv4 address can be retrieved from a pool of IPv4 addresses defined for the network's DHCP server. The address is assigned to the client for a specified time period known as a *lease*. When the lease is approximately 50 percent expired, the client tries to renew it. If the client can't renew the lease at that time, it tries again before the lease expires. If this attempt fails, the client tries to contact an alternate DHCP server. IPv4 addresses that aren't renewed are returned to the address pool. If the client is able to contact the DHCP server but the current IP address can't be reassigned, the DHCP server assigns a new IPv4 address to the client.

The availability of a DHCP server doesn't affect startup or logon (in most cases). DHCPv4 clients can start and users can log on to the local computer even if a DHCP server isn't available. During startup, the DHCPv4 client looks for a DHCP server. If a DHCP server is available, the client gets its configuration information from the server. If a DHCP server isn't available and the client's previous lease is still valid, the client pings the default gateway listed in the lease. A successful ping tells the client that it's probably on the same network it was on when it was issued the lease, and the client continues to use the lease as described previously. A failed ping tells the client that it might be on a different network. In this case, the client uses IPv4 autoconfiguration. The client also uses IPv4 autoconfiguration if a DHCP server isn't available and the previous lease has expired.

IPv4 autoconfiguration works like this:

1. The client computer selects an IP address from the Microsoft-reserved class B subnet 169.254.0.0 and uses the subnet mask 255.255.0.0. Before using the IPv4 address, the client performs an Address Resolution Protocol (ARP) test to be sure that no other client is using this IPv4 address.

2. If the IPv4 address is in use, the client repeats step 1, testing up to 10 IPv4 addresses before reporting failure. When a client is disconnected from the network, the ARP test always succeeds. As a result, the client uses the first IPv4 address it selects.

3. If the IPv4 address is available, the client configures the NIC with this address. The client then attempts to contact a DHCP server, sending out a broadcast every five minutes to the network. When the client successfully contacts a server, the client obtains a lease and reconfigures the network interface.

As part of your planning, you need to consider how many DHCP servers should be installed on the network. Typically, you'll want to install at least two DHCP servers on each physical network segment. Windows Server 2016 includes DHCP failover for IPv4. DHCP failover enables high availability of DHCP services by synchronizing IPv4 address leases between two DHCP servers in one of two modes:

- **Load Balance** When you load balance the servers, you specify the percentage of the load each server should handle. Typically, you use a 50/50 approach to make each server equally share the load. You also could use other approaches, such as 60/40 to make one server carry 60 percent of the load and the other 40 percent of the load.
- **Hot Standby** With hot standby, one of the servers acts as the primary server and handles the DHCP services. The other acts as a standby server in case the primary

fails or runs out of addresses to lease. A specific percentage of available IP addresses are reserved for the hot standby—5 percent by default.

The configuration of DHCP failover is simple and straightforward, and it does not require clustering or any advanced configuration. To configure DHCP failover, all you need to do is complete the following steps:

1. Install and configure two DHCP servers. The servers should be on the same physical network.
2. Create a DHCPv4 scope on one of the servers. Scopes are pools of IPv4 or IPv6 addresses you can assign to clients through leases.
3. When you establish the other server as a failover partner for the DHCPv4 scope, the scope is replicated to the partner.

Using Dynamic IPv6 Addressing and Configuration

Both IPv4 and IPv6 are enabled by default when networking hardware is detected during installation. As discussed in Chapter 2, "Implementing TCP/IP networking," IPv4 is the primary version of IP used on most networks, and IPv6 is the next generation version of IP. IPv6 uses 128-bit addresses. In a standard configuration, the first 64 bits represent the network ID, and the last 64 bits represent the network interface on the client computer.

You can use DHCP to configure IPv6 addressing in two key ways:

- **DHCPv6 stateful mode**   In DHCPv6 stateful mode, a client acquires its IPv6 address in addition to its network configuration parameters through DHCPv6.
- **DHCPv6 stateless mode**   In DHCPv6 stateless mode, a client uses autoconfiguration to acquire its IP address and acquires its network configuration parameters through DHCPv6.

A computer that uses dynamic IPv6 addressing, configuration, or both mechanisms is called a *DHCPv6 client*. As with DHCPv4, the components of the DHCPv6 infrastructure consist of DHCPv6 clients that request configuration, DHCPv6 servers that provide configuration, and DHCPv6 relay agents that convey messages between clients and servers when clients are on subnets that do not have a DHCPv6 server.

Unlike in DHCPv4, you must also configure your IPv6 routers to support DHCPv6. A DHCPv6 client performs autoconfiguration based on the following flags in the Router Advertisement message sent by a neighboring router:

- Managed Address Configuration flag, which is also known as the *M flag*. When set to 1, this flag instructs the client to use a configuration protocol to obtain stateful addresses.
- Other Stateful Configuration flag, which is also known as the *O flag*. When set to 1, this flag instructs the client to use a configuration protocol to obtain other configuration settings.

Windows includes a DHCPv6 client. The DHCPv6 client attempts DHCPv6-based configuration depending on the values of the M and O flags in the Router Advertisement messages it receives. If there is more than one advertising router for a given subnet, the additional router or routers should be configured to advertise the same stateless address prefixes and the same values for the M and O flags. All current Windows desktop and server operating systems include IPv6 clients and, therefore, accept the values of the M and O flags in router advertisements they receive.

You can configure an IPv6 router to set the M flag to 1 in router advertisements by entering the following command at an administrator command prompt, where *Inter-faceName* is the actual name of the interface:

```
netsh interface ipv6 set interface InterfaceName managedaddress=enabled
```

Similarly, you can set the O flag to 1 in router advertisements by entering the following command at an administrator command prompt:

```
netsh interface ipv6 set interface InterfaceName otherstateful=enabled
```

If the interface name contains spaces, enclose the related value in quotation marks, as shown in the following example:

```
netsh interface ipv6 set interface "Wired Ethernet Connection 2"
managedaddress=enabled
```

Keep the following in mind when you are working with the M and O flags:

- If the M and O flags are both set to 0, the network is considered not to have DHCPv6 infrastructure. Clients use router advertisements for non-link-local addresses and manual configuration to configure other settings.
- If the M and O flags are both set to 1, DHCPv6 is used for both IP addressing and other configuration settings. This combination is known as *DHCPv6 stateful mode*, in which DHCPv6 assigns stateful addresses to IPv6 clients.
- If the M flag is set to 0 and the O flag is set to 1, DHCPv6 is used only to assign other configuration settings. Neighboring routers are configured to advertise non-link-local address prefixes from which IPv6 clients derive stateless addresses. This combination is known as *DHCPv6 stateless mode*.
- If the M flag is set to 1 and the O flag is set to 0, DHCPv6 is used for IP address configuration but not for other settings. Because IPv6 clients typically need to be configured with other settings, such as the IPv6 addresses of DNS servers, this combination typically is not used.

Windows obtains dynamic IPv6 addresses by using a process similar to obtaining dynamic IPv4 addresses. Typically, IPv6 autoconfiguration for DHCPv6 clients in stateful mode works like this:

1. The client computer selects a link-local unicast IPv6 address. Before using the IPv6 address, the client performs an ARP test to make sure that no other client is using this IPv6 address.

2. If the IPv6 address is in use, the client repeats step 1. Keep in mind that when a client is disconnected from the network, the ARP test always succeeds. As a result, the client uses the first IPv6 address it selects.

3. If the IPv6 address is available, the client configures the NIC with this address. The client then attempts to contact a DHCP server, sending out a broadcast every five minutes to the network. When the client successfully contacts a server, the client obtains a lease and reconfigures the network interface.

This is not how IPv6 autoconfiguration works for DHCPv6 clients in stateless mode. In stateless mode, DHCPv6 clients configure both link-local addresses and additional non-link-local addresses by exchanging Router Solicitation and Router Advertisement messages with neighboring routers.

Like DHCPv4, DHCPv6 uses User Datagram Protocol (UDP) messages. DHCPv6 clients listen for DHCP messages on UDP port 546. DHCPv6 servers and relay agents listen for DHCPv6 messages on UDP port 547. The structure for DHCPv6 messages is much simpler than for DHCPv4, which had its origins in Bootstrap Protocol (BOOTP) to support diskless workstations.

DHCPv6 messages start with a 1-byte Msg-Type field that indicates the type of DHCPv6 message. This is followed by a 3-byte Transaction-ID field determined by a client and used to group together the messages of a DHCPv6 message exchange. Following the Transaction-ID field, DHCPv6 options are used to indicate client and server identification, addresses, and other configuration settings.

Three fields are associated with each DHCPv6 option. A 2-byte Option-Code field indicates a specific option. A 2-byte Option-Len field indicates the length of the Option-Data field in bytes. The Option-Data field contains the data for the option.

Messages exchanged between relay agents and servers use a different message structure to transfer additional information. A 1-byte Hop-Count field indicates the number of relay agents that have received the message. A receiving relay agent can discard the message if the message exceeds a configured maximum hop count. A 15-byte Link-Address field contains a non-link-local address that is assigned to an interface connected to the subnet on which the client is located. Based on the Link-Address field, the server can determine the correct address scope from which to assign an address. A 15-byte Peer-Address field contains the IPv6 address of the client that originally sent the message or the previous relay agent that relayed the message. Following the Peer-Address field are DHCPv6 options. A key option is the Relay Message option. This option provides an encapsulation of the messages being exchanged between the client and the server.

IPv6 does not have broadcast addresses. The use of the limited broadcast address for some DHCPv4 messages has been replaced with the use of the All_DHCP_Relay_Agents_and_Servers address of FF02::1:2 for DHCPv6. A DHCPv6 client attempting to discover the location of the DHCPv6 server on the network sends a Solicit message from its link-local address to FF02::1:2. If there is a DHCPv6 server on the client's subnet, it receives the Solicit message and sends an appropriate reply. If the client and server are on different subnets, a DHCPv6 relay agent on the client's subnet that receives the Solicit message forwards it to a DHCPv6 server.

Checking IP Address Assignment

You can use Ipconfig to check the currently assigned IP address and other configuration information. To obtain information for all network adapters on the computer, enter the command **ipconfig /all** at the command prompt. If the IP address has been assigned automatically, you'll notice an entry for Autoconfiguration IP Address. In the following example, the autoconfiguration IPv4 address is 169.254.98.59:

```
Windows IP Configuration
        Host Name ................: FRODO
        Primary DNS Suffix ........: tvpress.local
        Node Type ................: Hybrid
        IP Routing Enabled.........: No
        WINS Proxy Enabled.........: No
        DNS Suffix Search List.....: tvpress.local
Ethernet adapter Ethernet:
        Connection-specific DNS Suffix...:
        Description ...............: Intel Pro/1000 Network Connection
        Physical Address............: 23-15-C6-F8-FD-67
        DHCP Enabled...............: Yes
        Autoconfiguration Enabled...: Yes
        Autoconfiguration IP Address: 169.254.98.59
        Subnet Mask ...............: 255.255.0.0
        Default Gateway ...........:
        DNS Servers ...............:
```

Understanding Scopes

Scopes are pools of IPv4 or IPv6 addresses you can assign to clients through leases. DHCP also provides a way to permanently assign a lease on an address. To do this, you need to create a reservation by specifying the IPv4 address to reserve and the media access control (MAC) address of the computer that will hold the IPv4 address. The reservation thereafter ensures that the client computer with the specified MAC address always gets the designated IPv4 address. With IPv6, you can specify that a lease is temporary or nontemporary. A nontemporary lease is similar to a reservation.

You create scopes to specify IP address ranges that are available for DHCP clients. For example, you could assign the IP address range 192.168.12.2 to 192.168.12.250 to a scope called Enterprise Primary. Scopes can use public or private IPv4 addresses on the following networks:

- **Class A networks** IP addresses from 1.0.0.0 to 126.255.255.255
- **Class B networks** IP addresses from 128.0.0.0 to 191.255.255.255
- **Class C networks** IP addresses from 192.0.0.0 to 223.255.255.255
- **Class D networks** IP addresses from 224.0.0.0 to 239.255.255.255

> **NOTE** The IP address 127.0.0.1 is used for local loopback (and so are any other IP addresses in the 127.x.y.z address range).

Scopes can also use link-local unicast, global unicast, and multicast IPv6 addresses. Link-local unicast addresses begin with FE80. Multicast IPv6 addresses begin with FF00. Global (site-local) unicast addresses include all other addresses except :: (unspecified) and ::1 (loopback) addresses.

A single DHCP server can manage multiple scopes. With IPv4 addresses, four types of scopes are available:

- **Normal scopes** Used to assign IPv4 address pools for class A, B, and C networks.
- **Multicast scopes** Used to assign IP address pools for IPv4 class D networks. Computers use multicast IP addresses as secondary IP addresses in addition to a standard IP address.
- **Superscopes** Containers for other scopes that are used to simplify management of multiple scopes and also support DHCP clients on a single physical network where multiple logical IP networks are used.
- **Failover scopes** Scopes split between two DHCP servers to increase fault tolerance, provide redundancy, and enable load balancing.

With IPv6, only normal scopes are available. Although you can create scopes on multiple network segments, you'll usually want these segments to be in the same network class, such as all IP addresses that are class C.

> **TIP** Don't forget that you must configure DHCPv4 and DHCPv6 relays to relay DHCPv4 and DHCPv6 broadcast requests between network segments. You can configure relay agents with the Routing and Remote Access Service (RRAS) and the DHCP Relay Agent Service. You can also configure some routers as relay agents. These services can be installed as part of the Remote Access role. On a server with no other policy and access role services configured, you can install the Remote Access role by using the Add Roles And Features Wizard.

Installing a DHCP Server

Dynamic IP addressing is available only if a DHCP server is installed on the network. By using the Add Roles And Features Wizard, you install the DHCP server as a role service, configure its initial settings, and authorize the server in Active Directory Domain Services (AD DS). Only authorized DHCP servers can provide dynamic IP addresses to clients.

Installing DHCP Components

On a server running Windows Server 2016, follow these steps to enable the server to function as a DHCP server:

1. DHCP servers should be assigned a static IPv4 and IPv6 address on each subnet to which they are connected and will service. Be sure that the server has static IPv4 and IPv6 addresses.

2. In Server Manager, click Manage, and then click Add Roles And Features, or select Add Roles And Features in the Quick Start pane. This starts the Add Roles And Features Wizard. If the wizard displays the Before You Begin page, read the Welcome text, and then click Next.

3. On the Installation Type page, Role-Based Or Feature-Based Installation is selected by default. Click Next.

4. On the Server Selection page, you can choose to install roles and features on running servers or virtual hard disks. Either select a server from the server pool or select a server from the server pool on which to mount a virtual hard disk (VHD). If you are adding roles and features to a VHD, click Browse, and then use the Browse For Virtual Hard Disks dialog box to locate the VHD. When you are ready to continue, click Next.

NOTE Only servers running Windows Server 2016 and that have been added for management in Server Manager are listed.

5. On the Select Roles page, select DHCP Server. If additional features are required to install a role, you'll get an additional dialog box. Click Add Features to close the dialog box and add the required features to the server installation. When you are ready to continue, click Next three times.

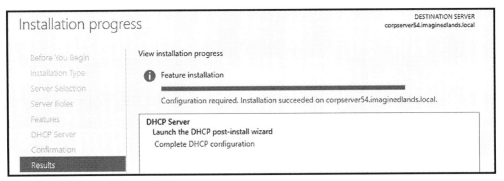

Select server roles

DESTINATION SERVER
corpserver54.imaginedlands.local

Select one or more roles to install on the selected server.

Before You Begin
Installation Type
Server Selection
Server Roles
Features
DHCP Server
Confirmation
Results

Roles

- [ ] Active Directory Certificate Services
- [ ] Active Directory Domain Services
- [ ] Active Directory Federation Services
- [ ] Active Directory Lightweight Directory Services
- [ ] Active Directory Rights Management Services
- [ ] Device Health Attestation
- [x] DHCP Server
- [ ] DNS Server

Description

Dynamic Host Configuration Protocol (DHCP) Server enables you to centrally configure, manage, and provide temporary IP addresses and related information for client computers.

6. If the server on which you want to install the DHCP Server role doesn't have all the required binary source files, the server gets the files via Windows Update by default or from a location specified in Group Policy.

NOTE You also can specify an alternate path for the required source files. To do this, click the Specify An Alternate Source Path link, enter that alternate path in the box provided, and then click OK. For network shares, enter the UNC path to the share, such as \\Server23\WinServer2016\. For mounted Windows images, enter the WIM path prefixed with *WIM:* and including the index of the image to use, such as WIM:\\Server23\WS16\install.wim:4.

7. After you review the installation options and save them as necessary, click Install to begin the installation process. The Installation Progress page tracks the progress of the installation. If you close the wizard, click the Notifications icon in Server Manager, and then click the link provided to reopen the wizard.

8. When Setup finishes installing the DHCP Server role, the Installation Progress page will be updated to reflect this. Review the installation details to ensure that all phases of the installation were completed successfully.

9. Additional configuration is required for the DHCP server. Click the Complete DHCP Configuration link to start the DHCP Post-Install Configuration Wizard. If you closed the wizard, click Notifications on Server Manager's toolbar and then click the Complete DHCP Configuration link in the Post-Deployment Configuration task panel.

Installation progress

DESTINATION SERVER
corpserver54.imaginedlands.local

View installation progress

Before You Begin
Installation Type
Server Selection
Server Roles
Features
DHCP Server
Confirmation
Results

🛈 Feature installation

Configuration required. Installation succeeded on corpserver54.imaginedlands.local.

DHCP Server
Launch the DHCP post-install wizard
Complete DHCP configuration

10. The Description page states that the DHCP Administrators and DHCP Users groups will be created in the domain for delegation of DHCP Server administration. Additionally, if the DHCP server is joined to a domain, the server will be authorized in Active Directory. Click Next.

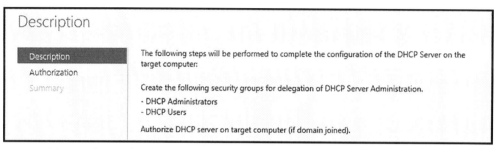

11. On the Authorization page, do one of the following to specify the credentials to use to authorize the DHCP server in Active Directory:

- Your current user name is shown in the User Name text box. If you have administrator privileges in the domain that the DHCP server is a member of and you want to use your current credentials, click Commit to attempt to authorize the server by using these credentials.

- If you want to use alternate credentials or if you are unable to authorize the server by using your current credentials, select Use Alternate Credentials, and then click Specify. In the Windows Security dialog box, enter the user name and password for the authorized account, and then click OK. Click Commit to attempt to authorize the server by using these credentials.

- If you want to authorize the DHCP server later, select Skip AD Authorization, and then click Commit. Keep in mind that in domains, only authorized DHCP servers can provide dynamic IP addresses to clients.

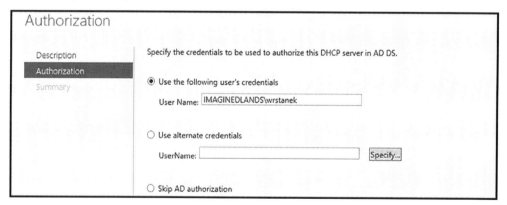

12. When the wizard finishes the post-install configuration, review the installation details to ensure that tasks were completed successfully, and then click Close.

13. Next, you need to restart the DHCP Server service on the DHCP server so that the DHCP Administrators and DHCP Users groups can be used. To do this,

click DHCP in the left pane of Server Manager. Next, in the main pane, on the Servers panel, select the DHCP server. Finally, on the Services panel, right-click the entry for the DHCP Server, and then click Restart Service.

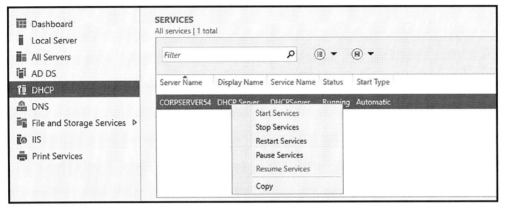

14. To complete the installation, you need to do the following:

- If the server has multiple network cards, review the server bindings and specify the connections that the DHCP server supports for servicing clients. See "Configuring Server Bindings" later in this chapter.
- Configure server options to assign common configuration settings for DHCPv4 and DHCPv6 clients, including 003 Router, 006 DNS Servers, 015 DNS Domain Name, and 044 WINS/NBNS Servers. See "Setting Scope Options" in Chapter 17.
- Create and activate any DHCP scopes that the server will use, as discussed in "Creating and Managing Scopes" in Chapter 17.

Starting and Using the DHCP Console

After you install a DHCP server, you use the DHCP console to configure and manage dynamic IP addressing. In Server Manager, click Tools, and then click DHCP to open the DHCP console. Alternatively, enter **Dhcpmgmt.msc** in the Search box or at a prompt.

The main window for the DHCP console is divided into two panes. The left pane lists the DHCP servers in the domain according to their fully qualified domain name (FQDN). You can expand a server listing to show subnodes for IPv4 and IPv6. If you expand the IP nodes, you'll find the scopes and options defined for the related IP version. The right pane shows the expanded view of the current selection.

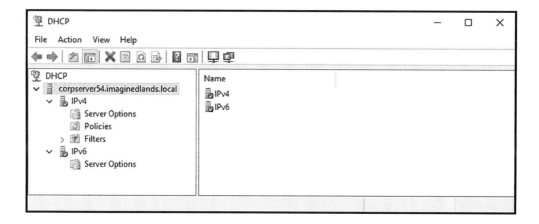

Icons on the various nodes show the current status of the nodes. For server and IP nodes, you might find the following icons:

- A server icon with a green circle with a check mark indicates that the DHCP service is running and the server is active.
- A server icon with red circle with an X through it indicates that the console can't connect to the server. The DHCP service has been stopped or the server is inaccessible.
- A red down arrow indicates that the DHCP server hasn't been authorized.
- A blue warning icon indicates that the server's state has changed or a warning has been issued.

For scopes, you might find the following icons:

- A red down arrow indicates that the scope hasn't been activated.
- A blue warning icon indicates that the scope's state has changed or a warning has been issued.

Connecting to Remote DHCP Servers

When you start the DHCP console, you are connected directly to a local DHCP server, but you won't find entries for remote DHCP servers. You can connect to remote servers by following these steps:

1. Right-click DHCP in the console tree, and then click Add Server.
2. Select This Server, and then enter the IP address or computer name of the DHCP server you want to manage.
3. Click OK. An entry for the DHCP server is added to the console tree.

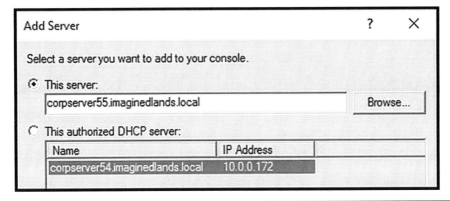

Starting and Stopping a DHCP Server

You manage DHCP servers through the DHCP Server service. As with any other service, you can start, stop, pause, and resume the DHCP Server service in the Services node of Computer Management or from the command line. You can also manage the DHCP Server service in the DHCP console. Right-click the server you want to manage in the DHCP console, point to All Tasks, and then click Start, Stop, Pause, Resume, or Restart, as appropriate.

Authorizing a DHCP Server in Active Directory

Before you can use a DHCP server in the domain, you must authorize it in Active Directory. By authorizing the server, you specify that the server is authorized to provide dynamic IP addressing in the domain. Windows Server 2016 requires authorization to prevent unauthorized DHCP servers from serving domain clients. This in turn ensures that network operations can run smoothly.

Only Enterprise Admins can authorize DHCP servers. In the DHCP console, you authorize a DHCP server by right-clicking the server entry in the tree view, and then selecting Authorize. To remove the authorization, right-click the server, and then select Unauthorize.

At an administrator PowerShell prompt, you can use Add-DhcpServerInDC to authorize DHCP servers. Use the –DnsName parameter to specify the name of the server to authorize or the –IpAddress to specify the IP address of the server to authorize as shown in the following examples:

```
Add-DhcpServerInDC -DnsName CorpSvr03.imaginedlands.com
Add-DhcpServerInDC -IpAddress 192.168.1.1
```

Use Remove-DhcpServerInDC to remove the authorization. The basic syntax is the same.

Configuring DHCP Servers

After you install a new DHCP server, you need to configure and optimize the server for the network environment. A separate set of options are provided for IPv4 and IPv6.

Configuring Server Bindings

A server with multiple NICs has multiple local area network connections and can provide DHCP services on any of these network connections. However, you might not want DHCP to be served over all available connections. For example, if the server has both a 100–megabits per second (Mbps) connection and a 1–gigabit per second (Gbps) connection, you might want all DHCP traffic to go over the 1-Gbps connection.

To bind DHCP to a specific network connection, follow these steps:

1. In the DHCP console, right-click the server with which you want to work, and then click Add/Remove Bindings.
2. Select the IPv4 or IPv6 tab as appropriate for the type of binding with which you want to work.

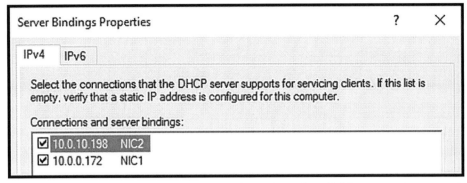

Server Bindings Properties   ?   ✕

IPv4   IPv6

Select the connections that the DHCP server supports for servicing clients. If this list is empty, verify that a static IP address is configured for this computer.

Connections and server bindings:

☑ 10.0.10.198   NIC2
☑ 10.0.0.172   NIC1

3. The Bindings dialog box displays a list of available network connections for the DHCP server.

- If you want the DHCP Server service to use a connection to service clients, select the check box for the connection.
- If you don't want the service to use a connection, clear the related check box.
- If there are no network connections listed for the protocol with which you are working, ensure that the server has a static address for that protocol.

4. Click OK when you have finished.

Updating DHCP Statistics

The DHCP console provides statistics concerning IPv4 and IPv6 address availability and usage. In the DHCP console, you can view these statistics by expanding the node for the server with which you want to work, right-clicking IPv4 or IPv6 as appropriate for the type of address with which you want to work, and then clicking Display Statistics.

By default, these statistics are updated only when you start the DHCP console or when you select the server and then click the Refresh button on the toolbar. If you monitor DHCP routinely, you might want these statistics to be updated automatically, which you can do by following these steps:

1. In the DHCP console, expand the node for the server with which you want to work, right-click IPv4 or IPv6 as appropriate for the type of address with which you want to work, and then click Properties.

2. On the General tab, select Automatically Update Statistics Every and enter an update interval in hours and minutes. Click OK.

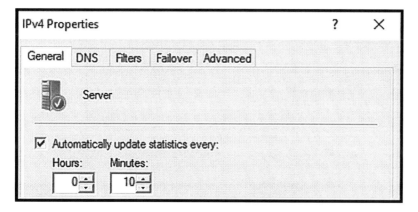

Auditing and Troubleshooting DHCP

Windows Server 2016 is configured to audit DHCP processes by default. Auditing tracks DHCP processes and requests in log files.

You can use audit logs to help you troubleshoot problems with a DHCP server. Just as you enable and configure logging separately for IPv4 and IPv6, the two protocols use different log files. %SystemRoot%\System32\DHCP is the default location for DHCP logs. In this directory, you'll find a different log file for each day of the week. The IPv4 log file for Monday is named DhcpSrvLog-Mon.log, the log file for Tuesday is named DhcpSrvLog-Tue.log, and so on. The IPv6 log file for Monday is named DhcpV6SrvLog-Mon.log, the log file for Tuesday is named DhcpV6SrvLog-Tue.log, and so on.

When you start the DHCP server or a new day arrives, a header message is written to the log file. This header provides a summary of DHCP events and their meanings. Stopping and starting the DHCP Server service doesn't clear a log file. Log data is kept for a week. For example, the DCHP Server service clears and starts over Monday's log the following Monday. You don't have to monitor space usage by the DHCP Server service. The service is configured to monitor itself and restricts disk space usage by default.

You can enable or disable DHCP auditing by following these steps:

1. In the DHCP console, expand the node for the server with which you want to work, right-click IPv4 or IPv6 as appropriate for the type of address with which you want to work, and then click Properties.

2. On the General tab, select or clear the Enable DHCP Audit Logging check box, and then click OK.

By default, DHCP logs are stored in %SystemRoot%\System32\DHCP. You can change the location of DHCP logs by following these steps:

1. In the DHCP console, expand the node for the server with which you want to work, right-click IPv4 or IPv6 as appropriate for the type of address with which you want to work, and then click Properties.

2. Click the Advanced tab. Audit Log File Path shows the current folder location for log files. Enter a new folder location, or click Browse to select a new location.

3. Click OK. Windows Server 2016 now needs to restart the DHCP Server service. When prompted to restart the service, click Yes. The service will be stopped and then started again.

The DHCP server has a self-monitoring system that checks disk space usage. By default, the maximum size of all DHCP server logs is 70 megabytes (MB), with each individual log being limited to one-seventh of this space. If the server reaches the 70-MB limit or an individual log grows beyond the allocated space, logging of DHCP activity stops until log files are cleared or space is otherwise made available. Typically, this happens at the beginning of a new day when the server clears the previous week's log file for that day.

Registry keys that control log usage and other DHCP settings are located under HKEY_LOCAL_MACHINE in:

SYSTEM\CurrentControlSet\Services\DHCPServer\Parameters

The following keys control the logging:

* **DhcpLogFilesMaxSize** Sets the maximum file size for all logs. The default is 70 MB.
* **DhcpLogDiskSpaceCleanupInterval** Determines how often DHCP checks disk space usage and cleans up as necessary. The default interval is 60 minutes.
* **DhcpLogMinSpaceOnDisk** Sets the free space threshold for writing to the log. If the disk has less free space than the value specified, logging is temporarily disabled. The default value is 20 MB.

DhcpLogMinSpaceOnDisk is considered an optional key and is not created automatically. You need to create this key as necessary and set appropriate values for your network.

Integrating DHCP and DNS

DNS is used to resolve computer names in Active Directory domains and on the Internet. Thanks to the DNS dynamic update protocol, you don't need to manually register DHCP clients in DNS. The protocol allows the client or the DHCP server to register the forward-lookup and reverse-lookup records in DNS as necessary. When configured by using the default setup for DHCP, current DHCP clients automatically update their own DNS records after receiving an IP address lease. You can modify this behavior globally for each DHCP server or on a per-scope basis.

Name protection is an additional feature in Windows Server 2016. With name protection, the DHCP server registers records on behalf of the client only if no other client with this DNS information is already registered. You can configure name protection for IPv4 and IPv6 at the network adapter level or at the scope level. Name protection settings configured at the scope level take precedence over the setting at the IPv4 or IPv6 level.

Name protection is designed to prevent name squatting. Name squatting occurs when a computer not based on the Windows operating system registers a name in DNS that is already registered to a computer running a Windows operating system. By enabling name protection, you can prevent name squatting by computers not based on the Windows operating system. Although name squatting generally does not present a problem when you use Active Directory to reserve a name for a single user or computer, it usually is a good idea to enable name protection on all Windows networks.

Name protection is based on the Dynamic Host Configuration Identifier (DHCID) and support for the DHCID RR (resource record) in DNS. The DHCID is a resource record stored in DNS that maps names to prevent duplicate registration. DHCP uses the DHCID resource record to store an identifier for a computer along with related information for the name, such as the A and AAAA records of the computer. The DHCP server can request a DHCID record match and then refuse the registration of a computer with a different address attempting to register a name with an existing DHCID record.

You can view and change the global DNS integration settings by following these steps:

1. In the DHCP console, expand the node for the server with which you want to work, right-click IPv4 or IPv6, and then click Properties.

2. Click the DNS tab. The default DNS integration settings for DHCP are as shown in the dialog box that follows. Because these settings are configured by default, you usually don't need to modify the configuration. However, if you only want host (A) records to be dynamically updated instead of both host (A) and pointer (PTR) records, select the Disable Dynamic Updates For DNS PTR Records check box.

> **IMPORTANT** The default configuration, which registers and maintains both A and PTR records, assumes that you've configured reverse lookup zones for your organization. If you haven't, attempts to register and update PTR records will fail. You can prevent repeated failed attempts to register and update PTR records by disabling dynamic updates for PTR records. If you disable this option in the IPv4 properties, you are disabling the option for all IPv4 scopes. Alternatively, you can use scope properties to disable the option on a per scope basis.

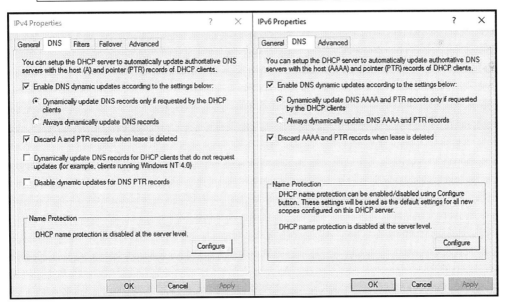

3. Optionally, you can enable or disable the name protection feature. With name protection, the DHCP server registers records on behalf of the client only if no other client with this DNS information is already registered. To

enable or disable name protection, click Configure. In the Name Protection dialog box, select or clear Enable Name Protection, and then click OK.

You can view and change the per-scope DNS integration settings by following these steps:

1. In the DHCP console, expand the node for the server with which you want to work, and then expand IPv4 or IPv6.

2. Right-click the scope with which you want to work, and then click Properties.

3. Click the DNS tab. The options available are the same as those shown in the previous figure. Because these settings are configured by default, you usually don't need to modify the configuration.

4. Optionally, you can enable or disable the name-protection feature. Click Configure. In the Name Protection dialog box, select or clear Enable Name Protection, and then click OK.

Avoiding IP Address Conflicts

IPv4 address conflicts are a common cause of problems with DHCP. No two computers on the network can have the same unicast IP address. If a computer is assigned the same unicast IPv4 address as another, one or both of the computers might become disconnected from the network. More specifically, the computer already using the IPv4 address can continue using the address and any other computer that tries to use that IPv4 address is blocked from using it.

To better detect and avoid potential conflicts, you can enable IPv4 address conflict detection by following these steps:

1. In the DHCP console, expand the node for the server with which you want to work, right-click IPv4, and then click Properties.

2. On the Advanced tab, set Conflict Detection Attempts to a value other than 0. The value you enter determines the number of times the DHCP server checks an IP address before leasing it to a client. The DHCP server checks IP addresses by sending a ping request over the network.

REAL WORLD A unicast IPv4 address is a standard IP address for class A, B, and C networks. When a DHCP client requests a lease, a DHCP server checks its pool of available addresses and assigns the client a lease on an available IPv4 address. By default, the server checks only the list of current leases to determine whether an address is available. It doesn't actually query the network to determine whether an address is in use. Unfortunately, in a busy network environment, an administrator might have assigned this IPv4 address to another computer or an offline computer might have been brought online with a lease that it believes hasn't expired, even though the DHCP server believes the lease has expired. Either way, you have an address conflict that will cause problems on the network. To reduce these types of conflicts, set the conflict detection to a value greater than 0.

Saving and Restoring the DHCP Configuration

After you configure all the necessary DHCP settings, you might want to save the DHCP configuration so that you can restore it on the DHCP server. To save the configuration, enter the following command at the command prompt:

```
netsh dump DHCP > dhcpconfig.dmp
```

In this example, *dhcpconfig.dmp* is the name of the configuration script you want to create. By default, the script is created in the current working directory. Alternatively, you can specify the full file path in which to save the script. After you create this script, you can restore the configuration by executing the script. If you saved the script in the current working directory, you can enter the following command at the command prompt:

```
netsh exec dhcpconfig.dmp
```

If you saved the script in another directory, you can specify the full path to the script, such as:

```
netsh exec d:\dhcp\scripts\dhcpconfig.dmp
```

> **TIP** You can also use this technique to set up another DHCP server with the same configuration. Just copy the configuration script to a folder on the destination computer, and then execute it.

You can save or restore the DHCP configuration by using the DHCP console as well. To save the configuration, right-click the DHCP server entry, click Backup, use the dialog box provided to select the folder for the backup, and then click OK. To restore the configuration, right-click the DHCP server entry, click Restore, use the dialog box provided to select the backup folder, and then click OK. When prompted to confirm, click Yes.

At an administrator PowerShell prompt, you use Export-DhcpServer to save the configuration settings. The basic syntax is:

```
Export-DhcpServer -ComputerName ServerID -File SavePath
```

Here, *ServerID* is the DNS name or IP address of the DHCP server and *SavePath* is the path and name of the file in which you want to store the configuration settings. If you omit the name of the server to work with, the local server is used. If you don't specify a save path along with the file name, the configuration file is created in the current working directory. In the following example, you store the configuration settings in the d:\dhcp\scripts directory with the name dhcpconfig.dmp:

```
Export-DhcpServer-File d:\dhcp\scripts\dhcpconfig.dmp
```

You can restore the configuration using Import-DhcpServer. The basic syntax is:

```
Import-DhcpServer -ComputerName ServerID -BackupPath CurrentConfigSavePath
-File SavePath
```

Here, *SavePath* is the path and name of the file in which you stored the configuration settings and *CurrentConfigSavePath* specifies the path where the current configuration should be saved prior to importing and overwriting existing settings. In the following example, you back up the settings to d:\dhcp\backup\origconfig.dmp and then apply the saved configuration from d:\dhcp\scripts\dhcpconfig.dmp:

```
Import-DhcpServer-BackupPath d:\dhcp\backup\origconfig.dmp
-File d:\dhcp\scripts\dhcpconfig.dmp
```

Chapter 17. Managing and Maintaining DHCP

After you install a DHCP server, you need to configure the scopes that the DHCP server will use, manage addressing, and perform basic maintenance tasks. Scopes are pools of IP addresses you can lease to clients. For each scope you define, you can add reservations, exclusions and filters to control which IP addresses are available and used. You can create superscopes, normal scopes, multicast scopes, and failover scopes with IPv4 addresses, but you can create only normal scopes with IPv6 addresses.

Creating and Managing Scopes

Scopes provide a pool of IP addresses for DHCP clients. A normal scope is a scope with class A, B, or C network addresses. A multicast scope is a scope with class D network addresses. Although you create normal scopes and multicast scopes differently, you manage them in much the same way. The key differences are that multi-cast scopes can't use reservations, and you can't set additional options for WINS, DNS, routing, and so forth.

Creating Normal Scopes for IPv4 Addresses

You can create a normal scope for IPv4 addresses by following these steps:

1. In the DHCP console, expand the node for the server with which you want to work, and then right-click IPv4. If you want to add the new scope to a superscope automatically, right-click the superscope instead.

2. On the shortcut menu, click New Scope to start the New Scope Wizard. Click Next.

3. Enter a name and description for the scope, and then click Next.

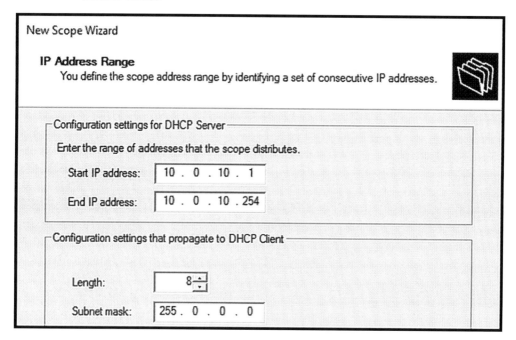

New Scope Wizard

Scope Name
You have to provide an identifying scope name. You also have the option of providing a description.

Type a name and description for this scope. This information helps you quickly identify how the scope is to be used on your network.

Name: Primary Scope - 10.0.10.x

Description:

4.   The Start IP Address and End IP Address boxes define the valid IP address range for the scope. On the IP Address Range page, enter a start address and an end address in these boxes.

> **NOTE**   Generally, the scope doesn't include the x.x.x.0 and x.x.x.255 addresses, which are usually reserved for network addresses and broadcast messages, respectively. Accordingly, you would use a range such as 192.168.10.1 to 192.168.10.254 rather than 192.168.10.0 to 192.168.10.255.

5.   When you enter an IP address range, the bit length and subnet mask are filled in for you automatically. Unless you use subnets, you should use the default values.

New Scope Wizard

IP Address Range
You define the scope address range by identifying a set of consecutive IP addresses.

Configuration settings for DHCP Server

Enter the range of addresses that the scope distributes.

Start IP address: 10 . 0 . 10 . 1

End IP address: 10 . 0 . 10 . 254

Configuration settings that propagate to DHCP Client

Length: 8

Subnet mask: 255 . 0 . 0 . 0

6. Click Next. If the IP address range you entered is too large for a single scope, you're given the opportunity to create a superscope that contains separate scopes for each network and, in this case, select the Yes option button to continue, and then move on to step 8. If you make a mistake, click Back, and then modify the IP address range you entered.

7. Use the Start IP Address and End IP Address boxes on the Add Exclusions And Delay page to define IP address ranges that are to be excluded from the scope. You can exclude multiple address ranges as follows:

* To define an exclusion range, enter a start address and an end address in the Exclusion Range's Start IP Address and End IP Address boxes, and then click Add. To exclude a single IP address, use that address as both the start IP address and the end IP address.
* To track which address ranges are excluded, use the Excluded Address Range list.
* To delete an exclusion range, select the range in the Excluded Address Range list, and then click Remove.

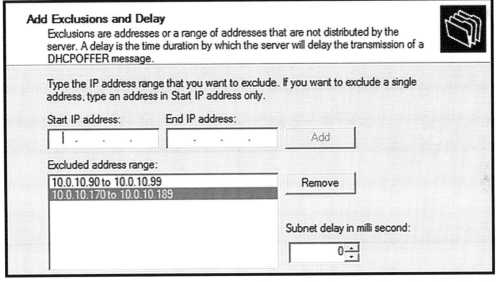

8. Click Next. Specify the duration of leases for the scope by using the Day(s), Hour(s), and Minutes boxes. The default duration is eight days. Click Next.

NOTE A lease duration that's set too long can reduce the effectiveness of DHCP and might eventually cause you to run out of available IP addresses, especially on networks with mobile users or other types of computers that aren't fixed members of the network. A good lease duration for most networks is from one to three days.

9. You have the opportunity to configure common DHCP options for DNS, WINS, gateways, and more. If you want to set these options now, select Yes, I Want To Configure These Options Now; otherwise, select No, I Will Configure These Options Later and skip steps 10–15.

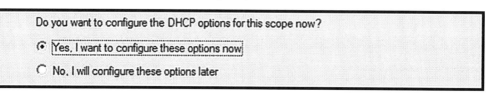

Do you want to configure the DHCP options for this scope now?

⦿ Yes, I want to configure these options now

◯ No, I will configure these options later

10. Click Next. The first option you can configure is the default gateway. In the IP Address box, enter the IP address of the primary default gateway, and then click Add. Repeat this process for other default gateways.

11. The first gateway listed is the one clients try to use first. If the gateway isn't available, clients try to use the next gateway, and so on. Use the Up and Down buttons to change the order of the gateways, as necessary.

12. Click Next. Configure default DNS settings for DHCP clients. Enter the name of the parent domain to use for DNS resolution of computer names that aren't fully qualified.

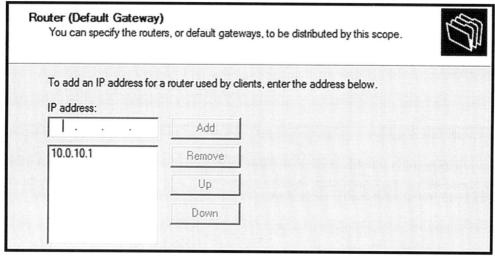

Router (Default Gateway)
You can specify the routers, or default gateways, to be distributed by this scope.

To add an IP address for a router used by clients, enter the address below.

IP address:

	Add
10.0.10.1	Remove
	Up
	Down

13. In the IP Address box, enter the IP address of the primary DNS server, and then click Add. Repeat this process to specify additional DNS servers. Again,

the order of the entries determines which IP address is used first. Change the order as necessary by using the Up and Down buttons. Click Next.

Domain Name and DNS Servers
The Domain Name System (DNS) maps and translates domain names used by clients on your network.

You can specify the parent domain you want the client computers on your network to use for DNS name resolution.

Parent domain: imaginedlands.local

To configure scope clients to use DNS servers on your network, enter the IP addresses for those servers.

Server name: IP address:

[   ]   [.   .   .   ]   Add

                Resolve   10.0.0.171   Remove
                                 10.0.10.175
                                                          Up

                                                          Down

TIP If you know the name of a server instead of its IP address, enter the name in the Server Name box, and then click Resolve. The IP address is then entered in the IP Address box, if possible. Add the server by clicking Add. Using this approach helps to ensure you've entered the correct information.

14. Configure default WINS settings for the DHCP clients. The techniques you use are the same as those previously described. Click Next.

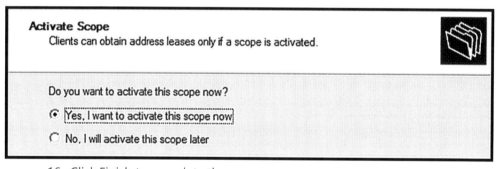

15. If you want to activate the scope, select Yes, I Want To Activate This Scope Now, and then click Next. Otherwise, select No, I Will Activate This Scope Later and then click Next.

16. Click Finish to complete the process.

Creating Normal Scopes for IPv6 Addresses

You create normal scopes for IPv6 addresses by using the New Scope Wizard. When you are configuring DHCP for IPv6 addresses, you must enter the network ID and a preference value. Typically, the first 64 bits of an IPv6 address identify the network, and a 64-bit value is what the New Scope Wizard expects you to enter. The preference value sets the priority of the scope relative to other scopes. The scope with the lowest preference value will be used first. The scope with the second-lowest preference will be used second, and so on.

You can create a normal scope for IPv6 addresses by following these steps:

1. In the DHCP console, expand the node for the server with which you want to work and then expand the IPv6 node.

2. Right-click IPv6. On the shortcut menu, click New Scope to start the New Scope Wizard. Click Next.

3. Enter a name and description for the scope, and then click Next.

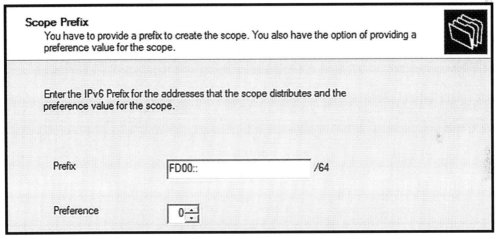

4. On the Scope Prefix page, enter the 64-bit network prefix, and then set a preference value. Click Next.

5. Use the Start IPv6 Address and End IPv6 Address boxes on the Add Exclusions page to define IPv6 address ranges that are to be excluded from the scope. You can exclude multiple address ranges as follows:

- To define an exclusion range, enter a start address and an end address in the Exclusion Range's Start IPv6 Address and End IPv6 Address boxes, and then click Add. To exclude a single IPv6 address, use that address as the start IPv6 address, and then click Add.
- To track which address ranges are excluded, use the Excluded Address Range list.
- To delete an exclusion range, select the range in the Excluded Address Range list, and then click Remove.

Add Exclusions
Exclusions are addresses or a range of addresses that are not distributed by the server.

Type the IPv6 address range that you want to exclude for the given scope. If you want to exclude a single address, type an identifier in Start IPv6 Address only.

Start IPv6 Address: fd00::

End IPv6 Address: fd00::   Add

Excluded address range:
fd00::100 to fd00::199   Remove

6. Click Next. Dynamic IPv6 addresses can be temporary or nontemporary. A nontemporary address is similar to a reservation. On the Scope Lease page, specify the duration of leases for nontemporary addresses by using the Days, Hours, and Minutes boxes under Preferred Life Time and Valid Life Time. The preferred lifetime is the preferred amount of time the lease should be valid. The valid lifetime is the maximum amount of time the lease is valid. Click Next.

Non Temporary Address(IANA)

Preferred Life Time
Days: Hours: Minutes:
8   0   0

Valid Life Time
Days: Hours: Minutes:
12   0   0

NOTE A lease lifetime that's set too long can reduce the effectiveness of DHCP. A good lease duration for nontemporary leases is from 8 to 30 days.

7. If you want to activate the scope, select Yes under Activate Scope Now, and then click Finish. Otherwise, select No under Activate Scope Now, and then click Finish.

Creating Multicast Scopes

To create a multicast scope, follow these steps:

1. In the DHCP console, expand the node for the server with which you want to work. Select and then right-click IPv4. If you want to add the new scope to a superscope, select and then right-click the superscope instead.

2. On the shortcut menu, click New Multicast Scope to start the New Multicast Scope Wizard. Click Next.

3. Enter a name and description for the scope, and then click Next.

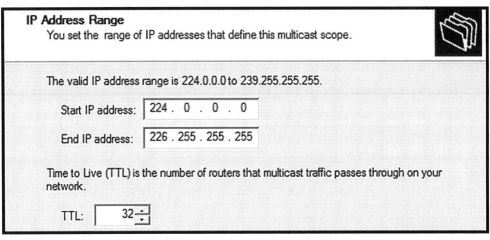

4. The Start IP Address and End IP Address boxes define the valid IP address range for the scope. Enter a start address and an end address in these boxes. You must define multicast scopes by using Class D IP addresses. This means the valid IP address range is 224.0.0.0 to 239.255.255.255.

5. Messages sent by computers using multicast IP addresses have a specific time-to-live (TTL) value. The TTL value specifies the maximum number of routers the message can go through. The default value is 32, which is

sufficient on most networks. If you have a large network, you might need to increase this value to reflect the actual number of routers that might be used.

6. Click Next. If you make a mistake, click Back, and then modify the IP address range you entered.

7. Use the exclusion range to define IP address ranges that are to be excluded from the scope. You can exclude multiple address ranges as follows:

- To define an exclusion range, enter a start address and an end address in the Start IP Address and End IP Address boxes, and then click Add.
- To track which address ranges are excluded, use the Excluded Addresses list.
- To delete an exclusion range, select the range in the Excluded Addresses list, and then click Remove.

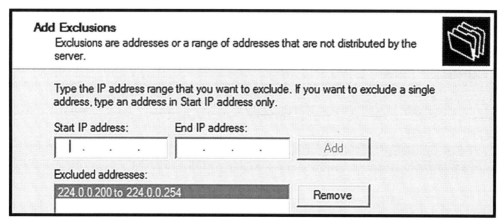

8. Click Next. Specify the duration of leases for the scope by using the Day(s), Hour(s), and Minutes boxes. The default duration is 30 days. Click Next.

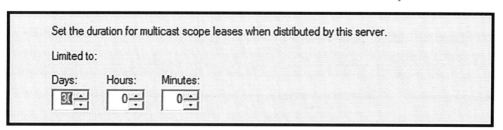

TIP If you haven't worked a lot with multicast, you shouldn't change the default value. Multicast leases aren't used in the same way as normal leases. Multiple computers can use a multicast IP address, and all of these computers can have a lease on the IP address. A good multicast lease duration for most networks is from 30 to 60 days.

9. If you want to activate the scope, select Yes, and then click Next. Otherwise, select No, and then click Next.

10. Click Finish to complete the process.

Setting Scope Options

Scope options enable you to precisely control a scope's functioning and to set default TCP/IP settings for clients that use the scope. For example, you can use scope options to enable clients to automatically find DNS servers on the network. You can also define settings for default gateways, WINS, and more. Scope options apply only to normal scopes, not to multicast scopes.

You can set scope options in any of the following ways:

- Globally for all scopes by setting default server options
- On a per-scope basis by setting scope options
- On a per-client basis by setting reservation options
- On a client-class basis by configuring user-specific or vendor-specific classes

IPv4 and IPv6 have different scope options. Scope options use a hierarchy to determine when certain options apply. The previous list shows the hierarchy. Basically, this means the following:

- Per-scope options override global options
- Per-client options override per-scope and global options
- Client-class options override all other options

Assigning Server Options

Server options are applied to all scopes configured on a particular DHCP server. You can view and assign server options by following these steps:

1. In the DHCP console, double-click the server with which you want to work, and then expand its IPv4 and IPv6 folders in the tree view.

2. To view current settings, select the Server Options node under IPv4 or IPv6, depending on the type of address with which you want to work. Currently configured options are displayed in the right pane.

3. To assign new settings, right-click Server Options, and then click Configure Options to open the Server Options dialog box. Under Available Options, select the check box for the first option you want to configure. Then, with the option selected, enter any required information in the Data Entry panel. Repeat this step to configure other options.

4. Click OK to save your changes.

Assigning Scope Options

Scope options are specific to an individual scope and override the default server options. You can view and assign scope options by following these steps:

1. In the DHCP console, expand the entry for the scope with which you want to work.

2. To view current settings, select Scope Options. Currently configured options are displayed in the right pane.

3. To assign new settings, right-click Scope Options, and then click Configure Options. This opens the Scope Options dialog box. Under Available Options, select the check box for the first option you want to configure. Then, with the option selected, enter any required information in the Data Entry panel. Repeat this step to configure other options.

4. Click OK.

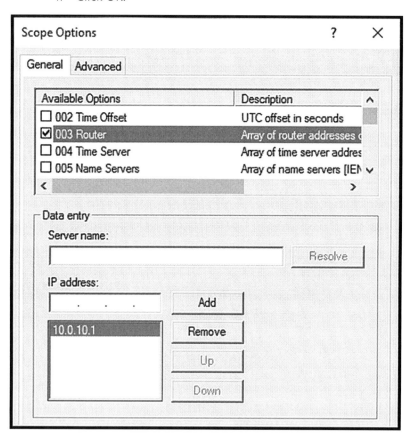

Assigning Reservation Options

You can assign reservation options to a client that has a reserved IPv4 or IPv6 address. These options are specific to an individual client and override server-specific and scope-specific options. To view and assign reservation options, follow these steps:

1. In the DHCP console, expand the entry for the scope with which you want to work.

2. Double-click the Reservations folder for the scope.

3. To view current settings, click the reservation you want to examine. Currently configured options are displayed in the right pane.

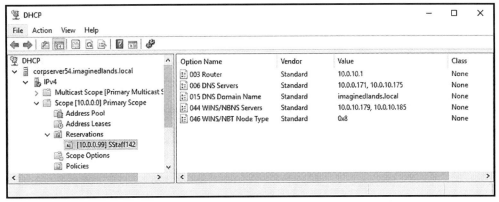

4. To assign new settings, right-click the reservation, and then click Configure Options to open the Reservation Options dialog box. Under Available Options, select the check box for the first option you want to configure. Then, with the option selected, enter any required information in the Data Entry panel. Repeat this step to configure other options.

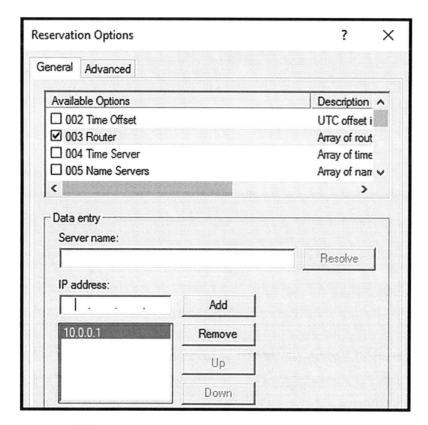

Modifying Scopes

You can modify an existing scope by following these steps:

1. In the DHCP console, double-click the server with which you want to work, and then expand its IPv4 and IPv6 folders in the tree view. This should display the currently configured scopes for the server.

2. Right-click the scope you want to modify, and then click Properties.

3. You can now modify the scope properties. Keep the following in mind:

- When you modify normal IPv4 scopes, you have the option of setting an unlimited lease expiration time. If you do, you create permanent leases that reduce the effectiveness of pooling IP addresses with DHCP. Permanent leases aren't released unless you physically release them or deactivate the scope. As a result, you might eventually run out of addresses, especially as your network grows. A better alternative to unlimited leases is to use address reservations, and then only for specific clients that need fixed IP addresses.

- When you modify multicast scopes, you have the option of setting a life-time for the scope. The scope lifetime determines the amount of time the scope is valid. By default, multicast scopes are valid as long as they're activated. To change this setting, click the Lifetime tab, select Multicast Scope Expires On, and then set an expiration date.

Activating and Deactivating Scopes

In the DHCP console, inactive scopes are displayed with an icon showing a red arrow pointing down. Active scopes display the standard folder icon.

You can activate an inactive scope by right-clicking it in the DHCP console, and then selecting Activate. You can deactivate an active scope by right-clicking it in the DHCP console, and then selecting Deactivate.

> **IMPORTANT** Deactivating turns off a scope but doesn't terminate current client leases. If you want to terminate leases, follow the instructions in "Deleting Leases and Reservations" later in this chapter.

Enabling the Bootstrap Protocol

Bootstrap Protocol (BOOTP) is a dynamic IPv4 addressing protocol that predates DHCP. Normal scopes don't support BOOTP. To enable a scope to support BOOTP, follow these steps:

1. Right-click the normal scope for IPv4 addresses that you want to modify, and then click Properties.
2. On the Advanced tab, click Both to support DHCP and BOOTP clients.
3. As necessary, set a lease duration for BOOTP clients, and then click OK.

> **NOTE** The typical lease duration for a BOOTP address is much longer than for a DHCP address. For BOOTP, the default of 30 days is a good compromise, though some scenarios may lend themselves to an unlimited lease duration.

Removing a Scope

Removing a scope permanently deletes the scope from the DHCP server. To remove a scope, follow these steps:

1. In the DHCP console, right-click the scope you want to remove, and then click Delete.
2. When prompted to confirm that you want to delete the scope, click Yes.

Configuring Multiple Scopes on a Network

You can configure multiple scopes on a single network. A single DHCP server or multiple DHCP servers can serve these scopes. However, any time you work with multiple scopes, it's extremely important that the address ranges used by different scopes not overlap. Each scope must have a unique address range. If it doesn't, the same IP address might be assigned to different DHCP clients, which can cause severe problems on the network.

To understand how you can use multiple scopes, consider the following scenario, in which each server has its respective DHCP scope IP address range on the same subnet:

* **Server A**   192.168.10.1 to 192.168.10.99
* **Server B**   192.168.10.100 to 192.168.10.199
* **Server C**   192.168.10.200 to 192.168.10.254

Each of these servers responds to DHCP discovery messages, and any of them can assign IP addresses to clients. If one of the servers fails, the other servers can continue to provide DHCP services to the network. To introduce fault tolerance and provide redundancy, you can use failover scopes as discussed in the next section.

Creating and Managing Failover Scopes

Failover scopes are split between two DHCP servers to increase fault tolerance, provide redundancy over using a single DHCP server, and enable load balancing. With a failover scope, you identify the two DHCP servers that split the scope. If one of the servers becomes unavailable or overloaded, the other server can take its place by continuing to lease new IP addresses and renew existing leases. A failover scope can also help to balance server loads.

Creating Failover Scopes

Failover scopes apply only to IPv4 addresses. You can split a single scope or a superscope that contains multiple scopes.

You create a failover scope on the DHCP server that you want to designate as the primary server by splitting an existing scope or superscope. During the failover-scope creation process, you need to specify the partner server with which you want to split the primary server's scope. This additional server acts as the secondary server for the scope. Because failover scopes are a server-side enhancement, no additional configuration is required for DHCP clients.

The way scope splitting works depends on the failover scope configuration settings. You do one of the following:

* **Optimize for load balancing**   A failover scope optimized for load balancing has little or no time delay configured in its scope properties. With no time delay, both the primary and the secondary servers can respond to DHCP DISCOVER requests from DHCP clients. This enables the fastest server to respond to and accept a DHCPOFFER first. Fault tolerance continues to be a part of the scope. If one of the servers becomes unavailable or overloaded and is unable to respond to requests, the other server handles requests and continues distributing addresses until the normal process is restored. For load balancing, set Load Balance as the failover mode.
* **Optimize for fault tolerance**   A failover scope optimized for fault tolerance has an extended time delay configured in its scope properties. The time delay on the secondary DHCP server causes the server to respond with a delay to DHCP DISCOVER requests from DHCP clients. The delay on the secondary server enables the primary DHCP server to respond to and accept the DHCPOFFER first. However, if the primary server becomes unavailable or overloaded and is unable to respond to requests, the secondary server handles requests and continues distributing addresses until the primary server is available to service clients again. For fault tolerance, set Hot Standby as the failover mode.

You can create a failover scope by completing the following steps:

1. In the DHCP console, connect to the primary DHCP server for the failover scope. Double-click the entry for the primary server, and then expand its IPv4 folder in the tree view.

2. The scope with which you want to work must already be defined. Right-click the scope or superscope that you want to configure for failover, and then click Configure Failover to start the Configure Failover Wizard.

3. The scope you right-clicked previously is selected by default. Click Next.

Configure Failover

Introduction to DHCP Failover

DHCP Failover enables high availability of DHCP services by synchronizing IP address lease information between two DHCP servers. DHCP failover also provides load balancing of DHCP requests.

This wizard will guide you through setup of DHCP failover. Select from the following list of scopes which are available to be configured for high availability. Scopes which are already configured for high availability are not displayed in the list below.

Available scopes: ☑ Select all.

10.0.0.0

4. Next, you need to specify the partner server to use for failover. Click Add Server. Use the options in the Add Server dialog box to select the secondary DHCP server for the failover scope, and then click OK. Clear the Reuse Existing Failover Relationships check box, and then click Next to continue.

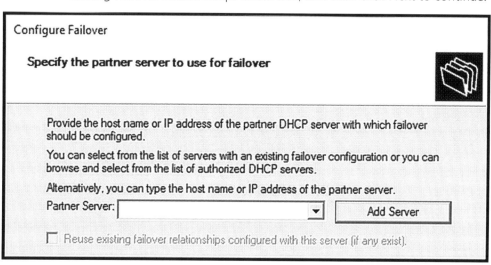

Configure Failover

Specify the partner server to use for failover

Provide the host name or IP address of the partner DHCP server with which failover should be configured.

You can select from the list of servers with an existing failover configuration or you can browse and select from the list of authorized DHCP servers.

Alternatively, you can type the host name or IP address of the partner server.

Partner Server: [▼] [Add Server   ]

☐ Reuse existing failover relationships configured with this server (if any exist).

```
┌─────────────────────────────────────────────────────────────┐
│ Add Server                                       ?    ✕       │
│                                                               │
│ Select a server you want to add to your console.              │
│                                                               │
│ ◯ This server:                                                │
│   ┌──────────────────────────────────────┐  ┌──────────┐     │
│   │                                      │  │ Browse…  │     │
│   └──────────────────────────────────────┘  └──────────┘     │
│                                                               │
│ ◉ This authorized DHCP server:                                │
│   ┌────────────────────────────┬──────────────┬─────────┐    │
│   │ Name                       │ IP Address   │         │    │
│   ├────────────────────────────┼──────────────┼─────────┤    │
│   │ corpserver12.imaginedlands.local │ 10.0.0.171 │       │   │
│   │ corpserver54.imaginedlands.local │ 10.0.0.172 │       │   │
│   └────────────────────────────┴──────────────┴─────────┘    │
└─────────────────────────────────────────────────────────────┘
```

> **NOTE**   If the scopes you are configuring already exists on the partner server, you'll see a warning that the scopes will need to be deleted on the partner server before you can continue. You'll need to open the DHCP console on the partner server and then delete the duplicated scope.

5. You'll next need to create a new failover relationship. Several parameters are set for you automatically, including:

* **Relationship name**   A descriptor used to differentiate failover relationships. The default name is based on the name and domain of the servers in the partnership. Although you can change the name if you want, the default value usually is sufficient.

* **Maximum Client Lead Time**   Sets the lead time for assigning leases to clients. When a client is first assigned a lease, the lease is valid only for the interval defined by the maximum lead time and must be validated before the lead time expires. The lease is validated when the client contacts the originating DHCP server within the lead time interval. Once validated, the client is assigned the lease for the normal lease interval. For example, if the maximum lead time is 10 minutes and the normal lease duration is 8 days, the client is initially assigned a lease for 10 minutes and must contact the server again before the lead time interval expires to receive a full lease of 8 days. However, if the originating server is unavailable for some reason, the client will send out a message to which any available DHCP server can respond to confirm the full 8-day lease.

> **REAL WORLD**   Wondering why this lead time process is used? This process is designed to ensure client leases aren't inadvertently duplicated or lost should failover partners lose communication with each other. Normally, if two DHCP servers share a failover partnership, partner A and B share information about leases with each other. However, if partner A assigns a lease and then goes offline before telling partner B about it, partner B will learn about the lease when the client tries to renew the lease before the lead time expires. Partner B will then register the lease and assign the client a full lease. As a best practice, you'll want to use a maximum lead time of 5 to 60 minutes. A shorter duration ensures clients are more quickly assigned full leases.

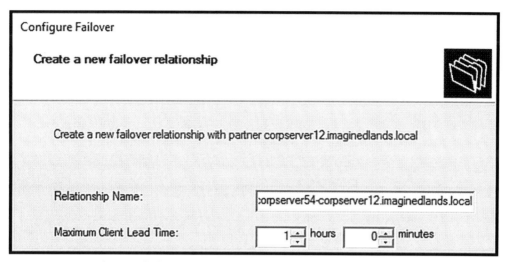

Configure Failover

Create a new failover relationship

Create a new failover relationship with partner corpserver12.imaginedlands.local

Relationship Name: corpserver54-corpserver12.imaginedlands.local

Maximum Client Lead Time: 1 hours   0 minutes

6. Use the Mode list to set the failover mode as Load Balance or Hot Standby.

7. If you set the failover mode for Load Balance, use the Load Balance Percentage combo boxes to specify the relative percentage for how to allocate the IP addresses to each of the servers. Here are configuration examples:

- An 80/20 split works best when you want one server to handle most of the workload and want another server to be available as needed.
- An 60/40 split works best when you want one server to handle a little more of the workload than the other, but you want both servers to have regular workloads.
- A 50/50 split works best when you want to evenly balance the load between two servers.

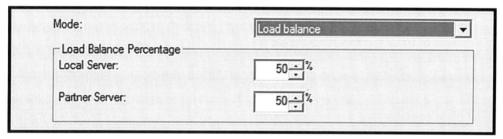

Mode: Load balance

Load Balance Percentage
Local Server: 50 %

Partner Server: 50 %

8. If you set the failover mode to Hot Standby, set the role of the partner as either Active or Standby and then specify the relative percentage of IP addresses to reserve for the standby partner. By default, 5 percent of the IP addresses are reserved for the standby partner.

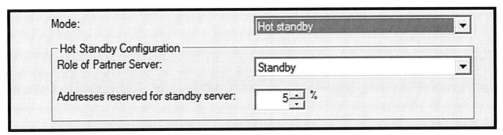

9. The State Switchover Interval enables automatic switchover by setting the amount of time a DHCP server waits before assuming control of an address range in the event a failover partner becomes unavailable. For automatic transition to occur, you must enable and set the State Switchover Interval to a specific value. Otherwise, if a server is unable to communicate with a failover partner, the server remains in a communication interrupted state until an administrator manually changes the server to a partner down state, which allows the server to respond to all DHCP client requests. As a best practice, you'll want to use a switchover interval of 30 to 90 minutes. This interval ensures switchover is handled in a timely manner while allowing for intermittent communication outages that may occur.

10. Message authentication is enabled by default to ensure all DHCP messages are authenticated. Authentication prevents spoofing and other attacks against your servers.

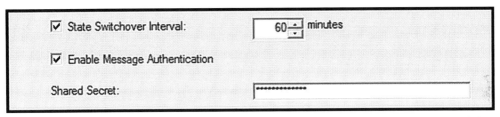

11. Enter a shared secret for the partners. The shared secret is a password that the partners use when synchronizing the DHCP database and performing other tasks related to maintaining the DHCP failover partnership. Like other passwords, the shared secret should be relatively complex to prevent spoofing and other attacks against your servers. When you are ready to continue, click Next.

12. Click Next and then click Finish. Review the summary of the failover scope configuration. If any errors were encountered, you might need to take corrective action. Click Close.

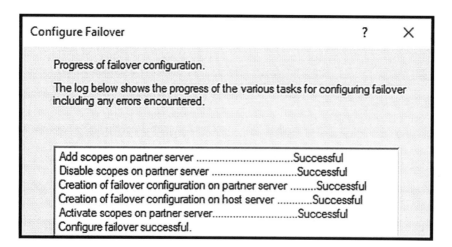

Configure Failover ? ✕

Progress of failover configuration.

The log below shows the progress of the various tasks for configuring failover including any errors encountered.

Add scopes on partner server ....Successful
Disable scopes on partner server ....Successful
Creation of failover configuration on partner server ....Successful
Creation of failover configuration on host server ....Successful
Activate scopes on partner server.............................Successful
Configure failover successful.

Modifying or Removing Failover Scopes

Failover scopes are not identified as such in the DHCP console. You can identify a failover scope by its network ID and IP address pool. Generally, you'll find a scope with the same network ID on two DHCP servers, and the scope properties will include information about the failover partnership. To view this information, right-click the scope, and then select Properties. In the Properties dialog box, select the Failover tab.

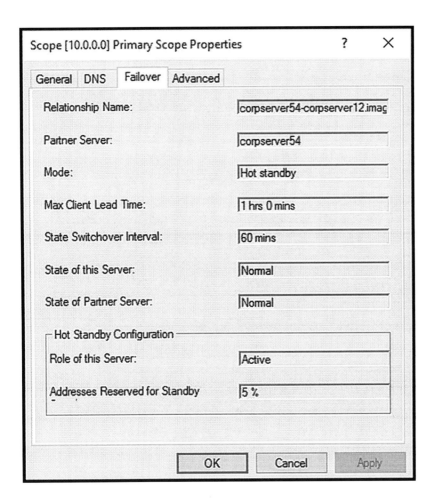

Scope [10.0.0.0] Primary Scope Properties

General | DNS | Failover | Advanced

Relationship Name:	corpserver54-corpserver12.imag
Partner Server:	corpserver54
Mode:	Hot standby
Max Client Lead Time:	1 hrs 0 mins
State Switchover Interval:	60 mins
State of this Server:	Normal
State of Partner Server:	Normal

Hot Standby Configuration

| Role of this Server: | Active |
| Addresses Reserved for Standby | 5 % |

OK | Cancel | Apply

You can manage the partnership in several ways:

- If you suspect the configuration details related to the partnership are out of sync, right-click the scope, and then select Replicate Partnership.
- If you suspect the DHCP database that the partners share is out of sync, right-click the scope, and then select Replicate Scope.
- If you no longer want the scope to fail over, you can deconfigure failover by right-clicking the scope, and then selecting Deconfigure Failover.

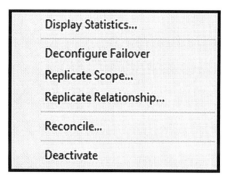

| Display Statistics... |
| Deconfigure Failover |
| Replicate Scope... |
| Replicate Relationship... |
| Reconcile... |
| Deactivate |

You can't modify the failover settings after the partnership is established; however, you can deconfigure failover and then reconfigure failover.

Creating and Managing Superscopes

A superscope is a container for IPv4 scopes in much the same way that an organizational unit is a container for Active Directory objects. Superscopes help you manage scopes available on the network by grouping them into a single point of management. For example, with a superscope, you can activate or deactivate multiple scopes through a single action. You can also view statistics for all scopes in the superscope rather than having to check statistics for each scope. Superscopes also support DHCP clients on a single physical network where multiple logical IP networks are used, or put another way, you can create superscopes to distribute IP addresses from different logical networks to the same physical network segment.

Creating Superscopes

After you create at least one normal or multicast IPv4 scope, you can create a superscope by following these steps:

1. In the DHCP console, expand the node for the server with which you want to work, right-click IPv4, and then click New Superscope to start the New Superscope Wizard. Click Next.

2. Enter a name for the superscope, and then click Next.

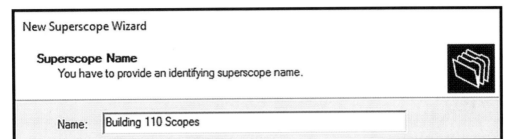

New Superscope Wizard

Superscope Name
 You have to provide an identifying superscope name.

Name: `Building 110 Scopes`

3. Select scopes to add to the superscope. Select individual scopes by clicking their entry in the Available Scopes list. Select multiple scopes by clicking entries while holding down Shift or Ctrl.

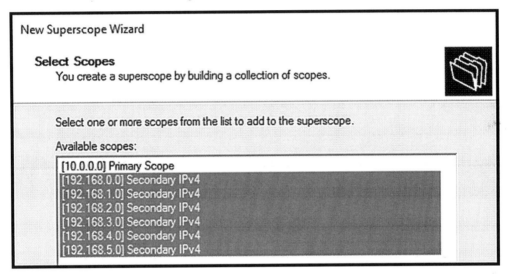

New Superscope Wizard

Select Scopes
 You create a superscope by building a collection of scopes.

Select one or more scopes from the list to add to the superscope.

Available scopes:

[10.0.0.0] Primary Scope
[192.168.0.0] Secondary IPv4
[192.168.1.0] Secondary IPv4
[192.168.2.0] Secondary IPv4
[192.168.3.0] Secondary IPv4
[192.168.4.0] Secondary IPv4
[192.168.5.0] Secondary IPv4

4. Click Next, and then click Finish.

Adding Scopes to a Superscope

You can add scopes to a superscope when you create it, or you can add the scopes later. To add a scope to a superscope, follow these steps:

1. Right-click the scope you want to add to a superscope, and then click Add To Superscope.

2. In the Add Scope To A Superscope dialog box, select a superscope.

3. Click OK. The scope is then added to the superscope.

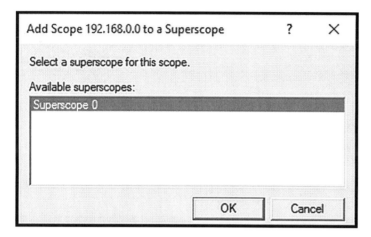

Removing Scopes From a Superscope

To remove a scope from a superscope, follow these steps:

1. Right-click the scope you want to remove from a superscope, and then click Remove From Superscope.

2. Confirm the action by clicking Yes when prompted. If this is the last scope in the superscope, the superscope is deleted automatically.

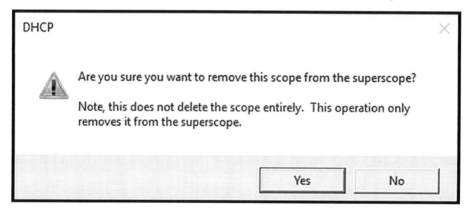

Activating and Deactivating a Superscope

When you activate or deactivate a superscope, you make all the scopes within the superscope active or inactive. To activate a superscope, right-click the superscope, and then select Activate. To deactivate a superscope, right-click the superscope, and then select Deactivate.

Deleting a Superscope

Deleting a superscope removes the superscope container but doesn't delete the scopes it contains. If you want to delete the member scopes, you'll need to do that separately. To delete a superscope, right-click the superscope, and then select Delete. When prompted, click Yes to confirm the action.

Managing Addressing

Scopes have separate folders for address pools, leases, and reservations. By accessing these folders, you can view current statistics for the related data and manage existing entries.

Viewing Scope Statistics

Scope statistics provide summary information about the address pool for the current scope or superscope. To view statistics, right-click the scope or superscope, and then select Display Statistics.

The primary columns in the Scope Statistics dialog box are used as follows:

- **Total Scopes**   Shows the number of scopes in a superscope.
- **Total Addresses**   Shows the total number of IP addresses assigned to the scope.
- **In Use**   Shows the total number (as a numerical value and as a percentage of the total available addresses) of addresses being used. If the total reaches 85 percent or more, you might want to consider assigning additional addresses or freeing up addresses for use.
- **Available**   Shows the total number (as a numerical value and as a percentage of the total available addresses) of addresses available for use.

Enabling and Configuring MAC Address Filtering

MAC address filtering (aka *link-layer filtering*) is a feature for IPv4 addresses that enables you to include or exclude computers and devices based on their MAC address. When you configure MAC address filtering, you can specify the hardware types that are exempted from filtering. By default, all hardware types defined in RFC 1700 are exempted from filtering. To modify hardware type exemptions, follow these steps:

1. In the DHCP console, right-click the IPv4 node, and then click Properties.

2. On the Filters tab, click Advanced. In the Advanced Filter Properties dialog box, select the check box for hardware types to exempt from filtering. Clear the check box for hardware types to filter.

3. Click OK to save your changes.

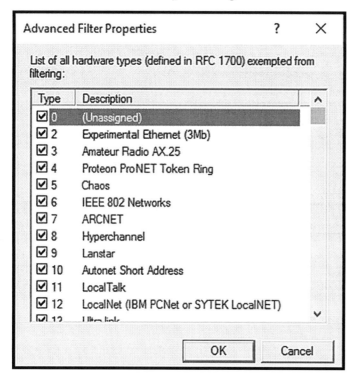

Before you can configure MAC address filtering, you must do one of the following:

- Enable and define an explicit allow list. The DHCP server provides DHCP services only to clients whose MAC addresses are in the allow list. Any client that previously received IP addresses is denied address renewal if its MAC address isn't on the allow list.
- Enable and define an explicit deny list. The DHCP server denies DHCP services only to clients whose MAC addresses are in the deny list. Any client that previously received IP addresses is denied address renewal if its MAC address is on the deny list.
- Enable and define an allow list and a block list. The block list has precedence over the allow list. This means that the DHCP server provides DHCP services only to clients whose MAC addresses are in the allow list, if no corresponding matches are in the deny list. If a MAC address has been denied, the address is always blocked even if the address is on the allow list.

To enable an allow list, deny list, or both, follow these steps:

1. In the DHCP console, right-click the IPv4 node, and then click Properties.

2. On the Filters tab, you'll find the current filter configuration details. To use an allow list, select Enable Allow List. To use a deny list, select Enable Deny List.

3. Click OK to save your changes.

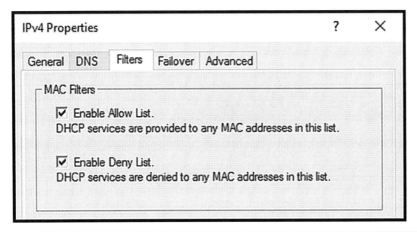

> **NOTE** As an alternative, you can right-click the Allow or Deny node, under the Filters node, and then select Enable to enable allow or deny lists. If you right-click the Allow or Deny node and then select Disable, you disable allow or deny lists.

After you enable filtering, you define your filters by using the MAC address for the client computer or device's network adapter. On a client computer, you can obtain the MAC address by entering the command **ipconfig /all** at the command prompt. The Physical Address entry shows the client's MAC address. You must enter this value exactly for the address filter to work.

A MAC address is defined by eight pairings of two-digit hexadecimal numbers separated by a hyphen, as shown here:

```
FE-01-56-23-18-94-EB-F2
```

When you define a filter, you can specify the MAC address with or without the hyphens. This means that you could enter FE-01-56-23-18-94-EB-F2 or FE0156231894EBF2.

You also can use an asterisk (*) as a wildcard for pattern matching. To allow any value to match a specific part of the MAC address, you can insert * where the values usually would be, as shown here:

FE-01-56-23-18-94-*-F2

FE-*-56-23-18-94-*-*

FE-01-56-23-18-*-*-*

FE01*

To configure a MAC address filter, follow these steps:

1. In the DHCP console, double-click the IPv4 node, and then double-click the Filters node.

2. Right-click Allow or Deny as appropriate for the type of filter you are creating, and then click New Filter.

3. Enter the MAC address to filter, and then if you want to you can enter a comment in the Description text box. Click Add. Repeat this step to add other filters.

4. Click Close when you have finished.

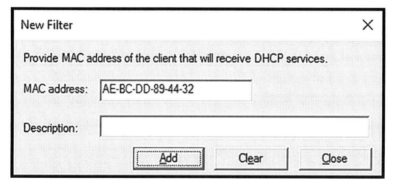

Setting a New Exclusion Range

You can exclude IPv4 or IPv6 addresses from a scope by defining an exclusion range. Scopes can have multiple exclusion ranges. To define an exclusion range for a scope with IPv4 addresses, follow these steps:

1. In the DHCP console, expand the scope with which you want to work, and then right-click the Address Pool folder or Exclusions folder. On the shortcut menu, click New Exclusion Range.

2. Enter a start address and an end address in the Start IP Address and End IP Address boxes, and then click Add. The range specified must be a subset of the range set for the current scope and must not be currently in use. Repeat this step to add other exclusion ranges.

3. Click Close when you have finished.

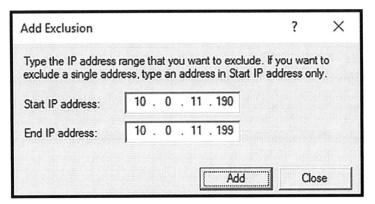

> **TIP** To exclude a single IP address, enter a start address and leave the end address blank.

To define an exclusion range for a scope with IPv6 addresses, follow these steps:

1. In the DHCP console, expand the scope with which you want to work, and then right-click the Exclusions folder. On the shortcut menu, click New Exclusion Range.

2. Enter a start address and an end address in the Start IPv6 Address and End IPv6 Address boxes, and then click Add. The range specified must be a subset of the range set for the current scope and must not be currently in use. Repeat this step to add other exclusion ranges.

3. Click Close when you have finished.

If you don't need an exclusion anymore, you can delete it. Select Address Pool or Exclusions as appropriate. In the main pane, right-click the exclusion, select Delete, and then click Yes in response to the confirmation message.

Reserving DHCP Addresses

DHCP provides several ways to assign permanent addresses to clients. One way is to use the Unlimited setting in the Scope dialog box to assign permanent addresses to all clients that use the scope. Another way is to reserve DHCP addresses on a per-client basis. When you reserve a DHCP address, the DHCP server always assigns the client the same IP address, and you can do so without sacrificing the centralized management features that make DHCP so attractive.

If the client is on the network and has a current IPv4 or IPv6 lease, you can create a reservation by completing the following steps:

1. In the DHCP console, expand the scope with which you want to work, and then select the Address Leases folder.
2. Right-click the lease you want to work with. On the shortcut menu, click Add To Reservation.

Otherwise, to manually reserve an IPv4 address for a client, follow these steps:

1. In the DHCP console, expand the scope with which you want to work, and then right-click the Reservations folder. On the shortcut menu, click New Reservation.
2. In the Reservation Name text box, enter a short but descriptive name for the reservation. This name is used only for identification purposes.
3. In the IP Address box, enter the IPv4 address you want to reserve for the client.

> **NOTE** This IP address must be within the valid range of addresses for the currently selected scope.

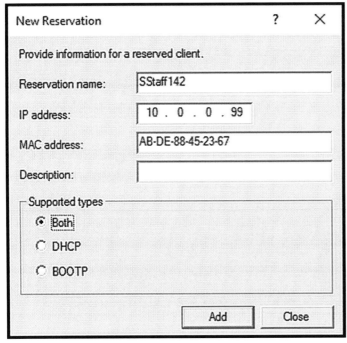

New Reservation   ?   ✕

Provide information for a reserved client.

Reservation name: │SStaff142   │

IP address: │ 10 . 0 . 0 . 99 │

MAC address: │AB-DE-88-45-23-67   │

Description: │   │

┌─ Supported types ──────────────────────────────────┐
│ ⦿ Both   │
│ ○ DHCP   │
│ ○ BOOTP   │
└───┘

                          [Add   ]   [Close   ]

4. The MAC Address box specifies the MAC address for the client computer's NIC. You can obtain the MAC address by entering the command **ipconfig /all** at the command prompt on the client computer. The Physical Address entry shows the client's MAC address. You must enter this value exactly for the address reservation to work.

5. Enter an optional comment in the Description text box.

6. By default, both DHCP and BOOTP clients are supported. This option is fine, and you need to change it only if you want to exclude a particular type of client.   .

7. Click Add to create the address reservation. Repeat this step to add other address reservations.

8. Click Close when you have finished.

To manually reserve an IPv6 address for a client, follow these steps:

1. In the DHCP console, expand the scope with which you want to work, and then right-click the Reservations folder. On the shortcut menu, click New Reservation.

2. In the Reservation text box, enter a short but descriptive name for the reservation. This information is used only for identification purposes.

3. In the IPv6 Address box, enter the IPv6 address you want to reserve for the client.

> **NOTE** This IP address must be within the valid range of addresses for the currently selected scope.

4. The device unique identifier (DUID) box specifies the MAC address for the client computer's NIC. You can obtain the MAC address by entering the command **ipconfig /all** at the command prompt on the client computer. The Physical Address entry shows the client's MAC address. You must enter this value exactly for the address reservation to work.

5. The identity association identifier (IAID) sets a unique identifier prefix for the client. Typically, this is a nine-digit value.

6. Enter an optional comment in the Description text box.

7. Click Add to create the address reservation. Repeat this step to add other address reservations.

8. Click Close when you have finished.

When you work with reserved addresses, you should take note of a couple caveats:

* Reserved addresses aren't automatically reassigned. If the address is already in use, you need to release the address to ensure that the appropriate client can obtain it. You can force a client to release an address by terminating the client's lease or by logging on to the client and entering the command **ipconfig /release** at an administrator command prompt.
* Clients don't automatically switch to the reserved address. If the client is using a different IP address, you need to force the client to release the current lease and request a new one. You can do this by terminating the client's lease or by logging on to the client and entering the command **ipconfig /renew** at an administrator command prompt.

Modifying Reservation Properties

You can modify the properties of reservations by following these steps:

1. In the DHCP console, expand the scope with which you want to work, and then click the Reservations folder.

2. Right-click a reservation, and then click Properties. You can now modify the reservation properties. You can't modify options that are shaded, but you can modify other options. These options are the same options described in the previous section.

Deleting Leases and Reservations

You can delete active leases and reservations by following these steps:

1. In the DHCP console, expand the scope with which you want to work, and then click the Address Leases folder or Reservations folder, as appropriate.
2. Right-click the lease or reservation you want to delete, and then click Delete.
3. Confirm the deletion by clicking Yes.
4. The lease or reservation is now removed from DHCP; however, the client isn't forced to release the IP address. To force the client to release the IP address, log on to the client that holds the lease or reservation and enter the command **ipconfig /release** at an administrator command prompt.

Backing Up and Restoring the DHCP Database

DHCP servers store DHCP lease and reservation information in database files. By default, these files are stored in the %SystemRoot%\System32\DHCP directory. The key files in this directory are used as follows:

- **Dhcp.mdb** The primary database file for the DHCP server
- **J50.log** A transaction log file used to recover incomplete transactions in case of a server malfunction
- **J50.chk** A checkpoint file used in truncating the transaction log for the DHCP server
- **J50000NN.log** A reserved log file for the DHCP server
- **Tmp.edb** A temporary working file for the DHCP server

Backing Up the DHCP Database

The %SystemRoot%\System32\DHCP\Backup folder contains the backup information for the DHCP configuration and the DHCP database. By default, the DHCP database is backed up every 60 minutes automatically. To manually back up the DHCP database at any time, follow these steps:

1. In the DHCP console, right-click the server you want to back up, and then click Backup.
2. In the Browse For Folder dialog box, select the folder that will contain the backup DHCP database, and then click OK.

Registry keys that control the location and timing of DHCP backups, in addition to other DHCP settings, are located under HKEY_LOCAL_MACHINE in SYSTEM\CurrentControlSetServices\DHCPServer\Parameters.

The following keys control the DHCP database and backup configuration:

- **BackupDatabasePath**   Sets the location of the DHCP database. You should set this option through the DHCP Properties dialog box. Click the Advanced tab, and then set the Database Path as appropriate.
- **DatabaseName**   Sets the name of the primary DHCP database file. The default value is DHCP.mdb.
- **BackupInterval**   Determines how often the DHCP client information database is backed up. The default is 60 minutes.
- **DatabaseCleanupInterval**   Determines how often the DHCP service deletes expired records from the DHCP client information database. The default is four hours.

Restoring the DHCP Database From Backup

In the case of a server crash and recovery, you might need to restore and then reconcile the DHCP database. To force DHCP to restore the database from backup, follow these steps:

1. If necessary, restore a good copy of the %SystemRoot%\System32\DHCP\Backup directory from the archive. Afterward, start the DHCP console, right-click the server you want to restore, and then click Restore.

2. In the Browse For Folder dialog box, select the folder that contains the backup you want to restore, and then click OK.

3. During the restoration of the database, the DHCP Server service is stopped. As a result, DHCP clients are temporarily unable to contact the DHCP server to obtain IP addresses.

Using Backup and Restore to Move the DHCP Database to a New Server

If you need to rebuild a server providing DHCP services, you might want to move the DHCP services to another server prior to rebuilding the server. To do this, you need to perform several tasks on the source and destination servers. On the destination server, do the following:

1. Install the DHCP Server service on the destination server, and then restart the server.
2. Stop the DHCP Server service in the Services console.
3. Delete the contents of the %SystemRoot%\System32\DHCP folder.

On the source server, do the following:

1. Stop the DHCP Server service in the Services console.
2. After the DHCP Server service is stopped, disable the service so that it can no longer be started.
3. Copy the entire contents of the %SystemRoot%\System32\DHCP folder to the %SystemRoot%\System32\DHCP folder on the destination server.

Now all the necessary files are on the destination server. Start the DHCP Server service on the destination server to complete the migration.

Forcing the DHCP Server Service to Regenerate the DHCP Database

If the DHCP database becomes corrupt and Windows is unable to repair the database when you stop and restart the DHCP Server service, you can attempt to restore the database as described in "Restoring the DHCP Database From Backup" earlier in this chapter. If this fails or you prefer to start with a fresh copy of the DHCP database, follow these steps:

1. Stop the DHCP Server service in the Services console.
2. Delete the contents of the %SystemRoot%\System32\DHCP folder. If you want to force a complete regeneration of the database and not allow the server to restore from a previous backup, you should also delete the contents of the Backup folder.

> **CAUTION** Don't delete DHCP files if the DHCPServer registry keys aren't intact. These keys must be available to restore the DHCP database.

3. Restart the DHCP Server service.
4. No active leases or other information for scopes are displayed in the DHCP console. To regain the active leases for each scope, you must reconcile the server scopes as discussed in the next section.

5. To prevent conflicts with previously assigned leases, you should enable address conflict detection for the next few days, as discussed in "Avoiding IP Address Conflicts" earlier in Chapter 16.

Reconciling Leases and Reservations

Reconciling checks the client leases and reservations against the DHCP database on the server. If inconsistencies are found between what is registered in the Windows registry and what is recorded in the DHCP server database, you can select and reconcile any inconsistent entries. After the entries you select are reconciled, DHCP either restores the IP address to the original owner or creates a temporary reservation for the IP address. When the lease time expires, the address is recovered for future use.

You can reconcile scopes individually, or you can reconcile all scopes on a server. To reconcile a scope individually, follow these steps:

1. In the DHCP console, right-click the scope with which you want to work, and then click Reconcile.
2. In the Reconcile dialog box, click Verify.
3. Inconsistencies are reported in the status window. Select the displayed addresses, and then click Reconcile to repair inconsistencies.
4. If no inconsistencies are found, click OK.

To reconcile all scopes on a server, follow these steps:

1. In the DHCP console, expand the server entry, right-click the IPv4 node, and then click Reconcile All Scopes.
2. In the Reconcile All Scopes dialog box, click Verify.
3. Inconsistencies are reported in the status window. Select the displayed addresses, and then click Reconcile to repair inconsistencies.
4. If no inconsistencies are found, click OK.

Chapter 18. Implementing DNS

DNS is a name-resolution service that resolves computer names to IP addresses. When you use DNS, a fully qualified host name—pc15.tvpress.com, for example—can be resolved to an IP address, which enables computers to find one another. DNS operates over the TCP/IP protocol stack and can be integrated with Windows Internet Name Service (WINS), Dynamic Host Configuration Protocol (DHCP), and Active Directory Domain Services (AD DS). Fully integrating DNS with these Windows networking features enables you to optimize DNS for Windows Server domains.

Understanding DNS

DNS organizes groups of computers into domains. These domains are organized into a hierarchical structure that can be defined on an Internet-wide basis for public networks or on an enterprise-wide basis for private networks (also known as *extranets* and *intranets*, respectively). The various levels within the hierarchy identify individual computers, organizational domains, and top-level domains. For the fully qualified host name server4.reagentpress.com, *server4* represents the host name for an individual computer, *reagentpress* is the organizational domain, and *com* is the top-level domain.

Top-level domains are at the root of the DNS hierarchy and are also called *root domains*. These domains are organized geographically, by organization type, and by function. Typical corporate domains, such as microsoft.com, are also referred to as *parent domains* because they're the parents of an organizational structure. You can divide parent domains into subdomains you can use for groups or departments within your organization.

Subdomains are often referred to as *child domains*. For example, the fully qualified domain name (FQDN) for a computer within a human resources group could be designated as beowulf.hr.reagentpress.com. Here, *beowulf* is the host name, *hr* is the child domain, and *reagentpress.com* is the parent domain.

Integrating Active Directory and DNS

Active Directory domains use DNS to implement their naming structure and hierarchy. Active Directory and DNS are tightly integrated, so much so that you should install DNS on the network before you can install Active Directory Domain Services.

During installation of the first domain controller on an Active Directory network, you have the opportunity to automatically install DNS if a DNS server can't be found on the network. You can also specify whether DNS and Active Directory should be integrated fully. In most cases, you should respond affirmatively to both requests. With full integration, DNS information is stored directly in Active Directory, which enables you to take advantage of Active Directory's capabilities.

Understanding the difference between partial integration and full integration is very important:

- **Partial integration** With partial integration, the domain uses standard file storage. DNS information is stored in text-based files that end with the .dns extension. The default location of these files is %SystemRoot%\System32\Dns. Updates to DNS are handled through a single authoritative DNS server. This server is designated as the primary DNS server for the particular domain or an area within a domain called a *zone*. Clients that use dynamic DNS updates through DHCP must be configured to use the primary DNS server in the zone. If they aren't, their DNS information won't be updated. Likewise, dynamic updates through DHCP can't be made if the primary DNS server is offline.
- **Full integration** With full integration, the domain uses directory-integrated storage. DNS information is stored directly in Active Directory and is available through the container for the *dnsZone* object. Because the information is part of Active Directory, any domain controller can access the data, and you can use a multimaster approach for dynamic updates through DHCP. This enables any domain controller running the DNS Server service to handle dynamic updates. Furthermore, clients that use dynamic DNS updates through DHCP can use any DNS server within the zone. An added benefit of directory integration is the ability to use directory security to control access to DNS information.

If you look at the way DNS information is replicated throughout the network, you will find more advantages to full integration with Active Directory. With partial integration, DNS information is stored and replicated separately from Active Directory. By having two separate structures, you reduce the effectiveness of both

DNS and Active Directory and make administration more complex. Because DNS is less efficient than Active Directory at replicating changes, you might also increase network traffic and the amount of time required to replicate DNS changes throughout the network.

In early releases of the DNS Server service for Windows servers, restarting a DNS server could take an hour or more in large organizations with extremely large AD DS–integrated zones. The operation took this much time because the zone data was loaded in the foreground while the server was starting the DNS service. To ensure that DNS servers can be responsive after a restart, the DNS Server service loads zone data from AD DS in the background while the service restarts. This ensures that the DNS server is responsive and can handle requests for data from other zones.

At startup, DNS servers perform the following tasks:

- Enumerate all zones to be loaded
- Load root hints from files or AD DS storage
- Load all zones that are stored in files rather than in AD DS
- Begin responding to queries and Remote Procedure Calls (RPCs)
- Create one or more threads to load the zones that are stored in AD DS

Because separate threads load zone data, the DNS server is able to respond to queries while zone loading is in progress. If a DNS client performs a query for a host in a zone that has already been loaded, the DNS server responds appropriately. If the query is for a host that has not yet been loaded into memory, the DNS server reads the host's data from AD DS and updates its record list accordingly.

Enabling DNS on the Network

To enable DNS on the network, you need to configure DNS clients and servers. When you configure DNS clients, you tell the clients the IP addresses of DNS servers on the network. By using these addresses, clients can communicate with DNS servers anywhere on the network, even if the servers are on different subnets.

The DNS client built into computers running Windows supports DNS traffic over Internet Protocol version 4 (IPv4) and Internet Protocol version 6 (IPv6). By default, IPv6 automatically configures the site-local address of DNS servers. To add the IPv6 addresses of your DNS servers, use the properties of the Internet Protocol Version 6 (TCP/IPv6) component in Network Connections or the following command:

```
netsh interface IPV6 ADD DNSSERVERS
```

In Windows PowerShell, you can use Get-NetIPInterface to list the available interfaces and then use Set-DNSClientServerAddress to set the IPv6 address on a specified interface.

DNS servers support IPv6 addresses as fully as they support IPv4 addresses. In the DNS Manager console, host addresses are displayed as IPv4 or IPv6 addresses. The Dnscmd command-line tool also accepts addresses in either format. Additionally, DNS servers can now send recursive queries to IPv6-only servers, and the server forwarder list can contain both IPv4 and IPv6 addresses. Finally, DNS servers now support the ip6.arpa domain namespace for reverse lookups.

When the network uses DHCP, you should configure DHCP to work with DNS. DHCP clients can register IPv6 addresses along with or instead of IPv4 addresses. To ensure proper integration of DHCP and DNS, you need to set the DHCP scope options as specified in "Setting Scope Options" in Chapter 17, "Managing and Maintaining DHCP." For IPv4, you should set the 006 DNS Servers and 015 DNS Domain Name scope options. For IPv6, you should set the 00023 DNS Recursive Name Server IPV6 Address List and 00024 Domain Search List scope options. Additionally, if computers on the network need to be accessible from other Active Directory domains, you need to create records for them in DNS. DNS records are organized into zones, where a *zone* is simply an area within a domain.

DNS client computers running Windows can use Link-Local Multicast Name Resolution (LLMNR) to resolve names on a local network segment when a DNS server is not available. They also periodically search for a domain controller in the domain to which they belong. This functionality helps avoid performance problems that might occur if a network or server failure causes a DNS client to create an association with a distant domain controller located on a slow link rather than a local domain controller. Previously, this association continued until the client was forced to seek a new domain controller, such as when the client computer was disconnected from the network for a long period of time. By periodically renewing its association with a domain controller, a DNS client can reduce the probability that it will be associated with an inappropriate domain controller.

The DNS client service for current versions of Windows has several interoperability and security enhancements specific to LLMNR and NetBIOS. To improve security for mobile networking, the service

* Does not send outbound LLMNR queries over mobile broadband or VPN interfaces
* Does not send outbound NetBIOS queries over mobile broadband

For better compatibility with devices in power-saving mode, the LLMNR query timeout is set to 410 milliseconds (msec) for the first retry and 410 msec for the second retry, making the total timeout value 820 msec. To improve response times for all queries, the DNS client service does the following:

* Issues LLMNR and NetBIOS queries in parallel, and optimizes for IPv4 and IPv6
* Divides interfaces into networks to send parallel DNS queries
* Uses asynchronous DNS cache with an optimized response timing

> **NOTE**   You can configure a DNS client computer running Windows 7 or later, in addition to Windows Server 2008 R2 or later, to locate the nearest domain controller instead of searching randomly. This can improve performance in networks containing domains that exist across slow links. However, because of the network traffic this process generates, locating the nearest domain controller can have a negative impact on network performance.

Windows Server supports read-only primary zones and the GlobalNames zone. To support read-only domain controllers (RODCs), the primary read-only zone is created automatically. When a computer becomes an RODC, it replicates a full read-only copy of all the application directory partitions that DNS uses, including the domain partition, ForestDNSZones, and DomainDNSZones. This ensures that the DNS server running on the RODC has a full read-only copy of any DNS zones. As an administrator of an RODC, you can view the contents of a primary read-only zone. You cannot, however, change the contents of a zone on the RODC. You can change the contents of the zone only on a standard domain controller.

To support all DNS environments and single-label name resolution, you can create a zone named *GlobalNames*. For optimal performance and cross-forest support, you should integrate this zone with AD DS and configure each authoritative DNS server with a local copy. When you use Service Location (SRV) resource records to publish the location of the GlobalNames zone, this zone provides unique, single-label computer names across the forest. Unlike WINS, the GlobalNames zone is intended to provide single-label name resolution for a subset of host names—typically, the CNAME resource records for your corporate servers. The GlobalNames zone is not intended to be used for peer-to-peer name resolution, such as name resolution for workstations. This is what LLMNR is for.

When the GlobalNames zone is configured appropriately, single-label name resolution works as follows:

1. The client's primary DNS suffix is appended to the single-label name that the client is looking up, and the query is submitted to the DNS server.

2. If that computer's full name is not resolved, the client requests resolution by using its DNS suffix search lists, if any.

3. If none of those names can be resolved, the client requests resolution by using the single-label name.

4. If the single-label name appears in the GlobalNames zone, the DNS server hosting the zone resolves the name. Otherwise, the query fails over to WINS.

Dynamic updates in the GlobalNames zone are not supported.

Configuring Name Resolution on DNS Clients

The best way to configure name resolution for DNS clients depends on the configuration of your network. If computers use DHCP, you probably want to configure DNS through settings on the DHCP server. If computers use static IP addresses or you want to configure DNS specifically for an individual system, you should configure DNS manually.

You can configure DNS settings on the DNS tab of the Advanced TCP/IP Settings dialog box. To access this dialog box, follow these steps:

1. In Settings, click Network & Internet on the home page and then click Ethernet. On the Ethernet page, click Change Adapter Options.

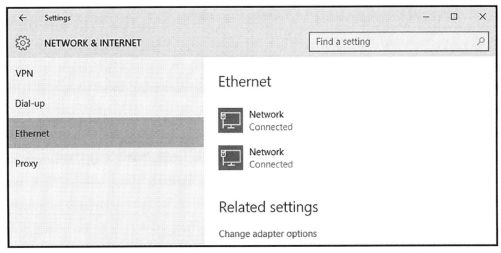

2. In Network Connections, right-click the connection with which you want to work, and then click Properties.

3. Double-click Internet Protocol Version 6 (TCP/IPv6) or Internet Protocol Version 4 (TCP/IPv4), depending on the type of IP address you are configuring.

4. If the computer is using DHCP and you want DHCP to specify the DNS server address, select Obtain DNS Server Address Automatically. Otherwise, select Use The Following DNS Server Addresses, and then enter primary and alternate DNS server addresses in the text boxes provided.

5. Click Advanced to display the Advanced TCP/IP Settings dialog box. In this dialog box, click the DNS tab.

You use the options of the DNS tab as follows:

- **DNS Server Addresses, In Order Of Use**   Use this area to specify the IP address of each DNS server that is used for domain name resolution. Click Add if you want to add a server IP address to the list. Click Remove to remove a selected server address from the list. Click Edit to edit the selected entry. You can specify multiple servers for DNS resolution. Their priority is determined by the order. If the first server isn't available to respond to a host name resolution request, the next DNS server in the list is accessed, and so on. To change the position of a server in the list box, select it, and then use the up or down arrow.

- **Append Primary And Connection Specific DNS Suffixes**   Typically, this option is selected by default. Select this option to resolve unqualified computer names in the primary domain. For example, if the computer name Gandolf is used and the parent domain is microsoft.com, the computer name would resolve to gandolf.microsoft.com. If the fully qualified computer name doesn't exist in the parent domain, the query fails. The parent domain used is the one set on the

Computer Name tab in the System Properties dialog box. (Click System And Security\System in Control Panel, click Change Settings, and then display the Computer Name tab to check the settings.)

- **Append Parent Suffixes Of The Primary DNS Suffix**   This option is selected by default. Select this option to resolve unqualified computer names by using the parent/child domain hierarchy. If a query fails in the immediate parent domain, the suffix for the parent of the parent domain is used to try to resolve the query. This process continues until the top of the DNS domain hierarchy is reached. For example, if the computer name Gandolf is used in the dev.microsoft.com domain, DNS would attempt to resolve the computer name to gandolf.dev.microsoft.com. If this didn't work, DNS would attempt to resolve the computer name to gandolf.microsoft.com.

- **Append These DNS Suffixes (In Order)**   Select this option to set specific DNS suffixes to use rather than resolving through the parent domain. Click Add if you want to add a domain suffix to the list. Click Remove to remove a selected domain suffix from the list. Click Edit to edit the selected entry. You can specify multiple domain suffixes, which are used in order. If the first suffix is not resolved properly, DNS attempts to use the next suffix in the list. If this fails, the next suffix is used, and so on. To change the order of the domain suffixes, select the suffix, and then use the up or down arrow to change its position. This option is especially useful in hybrid namespaces where there are multiple parent domain names.

- **DNS Suffix For This Connection**   This option sets a specific DNS suffix for the connection that overrides DNS names already configured for use on this connection. You usually set the DNS domain name on the Computer Name tab of the System Properties dialog box.

- **Register This Connection's Addresses In DNS**   Select this option if you want all IP addresses for this connection to be registered in DNS under the computer's fully qualified domain name. This option is selected by default.

> **NOTE**   Dynamic DNS updates are used in conjunction with DHCP to enable a client to update its A (Host Address) record if its IP address changes and to enable the DHCP server to update the PTR (Pointer) record for the client on the DNS server. You can also configure DHCP servers to update both the A and PTR records on the client's behalf. Dynamic DNS updates are supported by DNS servers with BIND 8.2.1 or later in addition to all server versions of Windows.

- **Use This Connection's DNS Suffix In DNS Registration**   Select this option if you want all IP addresses for this connection to be registered in DNS under the parent domain.

Installing DNS Servers

You can configure any Windows Server 2016 system as a DNS server. Four types of DNS servers are available:

- **Active Directory–integrated primary server** A DNS server that's fully integrated with Active Directory. All DNS data is stored directly in Active Directory.
- **Primary server** The main DNS server for a domain that is partially integrated with Active Directory. This server stores a master copy of DNS records and the domain's configuration files. These files are stored as text files with the .dns extension.
- **Secondary server** A DNS server that provides backup services for the domain. This server stores a copy of DNS records obtained from a primary server and relies on zone transfers for updates. Secondary servers obtain their DNS information from a primary server when they are started, and they maintain this information until the information is refreshed or expired.
- **Forwarding-only server** A server that caches DNS information after lookups and always passes requests to other servers. These servers maintain DNS information until it's refreshed or expired or until the server is restarted. Unlike secondary servers, forwarding-only servers don't request full copies of a zone's database files. This means that when you start a forwarding-only server, its database contains no information.

Before you configure a DNS server, you must install the DNS Server service. Then you can configure the server to provide integrated, primary, secondary, or forwarding-only DNS services.

Installing and Configuring the DNS Server Service

All domain controllers can act as DNS servers, and you might be prompted to install and configure DNS during installation of the domain controller. If you respond affirmatively to the prompts, DNS is already installed, and the default configuration is set automatically. You don't need to reinstall.

If you're working with a member server instead of a domain controller, or if you haven't installed DNS, follow these steps to install DNS:

1. In Server Manager, click Manage, and then click Add Roles And Features, or select Add Roles And Features in the Quick Start pane to start the Add Roles And Features Wizard. If the wizard displays the Before You Begin page, read the Welcome text, and then click Next.

2. On the Installation Type page, Role-Based Or Feature-Based Installation is selected by default. Click Next.

3. On the Server Selection page, you can choose to install roles and features on running servers or virtual hard disks. Either select a server from the server pool or select a server from the server pool on which to mount a virtual hard disk (VHD). If you are adding roles and features to a VHD, click Browse and then use the Browse For Virtual Hard Disks dialog box to locate the VHD. When you are ready to continue, click Next.

4. On the Server Roles page, select DNS Server. If additional features are required to install a role, you'll get an additional dialog box. Click Add Features to close the dialog box, and add the required features to the server installation. When you are ready to continue, click Next three times.

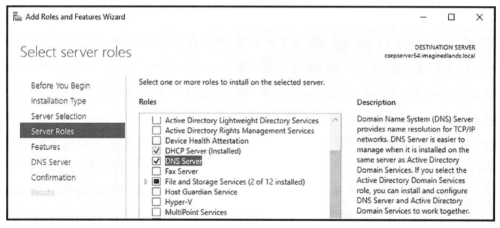

5. If the server on which you want to install the DNS Server role doesn't have all the required binary source files, the server gets the files via Windows Update by default or from a location specified in Group Policy.

> **NOTE** You also can specify an alternate path for the required source files. To do this, click the Specify An Alternate Source Path link, enter that alternate path in the box provided, and then click OK. For network shares, enter the UNC path to the share, such as \\CorpServer82\WinServer2012\. For mounted Windows images, enter the WIM path prefixed with WIM: and including the index of the image to use, such as WIM:\\CorpServer82\WinServer2012\install.wim:4.

6. Click Install to begin the installation process. The Installation Progress page tracks the progress of the installation. If you close the wizard, click the Notifications icon in Server Manager, and then click the link provided to reopen the wizard.

7. When Setup finishes installing the DNS Server role, the Installation Progress page will be updated to reflect this. Review the installation details to ensure that the installation was successful.

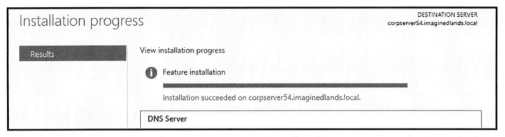

8. From now on, the DNS Server service should start automatically each time you restart the server. If it doesn't start, you need to start it manually. (See "Starting and Stopping a DNS Server" later in Chapter 19.)

9. After you install a DNS server, you use the DNS console to configure and manage DNS. In Server Manager, click Tools, and then click DNS to open the DNS Manager console.

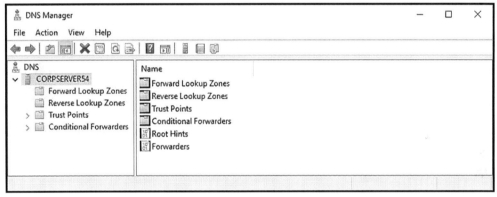

10. If the server you want to configure isn't listed in the tree view, you need to connect to the server. Right-click DNS in the tree view, and then click Connect To DNS Server. Now do one of the following:

- If you're trying to connect to a local server, select This Computer, and then click OK.
- If you're trying to connect to a remote server, select The Following Computer, enter the server's name or IP address, and then click OK.

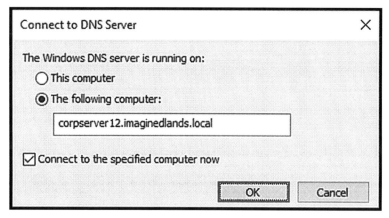

11. An entry for the DNS server should be listed in the tree view pane of the DNS Manager console. Right-click the server entry, and then click Configure A DNS Server to start the Configure A DNS Server Wizard. Click Next.

12. On the Select Configuration Action page, select Configure Root Hints Only to specify that only the base DNS structures should be created at this time.

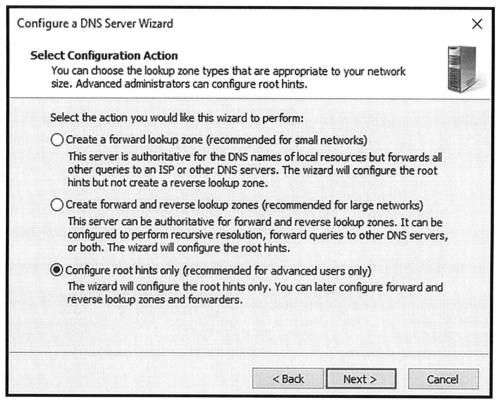

13. Click Next. The wizard searches for existing DNS structures and modifies them as necessary.

14. Click Finish to complete the process.

> **REAL WORLD** If the wizard wasn't able to configure the root hints, you might need to configure them manually or copy them from another server. However, a default set of root hints is included with DNS Server, and these root hints should be added automatically. To confirm, right-click the server entry in the DNS console, and then select Properties. In the Properties dialog box, the currently configured root hints are shown on the Root Hints tab.

Configuring a Primary DNS Server

Every domain should have a primary DNS server. You can integrate this server with Active Directory, or it can act as a standard primary server. Primary servers should have forward lookup zones and reverse lookup zones. You use forward lookups to resolve domain names to IP addresses. You need reverse lookups to authenticate DNS requests by resolving IP addresses to domain names or hosts.

After you install the DNS Server service on the server, you can configure a primary server by following these steps:

1. Start the DNS Manager console. If the server you want to configure isn't listed, connect to it as described previously in "Installing and configuring the DNS Server service."

2. An entry for the DNS server should be listed in the tree view pane of the DNS Manager console. Right-click the server entry, and then click New Zone to start the New Zone Wizard. Click Next.

3. You can now select the zone type. If you're configuring a primary server integrated with Active Directory (on a domain controller), select Primary Zone and be sure that the Store The Zone In Active Directory check box is selected. If you don't want to integrate DNS with Active Directory, select Primary Zone, and then clear the Store The Zone In Active Directory check box. Click Next.

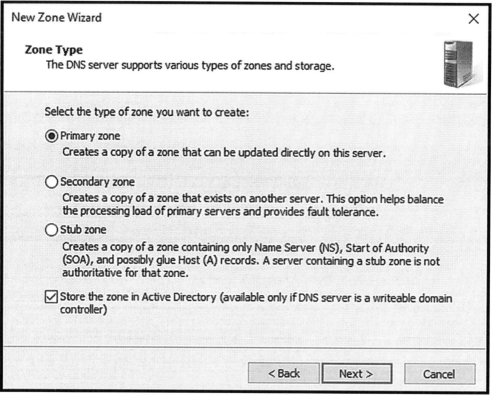

New Zone Wizard

Zone Type
The DNS server supports various types of zones and storage.

Select the type of zone you want to create:

◉ Primary zone
Creates a copy of a zone that can be updated directly on this server.

○ Secondary zone
Creates a copy of a zone that exists on another server. This option helps balance the processing load of primary servers and provides fault tolerance.

○ Stub zone
Creates a copy of a zone containing only Name Server (NS), Start of Authority (SOA), and possibly glue Host (A) records. A server containing a stub zone is not authoritative for that zone.

☑ Store the zone in Active Directory (available only if DNS server is a writeable domain controller)

[< Back] [Next >] [Cancel]

4. If you're integrating the zone with Active Directory, choose one of the following replication strategies; otherwise, proceed to step 6.

- **To All DNS Servers Running On Domain Controllers In This Forest**   Choose this strategy if you want the widest replication strategy. Remember, the Active Directory forest includes all domain trees that share the directory data with the current domain.
- **To All DNS Servers Running On Domain Controllers In This Domain**   Choose this strategy if you want to replicate DNS information within the current domain.
- **To All Domain Controllers In This Domain**   Choose this strategy if you want to replicate DNS information to all domain controllers within the current domain, as needed for legacy compatibility. Although this strategy gives wider replication for DNS information within the domain and supports compatibility with legacy Windows, not every domain controller is a DNS server as well (nor do you need to configure every domain controller as a DNS server).

5. Click Next. Select Forward Lookup Zone, and then click Next.

6. Enter the full DNS name for the zone. The zone name should help determine how the server or zone fits into the DNS domain hierarchy. For example, if you're creating the primary server for the imaginedlands.local domain, you would enter **imaginedlands.local** as the zone name. Click Next.

7. If you're configuring a primary zone that isn't integrated with Active Directory, you need to set the zone file name. A default name for the zone's DNS database file should be filled in for you. You can use this name or enter a new file name. Click Next.

8. Specify whether dynamic updates are allowed. You have three options:

- **Allow Only Secure Dynamic Updates**   When the zone is integrated with Active Directory, you can use access control lists (ACLs) to restrict which clients can perform dynamic updates. With this option selected, only clients with authorized computer accounts and approved ACLs can dynamically update their resource records in DNS when changes occur.
- **Allow Both Nonsecure And Secure Dynamic Updates**   Choose this option to allow any client to update its resource records in DNS when changes occur. Clients can be secure or nonsecure.
- **Do Not Allow Dynamic Updates**   Choose this option to disable dynamic updates in DNS. You should use this option only when the zone isn't integrated with Active Directory.

9. Click Next, and then click Finish to complete the process. The new zone is added to the server, and basic DNS records are created automatically.

10. A single DNS server can provide services for multiple domains. If you have multiple parent domains, such as microsoft.com and msn.com, you can repeat this process to configure other forward lookup zones. You also need to configure reverse lookup zones. Follow the steps listed in "Configuring Reverse Lookups" later in this chapter.

11. You need to create additional records for any computers you want to make accessible to other DNS domains. To do this, follow the steps listed in "Managing DNS Records" in Chapter 19.

REAL WORLD   Most organizations have private and public areas of their network. The public network areas might be where web and external email servers reside. Your organization's public network areas shouldn't allow unrestricted access. Instead, public network areas should be configured as part of perimeter networks. (Perimeter networks are also known as *DMZs*, demilitarized zones, and *screened subnets*. These are areas protected by your organization's firewall that have restricted external access and no access to the internal network.) Otherwise, public network areas should be in a completely separate and firewall-protected area.

The private network areas are where the organization's internal servers and work stations reside. On the public network areas, your DNS settings are in the public Internet space. Here, you might use a .com, .org, or .net DNS name that you've registered with an Internet registrar and public IP addresses that you've purchased or leased. On the private network areas, your DNS settings are in

---

the private network space. Here, you might use a local DNS name and private IP addresses, as discussed in Chapter 2.

Configuring a Secondary DNS Server

Secondary servers provide backup DNS services on the network. If you're using full Active Directory integration, you don't really need to configure secondaries. Instead, you should configure multiple domain controllers to handle DNS services. Active Directory replication will then handle replicating DNS information to your domain controllers. On the other hand, if you're using partial integration, you might want to configure secondaries to lessen the load on the primary server. On a small or medium-size network, you might be able to use the name servers of your Internet service provider (ISP) as secondaries. In this case, you should contact your ISP to configure secondary DNS services for you. Alternatively, you can put your public DNS records on a dedicated, external DNS service while hosting your private DNS records entirely on your internal DNS servers.

Because secondary servers use forward lookup zones for most types of queries, you might not need reverse lookup zones. But reverse lookup zone files are essential for primary servers, and you must configure them for proper domain name resolution.

If you want to set up your own secondaries for backup services and load balancing, follow these steps:

1. Start the DNS Manager console. If the server you want to configure isn't listed, connect to it as described previously.
2. Right-click the server entry, and then click New Zone to start the New Zone Wizard. Click Next.
3. For Zone Type, select Secondary Zone. Click Next.

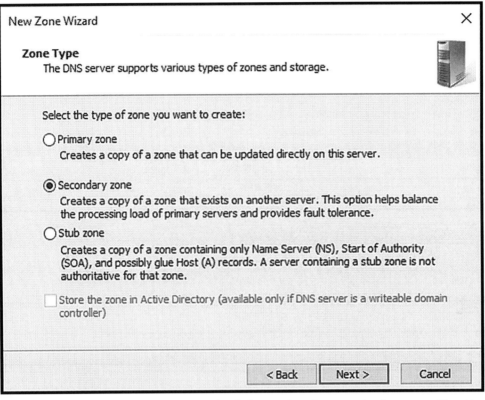

New Zone Wizard   ✕

Zone Type
The DNS server supports various types of zones and storage.

Select the type of zone you want to create:

○ Primary zone
Creates a copy of a zone that can be updated directly on this server.

⦿ Secondary zone
Creates a copy of a zone that exists on another server. This option helps balance the processing load of primary servers and provides fault tolerance.

○ Stub zone
Creates a copy of a zone containing only Name Server (NS), Start of Authority (SOA), and possibly glue Host (A) records. A server containing a stub zone is not authoritative for that zone.

☐ Store the zone in Active Directory (available only if DNS server is a writeable domain controller)

[< Back]   [Next >]   [Cancel]

4. Secondary servers can use both forward and reverse lookup zone files. You create the forward lookup zone first, so select Forward Lookup Zone, and then click Next.

5. As you are creating a copy of an existing zone, click Browse when prompted to enter the zone name and then use the dialog box provided to select the zone you are copying on the source server. Note the name of the source server for the next step. When you are ready to continue, click Next.

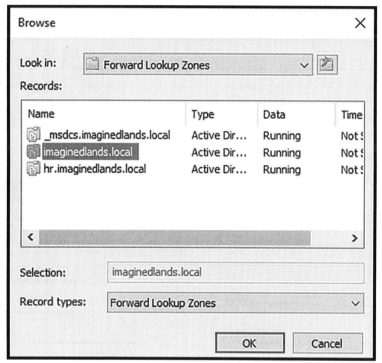

Browse

Look in: Forward Lookup Zones

Records:

Name	Type	Data	Time
_msdcs.imaginedlands.local	Active Dir...	Running	Not !
imaginedlands.local	Active Dir...	Running	Not !
hr.imaginedlands.local	Active Dir...	Running	Not !

Selection: imaginedlands.local

Record types: Forward Lookup Zones

OK   Cancel

6. Click in the Master Servers list, type name or IP address of the primary server for the zone, and then press Enter. The wizard then attempts to validate the server. If an error occurs, be sure the server is connected to the network and that you've entered the correct IP address. Also ensure you've enabled zone transfers on the primary. If you want to copy zone data from other servers in case the first server isn't available, repeat this step.

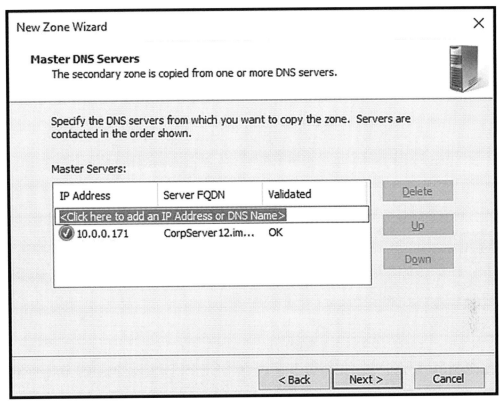

7. Click Next, and then click Finish. On a busy or large network, you might need to configure reverse lookup zones on secondaries. If so, follow the steps listed in the next section.

Configuring Reverse Lookups

Forward lookups are used to resolve domain names to IP addresses. Reverse lookups are used to resolve IP addresses to domain names. Each segment on your network should have a reverse lookup zone. For example, if you have the subnets 192.168.10.0, 192.168.11.0, and 192.168.12.0, you should have three reverse lookup zones.

The standard naming convention for reverse lookup zones is to enter the network ID in reverse order and then use the suffix *in-addr.arpa*. With the previous example, you'd have reverse lookup zones named 10.168.192.in-addr.arpa, 11.168.192.in-addr.arpa, and 12.168.192.in-addr.arpa. Records in the reverse lookup zone must be in sync with the forward lookup zone. If the zones get out of sync, authentication might fail for the domain.

You create reverse lookup zones by following these steps:

1. Start the DNS Manager console. If the server you want to configure isn't listed, connect to it as described previously.

2. Right-click the server entry, and then click New Zone to start the New Zone Wizard. Click Next.

3. If you're configuring a primary server integrated with Active Directory (a domain controller), select Primary Zone and be sure that Store The Zone In Active Directory is selected. If you don't want to integrate DNS with Active Directory, select Primary Zone, and then clear the Store The Zone In Active Directory check box. Click Next.

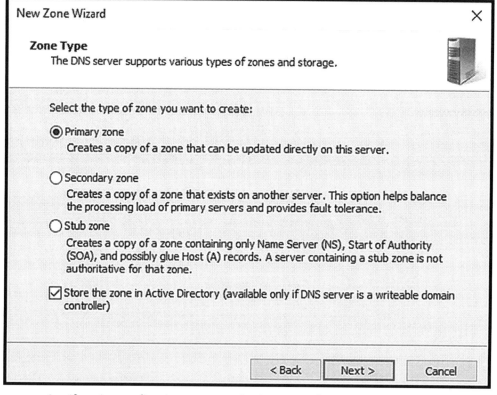

4. If you're configuring a reverse lookup zone for a secondary server, select Secondary Zone, and then click Next.

5. If you're integrating the zone with Active Directory, choose one of the following replication strategies:

- **To All DNS Servers Running On Domain Controllers In This -Forest** Choose this strategy if you want the widest replication strategy. Remember, the Active

Directory forest includes all domain trees that share the directory data with the current domain.

- **To All DNS Servers Running On Domain Controllers In This -Domain** Choose this strategy if you want to replicate DNS information within the current domain.
- **To All Domain Controllers In This Domain (For Windows 2000 -Compatibility)** Choose this strategy if you want to replicate DNS information to all domain controllers within the current domain, as needed for Windows 2000 compatibility. Although this strategy gives wider replication for DNS information within the domain, not every domain controller is a DNS server as well (and you don't need to configure every domain controller as a DNS server either).

6. Select Reverse Lookup Zone, and then click Next.

7. Choose whether you want to create a reverse lookup zone for IPv4 or IPv6 addresses, and then click Next. Do one of the following:

- If you are configuring a reverse lookup zone for IPv4, enter the network ID for the reverse lookup zone. The values you enter set the default name for the reverse lookup zone. Click Next.

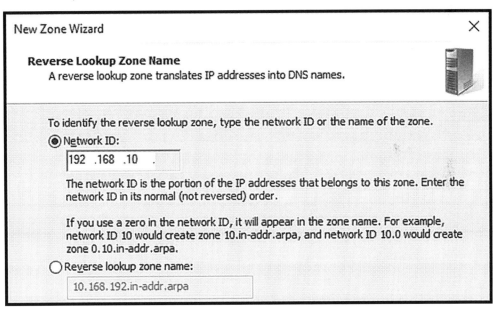

TIP If you have multiple subnets on the same network, such as 192.168.10 and 192.168.11, you can enter only the network portion for the zone name. For example, you could enter 192.168. In this case, you'd have 168.192.in-addr.arpa as the zone name and allow the DNS Manager console to create the necessary subnet zones when needed.

- If you are configuring a reverse lookup zone for IPv6, Enter the IPv6 prefix for the addresses and networks that are part of the reverse lookup zone. Be sure to use full prefix notation, such as FE80::/64. The values you enter are used to automatically generate the related zone names. Depending on the prefix you enter, the New Zone wizard will create up to eight zones. Click Next.

> **NOTE** Although DHCP for Windows Server will only work with address ranges and networks that use the /64 network prefix, DNS for Windows Server doesn't have these limitations. You can use subnetting as appropriate.

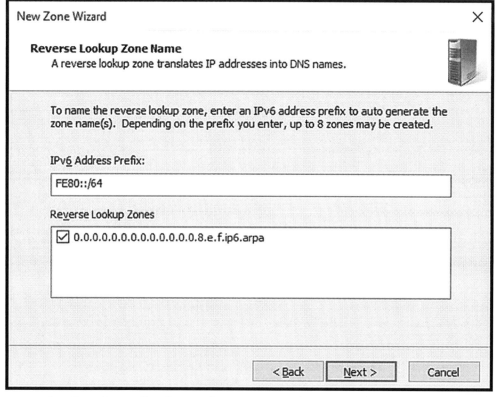

8. If you're configuring a primary or secondary server that isn't integrated with Active Directory, you need to set the zone file name. A default name for the zone's DNS database file should be filled in for you. You can use this name or enter a new file name. Click Next.

9. Specify whether dynamic updates are allowed. You have three options:

- **Allow Only Secure Dynamic Updates**   When the zone is integrated with Active Directory, you can use ACLs to restrict which clients can perform dynamic updates. With this option selected, only clients with authorized computer accounts and approved ACLs can dynamically update their resource records in DNS when changes occur.

- **Allow Both Nonsecure And Secure Dynamic Updates**   Choose this option to allow any client to update its resource records in DNS when changes occur. Clients can be secure or nonsecure.
- **Do Not Allow Dynamic Updates**   Choosing this option disables dynamic updates in DNS. You should use this option only when the zone isn't integrated with Active Directory.

   10. Click Next, and then click Finish. The new zone is added to the server, and basic DNS records are created automatically.

After you set up the reverse lookup zones, you need to ensure that delegation for the zones is handled properly. Contact your networking team or your ISP to ensure that the zones are registered with the parent domain.

Configuring Global Names

The GlobalNames zone is a specially named forward lookup zone that should be integrated with AD DS. Deploying a GlobalNames zone creates static, global records with single-label names, without relying on WINS. This enables users to access hosts by using single-label names rather than fully qualified domain names. You should use the GlobalNames zone when name resolution depends on DNS, such as when your organization is no longer using WINS and you are planning to deploy only IPv6. Because dynamic updates cannot be used to register updates in the GlobalNames zone, you should configure single-label name resolution only for your primary servers.

You can deploy a GlobalNames zone by completing the following steps:

1. In the DNS Manager console, select a DNS server that is also a domain controller. If the server you want to configure isn't listed, connect to it as described previously in "Installing and Configuring the DNS Server Service."

2. Right-click the Forward Lookup Zones node, and then click New Zone. In the New Zone Wizard, click Next to accept the defaults to create a primary zone integrated with AD DS. On the Active Directory Zone Replication Scope page, choose to replicate the zone throughout the forest, and then click Next. On the Zone Name page, enter **GlobalNames** as the zone name. Click Next twice, and then click Finish.

New Zone Wizard

Zone Name
What is the name of the new zone?

The zone name specifies the portion of the DNS namespace for which this server is authoritative. It might be your organization's domain name (for example, microsoft.com) or a portion of the domain name (for example, newzone.microsoft.com). The zone name is not the name of the DNS server.

Zone name:

GlobalNames

3. On every authoritative DNS server in the forest now and in the future, you need to enter the following at an administrator shell prompt:

```
Set-DnsServerGlobalNameZone -ComputerName ServerName -Enable $True
```

ServerName is the name of the DNS server that hosts the GlobalNames zone. To specify the local computer, simply omit the –ComputerName parameter, such as

```
Set-DnsServerGlobalNameZone -Enable $True
```

4. For each server that you want users to be able to access by using a single-label name, add an alias (CNAME) record to the GlobalNames zone. In the DNS Manager console, right-click the GlobalNames node, select New Alias (CNAME), and then use the dialog box provided to create the new resource record.

> **NOTE** An authoritative DNS server tries to resolve queries in the following order: byusing local zone data, by using the GlobalNames zone, by using DNS suffixes, by using WINS. For dynamic updates, an authoritative DNS server checks the GlobalNames zone before checking the local zone data.
>
> **TIP** If you want DNS clients in another forest to use the GlobalNames zone for resolving names, you need to add an SRV resource record with the service name _-globalnames._msdcs to that forest's forestwide DNS partition. The record must specify the FQDN of the DNS server that hosts the GlobalNames zone.

Chapter 19. Managing and Maintaining DNS

After installing a DNS server, you'll need to create records, manage zone properties, the Start Of Authority (SOA) Record, and other options to ensure smooth operations. You may also need to review and modify the server's configuration and security settings. Related tasks are discussed in this chapter.

Managing DNS Servers

The DNS Manager console is the tool you use to manage local and remote DNS servers. The DNS Manager console's main window is divided into two panes. The left pane makes it possible for you to access DNS servers and their zones. The right pane shows the details for the currently selected item. You can work with the DNS Manager console in three ways:

* Double-click an entry in the left pane to expand the list of files for the entry.
* Select an entry in the left pane to display details such as zone status and domain records in the right pane.
* Right-click an entry to display a context menu.

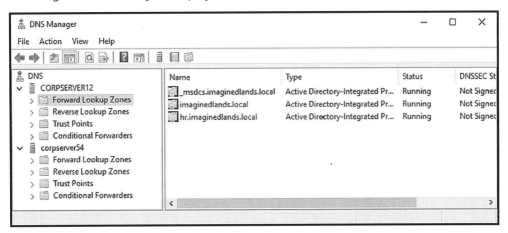

The Forward Lookup Zones and Reverse Lookup Zones folders provide access to the domains and subnets configured for use on this server. When you select domain or subnet folders in the left pane, you can manage DNS records for the domain or subnet.

Adding and Removing Servers to Manage

You can use the DNS Manager console to manage servers running DNS by following these steps:

1. Right-click DNS in the console tree, and then click Connect To DNS Server.

2. If you're trying to connect to the local computer, select This Computer. Otherwise, select The Following Computer, and then enter the IP address or fully qualified host name of the remote computer with which you want to connect.

3. Click OK. Windows Server 2016 attempts to contact the server. If it makes contact, it adds the server to the console.

> **NOTE**   If a server is offline or otherwise inaccessible because of security restrictions or problems with the Remote Procedure Call (RPC) service, the connection fails. You can still add the server to the console by clicking Yes when prompted.

In the DNS Manager console, you can delete a server by selecting its entry and then pressing Delete. When prompted, click Yes to confirm the deletion. Deleting a server only removes it from the server list in the console tree. It doesn't actually delete the server.

Starting and Stopping a DNS Server

To manage DNS servers, you use the DNS Server service. You can start, stop, pause, resume, and restart the DNS Server service in the Services node of Server Manager or from the command line. You can also manage the DNS Server service in the DNS Manager console. Right-click the server you want to manage in the DNS Manager console, point to All Tasks, and then click Start, Stop, Pause, Resume, or Restart as appropriate.

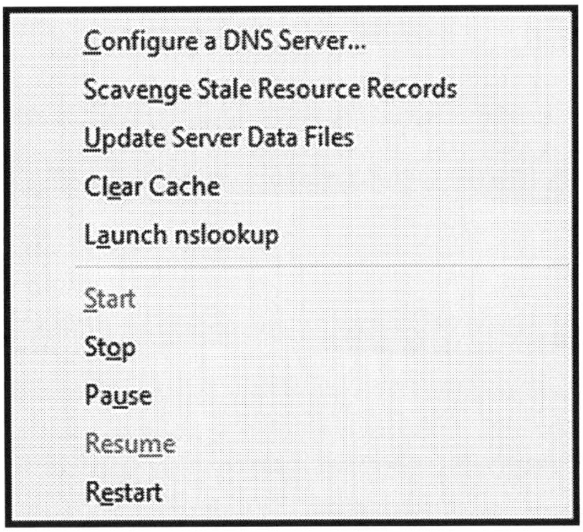

```
Configure a DNS Server...

Scavenge Stale Resource Records

Update Server Data Files

Clear Cache

Launch nslookup

Start

Stop

Pause

Resume

Restart
```

> **NOTE**   In Server Manager, under the DNS Server node, expand the DNS
> node and then right-click the server with which you want to work. On the
> shortcut menu, select Start Service, Stop Service, Pause Service, Resume
> Service, or Restart Service as appropriate.

Using DNSSEC and Signing Zones

All current versions of Windows support DNS Security Extensions (DNSSEC). DNSSEC
is defined in several Request For Comments (RFCs), including RFCs 4033, 4034, and
4035. These RFCs add origin authority, data integrity, and authenticated denial of
existence to DNS. With DNSSEC, there are the following additional resource records
to learn about:

* DNSKEY (Domain Name System Key)
* RRSIG (Resource Record Signature)
* NSEC (NextSECure)
* DS (Domain Services)

The DNS client running on these operating systems can send queries that indicate
support for DNSSEC, process related records, and determine whether a DNS server
has validated records on its behalf. On Windows servers, DNSSEC allows your DNS
servers to securely sign zones, to host DNSSEC-signed zones, to process related
records, and to perform both validation and authentication. The way a DNS client
works with DNSSEC is configured through the Name Resolution Policy Table (NRPT),
which stores settings that define the DNS client's behavior. Typically, you manage the
NRPT through Group Policy.

When a DNS server hosting a signed zone receives a query, the server returns the digital signatures in addition to the requested records. A resolver or another server configured with a trust anchor for a signed zone or for a parent of a signed zone can obtain the public key of the public/private key pair and validate that the responses are authentic and have not been tampered with.

As part of your predeployment planning, you need to identify the DNS zones to secure with digital signatures. DNS Server for Windows Server 2016 has the following significant enhancements for DNSSEC:

- Support for dynamic updates in Active Directory–integrated zones. Previously, if an Active Directory domain zone was signed, you needed to manually update all SRV records and other resource records. This is no longer required because DNS Server now does this automatically.
- Support for online signing, automated key management, and automated trust anchor distribution. Previously, you needed to configure and manage signings, keys, and trust anchors. This is no longer required because DNS Server now does this automatically.
- Support for validations of records signed with updated DNSSEC standards including NSEC3 and RSA/SHA-2.

With Windows Server 2016, an authoritative DNS server also can act as the Key Master for DNSSEC. The Key Master generates and manages signing keys for both Active Directory-integrated zones protected by DNSSEC and standard (file-backed) zones protected by DNSSEC. When a zone has a designated Key Master, the Key Master is responsible for the entire key signing process from key generation to storage, rollover, retirement, and deletion.

Although key signing and management tasks can only be initiated from the Key Master, other primary DNS servers can continue to use zone signing—they just do so via the Key Master. You must choose a key master when you sign a zone with DNSSEC. You can transfer the key master role to another DNS server that hosts the zone at any time.

Additionally, keep the following in mind:

- For file-backed zones, the primary server and all secondary servers hosting the zone must be a Windows Server or a DNSSEC-aware server that is running an operating system other than Windows.

- For Active Directory–integrated zones, every domain controller that is a DNS server in the domain must be running Windows Server if the signed zone is set to replicate to all DNS servers in the domain. Every domain controller that is a DNS server in the forest must be running Windows Server if the signed zone is set to replicate to all DNS servers in the forest.
- For mixed environments, all servers that are authoritative for a DNSSEC-signed zone must be DNSSEC-aware servers. DNSSEC-aware Windows clients that request DNSSEC data and validation must be configured to issue DNS queries to a DNSSEC-aware server. Non-DNSSEC-aware Windows clients can be configured to issue DNS queries to DNSSEC-aware servers. DNSSEC-aware servers can be configured to recursively send queries to a non-DNSSEC-aware DNS server.

Securing DNS zones with digital signatures is a multistep process. As part of that process, you need to designate a *key master*. Any authoritative server that hosts a primary copy of a zone can act as the key master. Next, you need to generate a Key Signing Key and a Zone Signing Key. A Key Signing Key (KSK) that is an authentication key has a private key and a public key associated with it. The private key is used for signing all of the DNSKEY records at the root of the zone. The public key is used as a trust anchor for validating DNS responses. A Zone Signing Key (ZSK) is used for signing zone records.

After you generate keys, you create resource records for authenticated denial of existence by using either the more secure NSEC3 standard or the less secure NSEC standard. Because trust anchors are used to validate DNS responses, you also need to specify how trust anchors are updated and distributed. Typically, you'll want to automatically update and distribute trust anchors. By default, records are signed with SHA-1 and SHA-256 encryption. You can select other encryption algorithms as well.

You don't need to go through the configuration process each time you sign a zone. The signing keys and other signing parameters are available for reuse.

To sign a zone while customizing the signing parameters, follow these steps:

1. In the DNS Manager console, right-click the zone you want to secure. On the shortcut menu, select DNSSEC, and then select Sign The Zone. This starts the Zone Signing Wizard. If the wizard displays a welcome page, read the Welcome text, and then click Next.

2. On the Signing Options page, select Customize Zone Signing Parameters, and then click Next.

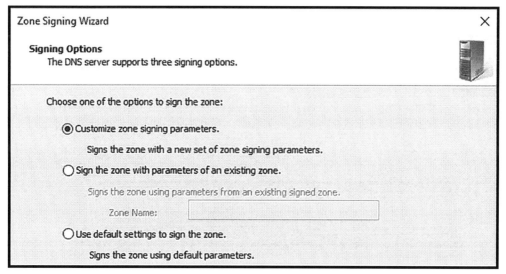

3. Select a key master for the zone. Any authoritative server that hosts a primary copy of a zone can act as the key master. When you are ready to continue, click Next twice.

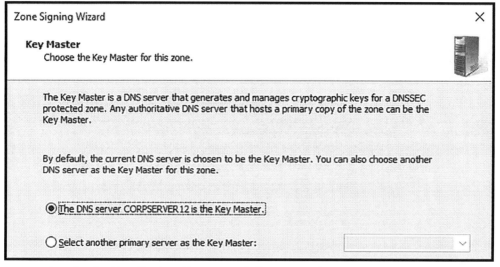

4. On the Key Signing Key page, define up to three Key Signing Keys. Configure a KSK by clicking Add, accepting or changing the default values for key properties and rollover, and then clicking OK. When you are ready to continue, click Next twice.

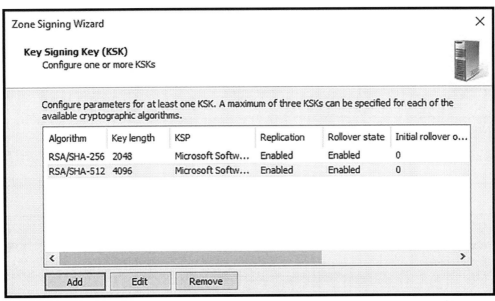

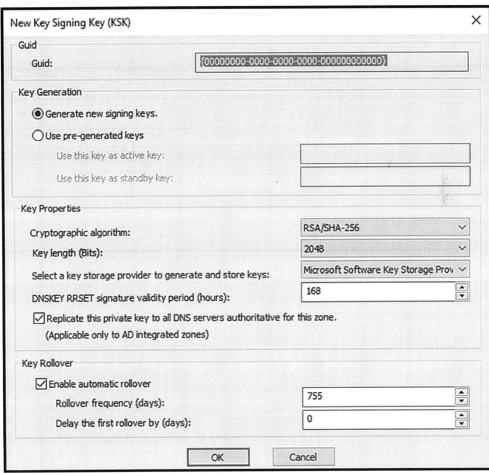

5. On the Zone Signing Key page, define up to three Zone Signing Keys. Configure a ZSK by clicking Add, accepting or changing the default values for key properties and rollover, and then clicking OK. When you are ready to continue, click Next five times.

6. After the wizard signs the zone, click Finish.

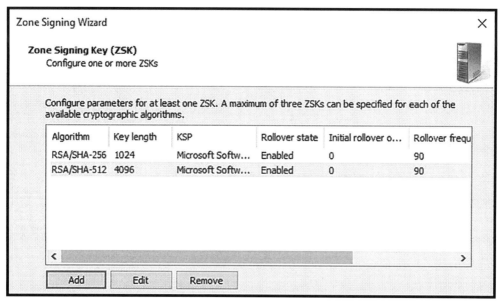

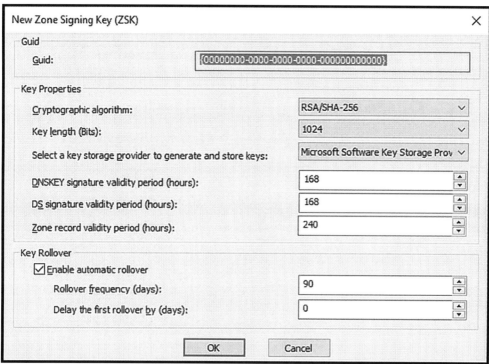

To sign a zone and use existing signing parameters, follow these steps:

1. In the DNS Manager console, right-click the zone you want to secure. On the shortcut menu, select DNSSEC and then select Sign The Zone. This starts the Zone Signing Wizard. If the wizard displays a welcome page, read the Welcome text, and then click Next.

2. On the Signing Options page, select Sign The Zone With Parameters Of An Existing Zone. Enter the name of an existing signed zone, such as **imaginedlands.local**, and then click Next.

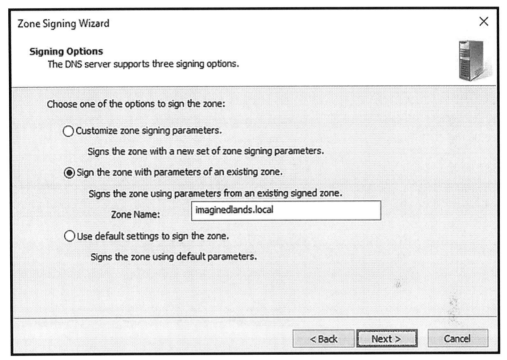

3. On the Key Master page, select a key master for the zone. Any authoritative server that hosts a primary copy of a zone can act as the key master. Click Next twice.

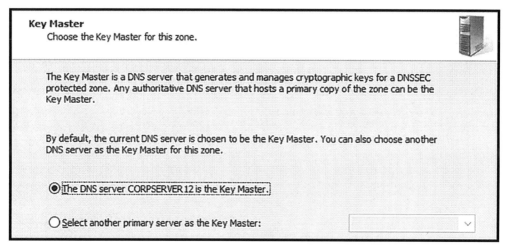

Key Master
Choose the Key Master for this zone.

The Key Master is a DNS server that generates and manages cryptographic keys for a DNSSEC protected zone. Any authoritative DNS server that hosts a primary copy of the zone can be the Key Master.

By default, the current DNS server is chosen to be the Key Master. You can also choose another DNS server as the Key Master for this zone.

◉ The DNS server CORPSERVER12 is the Key Master.

○ Select another primary server as the Key Master:

4. After the wizard signs the zone, click Finish.

Creating Child Domains Within Zones

By using the DNS Manager console, you can create child domains within a zone. For example, if you create the primary zone microsoft.com, you could create the subdomains hr.microsoft.com and mis.microsoft.com for the zone. You create child domains by following these steps:

1. In the DNS Manager console, expand the Forward Lookup Zones folder for the server with which you want to work.

2. Right-click the parent domain entry, and then click New Domain.

3. Enter the name of the new domain, and then click OK. For tech.imaginedlands.local, you would enter **tech**. For mis.imaginedlands.local, you would enter **mis**.

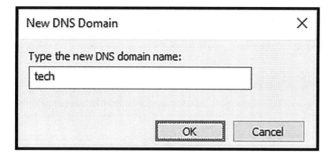

New DNS Domain ✕

Type the new DNS domain name:

tech

OK   Cancel

Creating Child Domains in Separate Zones

As your organization grows, you might want to organize the DNS namespace into separate zones. At your corporate headquarters, you could have a zone for the parent domain microsoft.com. At branch offices, you could have zones for each office, such as memphis.microsoft.com, newyork.microsoft.com, and la.microsoft.com.

You create child domains in separate zones by following these steps:

1. Install a DNS server in each child domain, and then create the necessary forward and reverse lookup zones for the child domain as described earlier in "Installing DNS Servers."

2. On the authoritative DNS server for the parent domain, you delegate authority to each child domain. Delegating authority enables the child domain to resolve and respond to DNS queries from computers inside and outside the local subnet.

You delegate authority to a child domain by following these steps:

1. In the DNS Manager console, expand the Forward Lookup Zones folder for the server with which you want to work.

2. Right-click the parent domain entry, and then click New Delegation to start the New Delegation Wizard. Click Next.

3. Enter the name of the delegated domain, such as **resources**, and then click Next. The name you enter updates the value in the Fully Qualified Domain Name text box.

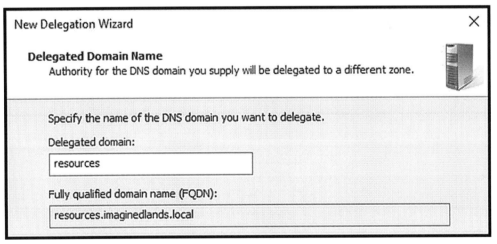

4. Click Add. This displays the New Name Server Record dialog box.

5. In the Server Fully Qualified Domain Name text box, type the fully qualified host name of a DNS server for the child domain, such as **corpserver01.tn.tvpress.local**, and then click Resolve. The server then

performs a lookup query and adds the resolved IP address to the IP Address list.

6. Repeat step 5 to specify additional name servers. The order of the entries determines which IP address is used first. Change the order as necessary by using the Up and Down buttons. When you are ready to continue, click OK to close the New Name Server Record dialog box.

7. Click Next, and then click Finish.

Deleting a Domain or Subnet

Deleting a domain or subnet permanently removes it from the DNS server. To delete a domain or subnet, follow these steps:

1. In the DNS Manager console, right-click the domain or subnet entry.

2. On the shortcut menu, click Delete, and then confirm the action by clicking Yes.

3. If the domain or subnet is integrated with Active Directory, you'll receive a warning prompt. Confirm that you want to delete the domain or subnet from Active Directory by clicking Yes.

> **NOTE** Deleting a domain or subnet deletes all DNS records in a zone file but doesn't actually delete the zone file on a primary or secondary server that isn't integrated with Active Directory. The actual zone file remains in the %SystemRoot%\System32\Dns directory. You can delete this file after you have deleted the zones from the DNS Manager console.

Managing DNS Records

After you create the necessary zone files, you can add records to the zones. Computers that need to be accessed from Active Directory and DNS domains must have DNS records. Although there are many types of DNS records, most of these record types aren't commonly used. So rather than focus on record types you probably won't use, let's focus on the ones you will use:

- **A (IPv4 address)** Maps a host name to an IPv4 address. When a computer has multiple adapter cards, IPv4 addresses, or both, it should have multiple address records.
- **AAAA (IPv6 address)** Maps a host name to an IPv6 address. When a computer has multiple adapter cards, IPv6 addresses, or both, it should have multiple address records.

- **CNAME (canonical name)**   Sets an alias for a host name. For example, by using this record, zeta.microsoft.com can have an alias of www.microsoft.com.
- **MX (mail exchanger)**   Specifies a mail exchange server for the domain, which enables email messages to be delivered to the correct mail servers in the domain.
- **NS (name server)**   Specifies a name server for the domain, which enables DNS lookups within various zones. Each primary and secondary name server should be declared through this record.
- **PTR (pointer)**   Creates a pointer that maps an IP address to a host name for reverse lookups.
- **SOA (start of authority)**   Declares the host that's the most authoritative for the zone and, as such, is the best source of DNS information for the zone. Each zone file must have an SOA record (which is created automatically when you add a zone). Also declares other information about the zone, such as the responsible person, refresh interval, retry interval, and so on.
- **SRV (service location)**   Locates a server providing a specific service. Active Directory uses SRV records to locate domain controllers, global catalog servers, LDAP servers, and Kerberos servers. Most SRV records are created automatically. For example, Active Directory creates an SRV record when you promote a domain controller. LDAP servers can add an SRV record to indicate they are available to handle LDAP requests in a particular zone.

Adding Address and Pointer Records

You use the A and AAAA records to map a host name to an IP address, and the PTR record creates a pointer to the host for reverse lookups. You can create address and pointer records at the same time or separately.

You create a new host entry with address and pointer records by following these steps:

1. In the DNS Manager console, expand the Forward Lookup Zones folder for the server with which you want to work.

2. Right-click the domain you want to update, and then click New Host (A Or AAAA). This opens the New Host dialog box.

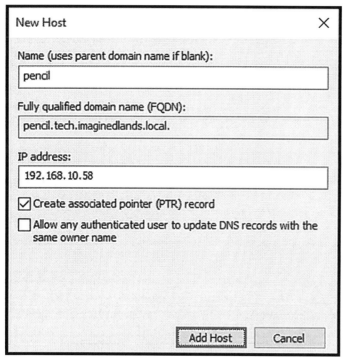

New Host   ✕

Name (uses parent domain name if blank):
pencil

Fully qualified domain name (FQDN):
pencil.tech.imaginedlands.local.

IP address:
192.168.10.58

☑ Create associated pointer (PTR) record
☐ Allow any authenticated user to update DNS records with the
  same owner name

                          Add Host   Cancel

3. Enter the single-part computer name, such as **pencil**, and then the IP address, such as **192.168.10.58**.

4. Select the Create Associated Pointer (PTR) Record check box.

> **NOTE** You can create PTR records only if the corresponding reverse lookup zone is available. You can create this file by following the steps listed in "Configuring Reverse Lookups" in Chapter 18. The Allow Any Authenticated User option is available only when a DNS server is configured on a domain controller.

5. Click Add Host, and then click OK. Repeat these steps as necessary to add other hosts.

6. Click Done when you have finished.

Adding a PTR Record Later

If you need to add a PTR record later, you can do so by following these steps:

1. In the DNS Manager console, expand the Reverse Lookup Zones folder for the server with which you want to work.

2. Right-click the subnet you want to update, and then click New Pointer (PTR).

3. Complete the host IP address. For example, if you are configuring the host IP address 192.168.10.42 for the 192.168.10 network, type **42**. Then enter the host name, such as **tnpc14**. Click OK.

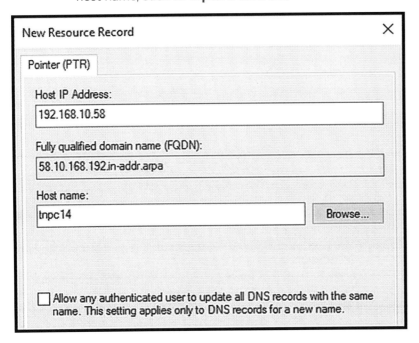

Adding DNS Aliases with CNAME

You specify host aliases by using CNAME records. Aliases enable a single host computer to appear to be multiple host computers. For example, the host matrix.imaginedlands.com can be made to appear as www.imaginedlands.com and ftp.imaginedlands.com.

To create a CNAME record, follow these steps:

1. In the DNS Manager console, expand the Forward Lookup Zones folder for the server with which you want to work.

2. Right-click the domain you want to update, and then click New Alias (CNAME).

3. In the Alias Name text box, enter the alias. The alias is a single-part host name, such as *www* or *ftp*.

New Resource Record

Alias (CNAME)

Alias name (uses parent domain if left blank):

intranet

Fully qualified domain name (FQDN):

intranet.tech.imaginedlands.local.

Fully qualified domain name (FQDN) for target host:

fileserver82b4.imaginedlands.local   Browse...

☐ Allow any authenticated user to update all DNS records with the same
name. This setting applies only to DNS records for a new name.

4. In the Fully Qualified Domain Name (FQDN) For Target Host text box, enter
    the full host name of the computer for which the alias is to be used.

5. Click OK.

Adding Mail Exchange Servers

MX records identify mail exchange servers for the domain. These servers are
responsible for processing or forwarding email within the domain. When you create
an MX record, you must specify a preference number for the mail server. A preference
number is a value from 0 to 65,535 that denotes the mail server's priority within the
domain. The mail server with the lowest preference number has the highest priority
and is the first to receive mail. If mail delivery fails, the mail server with the next
lowest preference number is tried.

You create an MX record by following these steps:

1. In the DNS Manager console, expand the Forward Lookup Zones folder for
    the server with which you want to work.

2. Right-click the domain you want to update, and then click New Mail
    Exchanger (MX).

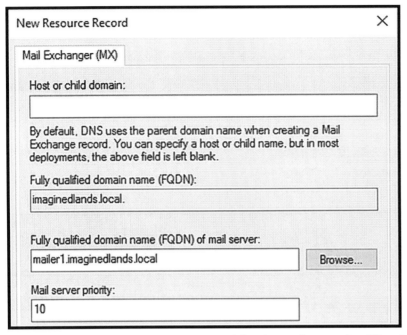

New Resource Record ✕

Mail Exchanger (MX)

Host or child domain:

[   ]

By default, DNS uses the parent domain name when creating a Mail Exchange record. You can specify a host or child name, but in most deployments, the above field is left blank.

Fully qualified domain name (FQDN):

[imaginedlands.local.]

Fully qualified domain name (FQDN) of mail server:

[mailer1.imaginedlands.local]   [Browse...]

Mail server priority:

[10]

3. You can now create a record for the mail server by filling in these text boxes:

- **Host Or Child Domain** Using a single-part name, enter the name of the subdomain for which the server specified in this record is responsible. In most cases, you will leave this box blank, which specifies that there is no subdomain and the server is responsible for the domain in which this record is created.
- **Fully Qualified Domain Name (FQDN)** Enter the FQDN of the domain to which this mail exchange record should apply, such as **imaginedlands.com**.
- **Fully Qualified Domain Name (FQDN) Of Mail Server** Enter the FQDN of the mail server that should handle mail receipt and delivery, such as **corpmail.imaginedlands.com**. Email for the previously specified domain is routed to this mail server for delivery.
- **Mail Server Priority** Enter a preference number for the host from 0 to 65,535.

> **NOTE** Assign preference numbers that leave room for growth. For example, use 10 for your highest priority mail server, 20 for the next, and 30 for the one after that.
>
> **REAL WORLD** You can't enter a multipart name in the Host Or Child Domain text box. If you need to enter a multipart name, you are creating the MX record at the wrong level of the DNS hierarchy. Create or access the additional domain level, and then add an MX record at this level for the subdomain.

4. Click OK.

Adding Name Servers

NS records specify the name servers for the domain. Each primary and secondary name server should be declared through this record. If you obtain secondary name services from an ISP, be sure to insert the appropriate NS records.

You create an NS record by following these steps:

1. In the DNS Manager console, expand the Forward Lookup Zones folder for the server with which you want to work.

2. Display the DNS records for the domain by selecting the domain folder in the tree view.

3. Right-click an existing NS record in the view pane, and then click Properties. This opens the Properties dialog box for the domain with the Name Servers tab selected.

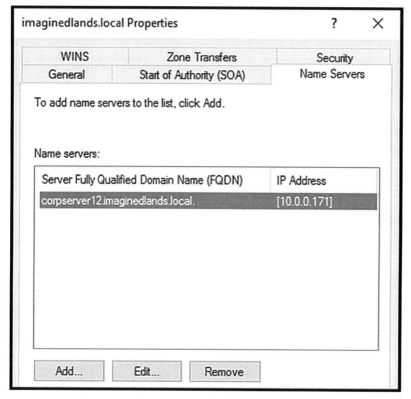

4. Click Add. This displays the New Name Server Record dialog box.

5. In the Server Fully Qualified Domain Name text box, enter the name of a DNS server for the child domain, such as **corpserver01.imaginedlands.local** and

then click Resolve. The server then performs a lookup query and adds the resolved IP address to the IP Address list.

6. Repeat step 5 to specify additional name servers. The order of the entries determines which IP address is used first. Change the order as necessary by using the Up and Down buttons. When you are ready to continue, click OK to close the New Name Server Record dialog box.

7. Click OK to save your changes.

Viewing and Updating DNS Records

To view or update DNS records, follow these steps:

1. Double-click the zone with which you want to work. Records for the zone should be displayed in the right pane.

2. Double-click the DNS record you want to view or update. This opens the record's Properties dialog box. Make the necessary changes, and then click OK.

Updating Zone Properties and the SOA Record

Each zone has separate properties you can configure. These properties set general zone parameters by using the SOA record, change notification, and WINS integration. In the DNS Manager console, you set zone properties by doing one of the following:

- Right-click the zone you want to update, and then click Properties.
- Select the zone, and then click Properties on the Action menu.

The Properties dialog boxes for forward and reverse lookup zones are identical except for the WINS and WINS-R tabs. In forward lookup zones, you use the WINS tab to configure lookups for NetBIOS computer names. In reverse lookup zones, you use the WINS-R tab to configure reverse lookups for NetBIOS computer names.

Modifying the SOA Record

An SOA record designates the authoritative name server for a zone and sets general zone properties, such as retry and refresh intervals. You can modify this information by following these steps:

1. In the DNS Manager console, right-click the zone you want to update, and then click Properties.

2. Click the Start Of Authority (SOA) tab, and then update the settings as appropriate.

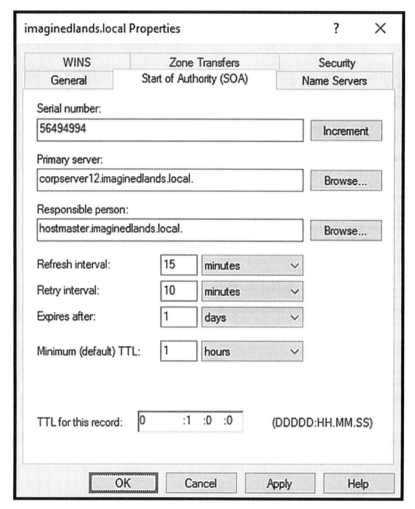

You use the text boxes on the Start Of Authority (SOA) tab as follows:

- **Serial Number** A serial number that indicates the version of the DNS database files. The number is updated automatically whenever you make changes to zone files. You can also update the number manually. Secondary servers use this number to determine whether the zone's DNS records have changed. If the primary server's serial number is larger than the secondary server's serial number, the records have changed, and the secondary server can request the DNS records for the zone. You can also configure DNS to notify secondary servers of changes (which might speed up the update process).

* **Primary Server**   The FQDN for the name server followed by a period. The period is used to terminate the name and ensure that the domain information isn't appended to the entry.
* **Responsible Person**   The email address of the person in charge of the domain. The default entry is *hostmaster* followed by a period followed by your domain name, meaning hostmaster@your_domain.com. If you change this entry, substitute a period in place of the @ symbol in the email address and terminate the address with a period.
* **Refresh Interval**   The interval at which a secondary server checks for zone updates. The default value is 15 minutes. You reduce network traffic by increasing this value. However, keep in mind that if the interval is set to 60 minutes, NS record changes might not be propagated to a secondary server for up to an hour.
* **Retry Interval**   The time the secondary server waits after a failure to download the zone database. If the interval is set to 10 minutes and a zone database transfer fails, the secondary server waits 10 minutes before requesting the zone database once more.
* **Expires After**   The period of time for which zone information is valid on the secondary server. If the secondary server can't download data from a primary server within this period, the secondary server lets the data in its cache expire and stops responding to DNS queries. Setting Expires After to seven days enables the data on a secondary server to be valid for seven days.
* **Minimum (Default) TTL**   The minimum time-to-live (TTL) value for cached records on a secondary server. The value can be set in days, hours, minutes, or seconds. When this value is reached, the secondary server causes the associated record to expire and discards it. The next request for the record needs to be sent to the primary server for resolution. Set the minimum TTL to a relatively high value, such as 24 hours, to reduce traffic on the network and increase efficiency. Keep in mind that a higher value slows down the propagation of updates through the Internet.
* **TTL For This Record**   The TTL value for this particular SOA record. The value is set in the format Days : Hours : Minutes : Seconds and generally should be the same as the minimum TTL for all records.

Allowing and Restricting Zone Transfers

Zone transfers send a copy of zone information to other DNS servers. These servers can be in the same domain or in other domains. For security reasons, Windows Server 2016 disables zone transfers. To enable zone transfers for secondaries you've configured internally or with ISPs, you need to permit zone transfers and then specify the types of servers to which zone transfers can be made.

Although you can allow zone transfers with any server, this opens the server to possible security problems. Instead of opening the floodgates, you should restrict access to zone information so that only servers you've identified can request updates from the zone's primary server. This enables you to funnel requests through a select group of secondary servers, such as your ISP's secondary name servers, and to hide the details of your internal network from the outside world.

To allow zone transfers and restrict access to the primary zone database, follow these steps:

1. In the DNS Manager console, right-click the domain or subnet you want to update, and then click Properties.

2. Click the Zone Transfers tab.

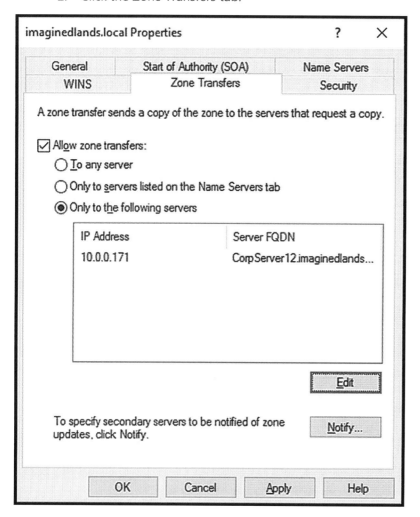

3. To restrict transfers to name servers listed on the Name Servers tab, select the Allow Zone Transfers check box, and then choose Only To Servers Listed On The Name Servers Tab.

4. To restrict transfers to designated servers, select the Allow Zone Transfers check box and then choose Only To The Following Servers. Then click Edit as appropriate to display the Allow Zone Transfers dialog box. Click in the IP Address list, enter the IP address of the secondary server for the zone, and then press Enter. Windows then attempts to validate the server. If an error occurs, make sure the server is connected to the network and that you've entered the correct IP address. If you want to copy zone data from other servers in case the first server isn't available, you can add IP addresses for other servers as well. Click OK.

5. Click OK to save your changes.

Notifying Secondaries of Changes

You set properties for a zone with its SOA record. These properties control how DNS information is propagated on the network. You can also specify that the primary server should notify secondary name servers when changes are made to the zone database. To do this, follow these steps:

1. In the DNS Manager console, right-click the domain or subnet you want to update, and then click Properties.

2. On the Zone Transfers tab, click Notify. This displays the Notify dialog box.

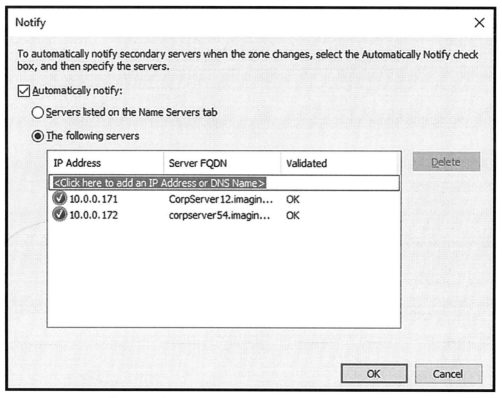

3. To notify secondary servers listed on the Name Servers tab, select the Automatically Notify check box, and then choose Servers Listed On The Name Servers Tab.

4. If you want to designate specific servers to notify, select the Automatically Notify check box, and then choose The Following Servers. Click in the IP Address list, enter the IP address of the secondary server for the zone, and then press Enter. Windows then attempts to validate the server. If an error occurs, make sure the server is connected to the network and that you entered the correct IP address. If you want to notify other servers, add IP addresses for those servers as well.

5. Click OK twice.

Setting the Zone Type

When you create zones, they're designated as having a specific zone type and an Active Directory integration mode. You can change the type and integration mode at any time by following these steps:

1. In the DNS Manager console, right-click the domain or subnet you want to update, and then click Properties.

2. Under Type on the General tab, click Change. In the Change Zone Type dialog box, select the new type for the zone.

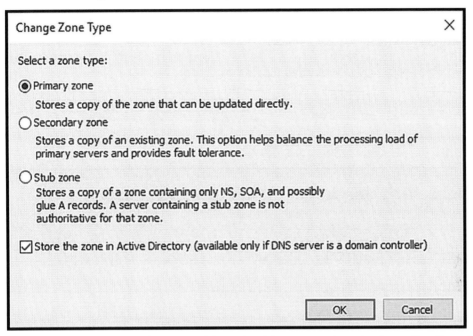

3. To integrate the zone with Active Directory, select the Store The Zone In Active Directory check box.

4. To remove the zone from Active Directory, clear the Store The Zone In Active Directory check box.

5. Click OK twice.

Enabling and Disabling Dynamic Updates

Dynamic updates enable DNS clients to register and maintain their own address and pointer records. This is useful for computers dynamically configured through DHCP. By enabling dynamic updates, you make it easier for dynamically configured computers to locate one another on the network. When a zone is integrated with Active Directory, you have the option of requiring secure updates. With secure updates, you use ACLs to control which computers and users can dynamically update DNS.

You can enable and disable dynamic updates by following these steps:

1. In the DNS Manager console, right-click the domain or subnet you want to update, and then click Properties.

2. Use the following options in the Dynamic Updates list on the General tab to enable or disable dynamic updates:

- **None**   Disable dynamic updates.
- **Nonsecure And Secure**   Enable nonsecure and secure dynamic updates.
- **Secure Only**   Enable dynamic updates with Active Directory security. This is available only with Active Directory integration.

3. Click OK.

> **NOTE**   DNS integration settings must also be configured for DHCP. See "Integrating DHCP and DNS" in Chapter 16.

Managing DNS Server Configuration and Security

You use the Server Properties dialog box to manage the general configuration of DNS servers. Through it, you can enable and disable IP addresses for the server and control access to DNS servers outside the organization. You can also configure monitoring, logging, and advanced options.

Enabling and Disabling IP Addresses for a DNS Server

By default, multihomed DNS servers respond to DNS requests on all available network interfaces and the IP addresses they're configured to use.

Through the DNS Manager console, you can specify that the server can answer requests only on specific IP addresses. Generally, you'll want to ensure that a DNS server has at least one IPv4 interface and one IPv6 interface.

To specify which IP addresses are used for answering requests, follow these steps:

1. In the DNS Manager console, right-click the server you want to configure, and then click Properties.

2. On the Interfaces tab, select Only The Following IP Addresses. Select an IP address that should respond to DNS requests, or clear an IP address that should not respond to DNS requests. Only the selected IP addresses will be used for DNS. All other IP addresses on the server will be disabled for DNS.

3. Click OK.

Controlling Access to DNS Servers Outside the Organization

Restricting access to zone information enables you to specify which internal and external servers can access the primary server. For external servers, this controls which servers can get in from the outside world. You can also control which DNS servers within your organization can access servers outside of your organization. To do this, you need to set up DNS forwarding within the domain.

With DNS forwarding, you configure DNS servers within the domain as one of the following:

- **Nonforwarders** Servers that must pass DNS queries they can't resolve to designated forwarding servers. These servers essentially act like DNS clients to their forwarding servers.
- **Forwarding-only** Servers that can only cache responses and pass requests to forwarders. These are also known as *caching-only* DNS servers.
- **Forwarders** Servers that receive requests from nonforwarders and forwarding-only servers. Forwarders use normal DNS communication methods to resolve queries and to send responses back to other DNS servers.
- **Conditional forwarders** Servers that forward requests based on the DNS domain. Conditional forwarding is useful if your organization has multiple internal domains.

> **NOTE** You can't configure the root server for a domain for forwarding (except for conditional forwarding used with internal name resolution). You can configure all other servers for forwarding.

Creating Nonforwarding and Forwarding-Only Servers

To create a nonforwarding or forwarding-only DNS server, follow these steps:

1. In the DNS Manager console, right-click the server you want to configure, and then click Properties.

2. Click the Advanced tab. To configure the server as a nonforwarder, ensure that the Disable Recursion check box is cleared, click OK, and then skip the remaining steps. To configure the server as a forwarding-only server, be sure that the Disable Recursion check box is selected.

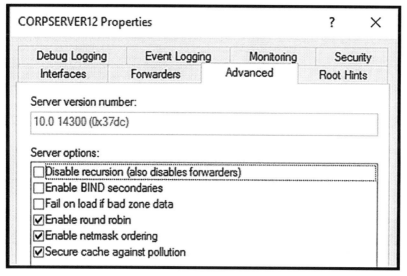

3. On the Forwarders tab, click Edit. This displays the Edit Forwarders dialog box.

4. Click in the IP Address list, type the IP address of a forwarder for the network, and then press Enter. Windows then attempts to validate the server. If an error occurs, make sure the server is connected to the network and that you've entered the correct IP address. Repeat this process to specify the IP addresses of other forwarders.

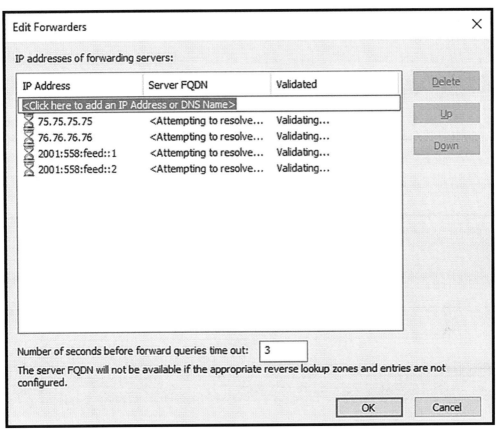

Edit Forwarders   ✕

IP addresses of forwarding servers:

IP Address	Server FQDN	Validated
<Click here to add an IP Address or DNS Name>		
75.75.75.75	<Attempting to resolve...	Validating...
76.76.76.76	<Attempting to resolve...	Validating...
2001:558:feed::1	<Attempting to resolve...	Validating...
2001:558:feed::2	<Attempting to resolve...	Validating...

Delete   Up   Down

Number of seconds before forward queries time out: 3

The server FQDN will not be available if the appropriate reverse lookup zones and entries are not configured.

OK   Cancel

5. Set the Forward Queries Time Out interval. This value controls how long the nonforwarder tries to query the current forwarder if it gets no response. When the Forward Time Out interval passes, the nonforwarder tries the next forwarder on the list. The default is three seconds. Click OK.

Creating Forwarding Servers

Any DNS server that isn't designated as a nonforwarder or a forwarding-only server will act as a forwarder. Thus, on the network's designated forwarders you should be sure that the Disable Recursion option is not selected and that you haven't configured the server to forward requests to other DNS servers in the domain.

Configuring Conditional Forwarding

If you have multiple internal domains, you might want to consider configuring conditional forwarding, which enables you to direct requests for specific domains to specific DNS servers for resolution. Conditional forwarding is useful if your organization has multiple internal domains and you need to resolve requests between these domains.

To configure conditional forwarding, follow these steps:

1. In the DNS Manager console, select and then right-click the Conditional Forwarders folder for the server with which you want to work. Click New Conditional Forwarder on the shortcut menu.

2. In the New Conditional Forwarder dialog box, enter the name of a domain to which queries should be forwarded, such as **tvpress.local**.

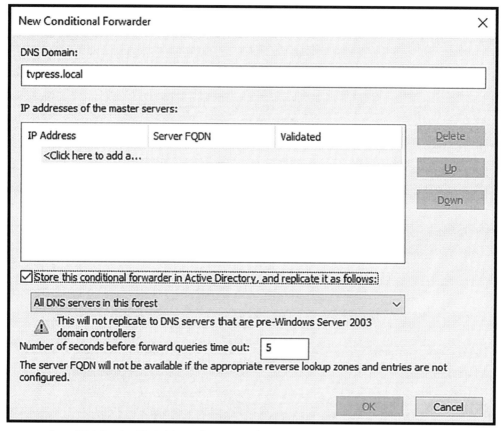

3. Click in the IP Address list, type the IP address of an authoritative DNS server in the specified domain, and then press Enter. Repeat this process to specify additional IP addresses.

4. If you're integrating DNS with Active Directory, select the Store This Conditional Forwarder In Active Directory check box, and then choose one of the following replication strategies:

- **All DNS Servers In This Forest** Choose this strategy if you want the widest replication strategy. Remember, the Active Directory forest includes all domain trees that share the directory data with the current domain.
- **All DNS Servers In This Domain** Choose this strategy if you want to replicate forwarder information within the current domain and child domains of the current domain.
- **All Domain Controllers In This Domain** Choose this strategy if you want to replicate forwarder information to all domain controllers within the current domain and child domains of the current domain. Although this strategy gives wider replication for forwarder information within the domain, not every domain controller is a DNS server as well (nor do you need to configure every domain controller as a DNS server).

5. Set the Forward Queries Time Out interval. This value controls how long the server tries to query the forwarder if it gets no response. When the Forward Time Out interval passes, the server tries the next authoritative server on the list. The default is five seconds. Click OK.

6. Repeat this procedure to configure conditional forwarding for other domains.

Enabling and Disabling Event Logging

By default, the DNS service tracks all events for DNS in the DNS Server event log. This log records all applicable DNS events and is accessible through the Event Viewer node in Computer Management. This means that all informational, warning, and error events are recorded. You can change the logging options by following these steps:

1. In the DNS Manager console, right-click the server you want to configure, and then click Properties.

2. Use the options on the Event Logging tab to configure DNS logging. To disable logging altogether, choose No Events.

3. Click OK.

Using Debug Logging to Track DNS Activity

You typically use the DNS Server event log to track DNS activity on a server. This log records all applicable DNS events and is accessible through the Event Viewer node in Computer Management. If you're trying to troubleshoot DNS problems, it's sometimes useful to configure a temporary debug log to track certain types of DNS events. However, don't forget to clear these events after you finish debugging.

To configure debugging, follow these steps:

1. In the DNS Manager console, right-click the server you want to configure, and then click Properties.

2. On the Debug Logging tab, select the Log Packets For Debugging check box, and then select the check boxes for the events you want to track temporarily.

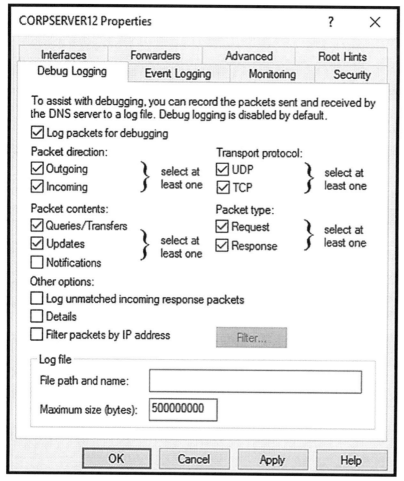

3. In the File Path And Name text box, enter the name of the log file, such as **dns.logs**. Logs are stored in the %SystemRoot%\System32\Dns directory by default.

4. Click OK. When finished debugging, turn off logging by clearing the Log Packets For Debugging check box.

Monitoring a DNS Server

Windows Server 2016 has built-in functionality for monitoring a DNS server. Monitoring is useful to ensure that DNS resolution is configured properly.

You can configure monitoring to occur manually or automatically by following these steps:

1. In the DNS Manager console, right-click the server you want to configure, and then click Properties.

2. Click the Monitoring tab. You can perform two types of tests. To test DNS resolution on the current server, select the A Simple Query Against This DNS Server check box. To test DNS resolution in the domain, select the A Recursive Query To Other DNS Servers check box.

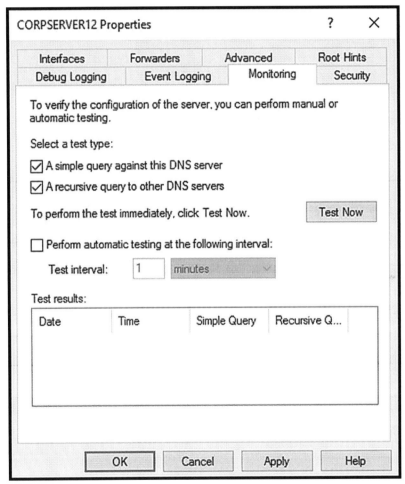

3. You can perform a manual test by clicking Test Now. You can schedule the server for automatic monitoring by selecting the Perform Automatic Testing At The Following Interval check box and then setting a time interval in seconds, minutes, or hours.

4. The Test Results panel shows the results of testing. You'll receive a date and time stamp indicating when the test was performed and a result, such as Pass or Fail. Although a single failure might be the result of a temporary outage, multiple failures typically indicate a DNS resolution problem.

NOTE   If all recursive query tests fail, the advanced server option Disable Recursion might be selected. Click the Advanced tab and check the server options.

REAL WORLD   If you're actively troubleshooting a DNS problem, you might want to configure testing to occur every 10–15 seconds. This interval will provide a rapid succession of test results. If you're monitoring DNS for problems as part of your daily administrative duties, you'll want a longer time interval, such as two or three hours.

Index

About the Author

William R. Stanek (*http://www.williamrstanek.com*) has more than 20 years of hands-on experience with advanced programming and development. He is a leading technology expert, an award-winning author, and a pretty-darn-good instructional trainer. Over the years, his practical advice has helped millions of programmers, developers, and network engineers all over the world. In 2013, William celebrated the publication of his 150th book.

William has been involved in the commercial Internet community since 1991. His core business and technology experience comes from more than 11 years of military service. He has substantial experience in developing server technology, encryption, and Internet solutions. He has written many technical white papers and training courses on a wide variety of topics. He frequently serves as a subject matter expert and consultant.

William has an MS with distinction in information systems and a BS in computer science, magna cum laude. He is proud to have served in the Persian Gulf War as a combat crewmember on an electronic warfare aircraft. He flew on numerous combat missions into Iraq and was awarded nine medals for his wartime service, including one of the United States of America's highest-flying honors, the Air Force Distinguished Flying Cross. Currently, he resides in the Pacific Northwest with his wife and children.

William recently rediscovered his love of the great outdoors. When he's not writing, he can be found hiking, biking, backpacking, traveling, or trekking in search of adventure with his family! In his spare time, William writes books for children, including *The Bugville Critters Explore the Solar System* and *The Bugville Critters Go on Vacation*.

Find William on Twitter at http://www.twitter.com/WilliamStanek and on Facebook at http://www.facebook.com/William.Stanek.Author.

Thank you for purchasing this book. If you found this book to be useful, helpful or informative, raise your voice and support William's work by sharing about this book online.

Unsure how to share? Here are some tips:

- Blog about the book
- Write a review at your favorite online store
- Post about the book on Facebook or elsewhere
- Tweet about the book

Stay in touch with William on Facebook and Twitter!

Made in the USA
Middletown, DE
28 January 2020